Resources, Environment and Agricultural Development

"Resources, Environment and Agricultural Development" series aim to provide an in-depth study of the challenges facing the world today, such as resource shortages and environmental pollution, as well as opportunities in agricultural modernization, technological progress, and income distribution, to focus on the critical issues of the balanced development in overall environment. Based on the central theme of overall sustainable and inclusive development in agriculture, the series' coverage includes but is not limited to studies in development economics, environmental & resource economics, agricultural economics, and public administration.

The series are positioned as a collection of scholarly books that aims to explore sustainable and inclusive development of agriculture under the constraints of resources and environmental conditions, under various predisposition of the resource environment and national contexts. We have incorporated many vivid and realistic agricultural development experiences into the book, such as lessons from China's agriculture, which provide a glimpses of China's rich practices and pathways for other countries worldwide.

Binlei Gong · Sujian Guo · Jun Xu ·
Channing Arndt
Editors

Chinese Governance and Transformation Towards Carbon Neutrality

Springer

Editors
Binlei Gong
School of Public Affairs
Zhejiang University
Hangzhou, China

Sujian Guo
Center for US-China Policy Studies
San Francisco State University
San Francisco, CA, USA

Jun Xu
School of Public Affairs
Zhejiang University
Hangzhou, China

Channing Arndt
IFPRI/CGIAR
Washington, DC, USA

ISSN 3059-2216 ISSN 3059-2224 (electronic)
Resources, Environment and Agricultural Development
ISBN 978-981-97-9995-4 ISBN 978-981-97-9996-1 (eBook)
https://doi.org/10.1007/978-981-97-9996-1

The original submitted manuscript has been translated into English. The translation was done using artificial intelligence. A subsequent revision was performed by the author(s) to further refine the work and to ensure that the translation is appropriate concerning content and scientific correctness. It may, however, read stylistically different from a conventional translation.

This Springer imprint is published by the registered company Springer Nature Singapore Pte Ltd.
The registered company address is: 152 Beach Road, #21-01/04 Gateway East, Singapore 189721, Singapore

Preface for the READ Series

In recent years, challenges such as resource depletion, environmental pollution, and food scarcity have persistently posed a threat to the realization of the sustainable development goals of the United Nations. In terms of resources, the world has witnessed a threefold increase in the consumption of our planet's resources in the past five decades, with a growth rate that is still continuing to expand at an average annual pace that exceeds 2.3%. The direct impact of chemical pollution in the world's air, soil, water, and workplaces is estimated to be causing 2 million deaths each year. In terms of food scarcity, about 9.2% of the global population—735 million people—faced chronic hunger in 2022, 122 million more than in 2019. And many of these issues may be becoming even more severe as they are being exacerbated by climate change, natural disasters, severe epidemics, conflicts, and civil unrest, which in turn often leads to other issues such as economic stagnation, inequality and health risks.

In this context, there is an urgent need for systematic research and international communication to tackle these problems because we have only one planet. I am delighted to see that the Resource, Environment and Agricultural Development (READ) team at Zhejiang University has established a collaboration with Springer Nature, one of the world's leading academic publishers, to launch the Resource, Environment, and Agricultural Development Book Series (READ Series). This series aims to provide in-depth studies of the most serious challenges facing the world today, such as resource scarcity and environmental pollution. The series will also seek to identify opportunities that can assist in the modernization of agriculture, help facilitate technological breakthroughs, and contribute to the reduction of income inequalities which are all needed to help the academic world to focus on the critical issues of the balanced development in the overall environment. Based on the central theme of overall sustainable and inclusive development in agriculture, the scope of the series includes, but is not limited to, studies in development economics, environmental and resource economics, agricultural economics, and public administration.

Resource, environment, and agricultural development constitute a multi-dimensional, interdisciplinary research field that encompasses a wide range of issues from agricultural production practices and policy-making to technological innovation and environmental management. As our guide to the future, resource environment and agricultural development are key areas that we cannot overlook or choose to ignore. For instance, how can we, the world, ensure global food security and sustainable development in a long run? How can policymakers across the planet mitigate and begin to adapt to the inevitable negative impacts of climate change? How can nations around the world maintain food output levels worldwide while using less resources and creating less polluting spillovers. How can governments—in developing and developed nations—launch successful and sustainable fights against poverty and hunger? How to enhance the sustainability and resilience of agri-food system? How can nations begin to accelerate the pace of green transition while simultaneously spurring economic growth? Is it possible to provide clean water and energy to everyone? These research questions relate to global challenges and to how to achieve future sustainable development goals. To achieve these goals, we need to work together across disciplinary boundaries to find solutions for the mutual development of resources, environment, and agriculture and to evaluate how the proposed solutions will affect the future of our world.

I am very pleased to see that Dr. Gong Binlei and Dr. Scott Rozelle will be serving as Editors of the READ Series. Dr. Gong is Qiushi Chair Professor in the School of Public Affairs and serves as Executive Vice Dean in the China Academy for Rural Development (CARD) at Zhejiang University. His own research agenda focuses on ways to optimize resource allocation and enhance the overall productivity growth in the economy as well as new approaches that can lead to successes in the green transition and rural development. Dr. Rozelle holdHelen F. Farnsworth Professorship of International Agricultural Policy and is Senior Fellow in Freeman Spogli Institute for International Studies at Stanford University. His research focuses on China's agricultural policy, poverty alleviation, and issues related to dealing with inequality, with an emphasis on the rural education, health, and early childhood development. I am convinced that their rich experience and profound knowledge in the field of sustainable development will be major assets to grow the READ book series into an important source of information with excellent reputation under their leadership as editors.

In summary, I extend my sincerest wishes for the READ series to become a valuable resource, offering theoretical underpinnings, empirical insights, and policy recommendations that can significantly support the pursuit of global sustainable development. Beyond the insights it provides, I hope the opportunity that this series provides will also encourages scholars to join this journey of discovery, to explore the future of resources, environment, and agricultural development—and indeed submit their own work for publication in the READ series, thereby contributing to the growth of the academic community in this series. Hence, this series should not only help readers gain both a broad and deep understanding of these issues but also inspire the engagement of all into working on successful ways to achieve sustainable development.

Johan Swinnen
Director General of the International
Food Policy Research Institute (IFPRI)
Managing Director of Systems
Transformation, CGIAR
Washington, DC, USA

Contents

Part I
Overview

Chapter 1
Introduction

Binlei Gong

Abstract Climate change poses a critical global challenge, with the Paris Agreement aiming to limit warming to 1.5 °C–2 °C this century. The IPCC's Sixth Assessment Report indicates that we may reach 1.5 °C within two decades, requiring "Net Zero" anthropogenic CO_2 emissions and substantial reductions in other greenhouse gases by 2050. As the largest developing country, China is committed to addressing climate change. In September 2020, President Xi Jinping announced goals to peak CO_2 emissions by 2030 and achieve climate neutrality by 2060, covering all GHGs. This commitment is supported by a "1+N" policy system, where "1" denotes the main policy framework and "N" includes sector-specific implementation plans, highlighting China's proactive role in global climate efforts. We first introduce achievements of climate governance in china from mitigation and adaption two aspects, and then point out there are still some challenges such like emergence for timeline, energy and industrial transition. Finally, we introduce five notable relationships of climate goverance in china. that is, the relationship between CO_2 reduction and non-CO_2 GHG Reduction, Green Governance and Climate Governance, Carbon Peaking and Climate Neutrality, China's Climate Neutrality and Global Net Zero Targets, Supply-side and Demand-side Reduction.

Keywords Climate change · Governance · Net Zero · Carbon neutrality

1.1 Background of Global Climate Governance

Climate change has emerged as one of the critical global issues facing humanity of our time. The Paris Agreement committed to controlling global warming within 1.5 °C–2 °C this century. However, according to IPCC's Sixth Assessment Report (AR6), published in 2021, the temperature rise may reach 1.5 °C in the next two decades, even under low emission scenarios. Achieving the 1.5 °C–2 °C warming target would

B. Gong (✉)
School of Public Affairs, Zhejiang University, Hangzhou, China
e-mail: gongbinlei@zju.edu.cn

B. Gong et al. (eds.), *Chinese Governance and Transformation Towards Carbon Neutrality*, Resources, Environment and Agricultural Development,
https://doi.org/10.1007/978-981-97-9996-1_1

require "Net Zero" global anthropogenic CO_2 emissions and reductions in other greenhouse gas emissions (GHGs) around 2050 or beyond. The world is entering an era of Climate Neutrality, and countries are working on setting their schedules. As shown in Table 1.1, more than 130 countries and regions have proposed "zero carbon" or "carbon neutral" targets, among which 14 countries, including Germany and Sweden, have set "carbon neutral" targets through legislation. More than 30 countries, including China and the United States, have declared policy strategy documents published by ministries, and nearly 20 countries, including Brazil and South Africa, have announced a target but have not yet institutionalized that pledge. However, nearly 60 countries have not yet taken steps to operationalize the pledge.

Table 1.1 Climate Neutrality targets and timetables for major countries and regions

Targets	Countries/regions (schedule)
In law	Germany (2045), Sweden (2045), Portugal (2045), Japan (2050), France (2050), United Kingdom (2050), South Korea (2050), Canada (2050), Spain (2050), Ireland (2050), Denmark (2050), Hungary (2050), New Zealand (2050), European Union (2050)
In policy document	Maldives (2030), Finland (2035), Iceland (2040), Antigua and Barbuda (2040), United States of America (2050), Italy (2050), Australia (2050), Belgium (2050), Romania (2050), Austria (2050), Chile (2050), Greece (2050), Ecuador (2050), Panama (2050), Croatia (2050), Lithuania (2050), Costa Rica (2050), Slovenia (2050), Uruguay (2050), Luxembourg (2050), Latvia (2050), Laos (2050), Malta (2050), Fiji (2050), Belize (2050), Marshall Islands (2050), Monaco (2050), Singapore (2050), Turkey (2053), China (2060), Ukraine (2060), Sri Lanka (2060)
Declaration/pledge	Brazil (2050), Thailand (2050), Argentina (2050), Malaysia (2050), Vietnam (2050), Colombia (2050), South Africa (2050), United Arab Emirates (2050), Kazakhstan (2050), Israel (2050), Estonia (2050), Malawi (2050), Cape Verde (2050), Andorra (2050), Russian Federation (2060), Saudi Arabia (2060), Nigeria (2060), Bahrain (2060), India (2070)
Proposed/in discussion	Bangladesh (2030), Guinea-Bissau (2030), Nepal (2045), Pakistan (2050), Switzerland (2050), Peru (2050), Ethiopia (2050), Myanmar (2050), Dominican Republic (2050), Sudan (2050), Slovakia (2050), Bulgaria (2050), Tanzania (2050), Uganda (2050), Lebanon (2050), Afghanistan (2050), Zambia (2050), Senegal (2050), Burkina Faso (2050), Mozambique (2050), Papua New Guinea (2050), Nicaragua (2050), Cyprus (2050), Trinidad and Tobago (2050), Haiti (2050), Niger (2050), Rwanda (2050), Jamaica (2050), Chad (2050), Mauritius (2050), Mauritania (2050), Namibia (2050), Togo (2050), Somalia (2050), Sierra Leone (2050), The Bahamas (2050), Burundi (2050), The Gambia (2050), Lesotho (2050), Central African Republic (2050), Timor-Leste (2050), Seychelles (2050), Solomon Islands (2050), Grenada (2050), Saint Vincent and the Grenadines (2050), Samoa (2050), Sao Tome and Principe (2050), Vanuatu (2050), Tonga (2050), Micronesia (2050), Palau (2050), Kiribati (2050), Nauru (2050), Tuvalu (2050), Eritrea (2050), Yemen (2050), Niue (2050), Indonesia (2060)

Source The Energy and Climate Intelligence Unit, derived in March 29, 2022

1.2 Overview of the Climate Policy System in China

China has been actively addressing climate change as the world's largest developing country. In September 2020, President Xi Jinping declared at the 75th General Debate of the UN General Assembly that China would increase its nationally determined contributions (NDCs), adopt more effective policies and measures, strive to peak CO_2 emissions by 2030 (carbon peaking), and achieve climate neutrality by 2060. It is worth noting that the climate neutrality target includes GHGs across the economy, which is distinct from the carbon peaking target. From CO_2 to all GHGs, China, as a responsible country, has been taking action to mitigate climate change. As shown in Table 1.2, the foundation of the "1 + N" policy system serves as a roadmap for carbon peaking and climate neutrality. The "1" here is the top-level policy design. The "N" includes implementation plans for energy, industry, transportation, urban and rural construction, and other sub-sectors, the scientific and technological support and energy security financial policies, and other guarantee plans.

1.3 Achievements of Climate Governance in China

1.3.1 Chinese Governance in Climate Mitigation

Pollution and Emission Reduction. China is determined to promote the green and low-carbon transition of the economy and society, maintaining stable economic and social development on the one hand and controlling pollution and emissions on the other. During the "13th Five-Year Plan" period, the quality of China's ecological environment improved significantly by implementing a series of environmental policies. The share of days with good air quality increased to 87% in 2020, and the average concentration of PM2.5 in cities above the prefecture-level not meeting the standard declined by 28.8% compared with 2015. Up to 98.2% of the black and odorous water bodies in built-up areas in cities at prefecture-level and above were eliminated, and the share of surface water with good quality was increased to 83.4%. In 2020, the carbon dioxide emission intensity of GDP dropped by 18.8% compared with 2015, which exceeded the 18% target of the "13th Five-Year Plan".

Energy and Industrial Transition. GHGs and conventional air pollutants are mainly emitted from fossil energy combustion and industrial production. China is actively promoting the transformation of energy and industry. On the one hand, China strictly controls coal consumption, and on the other hand, it strives to develop renewable energy. Restricted by its energy endowment, coal has long been Chin's primary energy source. China has endeavored to promote energy transformation, and the share of coal consumption declined rapidly from 72.4% in 2005 to 56.8% in 2020. During the same period, the share of primary electricity and other energy sources such as hydropower, nuclear power, and wind power increased from 7.4 to 15.9%.

Table 1.2 The "1 + N" policy system in China

1	The Central Committee of the Communist Party of China the State Council: on the complete and accurate implementation of the new development concept to do a good job of carbon peaking and carbon neutrality work				September 2021
N	Carbon reduction pathways	Energy	Opinions of the national development and reform commission national energy administration on improving institutional mechanisms and policy measures for green and low-carbon energy transition	Optimize the energy structure	January 2022
		Industry	Notice on carbon emission evaluation pilot in the planning and environmental assessment of industrial parks	Industrial optimization and upgrading	October 2021
		Urban and rural construction	Opinions on promoting the green development of urban and rural construction	Energy-efficient and low-carbon building facilities	October 2021
		Transportation	Guidance on accelerate the development of green low-carbon transportation guidance	Green low-carbon transportation system	May 2013
		Circular economy	Guidance on accelerating the establishment of green low-carbon cycle development of the economic system	Resource recycling	February 2021
	Safeguards	Green technology	Green technology driven		
		Green finance	Market capitalization driven		

(continued)

Table 1.2 (continued)

1	The Central Committee of the Communist Party of China the State Council: on the complete and accurate implementation of the new development concept to do a good job of carbon peaking and carbon neutrality work		September 2021
		Carbon Trading market	Market pricing driven
		Laws and regulations	Policy driven
		Actions and initiatives	Collaboration driven

China has strived to optimize its industrial structure by promoting green and low-carbon sectors in terms of industrial transition. The share of the tertiary industry increased to 54.5% of the GDP in 2020, which is 16.7 percentage points higher than the secondary industry. At the same time, the expansion of energy-intensive industries such as steel and chemical industries has been effectively controlled: 170 million tons of steel production capacity has been compressed since 2016, whereas 165.25 million tons of steel-making capacity has been withdrawn by 2020.

Carbon Sinks Enhancement. Forests, grasslands, wetlands, and oceans play essential roles in carbon sequestration. China has the largest area of artificial afforestation globally, which expanded by 36.3 million hectares during the "13th Five-Year Plan" period from 2016 to 2020. By the end of 2020, the national forest coverage rate reached 23.04%, the carbon reserve of forest vegetation reached 9.186 billion tons, the comprehensive vegetation coverage of grassland was up to 56.1%, and the wetland protection rate was over 50%. From 2000 to 2017, China contributed more newly forested land than any other country, which accounts for a quarter of the world's total increments. Moreover, China has established a system for monitoring the ecological environment of nature reserves, with 474 national nature reserves, 1200 km of shoreline remediation and restoration, and 23,000 hectares of coastal wetlands by 2020, which significantly increased the carbon sink capacity of the ecosystem.

1.3.2 Chinese Governance in Climate Adaption

Strategic Leadership. The Chinese government has made climate change adaptation a vital part of its national strategy to address the challenge of climate change. The National Strategy for Climate Change Adaptation enacted in 2013 clearly defines the principles and targets for climate change adaptation from 2014 to 2020. Moreover, implementing The National Strategy for Climate Change Adaptation 2035 in 2022 further strengthens top-level design and plays a strategic coordinating role for climate change adaptation.

Disaster Early Warning and Monitoring. The early warning of meteorological disaster risk offers basic information on climate change, providing helpful guidance for climate adaptation. Since the 12th Five-Year Plan, China has been actively establishing a nationwide long-run database of meteorological disasters, providing data support for natural disaster monitoring, disaster assessment, and disaster prevention and control to help the government make better and faster decisions.

Key Industries Responses. The agricultural sector suffers the most from climate change and meteorological disasters, and the No. 1 document of the Central Government in 2022 emphasized that "agriculture is a key area for promoting climate change adaptation." In terms of adaptation to climate change, the agricultural sector strives to develop and promote disaster prevention and mitigation technologies and increase the cultivation and extension of excellent resistant varieties. Agricultural infrastructure has improved significantly, especially the construction of farmland water conservancy facilities. In the forestry sector, the afforestation according to local conditions to enhance the ability of adaption has been implemented, which helps maintain ecological security. Flood control projects have been built to defend against flood and drought disasters in the water conservancy industry.

1.4 Challenges of Climate Governance in China

1.4.1 A Heavy Workload of Climate Commitments Under a Tight Timeline

From 2015 to 2021, the intensity of China's two NDCs to the UNFCCC has been gradually increasing. According to China's current "climate neutrality" target, the total emission reductions are by far the largest reduction commitment made by any country in the world. China's carbon emissions have not yet peaked, and China has only a 30-year transition period from carbon peaking to climate neutrality based on its climate commitments, which is a very tight timeline compared with the 70–80-year period for the EU's commitment. Moreover, China is in the midst of an economic transition, with the daunting task of balancing economic growth and reducing pollution and carbon emissions. China's low-carbon transition still faces three significant challenges: first, the manufacturing industry is still in the middle and low end of the international industrial value chain; second, coal consumption is still relatively high, and the task of optimizing the energy structure is arduous; third, energy consumption per unit of GDP is still too high, and the assignment of establishing a green low-carbon economic system is challenging.

1.4.2 A Difficult Task to Promote Energy and Industrial Transition

Energy is a traditional high-carbon industry, and China's energy consumption accounts for about 85% of the country's carbon emissions. China's energy structure has been dominated by coal in terms of energy consumption. Although it has been adjusting its energy structure in recent years, coal use still accounted for 58% of energy consumption in 2019, and clean energy accounted for only 15% of primary energy consumption, which is lower than the global average of 19%. In addition to increasing clean energy use, energy efficiency improvement is also a practical approach to reducing carbon emissions. However, China's energy consumption per unit of GDP is about 1.5 times the world average, indicating low energy efficiency from an international perspective. The energy structure determines the industrial structure. For a long period, China's economic growth has relied heavily on the industrial system with a foundation of fossil energy, which follows a strong path of dependence. At present, the domestic industrial transformation is still facing tremendous pressure: the manufacturing industry is at the low end of the global value chain, whereas some emerging sectors are still energy-intensive. The task of energy structure transition and industrial upgrading is arduous.

1.5 Five Notable Relationships of Climate Governance in China

1.5.1 The Relationship Between CO_2 Reduction and Non-CO_2 GHG Reduction

In climate mitigation, carbon emission reduction has the priority and draws much attention, but we should not overlook or choose to ignore non-CO_2 greenhouse gas (GHG) emissions. Carbon emission reduction refers to CO_2 emission reduction (narrowly defined). However, there is now relatively convincing evidence (IPCC) that human activities, especially the large amount of GHGs emitted by human activities since the industrial revolution, are the leading cause of global warming. According to the Kyoto Protocol, GHGs not only include carbon dioxide (CO_2) but also include methane (CH_4), nitrous oxide (N_2O), hydrofluorocarbons (HFCs), perfluorocarbons (PFCs), and sulfur hexafluoride (SF6). Although CO_2 accounts for about 80% of global GHG emissions, it is still essential to note that non-CO_2 GHGs (CH_4, N_2O, HFCs, and SF6) are also common industrial exhaust gases with even stronger greenhouse effects (see Table 1.3), which implies that the non-CO_2 GHGs can explain more than 20% of climate change. For example, the 20-year global warming potential (GWP) after emissions of N_2O is 289 times that of CO_2. Moreover, in some industries (e.g., the agricultural sector), non-CO_2 GHG emissions are much larger

Table 1.3 Lifetimes and GWPs relative to CO_2 for GHGs

Chemical formula	Lifetime (years)	Global warming potential for given time horizon		
		20 years	100 years	500 years
CO_2		1	1	1
CH_4	12	72	25	7.6
N_2O	114	289	298	153
HFC-23	270	12,000	14,800	12,200
HFC-32	4.9	2330	675	205
HFC-125	29	6350	3500	1100
PFC-14	50,000	5210	7390	11,220
PFC-116	10,000	8630	12,200	18,200
PFC-218	2600	6310	8830	12,500
SF6	3200	16,300	22,800	32,600

Source IPCC's forth Assessment Report (AR4), 2007

than CO_2 emissions and should draw the most attention. Reduction in non-CO_2 GHG emissions, rather than CO_2 emissions, might be the primary target in those sectors.

1.5.2 The Relationship Between Green Governance and Climate Governance

China's green transformation is a way to mitigate global climate change, but its purpose includes coping with climate change and resource conservation, environmental protection, public health, etc. It is a new development concept of a more systematic nature, in line with sustainable development. The climate crisis is an external factor forcing China to make a green transformation, and the green transformation is an inherent requirement for China's sustainable development. Since the 18th National Congress of the Communist Party of China (CPC), China has implemented the new development concept and contributed to combating air pollution, promoting ecological conservation, energy-saving, and emission reduction. The "Ten Atmospheric Regulations" and the "Winning the Blue-Sky Defense" are the epitome of China's environmental management in the past decade. With "carbon peaking and climate neutrality" targets proposed, the purpose of China's green transition will also include low-carbon economic and social development, in addition to environmental pollution prevention and control as well as natural ecological protection. To summarize, climate governance is part of Chinese green governance, and how to achieve a balanced act between pollution reduction and GHG reduction in addition to other economic and social targets (e.g., food security in agriculture and energy security in the energy sector) is the main task of Chinese green governance and transition.

1.5.3 The Relationship Between Carbon Peaking and Climate Neutrality

In China's "3060" targets, "carbon peaking" refers to the peaking of CO_2 emissions in 2030, whereas "climate neutrality" is the neutralization (or balance) of all GHG emissions and absorption, resulting in "net zero" emissions in 2060. Although CO_2 is the most emitted GHGs, other GHGs, such as CH_4 and N_2O, should also be considered in climate neutrality. The goal of carbon peaking lies on the emissions side and does not set a maximum on peak emissions. Climate neutrality is not only focused on emissions but also on balance between emissions and absorption. Therefore, carbon neutrality depends more on technical support and government governance and is more difficult to achieve. Moreover, carbon peaking is a prerequisite of climate neutrality. However, China has only a 30-year transition from carbon peaking to climate neutrality based on its climate commitments, which is a very tight timeline compared with the 70–80-year period for developed countries such as the United Kingdom and the United States. In order to achieve the final goal of climate neutrality, we should not only find the optimal peaking time (maybe earlier than 2030) and peaking volume of carbon emission but also take non-CO_2 emissions into account (although there is no strict constraint in 2030). To summarize, carbon peaking is a milestone, but we need to do more than that in 2030 to achieve the final goal of climate neutrality in 2060.

1.5.4 The Relationship Between China's Climate Neutrality and Global Net Zero Targets

As the largest developing country with a population of 1.4 billion, China proposed a 2060 climate neutrality target, a key contributor to global Net Zero Targets. Net Zero means offsetting anthropogenic GHG emissions and absorption to reach net zero emissions. Global 2050 Net Zero Targets is a requirement of the Paris Agreement, which indicates that emissions need to be reduced by 45% by 2030, and net zero emissions are to be achieved by 2050 to control global warming at no more than 1.5 °C. However, the current national plans of countries worldwide are far from meeting the global 2050 net zero emissions requirement. To further actively address climate change and fulfill the Paris Agreement commitments, in October 2021, the Chinese government submitted its second Nationally Determined Contributions to the United Nations Framework Convention on Climate Change (UNFCCC), updating its climate targets and significantly increasing the intensity of emission reductions

Table 1.4 China's NDCs in 2015 and 2021

Targets	The first NDC (2015)	The second NDC (2021)
Carbon dioxide emissions per unit of GDP	To lower in 2030 by 60 to 65% from the 2005 level	To lower in 2030 more than 65% from the 2005 level
The share of non-fossil fuels in primary energy consumption	To increase to around 20% in 2030	To increase to around 25% in 2030
The forest stock volume	To increase in 2030 by around 4.5 billion cubic meters on the 2005 level	To increase in 2030 by around 6 billion cubic meters on the 2005 level
Total installed capacity of wind and solar power generation	–	More than 1200 GW by 2030
Carbon dioxide emissions	To peak around 2030	To peak before 2030
GHG emissions	–	To achieve carbon neutrality in 2060

Source Collated from Enhanced Actions on Climate Change: China's Intended Nationally Determined Contributions (2015) and China's Implementation of National Independent Contributions Effective and New Goals & Initiatives (2021)

(see Table 1.4). To summarize, China strives to achieve climate neutrality, which greatly contributes to global net zero targets. Besides the clear target in 2030 and 2060, China also needs to set another goal in 2050 and work together with other nations to achieve the global target.

1.5.5 The Relationship Between Supply-Side and Demand-Side Reduction

Regarding the reduction cost, emission reduction on the supply-side is cheaper than demand-side. Production activities are the main emitters, and their GHG emissions are more concentrated than consumption activities. Hence, most countries, including China, implemented a series of policies mainly in energy, manufacturing, transportation, and other related industries to reduce GHG emissions. However, production is determined by consumption, and therefore the promotion of green and low-carbon consumption on the demand side is essential in achieving carbon peaking and climate neutrality goals. In designing the reduction mechanism of GHG emissions, we should consider both the supply-side and demand-side. To summarize, we should raise the awareness of green consumption to force the green transition on the supply side and use the green design of products to induce and foster green consumption behaviors on the demand side.

1.6 Summary

The global climate problem has intensified dramatically, and China, as the largest emitter of greenhouse gases, bears an important international responsibility. In order to meet this challenge, the Chinese Government has set a historic Dual-Carbon target in 2020, namely, to achieve carbon peaking by 2030 and carbon neutrality by 2060. However, realizing this goal faces many problems and challenges. China's Dual-Carbon governance and transformation is a systematic project, which inevitably requires a comprehensive discussion of issues and design of pathways from the national to the local level, and from the macro to the micro level.

First, the government and the market are the main tools of climate governance. The roles of the market, the "invisible" hand, and the government, the "visible" hand, are critical to achieving effective governance and a successful transition to climate neutrality. The government plays a leading and guiding role in the low-carbon transition, and promotes low-carbon development through the formulation and implementation of relevant policies, regulations and planning; the full utilization of market mechanisms is also key, and through measures such as the establishment of a carbon market and the promotion of carbon pricing, the market mechanism facilitates the innovation and application of low-carbon technologies. Second, industry and agriculture are key industries for climate governance. Industry accounts for a larger share of GDP in many countries around the world than agriculture, which (including forestry and fisheries) has the largest carbon sink capacity and the largest non-CO_2 greenhouse gas emissions. Finally, companies can also contribute to low-carbon development by promoting the efficient use of resources and the adoption of green production methods, as well as greener and cleaner living habits for individuals (Fig. 1.1).

The twelve papers in this book (Chaps. 2, 3, 4, 5, 6, 7, 8, 9, 10, 11, 12, and 13) explore China's Dual-Carbon governance and transition in a systematic manner at multiple levels, from macro to micro, emphasizing coordination and cooperation between all levels of government, between different fields, and between domestic and international levels, forming a multi-level governance system covering active participation by government, market, industry, and all sectors of society.

It is important to compare China's experience and performance in climate governance with that of other countries. So we start from this topic and open PART 2. In the Chapter 2, Chen et al. found that China and India, as huge developing countries, play different leadership positions in the carbon reduction process. Further, in the Chapter 3, Fang et al. discussed that China, after considering its own responsibility for the international carbon reduction process, based on its own national conditions, and combined with the "Belt and Road Initiative" initiative, put forward a green carbon neutralization path with its own characteristics. Achieving the goal of carbon peak and carbon neutralization is a major strategic decision made by China in coordinating the overall domestic and international situation.

However, China is faced with structural contradictions in terms of population structure, investment efficiency and energy supply and demand, which is a series of

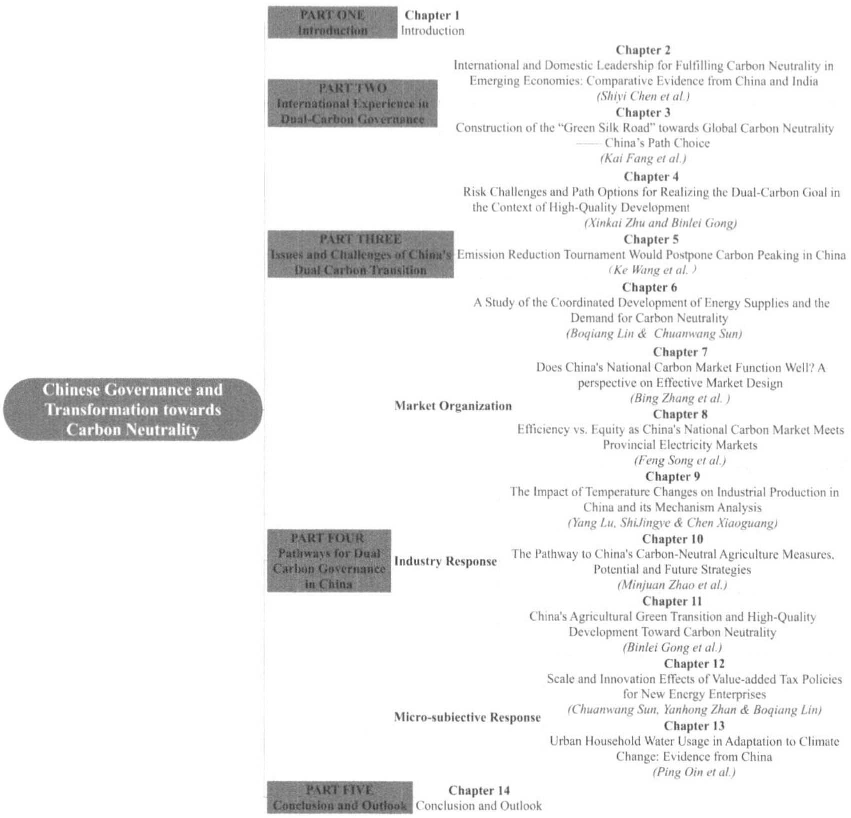

Fig. 1.1 Guide map of chapters

problems to achieve the goal of "Dual-Carbon". China needs to achieve the "Dual-Carbon" goal in a shorter time than the west, so it faces greater technical, economic, social and other challenges.

In the PART 3, through four articles from Chapters 4, 5, and 6, we explore the problems, challenges and path choices to achieve the dual-carbon goal in many aspects, such as Dual-Carbon policy guidance, market construction, industrial coordination, spatial coordination, technology research and development and so on.

On the basis of the macro-top-level design in China, the fourth part discusses the detailed path of dual-carbon governance in China from market, industry and micro-main body through Chapters 7, 8, 9, 10, 11, 12, and 13.

At the national level, Chapter 7 focuses on whether the carbon market is an effective mechanism for carbon reduction, and then turn to the local level, and whether the provincial electricity market reform takes into account both efficiency and fairness, which will be reflected in Chapter 8.

Different industries have different carbon reduction backgrounds, challenges and problems, so industry and agriculture, which play an important role in the national economy, are the main industries. Chapters 9, 10, and 11 discusses the industry adjustment and path planning made by industry and agriculture to deal with climate change respectively.

To sum up, carbon neutralization seems to be some huge plan and strategy, is it far away from our microscopic body? In Chapters 12 and 13, we answer this question from the perspective of enterprises and residents. Enterprises as to participate in market activities, residents as the microscopic body to participate in social governance, their carbon reduction behavior is equally important.

Part II
International Experience in Dual-Carbon Governance

Chapter 2
International and Domestic Leadership for Fulfilling Carbon Neutrality in Emerging Economies: Comparative Evidence from China and India

Shiyi Chen, Chang Wang, Yue Guo, Yu Yang, and Mathieu Blondeel

Abstract The socioeconomic impacts of potential climate policies are unevenly distributed across the globe, and different countries take different leading positions in fulfilling carbon neutrality. We select two top-emitting emerging economies, China and India, as our case studies. Considering structural, entrepreneurial, ideational, and exemplary leadership based on the leadership theory, we analyze the two countries' international and domestic positions in climate change mitigation after each became active climate action taker (i.e., during 2008–2021). We further rely on interest-based and norm-based approaches to explore the driving factors of their leading positions. We conclude that although China is generally more inclined to take the leading position, China and India currently both exert substantive leadership, especially prevalent in recent international climate negotiation rounds. China and India's consistency of international and domestic leadership evolves via different paths. China initially focused more on international rather than domestic leadership positions (symbolic leader), while India initially took the opposite approach (pioneer). An alignment between international and domestic leadership is found in both countries in more

S. Chen
School of Economics, Fudan University, Shanghai 200433, China

C. Wang (✉)
Ross School of Business, University of Michigan, Ann Arbor, MI 48109, USA
e-mail: wangchangqd@163.com

Y. Guo
School of International Relations, University of International Business and Economics, Beijing 100029, China

Y. Yang
Institute of Geographic Sciences and Natural Resources Research, Chinese Academy of Sciences, Beijing 100101, China

M. Blondeel
Department of Environmental Policy Analysis, Institute for Environmental Studies (IVM), Vrije Universiteit Amsterdam, 1081 HV Amsterdam, The Netherlands

B. Gong et al. (eds.), *Chinese Governance and Transformation Towards Carbon Neutrality*, Resources, Environment and Agricultural Development,
https://doi.org/10.1007/978-981-97-9996-1_2

recent years, making both countries substantive leaders. Compared with the interest-based approach, the norm-based approach has greater explanatory power for the two countries' leading position.

Keywords Climate leadership · China · India · Interest-based · Norm-based

2.1 Introduction

Substantial efforts are required for all countries to reduce carbon dioxide emissions (carbon emissions) towards the zero-carbon world in 2050, which is "a herculean task, involving rapid, dramatic changes in how governments, industries and societies function", according to the Intergovernmental Panel on Climate Change (IPCC) (Millar et al., 2017; Tollefson, 2018). However, currently the efforts made by different nations to cut emissions are quite diverse, which in total are not enough to limit the irreversible impacts of global warming (Rogelj et al., 2016). Although recent research suggests that realization of latest round of NDCs might be sufficient to meet at least the 2 °C target of the Paris Agreement, it is still uncertain whether the proposed pledges, especially the conditional ones, will be carried out by countries (Höhne et al., 2021; Meinshausen et al., 2022; Ou et al., 2021). The polarized efforts of countries in fulfilling carbon neutrality and changing related institutions are derived from disproportionate costs and benefits in climate change mitigation, and will hamper further international emission reduction negotiations and achievements (Duro & Padilla, 2008). One of the major reasons that some countries are reluctant to shift to a low-carbon economy is that the direct economic costs and other expected losses regarding climate change mitigation are more extensive than the economic benefits and gains at least in the short term. For example, international carbon pricing schemes frequently fail out of concerns for distributional unfairness and loss of efficiency and competitiveness (Klenert et al., 2018). Moreover, some oil producing countries are reluctant in climate change mitigation, because they suffer from effluent loss from reduced oil and gas production (Alizadeh et al., 2016; IEA, 2018).

Countries playing a leadership role in solving environmental and climate problems are key, since they can set the normative environment and stimulate laggard countries to emulate their behavior (Knill et al., 2012), as shown by some case studies (Kern, 2019; Vogel, 1997). This transnational common evolution of stringent environmental policy is a persistent topic for environmental studies, also known as *leader-laggard dynamics* (Knill et al., 2012). In the leader-laggard dynamics, leader countries are able to utilize institutional, politico-administrative, informational-cognitive and technological capacities to export their high domestic environmental standards to laggard countries through various innovative channels, such as stimulating bilateral and multilateral trade agreements and environmental treaties, and promoting green technological spillover by foreign direct investment (Holzinger et al., 2008a, 2008b; Jänicke, 2005; Liefferink & Andersen, 1998; Liefferink et al., 2009), thus achieving a strict environmental or climate policy regime. In the current bottom-up climate governance architecture where countries' pledges on carbon neutrality are based on their voluntary efforts, instead of predeterminate legally binding goals (Falkner, 2016), leadership countries are increasingly important, as they can launch innovative climate policy and boost other countries' emulation through transnational communications.

It is therefore not surprising that the identification of countries' position (i.e., leader or laggard) has received much research attention. The extant literature mostly focuses on identifying leader and laggard countries and the supranational organizations with small-n analysis and case studies (Oberthür & Dupont, 2021; Wiering et al., 2018; Wurzel et al., 2019a), but some studies also extend their research scope to a large-n sample and adopt quantitative analysis (Knill et al., 2012). However, existing scholarship usually focuses on the identification of leaders and laggards within the European Union (EU) and other developed countries, rather than developing countries, which are increasingly determining global climate change mitigation. According to the International Energy Agency's (IEA) stated policies scenario, China and India alone will account for 41% of global carbon emissions in 2030 (IEA, 2021). Moreover, existing studies generally consider earlier periods, neglecting the newly proposed carbon neutrality targets by China and India in 2020 and 2021, which could be pivotal to limit the peak of global warming. In fact, if China were to meet its 2060 carbon neutrality target, this could lower warming projections by around 0.2 °C (Chen et al., 2021). Therefore, international effort in mitigating climate change is increasingly determined by developing countries, as the carbon-intensive industries are relocated from the developed world to developing countries (Meng et al., 2018). Moreover, the diverging socioeconomic development and natural geographical condition have led to differentiation in climate change assertions among developing countries (Institute for Global Dialogue 2014). While the more affluent developing countries increase their economic capacity and political influence to mitigate climate change, some of them are reluctant to act. Partly because their mitigation efforts have diffused benefits across all developing countries but concentrated costs hindering the achievement of domestic economic objectives. As developing countries with large population, China and India are both in the development stage of heavy industrialization and urbanization, and face the problem of trade-offs between economic development and carbon emission reduction (Dubash, 2013; Mohan, 2017; Zhang et al., 2017; Zheng et al., 2019). China and India are generally viewed as the two most critical developing countries in fulfilling carbon neutrality, and are generally benchmarked against each other in climate ambition.

This paper makes the following contributions. Empirically, we first study the leadership position of the two largest developing countries, China and India, while existing literature focuses more on the developed countries. Given that China and India account for almost 50% global carbon emissions, it is essential to study the leadership position and specific actions of China and India with regards to climate change mitigation. Second, we focus on the most recent leadership positions of China and India, as well as the evolution and international-domestic discrepancy of leadership positions. The specific timeframe covered is 2008–2021. We focus on the period after 2008 because China and India started pursuing international and domestic leadership extensively and making quantitative emission-reduction plans around 2008, as the leading-up to the 15th UN Climate Change Conference of the Parties (COP15) in 2009 (Delman, 2011). Other studies, however, generally focus on the static leadership on a given time, and do not discuss the most recent leadership until 2021. Theoretically, in the first place, the study contributes to literature on global climate governance from a Southern perspective, while existing studies generally focus on the Global North, while marginalizing the Global South (Sapiains et al., 2021). Specifically, we find the following two traits of China and India's participation in climate governance that may be unique in emerging developing countries: (1) China and India are more inclined to combine carbon abatement and economic development, and look for the co-benefits between them; (2) China and India show enhanced leadership with the growth of economic power. Second, interest-based approaches in other studies generally focus on the aspects of abatement costs and expected economic losses on the cost side, and expected economic gains and ecological vulnerability abatement on the benefit side. We add security of energy supply as another factor on the benefit side in the interest-based approach, given that security of energy supply is an important consideration in the low-carbon plans of China and India. In terms of policy significance, the results of this paper have policy implications for China and India's respective climate action and climate cooperation. The emphasized importance of norm-based drivers in climate action also highlights the role of polycentric climate governance.

Against this backdrop of national zero-carbon proposals, we first conduct a leader-laggard assessment in the two largest developing countries based on their international and domestic climate position. Second, we identify and analyze the drivers of their leadership position, based on a classic framework of interest and norm-based approaches. We especially focus on the time period after 2008, when China and India started becoming active in international climate negotiations and formulated corresponding domestic policies. Our work finds that substantive leadership is revealed in both countries in recent international climate negotiation rounds, although China shows stronger international and domestic leadership. Inconsistency in China and India's international and domestic leadership is observed in earlier rounds of international climate negotiation: China initially shows great international leadership among the Global South, but the domestic action is relatively mild. India initially under-commits in international climate governance and shows greater domestic leadership. A posturing of, as well as an alignment between international and domestic leadership is shown by both countries in more recent years, making them substantive leaders. The norm-based approach rather than interest-based approach is more powerful in explaining the two countries' leading position.

The results of this paper not only enhance the understanding of the leading positions of the largest developing countries in climate change mitigation, but also reveal which factors are crucial in explaining leadership positions. Specifically, the analysis of the leading position of China and India highlights the essentiality of the two countries' international and domestic action, as well as the cooperation in achieving global temperature targets. The comparison between the interest-based and norm-based approaches offers insights on which parts should be stressed more to enhance climate governance. We find that interest-based explanations alone are not sufficient to account for the changes in leadership across the two selected countries. Rather, norm-based approaches provide a useful supplementary explanation and, combined with interests, result in a more comprehensive understanding of changes climate leadership. Therefore, the norms of climate change should be stressed more by environmental organizations, or during international climate negotiations. The article proceeds as follows: In Sect. 2.2, we give a thorough introduction on the theory (i.e., leadership theory), approaches (i.e., interest-based approach and norm-based approach) and data utilized in this article. In Sect. 2.3, we focus on analyzing China's and India's international positions from their international assertions and agreements and domestic positions from their national plans and actions based on the leadership theory. To explicitly explore the reasons behind their positions, we further rely on interest-based and norm-based approaches and socioeconomic data to explore the driving factors of their leading positions in Sect. 2.4. In Sect. 2.5, we discuss our findings and draw conclusions and policy implications.

2.2 Theory, Approaches and Data

2.2.1 Leadership Theory

Due to the disproportionate distribution of abatement cost and ecological vulnerability, different countries may hold different leading position to an environmental problem (Sprinz & Vaahtoranta, 1994). The countries' behaviors in dealing with climate change also have the characteristics of international and domestic inconsistency. For example, countries with structural leadership capacities (e.g. countries with strong economies) are more responsible for mitigating climate change for their historical emissions and are required to make more progress towards sustainable development. However, since some of these countries rely heavily on traditional carbon-intensive industries, they are reluctant to cut carbon emissions, and often impose less stringent climate policies than promised. Therefore, in order to distinguish such gaps between international and domestic climate leaderships, we categorize countries' particular positions in climate regime based on their international and domestic leaderships as low or high, as shown in Table 2.1 (Liefferink & Wurzel, 2017). As described by Liefferink and Wurzel (2017), international leadership refers to efforts to push for coherent international agreement or stringent international commitments, while domestic leadership means strong ambition in domestic climate policies. It is worth noting that our investigation of countries' leadership is rather heuristic, based on the ideal representation of leadership.

Liefferink and Wurzel (2017) have shown that the performance of a "leader (including symbolic leaders, substantive leaders, and pioneers)" or "laggard" varies

Table 2.1 International and domestic leading positions of countries in mitigating climate change

International climate leadership	Domestic climate leadership	
	Low	High
Low	**Laggard** (low international and low domestic ambitions)	**Pioneer** (low international and high domestic ambitions)
High	**Symbolic leader** (high international and low domestic ambitions)	**Substantive leader** (high international and high domestic ambitions)

*Source*Wurzel et al. (2019b)

across given points in time, also known as leader-laggard dynamics. In the leader-laggard dynamics, countries acting as leaders can export their high international ambitions or stringent domestic environmental standards to laggard countries through various channels, thus achieving a strict environmental or climate policy regime in the countries that were previously laggards.

Symbolic leaders, substantive leaders, and pioneers may exert their leadership in various ways. A country's leadership can be revealed by its commitments, actions, diplomacy skills, etc., and countries primarily exploit their leadership for different reasons. Based on how countries in leading positions act, we follow the most recent scholarship to further differentiate a country' leadership into four types, according to countries' roles and reasons in becoming climate leaders (Wurzel et al., 2019b). The four types include structural leadership, entrepreneurial leadership, ideational leadership, and exemplary leadership (displayed in Fig. 2.1). As noted by Wurzel et al. (2019b), symbolic or substantive leaders utilize all four types of leadership, while pioneers are inclined to offer primarily unintended exemplary leadership by unintentionally setting a good example without having the explicit intention of attracting followers.

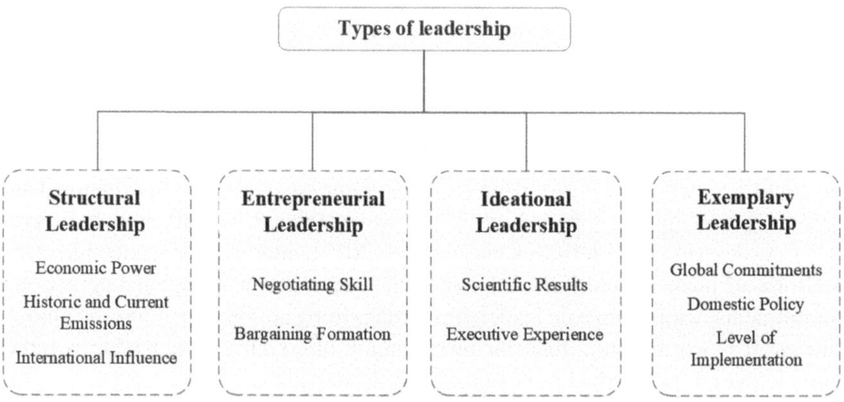

Fig. 2.1 Leadership theory: types and behaviors of leadership

Structural leadership is related to the nations' strengths in improving and contributing to climate change negotiation. Structural leadership is traditionally linked with strong military power, which is, however, not predominant in determining climate positions. We instead relate structural leadership to mainly three below aspects of comprehensive national strength: (i) economic capacity and (ii) historical and current emissions. An actor possessing national strength does not necessarily *act* as a structural leader. Structural leadership is only exercised when the country instrumentalizes its national strength in pursuit of global public good. An example of structural leadership towards environmental protection could be Germany successfully pushing forward stringent vehicle emissions regulations in the EU during the 1980s (Liefferink & Wurzel, 2017). Hosting both EU's largest domestic car industry and market, Germany used its structural power to get the new regulation accepted, bringing about the introduction of the catalytic converter and unleaded petrol against initial fierce opposition from other (major) EU economies (Klebaner & Ramírez Pérez, 2019).

Entrepreneurial leadership is the role of a broker in fostering a joint agreement that will benefit most of the participating parties. A country with entrepreneurial leadership is willing to use its negotiation skills to form a bargaining beneficial for the global climate change mitigation. Countries could also exercise entrepreneurial leadership through brokering deals among domestic parties. Therefore, entrepreneurial leadership can be revealed from nations' negotiating skills and bargaining formation results. Countries may exercise entrepreneurial leadership through coalition-building around a particular climate issue, especially by successfully solving the clashes between negotiating parties. For example, after the withdrawal of the US from the Paris Agreement in 2017, China and the EU released a joint statement stressing their commitment to the Agreement as well as the need for cooperation with other parties to achieve successful and meaningful outcomes of further multilateral negotiations.[1] This bilateral alliance can be viewed as an indication of entrepreneurial leadership.

Ideational leadership is related to the defining or redefining of interests through ideas. It involves scientific or experimental results that offer innovative climate solutions and executive experience of creating creative policies that may promote sustainable development. Ideational leadership can also relate to broader moral convictions of "what is right" (Blondeel & Graaf, 2018). Countries can offer ideational leadership through network formation, diffusion of ideas, and facilitating innovation and experimentation. An example can be the role of Netherland in forming the Natura 2000, a network of nature protection areas in the territory of the European Union (Wiering et al., 2018). The Dutch government successfully put forward the concept of National Ecological Network, which is a new aspect of the domestic nature policy of Netherland, as a model for Natura 2000.

Exemplary leadership means "setting example to others" intentionally or unintentionally, and is further divided into intentional exemplary leadership and unintentional exemplary leadership. While intentional exemplary leaders launch a stringent climate policy aiming to attract followers, unintentional exemplary leaders volunteer to provide the public good, with no intention in attracting others. Exemplary leadership relates to nations' actual actions towards carbon neutrality, including their global commitments, domestic policy, and specific level of implementation. The EU has shown exemplary leadership, as EU climate policies have increasingly become a benchmark and a source of inspiration for others. For example, the EU was the first region to launch emission trading system (ETS) in 2005, and is followed by New Zealand in 2008, the Northeastern United States in 2009, and China in 2010.

Different types of leadership are usually combined to achieve the goal. For example, countries with economic power (structural leadership) may facilitate coalition-building (entrepreneurial leadership), put forward a new concept (ideational leadership), and set a role model (exemplary leadership). Countries with limited structural leadership may have constrained capacity to facilitate coalition building but also exert substantial ideational and entrepreneurial leadership. The specific mix of types of leadership also varies with time. Entrepreneurial and ideational leadership is highly required during the phases of agenda-setting and planning, whereas structural leadership is crucial in the subsequent process of adoption and implementation (Naurin & Wallace, 2008).

Now that we have established which *types* of leadership exist, next, we discuss the drivers behind both international and domestic leadership on climate change mitigation.

2.2.2 Interest-Based Drivers of Action: A Logic of Consequence

Our interest-based approach is based on the interest-based explanation for environmental policy developed by Sprinz and Vaahtoranta (1994), focusing on domestic factors related to national interests. Their research suggests that high ecological vulnerability and low abatement costs are conclusive driving factors for international environmental policy (Sprinz & Vaahtoranta, 1994). This interest-driven explanation is further developed by Hickmann (2013), who argues that along with ecological vulnerability abatement and abatement costs, expected economic gains and losses of industries, especially energy industry, also influence environmental policies significantly. On the one hand, the fossil fuel industries may lobby the government to implement lighter emission mitigation goals and lower its transition pains, while on the other hand, renewable energy sector can advocate energy transition and enhance their economic benefits (Tørstad et al., 2020). In addition to the four aspects (i.e., ecological vulnerability abatement, abatement costs, expected economic gains, and expected economic losses), security of energy supply is also a very important benefit of mitigating climate change for both China and India. China and India are both highly reliant on oil and gas imports, and the development of renewable energy is used as a strategy in both countries to reduce the dependence on oil and gas (Wang et al., 2021). Security of energy supply, therefore, becomes a justification for climate change mitigation in both China and India.

In summary, five types of a country's cost/benefit are analyzed in this article: (i) abatement costs from economic transition, proxied by carbon emissions per unit of gross domestic product (GDP),[2] (ii) expected economic losses in competitiveness from carbon-intensive industries, proxied by the share of carbon-intensive sectors in GDP,[3] (iii) security of energy supply from reduced fossil fuel imports, proxied by the proportion of fuel imports in merchandise imports, (iv) expected economic gains from renewable energy sector, proxied by the proportion of renewables in electricity generation, and (v) ecological vulnerability abatement from mitigation, proxied by ecological vulnerability index. The detailed criterion and data description are shown in Table 2.2 in the next section.

2.2.3 *Norm-Based Drivers of Action: A Logic of Appropriateness*

Interests and norms can synthetically account for a country's efforts in climate change mitigation. While the interest-based approach analyzes countries' leading position based on the logic of consequences and the comparison between the cost and benefit, the norm-based approach generally follows a logic of appropriateness, in which countries behave according to their shared norms(March & Olsen, 1998). Shared norms can generate consensus on "what should be done", therefore "solve intractable problems and reform ineffective institutions". In the field of climate change, norm change is an essential strategy to tackle the global warming and complements the interest-based initiatives (Barbi, 2016). Utilizing the norm-based approach is a novel solution in dealing with the interest loss in climate change mitigation (Raymond et al., 2013). For instance, many advocates are using the Common But Differentiated Responsibilities (CBDR) principle to reframe public opinions on climate change, as the Global North historically has generated large amounts of carbon emissions to develop, leaving the Global South with the bulk of the economic, social and ecological losses (Blaxekjær & Nielsen, 2015). Norm reframing can lead countries that will not benefit from climate change mitigation to make pledges to take actions against global warming. To quantitatively evaluate socialization of climate norms, we measure climate-related norms in the following three aspects, (i) the share of citizens with public awareness of the severity of environmental problems, (ii) the share of citizens with the notion of sustainable development, and (iii) the share of citizens with public awareness (action) of climate change, to represent how norms about climate change are spread in a country. Evidence of norm acceptance can also be found in treaties and conventions, agreements, rules, and standards established by international organizations, resolutions, communiqués, and declarations (Bernstein, 2001; Blondeel et al., 2019). We also use government documents and the speeches by the leaders to illustrate the norms of climate change in China and India. Table 2.2 summarizes the types of interests and norms used in this paper.

Table 2.2 Logic, criterion, indicator, and data description of interest-based and norm-based approaches

Approach	Logic	Criterion	Indicator	Data description
Interest-based	Logic of consequences, what is beneficial/profitable	Costs	Carbon emissions intensity	Carbon emissions per unit of GDP
			Carbon-intensive industry interests	The share of carbon-intensive sectors in GDP
		Benefits	Fossil fuel imports	Proportion of fuel imports in merchandise imports
			Renewable electricity development	Proportion of renewables in electricity generation
			Ecological vulnerability towards climate change	Ecological vulnerability index
Norm-based	Logic of appropriateness, what should be done	Quantitative	Public environmental awareness	The share of citizens with public awareness of the severity of environmental problems
			Notion of sustainable development	The share of citizens with the notion of sustainable development
			Public climate awareness (action)	The share of citizens with public awareness (action) of climate change
		Qualitative	Government's attitude towards climate change	Government documents and the speeches by the leaders

Notes Carbon-intensive sectors are defined based on the scale of direct carbon emissions from fossil fuel combustion. Carbon-intensive sectors include petroleum processing, chemical products, steel and iron, non-ferrous metal, non-metallic products, electric power generation, and transportation. According to the data of IEA, the selected carbon-intensive sectors account for 84.12% of global total carbon emissions in 2019

2.2.4 Data Sources

The data in interest-based approach are mainly from the IEA, World Development Indicators (WDI) of World Bank, the Notre Dame Global Adaptation Initiative (ND-GAIN), and the Organization for Economic Cooperation and Development (OECD).

As for the norm-based approach, the first data source for the norm-based approach is the questionnaires collected by the wave six of World Value Survey (2010–2014).

The corresponding questions for the two measured aspects of environmental norms (i.e., (i) the public awareness of the severity of environmental problems (public awareness), and (ii) the notion of sustainable development (sustainable development)) are V80 and and V81, respectively. We calculate the proportion of questionnaire takers answering "5- environmental pollution" for question V80 and "1- Protecting the environment should be given priority" for question V81, respectively. However, World Value Survey only covers people's broad views about environmental problems, instead of specific opinions about climate change. To fill in the gap, we further supplement with 2010 Gallup Survey, and exploit the question "how much do you know about global warming or climate change". We use the proportion of people saying know "something" or "a great deal" about global warming or climate change to measure the public awareness of climate change. The next round of World Value Survey (2017–2022) or the most recent Gallup Survey do not include corresponding questions on environmental or climate change norms. To elucidate people's more recent norms of climate change, we therefore use a new survey conducted by Ipsos Global Advisor in 2022: The survey organizers ask individuals' willingness to combat climate change.[4] People are asked by the survey organizers. People were asked whether they agree with the following statement: "If individuals like me do not act now to combat climate change, we will be failing future generations."

2.3 International and Domestic Leadership Positions of Two Countries

In this section, we discuss *types* of leadership exercised by China and India, both internationally and domestically. Figure 2.2 summarizes the types of leadership and corresponding performance of China and India, which is discussed in detail in the following sessions, while Fig. 2.3 summarizes the shifts in international and domestic leadership towards carbon neutrality in China and India.

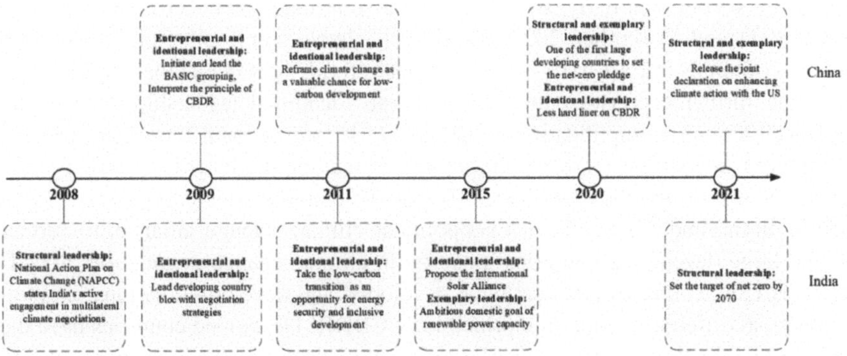

Fig. 2.2 Types of leadership China and India are exercising

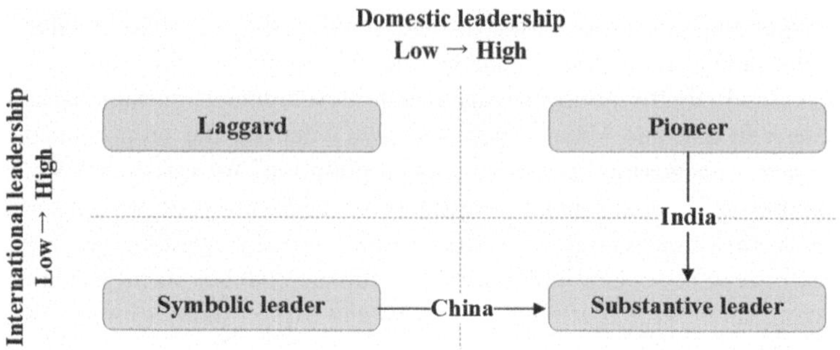

Fig. 2.3 The shifts in international and domestic leadership towards carbon neutrality in China and India

2.4 China's Climate Change Mitigation Leadership

2.4.1 International Leadership

According to a survey conducted during the COP14–17 concerning the perception of international leadership, China can be the most significant leader in the G77 + China group (Karlsson et al, 2011; Parker et al., 2015). China is the largest emerging market and a major contributor to global annual emissions, providing a basis for China's structural and exemplary leadership. With a significant share in global economic output and carbon emissions, China faces substantial international pressure from the EU and United States (US) to propose a quantitatively binding target for its emissions. Against this backdrop, China and the US also released the joint declaration on enhancing climate action during the COP26 in 2021, where China first suggested peaking coal consumption. China and the EU have a long-standing cooperation on climate change. China is one of the first developing countries to formulate explicit carbon neutrality policies not conditional on other countries behaviors, thus exercising an increased level of unconditional exemplary leadership. After China's pledge for carbon neutrality, Brazil and India soon made their net-zero pledges in April, 2021 and November, 2021, respectively. Japan and South Korea, two other major economies in East Asia, made their net-zero pledges in October, 2020.

China further exercises entrepreneurial and ideational leadership. One of the most well-known exemplifications of China's early international entrepreneurial and ideational leadership is its role in initiating and leading the BASIC grouping in the lead-up to and during the COP15 in 2009. BASIC countries (including Brazil, South Africa, India, and China) form a geopolitical climate change alliance, to further defend large developing countries' position in climate change negotiation. Specifically, BASIC countries interpret what developed and developing nations ought to accomplish differently under the principle of CBDR: Developed countries have the greatest historical responsibility in global warming and strongest capacity to solve it, while developing parties should also take nationally appropriate mitigation and adaptation actions with a financial mechanism and technology transfer from developed countries. BASIC countries' interpretation of CBDR strongly resonates with some members within the G77+China group, although it sometimes puts other members with greater vulnerability and adaptation to climate change at odds, such as the Alliance of Small Island States (AOSIS), some Least Developed Countries (LDCs), and African countries (Fuhr, 2021). Generally speaking, the alliance of BASIC countries manifests the emerging international influence of the Global South, and its later joint statements generate notable implications for the current "bottom-up" approach of determining emission budgets. In recent years, China has shifted its international entrepreneurial and ideational leadership, and put itself on a closer playfield with developed countries. China has been putting less hard liner on CBDR, as China's announcement on striving to achieve carbon neutrality before 2060 made no reference to China's traditionally hard-held bifurcation between developed and developing country responsibilities, or indeed linked China's actions in any way to the action of others. Therefore, China's pledge of achieving carbon neutrality by 2060 has become a signal of China's enhanced ideational leadership, indicating the central priority of China's climate policy.

2.4.2 Domestic Leadership

As the largest emerging country, China demonstrates substantial international and domestic climate leadership, although its international leadership is significantly higher than domestic leadership in its earlier climate change pledges. Domestically, China is also one of the first developing nations to integrate climate efforts into its national development plan. Demonstrating ideational leadership, the Chinese government has decided to reframe climate change as a valuable chance to develop renewable energy and address the problem of long-lasting dependence on imported oil. With China's entrepreneurial leadership, Chinese government spreads an understanding that with the upcoming of potential green technical trade barriers and air pollution coming along with carbon emissions, low-carbon technologies represent future economic and technological competitiveness (Pan, 2011; Zhai, 2011). Thus, China offers economic benefits for low-carbon enterprises utilizing various policy portfolios, providing an economic incentive to increase low-carbon competitiveness.

However, during the earlier rounds of climate change negotiations, China's emission reduction efforts were not a priority compared to economic growth, expressed in its emission reduction strategy that consisted of the relative decoupling of GDP growth and emission growth. In China's Five-Year Plans (a social and economic development initiative implemented in a five-year cycle), the government authorities proposed a mandatory target to abate carbon emissions per unit of GDP by 17%, 18%, and 18% during 2011–2015, 2016–2020, and 2021–2025, respectively. China is still paying more attention to settling its serious environmental problems, and treats carbon emission mitigation as a co-benefit for sustainable socioeconomic development. Low-carbon development in China still faces many implementation-level problems, such as the inter-region transfer of high-pollutants and top-emitting enterprises, and the curtailment of renewable energy, reflecting the inconsistent jurisdiction of different levels of government authorities (Fang et al., 2019).

We have witnessed an increase in China's domestic leadership in recent years, lending relatively strong domestic consistency for China's international leadership position. In 2020, especially, President Xi Jinping proposed striving to reach carbon neutrality by 2060 in the United Nations General Assembly, and corresponding domestic policies are being designed and implemented. While earlier pledges are mainly emission-intensity targets, which focus on the relative decoupling between carbon emissions and economic growth, the pledge of carbon peaking and carbon neutrality proposes absolute decoupling between carbon emissions and economic growth. China has proposed long-term carbon emission targets for achieving carbon emission peaking by 2030 and carbon neutrality by 2060 in China's Nationally Determined Contribution (NDC). The new pledges therefore call for a systematic and revolutionary shift in production and lifestyle. Existing literature largely shows that current policies could be sufficient to achieve carbon emissions peaking in advance around 2025 and carbon neutrality by 2060 (CAT, 2021; Duan et al., 2021; Yu et al., 2018). The Chinese central and local government has embarked on several key tasks, including establishing a low-carbon electricity supply system, implementing energy conservation and emission reduction actions in different sectors and regions, developing carbon emission trading market and green financing, and initiating green Belt and Road initiative (Chen et al., 2020; Liu et al., 2022).

2.5 India's Climate Change Mitigation Leadership

2.5.1 International Leadership

India is both among the countries that have the highest total carbon emissions and lowest carbon emissions per capita. India's carbon emissions have not increased as rapidly as China's. As a result, India is now faced with a challenge to exercise effective structural leadership that balances addressing total emissions and allowing emissions for individuals and households. On the one hand, because it is such a large emitter, India is expected by the international community to act a structural leader towards climate change mitigation, a position it sometimes is willing take up. In the National Action Plan on Climate Change (NAPCC) released in 2008, India stated its engagement in multilateral climate negotiations in a "positive, constructive and forward-looking manner" (as a symbol of Indian international structural leadership). On the other hand, with the low emission level per capita, India is often reluctant to take the position of "structural leader", emphasizing the country's needs to balance the relationship between poverty eradication, emission abatement, and economic development (Gupta et al., 2019; Wu, 2018). The priority of economic development and poverty eradication is consistently mentioned in government documents and speeches by leaders regarding emissions abatement. For example, in COP26, Prime Minister Modi promises the target of net zero by 2070, and also mentions that Indian government is "working to lift crores of people out of poverty".

India's ideational and entrepreneurial leadership in climate change efforts has become more prevalent over time (Atteridge et al., 2012). The conventional beliefs of India are that international climate negotiation is an aggressive attempt to environmentally colonize developing countries such as China and India, which started as early as 1991 (Agarwal & Narain, 1991). A nation's emission reduction responsibility, therefore, should be based on historical cumulative emissions and emissions per capita. This attitude towards climate change mitigation continued for more than 10 years, when India focused more on dealing with its domestic poverty and material limitation and stated refusal to take any climate obligations until its carbon emissions per capita reaches the OECD's level (Dubash, 2009; Jha, 2009). India is a long-term opinion leader in the developing country bloc, seeking to champion the needs from other developing countries, as well as to occupy the moral high ground as a protector of the Global South' benefits (Rajamani, 2008). India's negotiation strategy can be characterized by its "'civilizational' rhetoric, high opening demands, and an appeal to moral, 'Third Worldist' imperatives" (Michaelowa & Michaelowa, 2012). India has, however, transitioned from challenging the rules of global climate governance to formulating processes that shape international climate action (Mohan, 2017). For example, India proposed International Solar Alliance in 2015, aiming to promote solar power in developing countries. According to Ajar Mathur, India's principal spokesperson for the COP21, the alliance "represents a large market for solar energy". Out of the diminishing returns to scale of solar power generation, the alliance will lead to lower cost of solar power, benefiting especially countries with high solar resources but plagued by energy poverty.

Particularly following the announcement of the US withdrawal from the Paris Agreement, India is increasing its international leadership, and the international leadership is getting aligned with domestic leadership. With China's announcement of carbon neutrality by 2060, India is now clearly forecasted—for the first time—to become the world's largest emitter. Indian Prime Minister Modi announced a 2070 net zero target at the World Leaders Summit at COP26 in Glasgow.

2.5.2 Domestic Leadership

Contrast to China, India's position was initially pioneer, meaning that its international leadership was relatively modest compared with its domestic leadership. India proposes "hard" domestic targets on emissions reduction, but conservative targets in international pledges. The international and domestic inconsistency stems from the earlier national consensus that developing countries should not take the lead in climate change mitigation, whilst unilateral actions could be taken voluntarily without international commitments (Mohan & Wehnert, 2019; Vihma, 2011). India was among the first large developing countries to propose domestic emission-reduction plans, when it released the National Action Plan on Climate Change (NAPCC) in 2008. The targets in India's first NDC in 2015 are relatively modest given domestic contexts and offer plenty of room to increase ambition of action. India's first NDC pledges an emissions-intensity target of 33–35% by 2030 below 2005 levels and a share of non-fossil-based installed electric power capacity of 40% by 2030 (from 30%) with international support. However, both of the NDC targets could be reached under the mild low-carbon policies, lacking stronger clean transition pressure. The emissions intensity of India reduced by 31% between 2011 and 2016, and almost reached the emission-intensity target in the NDC. The non-fossil share target has already been reached, as the Indian government announces that non-fossil based electric power capacity takes up 40.1% of total capacity in 2021, much ahead of the 2030 deadline. The domestic climate targets are also more ambitious. India has a domestic goal in 2015 of increasing renewable power capacity from 35 GW (in March 2015) to 175 GW by 2022, which is a five-fold increase. This shows that India has the tendency of under-commitment in international climate change negotiations, while the domestic action is stronger. India therefore performs unintentional exemplary leadership, as it sets stringent domestic targets without the explicit intentions to attract followers. India is not explicitly inclined to attract followers, evidenced by its less stringent international commitments.

Domestically, India takes the transition to sustainable development as an opportunity to obtain domestic benefits of energy security and inclusive development, which can be viewed as ideational and entrepreneurial leadership. A large group of policy makers in India managed internalized climate objectives: By looking for climate co-benefits, they view decarbonization as a positive domestic policy objective (Vihma, 2011). Fossil fuel imports currently account for around 30% of merchandise imports of India, indicating a potential threat of international fossil fuel blockage which will hamper India's development. Furthermore, by developing domestic renewable energy sources as a major action regarding climate change mitigation, India can achieve the goal of inclusive development.

With the net-zero pledge by Prime Minister Modi in 2021, India is likely to improve the domestic leadership to meet the target. India also proposes to reduce the emissions intensity of its economy by 45% by 2030, an enhancement to the 33–35% of its first NDC goal. India's announcement is essential to keep the world on a 2 °C warming track, but should still be treated with caution: The announcement is short without sufficient details, and India has not updated its NDC to United Nations Framework Convention on Climate Change (UNFCCC).

2.5.3 Cooperation Between China and India

China and India have convergent interests with regard to climate change, thus, the two countries generally tend to cooperate in both international negotiations and domestic mitigation actions (Downie & Williams, 2018). The competition over climate leadership, on the other hand, is less obvious.[5] The types of cooperation include both bilateral and international cooperation.

In bilateral cooperation, China and India signed the Agreement on Cooperation on Addressing Climate Change in 2009, the Memorandum of Understanding (MoU) on Cooperation on Green Technologies in 2010, and a Joint Statement on Climate Change in 2015. The agreements generally invoke the principles of equity and CBDR, expressing a long-standing demand for China and India for a fair and just international climate change deal. For example, the joint statement issued by China and India in 2015 "calls for the leadership of developed countries in reducing greenhouse gas emissions and providing finance, technology and capacity building support to developing countries". China and India are also cooperating in specific areas, such as marine climate, polar scientific research, and natural disaster prevention and mitigation.

In international cooperation, China and India take common stands on issues of commitment in COPs. During the COP at Copenhagen in 2009, European countries urged to adopt a goal of a 50% reduction in global carbon emissions by 2050 (compared with a 1990 benchmark), whose passage is prevented by both China and India (Rapp et al., 2010). Such sentiment is noted at the first ever ministerial-level talks between India and China on climate change held at Beijing in August 2009 as Xie Zhenhua, Vice Chairman of the National Development and Reform Commission (NDRC) of China stated that, "both China and India are in complete agreement of views on certain critical items as it relates to Copenhagen". During the COP at Glasgow in 2021, China and India jointly opposed the commitment of "phasing out coal", and converted it into "phasing down coal".

China and India have used multilateral platforms to draw closer ties on climate change. Multilateral platforms include BASIC group, BRICS group, Asia–Pacific Partnership on Clean Development and Climate, the Clean Energy initiative, Like Minded Developing Countries on Climate Change, and the GLOBE G8 + 5 Climate Change Dialogue. They have also been pivotal in paving the way for a fairer negotiation process by garnering cooperation among like-minded countries of the developing Global South. The inevitability of climate change keeps forcing China and India to coordinate diplomatic positions at international forums.

2.6 Explaining Leadership Positions: Interests Versus Norms

From the above discussion, we can briefly summarize that China and India both have high leadership in addressing climate change. China and India both vigorously make pledges to address global warming in the international negotiation and domestic policy arena. Although not as significant as the EU and AOSIS, China and India are in a leading international position in defining and redefining CBDR and eventually help lead the world towards the current bottom-up approach. As the largest developing economy, China's international and domestic leadership is both higher than India's, evidenced in the first instance by China's initiation of the BASIC group, and secondly by China's issuing of climate policies ahead of India, which were more ambitious in its emission reduction goals. In initial rounds of international negotiation, there were discrepancies between international and domestic leadership initially, with China more inclined to take the international leading position, and India more frequently takes the domestic one. Starting around 2017, the alignment in international and domestic leadership is witnessed in both countries, as China and India both become substantive leaders.

What are the reasons contributing to countries' international and domestic positions? Why are different countries taking different positions in addressing climate change? Based on the interest-based and norm-based approaches, we attempt to analyze the two countries' interests and norms over climate change and other environmental problems (Mizo, 2016).

2.6.1 *Interest-Based Explanations*

Interest-based explanations are illustrated in Fig. 2.4. Specifically, Fig. 2.4 displays the costs and benefits in dealing with climate change for China and India, with corresponding statistics for the US, EU, and world average plotted for comparison. Our analysis mainly focuses on the statistics in 2008, the year before COP15, and how the number changes afterwards. The indicators used to show the costs of climate change mitigation include carbon emission intensity and the share of carbon-intensive sectors in GDP, which represent abatement costs and expected economic losses, respectively. The benefits of climate change mitigation can be revealed by a country's fossil fuel imports, renewable electricity development, and ecological vulnerability towards climate change. The corresponding indicators we use for benefits include proportion of fuel imports in merchandise imports, proportion of renewables in electricity generation, and ecological vulnerability index.

On the cost side, carbon emission intensity of China is significantly higher than that of other countries. China and India both face relatively lower marginal abatement costs, which is shown by their higher carbon emission intensity. In 2008, China's emission intensity was 0.65 kg/ 2015 USD, more than twofold higher than that of

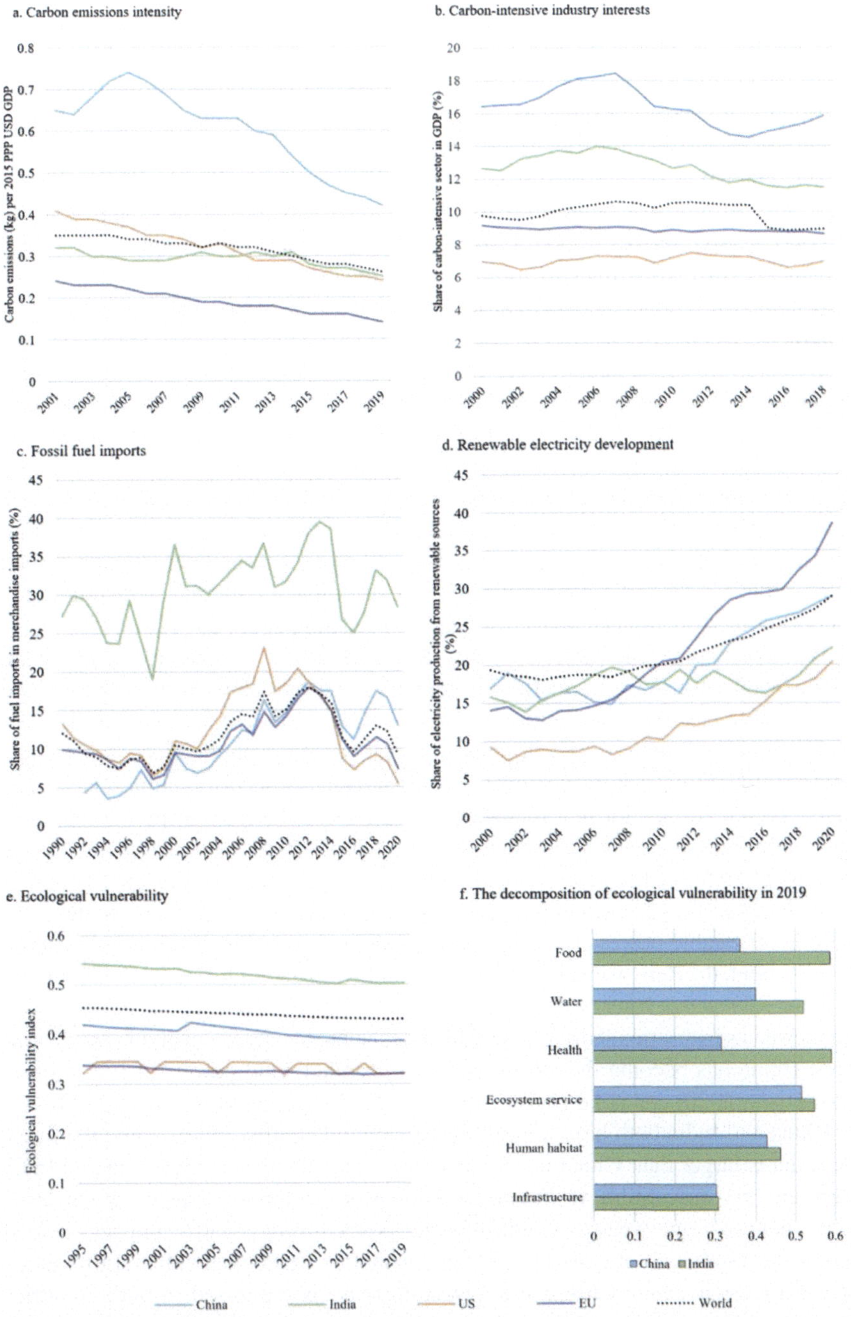

Fig. 2.4 Interest-based approach of countries in mitigating climate change. *Notes* The data are mainly from IEA, World Development Indicators (WDI) of World Bank, the Notre Dame Global Adaptation Initiative (ND-GAIN), and the Organization for Economic Cooperation and Development (OECD)

India. China's high emission intensity is partly driven by the carbon-intensive industrial structure, as carbon-intensive sectors take up about 17% of GDP in 2008 (Guan et al., 2018). India's share of carbon-intensive sectors is also above global average. The high share of carbon-intensive sectors suggests that both China and India depend on carbon-intensive industries for economic development and industrialization, so climate change mitigation poses high expected economic losses for the two countries. We also observe large decreases in carbon emissions intensity and share of carbon-intensive sectors in both China and India for most of the time since 2008.[6] Inevitably, low-carbon policies initially pose threats to their economic growth, but in the long run stimulate a more competitive, inclusive, and sustainable development pattern.

We next turn to the benefit side. The share of fossil fuel imports in merchandise imports for China and India is 16.27 and 36.69% in 2008, and 13.02 and 28.36% in 2020, respectively. While fossil fuel abundance may hinder nations' motivation in renewable energy development, fossil fuel dependency potentially causes energy security problem, and serves as an engine towards low-carbon innovation (Johnsson et al., 2019). China and India are known for being two large fossil fuel importing nations, but India's energy security problem is more serious than China's, which helps explain why India especially aims to substitute fossil fuel with renewable energy sources in climate change mitigation (Meckling et al., 2015).

We next analyze renewable electricity development of China and India. The share for renewable electricity production is higher for India than China in 2008, as the share of renewable electricity generation is 17.30% (China) and 19.07% (India), respectively. Renewable energy development has far-reaching implications for climate change mitigation, sustainable development, and energy security. India sets various energy policies to develop new renewables, so the share of electricity production from renewable sources rises with fluctuation during 2008–2020, with a moderate rate of increase of 16.56%. The increase in the share of renewables in total electricity output is much higher for China than India, which is a result for China's extensive development in renewable power generation. The guidelines for China's renewable energy development, the Renewable Energy Law and the Mid- and Long-Term Development Plan for Renewable Energy came into effect in 2006 and 2007, respectively, which are viewed as institutional drivers for China's renewable energy development. Nowadays, China has become the world leader in installed wind power (281.65 million kilowatts in 2020) and solar power capacity (253.56 million kilowatts in 2020).

China and India both have a high ecological vulnerability index, while the index for India is larger than China in all the sectors. This indicates that China and India are both very susceptible to the adverse impacts of climate change, which leads to frequent extreme weather conditions and poses strong negative impact on food and water resources, ecosystems, and human habitat. Ecological vulnerability index of India is higher than China, although a decrease is witnessed in both countries due to adaptation actions. Figure 2.3f further decomposes the ecological vulnerability index in 2019 in aspects of food, water, health, ecosystem, human habitat, and infrastructure. We find that India suffers from higher ecological vulnerability in all the aspects, but the stark difference only exists in aspects of food, water, and health.

Most of India's population is under threat of rising temperature, floods, storms, droughts, and sea level rise, and may suffer from bad health conditions. The spatial and temporal impact of climate change on water balance will restrain India's crops yield.

To sum up, via the interest-based approach, China and India both face large expected economic loss, evidenced by their carbon-intensive industry interest. The main benefits for China and India to take a strong climate position include security of energy supply, expected economic gains, and ecological vulnerability abatement. Among the benefits, renewable electricity development is an increasing benefit for both countries.

We also find that at the start of China and India's active participation in international climate change negotiation (i.e., year 2008), China has higher costs and lower benefits. Compared with India, China has both higher carbon emission intensity (lower marginal abatement cost), higher carbon-intensive industry interests (higher expected economic loss), fewer fossil fuel imports (lower security of energy supply), less renewable electricity generation (lower expected economic gains), and lower ecological vulnerability index (lower ecological vulnerability abatement) in 2008. Interest-based approach, as a result, has insufficient explanatory power for China's stronger climate leadership initially. However, China's strong climate leadership stimulates low-carbon transition, especially obvious in its large decrease in carbon emission intensity and increase in renewable electricity generation. The transition reshapes the nation's interest in climate mitigation, and may serve as a booster for the increased climate leadership in recent years.

2.6.2 Norm-Based Explanations

The above analysis reveals that interests alone cannot lead to enough justification to take actions (Stavins, 2011). Table 2.3 shows the norms of environmental problems in China and India in the aspects of public environmental awareness around 2010, notions of sustainable development around 2010, and public climate awareness (action) both around 2010 and in 2022. We find that around 2010, environmentally friendly norms are generally formed in both countries, but China has stronger norms in all the three aspects. For example, 65% surveyed people in China have climate awareness, while in India the corresponding ratio is 37%. Public climate awareness (action) increases significantly both in China and India during the period of 2010–2022. In China, the percentage of people with a willingness to combat climate change becomes 79% in 2022. In India, the corresponding percentage becomes 75%. We can see that China and India both show an increase in public climate awareness (action). The level of public climate awareness (action) in India rises more, and converges to China's level.

Aside from the statistical evidence, we also use speeches and documents from China's leader to show the consistent norm for environmental protection in China. The environmental norms of China's current leader originated early: In 2005, Xi

Table 2.3 Countries' norms in environmental problems

	Around year 2010			Year 2022
	Public environmental awareness	Notion of sustainable development	Public climate awareness (action)	Public climate awareness (action)
China	0.2187	0.5648	0.65	0.79
India	0.0917	0.5220	0.37	0.75

Notes The data are mainly from the wave six of World Value Survey, Gallup Survey, and a survey conducted by Ipsos Global Advisor

Jinping, the current president of China, was the party secretary of Zhejiang province. Xi published an article in a provincial newspaper, where he illustrated the norm that "lucid waters and lush mountains are invaluable assets":

> If [we] can turn these ecological and environmental advantages into the advantages of ecological agriculture, ecological industry, ecological tourism and ecological economy, then lucid waters and lush mountains can be turned into invaluable assets. Lucid waters and lush mountains can bring invaluable assets, but invaluable assets cannot buy lucid waters and lush mountains. Lucid waters and lush mountains and invaluable assets can produce not only contradictions, but also dialectical unity.

Xi later incorporated "lucid waters and lush mountains" into his thought on "ecological civilization" during the China Eco-environmental Conference in 2018. Specifically, principles that must be followed in order to promote "ecological civilization" include "maintaining harmonious coexistence between man and nature", "lucid waters and lush mountains are invaluable assets", "a good ecological environment is the most inclusive well-being", "fostering a community of life for man and nature", "using the strictest rules of law to protect the ecological environment", and "working together to build a global ecological civilization". Specifically, Xi said during the conference:

> [We] must deeply involve [ourselves] in global environmental governance, enhance our voice and influence in the global environmental governance system, actively guide the direction of change in the international order and form solutions for world environmental protection and sustainable development.

China also forms the norm that net-zero is an essential part of China's ecological civilization construction. China's policy documents for carbon neutrality specifically formulates that carbon neutrality be incorporated into the overall layout of building an ecological civilization. This could be considered evidence of the norm (and logic of appropriateness) informing climate mitigation efforts. This ecological civilization norm (as a logic of appropriateness) might be one of the drivers behind China's climate action. In India's case, linking development priorities with climate change has traditionally been the norm in India's policymaking. The Indian National Action Plan on Climate Change launched in 2008, formally at least, calls for a co-benefits approach where the linkages with development and the environment are explicitly considered. The approach also features prominently in the country's Twelfth Five

Year Plan and Low Carbon Strategies for Inclusive Growth (LCSIG) report. The Indian National Action Plan on Climate Change, for example, specifies:

> India is faced with the challenge of sustaining its rapid economic growth while dealing with the global threat of climate change. This threat emanates from accumulated greenhouse gas emissions in the atmosphere, anthropogenically generated through long-term and intensive industrial growth and high consumption lifestyles in developed countries. While engaged with the international community to deal with this threat collectively and cooperatively, India needs a national strategy to firstly, adapt to climate change and secondly, to further enhance the ecological sustainability of India's development path.

Later on, India also pivoted to a more productive attitude towards climate change. In COP26, although poverty eradication and economic development are still mentioned in India's National Statement, India also proposed a new norm, the Lifestyle For Environment (LIFE), advocating an environmental friendly lifestyle:

> [LIFE] can become a mass movement of Environmental Conscious Life Style. What is needed today is Mindful and Deliberate Utilization, instead of Mindless and Destructive Consumption. These movements together can set goals that can revolutionize many sectors in diverse areas such as Fishing, Agriculture, Wellness, Dietary Choices, Packaging, Housing, Hospitality, Tourism, Clothing, Fashion, Water Management and Energy.

2.7 Discussion and Conclusion

China and India are the two developing countries with the bulk of total emissions, both faced with the challenge of sustaining their rapid economic growth while dealing with the global threat of climate change. In this paper, we analyze the international and domestic climate leadership of China and India, and explain the leading positions using interest-based and norm-based approaches.

China has substantive international and domestic climate leadership, although it serves more like a symbolic leader (i.e., more inclined to be an international leader) for emerging economies during earlier rounds of climate negotiation. Evidence of China's earlier international leadership (after 2008) is its initiation of the BASIC group and defining of CBDR. Internally, China's major focus has been economic development, and mainly aims to achieve relative decoupling, i.e., the decrease in carbon emissions relative to GDP. In recent years, however, we witness China taking stronger international and domestic positions, and an alignment between China's international and domestic leading positions. This is most evidenced by its proposal of carbon neutrality by 2060 and the formulation of relevant policies. China has since then vigorously promoted carbon emission reduction with government policies, promulgated a series of systems and regulations for the construction of ecological civilization, and established stricter regional carbon intensity control objectives and assessment systems.

Compared with China, India primarily takes the pioneer position, exerting greater domestic leadership after 2008. India implements ambitious domestic policies to reduce emissions, but the emission targets are not as strong in the international commitment, as India believes that its responsibility should be taken more as a favor to global society, instead of a responsibility. India's development goal is to continuously improve people's well-being and increase the proportion of the middle-class population. It has designed energy and climate development policies around this goal. Therefore, India's carbon emission reduction policies are more focused on supporting renewable electricity industry. With President Modi's pledge of net zero by 2070, India is also starting to take a greater leading position, and align its international and domestic leadership.

China and India both receive benefits and have positive climate-related norms in dealing with climate change. Using the interest-based approach, we identify the main benefit for China and India in climate change mitigation is their enhanced energy security, fulfilled interests of renewable electricity industry, and ecological vulnerability abatement. On the other hand, the main cost for China and India is their transition pain into low-carbon economy, especially expected economic losses. An interest-based approach alone offers limited explanation for China's stronger leadership than India, since India has more interests in most aspects of climate change mitigation. The reason is that climate change essentially represents a "tragedy of commons" on a global scale; countries' benefits in climate change mitigation are generally smaller than their costs if they act alone. Therefore, interest-based approaches have insufficient explanatory power (Nordhaus, 1994). Using the norm-based approach, we find that the positive climate-related norms are formed in both countries, and China has higher environmentally friendly norms across the aspects of public environmental awareness, notion of sustainable development, and public climate awareness (action). This observation validates that in our cases, the norms towards climate change mitigation are more essential in explaining climate leadership.

Based on the conclusions of this paper, we offer the following policy recommendations with regards to climate governance.

First, China and India should actively take leading positions. Most developing countries are unwilling or unable to take the leading position, while China and India have stronger international pressure and the motivation and capability of climate action (Abubakar & Dano, 2020). The specific actions that should be taken include developing renewable electricity, reducing coal investment, enhancing green technology innovation, creating carbon market mechanism, and promoting environmentally friendly lifestyle. China and India should also keep the consistency of international ambition and domestic policy. In order for the wording to be backed up by practice, China and India must make promising commitments and take concrete actions. In practice, there is a particular need for a flexible combination of assertions and actions that together constitute a convincing impetus for the other parties, especially the US and EU, to support China and India's initiatives.

Second, China and India have a shared view on climate change objectives, so the climate cooperation between the two countries is very important. While our research shows that China and India are already cooperating in international negotiations and domestic mitigation actions, there remain directions for further cooperation: For example, carbon emission intensity of India's service industry is relatively low. China and India could therefore carry out cooperation in the information technology (IT) and financial service industry. The bilateral cooperation between China and India could also help to shape global climate governance agendas going forward and over time, providing a basis for more coordinated actions in multilateral platforms.

Third, a multi-level polycentric system of climate governance should be built to strengthen the participation of cities, society, and individuals (Torney, 2019; Wurzel et al., 2019b). In climate governance, the rise of transnational municipal networks allows cities to collaborate through information-sharing, capacity-building, implementation, and rule-setting (Liu & Lo, 2021). Cities should more actively engage in major transnational municipal networks, such as Local Governments for Sustainability (ICLEI) and C40 Cities Climate Leadership Group (C40). Non-governmental organizations (NGOs) play an influential role in the multi-level system of climate governance. Especially, based on our research findings, to enhance the climate change targets of countries towards the 1.5 °C global warming path, the norms, instead of interests of climate change should be emphasized more by NGOs. Individuals, especially those from higher income levels, should take the responsibility of sustainable consumption.

Notes

1. Source: https://climate-diplomacy.org/sites/default/files/2020-10/350072665-Final-Version-EU-China-Leaders-Joint-Statement-on-Climate-Change.pdf.
2. Abatement costs from economic transition are proxied by carbon emission intensity. This is based on the fact that the lower the carbon emission intensity, the more advanced technology should be used to reduce the remaining carbon emissions, thus the marginal abatement cost of carbon emissions becomes higher (Du et al., 2015).
3. According to Hickmann (2013), expected economic loss will occur for countries that have profited from the carbon-intensive products. Therefore, the share of carbon-intensive sectors in GDP is a direct representation of expected economic loss.
4. The results of the survey are available at https://www.ipsos.com/sites/default/files/ct/news/documents/2022-04/Ipsos%20-%20Global%20Advisor%20-%20Earth%20Day%202022%20-%20Release%201.pdf.
5. As mentioned above, the two countries have different national contexts in terms of geographic and demographic vulnerabilities, and the diplomatic situation is also different. Therefore, competition is an unavoidable existence. For example, as noted by Jayaram (2014), the two countries have diverged on a number of times, most notably over the topic of low-carbon Intellectual Property Rights (IPR). On broader issues, as neighboring countries, China and India face complex contradictions and competitions on issues such as territorial disputes, regional influence competition, and waterway control. However, with regards to the global challenge of climate change, the two countries have similar situations, positions, and national interests, and the cooperation has been more prominent compared to competition.
6. One exception is China's share of carbon-intensive sector increase since 2015. This is mainly driven by electric generation sector that went through restructuring reform in 2015. After the reform, power plants' revenue and value added both increase.

References

Abubakar, I. R., & Dano, U. L. (2020). Sustainable urban planning strategies for mitigating climate change in Saudi Arabia. *Environment, Development and Sustainability, 22*(6), 5129–5152.

Agarwal, A., & Narain, S. (1991). *Global warming in an unequal world: A case of environmental colonialism.* Centre for Science and Environment.

Alizadeh, R., Majidpour, M., Maknoon, R., & Kaleibari, S. S. (2016). Clean development mechanism in Iran: Does it need a revival? *International Journal of Global Warming, 10*(1–3), 196–215.

Atteridge, A., Shrivastava, M. K., Pahuja, N., & Upadhyay, H. (2012). Climate policy in India: What shapes international, national and state policy? *Ambio, 41*(1), 68–77.

Barbi, F. (2016). Governing climate change in China and Brazil: Mitigation strategies. *Journal of Chinese Political Science, 21*, 357–370.

Bernstein, S. (2001). *The compromise of liberal environmentalism.* Columbia University Press.

Blaxekjær, L. Ø., & Nielsen, T. D. (2015). Mapping the narrative positions of new political groups under the UNFCCC. *Climate Policy, 15*(6), 751–766.

Blondeel, M., Colgan, J., & Van de Graaf, T. (2019). What drives norm success? Evidence from anti-fossil fuel campaigns. *Global Environmental Politics, 19*(4), 63–84.

Blondeel, M., & Van de Graaf, T. (2018). Toward a global coal mining moratorium? A comparative analysis of coal mining policies in the USA, China, India and Australia. *Climatic Change, 150*(1), 89–101.

CAT. (2021). *Glasgow's 2030 credibility gap: Net zero's lip service to climate action.* The Climate Action Tracker. https://climateactiontracker.org/publications/glasgows-2030-credibility-gap-net-zeros-lip-service-to-climate-action/

Chen, J., Cui, H., Xu, Y., & Ge, Q. (2021). Long-term temperature and sea-level rise stabilization before and beyond 2100: Estimating the additional climate mitigation contribution from China's recent 2060 carbon neutrality pledge. *Environmental Research Letters, 16*, 074032.

Chen, M., Zhang, L., Teng, F., Dai, J., Li, Z., Wang, Z., & Li, Y. (2020). Climate technology transfer in BRI era: Needs, priorities, and barriers from receivers' perspective. *Ecosystem Health and Sustainability, 6*(1), 1780948.

Delman, J. (2011). China's 'radicalism at the center': Regime legitimation through climate politics and climate governance. *Journal of Chinese Political Science, 16*, 183–205.

Downie, C., & Williams, M. (2018). After the Paris agreement: What role for the BRICS in global climate governance? *Global Policy, 9*(3), 398–407.

Du, L., Hanley, A., & Wei, C. (2015). Estimating the marginal abatement cost curve of CO_2 emissions in China: Provincial panel data analysis. *Energy Economics, 48*, 217–229.

Dubash, N. K. (2009). *Toward a progressive Indian and global climate politics* (Centre for Policy Research Climate Initiative Working Paper, 2009).

Dubash, N. K. (2013). The politics of climate change in India: Narratives of equity and co-benefits. *Wiley Interdisciplinary Reviews: Climate Change, 4*(3), 191–201.

Duan, H., Zhou, S., Jiang, K., Bertram, C., Harmsen, M., Kriegler, E., Van Vuuren, D. P., Wang, S., Fujimori, S., Tavoni, M., & Ming, X. (2021). Assessing China's efforts to pursue the 1.5 °C warming limit. *Science, 372*, 378–385.

Duro, J. A., & Padilla, E. (2008). Analysis of the international distribution of per capita CO_2 emissions using the polarization concept. *Energy Policy, 36*, 456–466.

Falkner, R. (2016). The Paris agreement and the new logic of international climate politics. *International Affairs, 92*(5), 1107–1125.

Fang, D., Chen, B., Hubacek, K., Ni, R., Chen, L., Feng, K., & Lin, J. (2019). Clean air for some: Unintended spillover effects of regional air pollution policies. *Science Advances, 5*, 10.

Fuhr, H. (2021). The rise of the global south and the rise in carbon emissions. *Third World Quarterly, 42*(11), 2724–2746.

Guan, D., Meng, J., Reiner, D. M., Zhang, N., Shan, Y., Mi, Z., Shao, S., Liu, Z., Zhang, Q., & Davis, S. J. (2018). Structural decline in China's CO_2 emissions through transitions in industry and energy systems. *Nature Geoscience, 11*(8), 551–555.

Gupta, D., Ghersi, F., Vishwanathan, S. S., & Garg, A. (2019). Achieving sustainable development in India along low carbon pathways: Macroeconomic assessment. *World Development, 123*, 104623.

Hickmann, T. (2013). Science–policy interaction in international environmental politics: An analysis of the ozone regime and the climate regime. *Environmental Economics and Policy Studies, 16*, 21–44.

Höhne, N., Gidden, M. J., den Elzen, M., Hans, F., Fyson, C., Geiges, A., Jeffery, M. L., Gonzales-Zuñiga, S., Mooldijk, S., Hare, W., & Rogelj, J. (2021). Wave of net zero emission targets opens window to meeting the Paris agreement. *Nature Climate Change, 11*(10), 820–822.

Holzinger, K., Knill, C., & Arts, B. (2008a). *Environmental policy convergence in Europe: The impact of international institutions and trade*. Cambridge University Press.

Holzinger, K., Knill, C., & Sommerer, T. (2008b). Environmental policy convergence: The impact of international harmonization, transnational communication, and regulatory competition. *International Organization, 62*, 553–587.

IEA. (2018). *Outlook for producer economies: What do changing energy dynamics mean for major oil and gas exporters?* IEA Publication.

IEA. (2021). *World energy outlook 2021*. IEA Publication.

Jänicke, M. (2005). Trend-setters in environmental policy: The character and role of pioneer countries. *European Environment, 15*, 129–142.

Jayaram, D. (2014). Sino-Indian cooperation at the climate change negotiations: The past, the present and the future. *Chinese Journal of Urban and Environmental Studies, 2*(1), 1450010.

Johnsson, F., Kjärstad, J., & Rootzén, J. (2019). The Threat to climate change mitigation posed by the abundance of fossil fuels. *Climate Policy, 19*(2), 258–274.

Jha, P. (2009). Indian public perceptions of the international climate change negotiations. In D. Michel & A. Pandya (Eds.), *Indian climate policy: Choices and challenges*. Henry L. Stimson Centre.

Karlsson, C., Parker, C., Hjerpe, M., & Linnér, B. O. (2011). Looking for leaders: Perceptions of climate change leadership among climate change negotiation participants. *Global Environmental Politics, 11*(1), 89–107.

Kern, K. (2019). Cities as leaders in EU multilevel climate governance: Embedded upscaling of local experiments in Europe. *Environmental Politics, 28*(1), 125–145.

Klebaner, S., & Ramírez Pérez, S. M. (2019). Managing technical changes from the scales of legal regulation: German clean cars against the European pollutant emissions regulations in the 1980s. *Management & Organizational History, 1*(4), 442–468.

Klenert, D., Mattauch, L., Combet, E., Edenhofer, O., Hepburn, C., Rafaty, R., & Stern, N. (2018). Making carbon pricing work for citizens. *Nature Climate Change, 8*, 669–677.

Knill, C., Heichel, S., & Arndt, D. (2012). Really a front-runner, really a straggler? Of environmental leaders and laggards in the European Union and beyond—A quantitative policy perspective. *Energy Policy, 48*, 36–45.

Liefferink, D., & Andersen, M. S. (1998). Strategies of the 'green' member states in EU environmental policy-making. *Journal of European Public Policy, 5*(2), 254–270.

Liefferink, D., Arts, B., Kamstra, J., & Ooijevaar, J. (2009). Leaders and laggards in environmental policy: A quantitative analysis of domestic policy outputs. *Journal of European Public Policy, 16*, 677–700.

Liefferink, D., & Wurzel, R. (2017). Environmental leaders and pioneers: Agents of change? *Journal of European Public Policy, 24*(7), 951–968.

Liu, Z., Deng, Z., He, G., Wang, H., Zhang, X., Lin, J., Qi, Y., & Liang, X. (2022). Challenges and opportunities for carbon neutrality in China. *Nature Reviews Earth & Environment, 3*, 141–155.

Liu, M., & Lo, K. (2021). Pathways to international cooperation on climate governance in China: A comparative analysis. *Journal of Chinese Governance, 6*(3), 417–434.

March, J. G., & Olsen, J. P. (1998). The institutional dynamics of international political orders. *International Organization, 52*(4), 943–969.
Meckling, J., Kong, B., & Madan, T. (2015). Oil and state capitalism: Government-firm coopetition in China and India. *Review of International Political Economy, 22*(6), 1159–1187.
Meinshausen, M., Lewis, J., McGlade, C., Gütschow, J., Nicholls, Z., Burdon, R., Cozzi, L., & Hackmann, B. (2022). Realization of Paris agreement pledges may limit warming just below 2 °C. *Nature, 604*, 304–309.
Meng, J., Mi, Z., Guan, D., Li, J., Tao, S., Li, Y., Feng, K., Liu, J., Liu, Z., Wang, X., & Zhang, Q. (2018). The rise of south-south trade and its effect on global CO_2 emissions. *Nature Communications, 9*, 1871.
Michaelowa, K., & Michaelowa, A. (2012). India as an emerging power in international climate negotiations. *Climate Policy, 12*, 575–590.
Millar, R. J., Fuglestvedt, J. S., Friedlingstein, P., Rogelj, J., Grubb, M. J., Matthews, H. D., Skeie, R. B., Forster, P. M., Frame, D. J., & Allen, M. R. (2017). Emission budgets and pathways consistent with limiting warming to 1.5 °C. *Nature Geoscience, 10*(10), 741–747.
Mizo, R. (2016). India, China and climate cooperation. *India Quarterly, 72*(4), 375–394.
Mohan, A. (2017). From Rio to Paris: India in global climate politics. *Rising Powers Quarterly, 2*(3), 39–61.
Mohan, A., & Wehnert, T. (2019). Is India pulling its weight? India's nationally determined contribution and future energy plans in global climate policy. *Climate Policy, 19*(3), 275–282.
Naurin, D., & Wallace, H. (2008). Unveiling the Council of the European Union. In *Games governments play in Brussels*. Palgrave Macmillan.
Nordhaus, W. D. (1994). *Managing the global commons: The economics of climate change*. MIT Press.
Oberthür, S., & Dupont, C. (2021). The European Union's international climate leadership: Towards a grand climate strategy? *Journal of European Public Policy, 28*(7), 1095–1114.
Ou, Y., Iyer, G., Clarke, L., Edmonds, J., Fawcett, A. A., Hultman, N., McFarland, J. R., Binsted, M., Cui, R., Fyson, C., & Geiges, A. (2021). Can updated climate pledges limit warming well below 2 °C? *Science, 374*(6568), 693–695.
Pan, J. (2011). Carbon competitiveness is China's future. *Energy Conservation & Environmental Protection, 5*, 16–21. (in Chinese).
Parker, C. F., Karlsson, C., & Hjerpe, M. (2015). Climate change leaders and followers: Leadership recognition and selection in the UNFCCC negotiations. *International Relations, 29*(4), 434–454.
Rajamani, L. (2008). The Indian way: Exploring the synergies between development, energy and climate goals. In L. Barrera-Hernandez, Y. Omorogbe, C. Redgwell, & D. Zillman (Eds.), *Beyond the carbon economy*. Oxford University Press.
Rapp, T., Schwägerl, C., & Traufetter, G. (2010, May 5). The Copenhagen protocol, how China and India sabotaged the UN climate summit. *Spiegel*.
Raymond, L., Weldon, S. L., Kelly, D., Arriaga, X. B., & Clark, A. M. (2013). Making change: Norm-based strategies for institutional change to address intractable problems. *Political Research Quarterly, 67*, 197–211.
Rogelj, J., Den Elzen, M., Höhne, N., Fransen, T., Fekete, H., Winkler, H., Schaeffer, R., Sha, F., Riahi, K., & Meinshausen, M. (2016). Paris agreement climate proposals need a boost to keep warming well below 2 °C. *Nature, 534*, 631–639.
Sapiains, R., Ibarra, C., Jiménez, G., O'Ryan, R., Blanco, G., Moraga, P., & Rojas, M. (2021). Exploring the contours of climate governance: An interdisciplinary systematic literature review from a southern perspective. *Environmental Policy and Governance, 31*(1), 46–59.
Sprinz, D., & Vaahtoranta, T. (1994). The interest-based explanation of international environmental policy. *International Organization, 48*, 77–105.
Stavins, R. N. (2011). The problem of the commons: Still unsettled after 100 years. *American Economic Review, 101*(1), 81–108.
Tollefson, J. (2018). IPCC says limiting global warming to 1.5 °C will require drastic action. *Nature, 562*(7726), 172–173.

Torney, D. (2019). Follow the leader? Conceptualising the relationship between leaders and followers in polycentric climate governance. *Environmental Politics, 28*(1), 167–186.

Tørstad, V., Sælen, H., & Bøyum, L. S. (2020). The domestic politics of international climate commitments: Which factors explain cross-country variation in NDC ambition? *Environmental Research Letters, 15*(2), 024021.

Vihma, A. (2011). India and the global climate governance: Between principles and pragmatism. *The Journal of Environment & Development, 20*(1), 69–94.

Vogel, D. (1997). Trading up and governing across: Transnational governance and environmental protection. *Journal of European Public Policy, 4*, 556–571.

Wang, K. H., Su, C. W., Lobonţ, O. R., & Umar, M. (2021). Whether crude oil dependence and CO_2 emissions influence military expenditure in net oil importing countries? *Energy Policy, 153*(2021), 112281.

Wiering, M., Liefferink, D., & Beijen, B. (2018). The internal and external face of Dutch environmental policy: A case of fading environmental leadership? *Environmental Science & Policy, 81*, 18–25.

Wu, F. (2018). *Energy and climate policies in China and India: A two-level comparative study.* Cambridge University Press.

Wurzel, R. K. W., Liefferink, D., & Di Lullo, M. (2019a). The European Council, the Council and the member states: Changing environmental leadership dynamics in the European Union. *Environmental Politics, 28*, 248–270.

Wurzel, R. K., Liefferink, D., & Torney, D. (2019b). Pioneers, leaders and followers in multilevel and polycentric climate governance. *Environmental Politics, 28*(1), 1–21.

Yu, S., Zheng, S., Li, X., & Li, L. (2018). China can peak its energy-related carbon emissions before 2025: Evidence from industry restructuring. *Energy Economics, 73*, 91–107.

Zhai, Y. (2011). *Thoughts on low-carbon development.* http://www.npc.gov.cn/npc/c222/201111/f01f2a57703d4c139398b566bad84a56.shtml (in Chinese).

Zhang, X., Zhao, X., Jiang, Z., & Shao, S. (2017). How to achieve the 2030 CO_2 emission-reduction targets for China's industrial sector: Retrospective decomposition and prospective trajectories. *Global Environmental Change, 44*, 83–97.

Zheng, J., Mi, Z., Coffman, D. M., Milcheva, S., Shan, Y., Guan, D., & Wang, S. (2019). Regional development and carbon emissions in China. *Energy Economics, 81*, 25–36.

Chapter 3
Building the "Green Silk Road" Towards Global Carbon Neutrality—China's Path Choice

Kai Fang, Jixuan Xi, and Chenglin Li

Abstract The 'Belt and Road' Initiative (BRI) has made substantial progress. However, countries partnering in BRI face practical challenges, such as rapid growth in carbon emissions, severe carbon leakage, and various obstacles to carbon peak and neutrality. Climate change is increasingly hindering the BRI countries from achieving sustainable development. From a carbon neutrality perspective, it is significant to accelerate the builiding of the 'Green Silk Road'. Therefore, this paper presents the following policy recommendations: strengthen green and low-carbon cooperation with BRI countries at the national level, establish a green development system at the BRI level, propose a China's path choice to climate governance risks at the global level.

Keywords Carbon neutrality · The 'Belt and Road' Initiative · Green Silk Road

3.1 Research Background

The COVID-19 pandemic continues to wreak havoc globally, profoundly impacting the international political and economic landscape. From an ecological balance perspective, the pandemic outbreak is a consequence of the imbalance between humans and nature. While the economic downturn and pandemic control measures may temporarily reverse the upward trend in global carbon emissions (Liu et al., 2020), the enduring strategies to address climate change lie in the implementation of the concept of green development, the promotion of low-carbon societal transformation, and the strengthening of international climate cooperation. Against this backdrop, promoting a green recovery of the world economy is gradually becoming a global consensus. As the world's largest developing country and a major emitter of greenhouse gases, China should set an example in addressing climate change and

K. Fang (✉) · J. Xi · C. Li
School of Public Affairs, Zhejiang University, Hangzhou, China
e-mail: fangk@zju.edu.cn

B. Gong et al. (eds.), *Chinese Governance and Transformation Towards Carbon Neutrality*, Resources, Environment and Agricultural Development,
https://doi.org/10.1007/978-981-97-9996-1_3

leading climate governance. Since the 18th National Congress of the Communist Party of China, China has incorporated the concept of ecological civilization and building a beautiful country into its overall national strategic layout. It has adhered to sustainable development, prioritizing ecology and pursuing green, low-carbon development.[1]

Since its launch in 2013, the 'Belt and Road' Initiative (BRI) has attracted considerable attention from countries along the routes and the international community. It has provided a Chinese approach and solution for advancing global governance. It has also added new impetus to the realization of the United Nations '2030 Sustainable Development Agenda' and the 'Paris Agreement'.[2] As early as 2016, President Xi Jinping called for countries to work together to create a 'Green Silk Road'.[3] Chinese official departments have successively issued relevant policy documents (see Table 3.1), with green development becoming more prominent as the foundation of the BRI.

Nevertheless, most countries along the BRI are still in the early stages of industrialization and urbanization, experiencing rapid growth in carbon emissions. Achieving peak carbon emissions and carbon neutrality poses a significant challenge. At the same time, many sustainable development goals in this region remain incomplete. Many countries are situated in ecologically fragile areas, where their environmental footprint exceeds the corresponding carrying capacity, leading to generally low environmental sustainability (Fang et al., 2021a, 2021b, 2021c). This indicates inadequate implementation of green development concepts in the practical process of BRI and suggests that relevant theoretical research lags behind practical exploration. There is an urgent need to start from the global trend of carbon neutrality, conduct an in-depth analysis of the challenges faced in the building of the 'Green Silk Road', and propose systematic action measures to address climate change from a theoretical perspective. This will thus stimulate the enormous potential for joint efforts to overcome the crisis and achieve sustainable development. To address this, the second part of this paper discusses the main characteristics and causes of carbon emissions in countries along the BRI. The third part proposes essential tasks and implementation approaches for building the 'Green Silk Road', based on the current challenges, from three levels: China, the BRI, and the global perspective. The fourth part summarizes the main research findings.

3.2 Characteristics and Causes of Carbon Emissions in Countries Along the BRI

3.2.1 Rapid Growth in Carbon Emissions

Carbon emissions in countries along the BRI have increased rapidly. The carbon emissions of 65 countries along the route increased from 9.37 billion tons in 1992 to 21.13 billion tons in 2020, with an average annual growth rate of 4.5%. Their

Table 3.1 Relevant policy documents of the 'Green Silk Road'

Time	File name	Issuing authority	Main content
March 2015	Vision and Actions on Jointly Building Silk Road Economic Belt and 21st-Century Maritime Silk Road	National Development and Reform Commission, Ministry of Foreign Affairs, Ministry of Commerce	Emphasize the concept of ecological civilization in investment and trade, strengthen cooperation on ecological environment, biodiversity, and climate change adaptation, and jointly build the 'Green Silk Road'
November 2016	13th Five-Year Plan for Ecological and Environmental Protection	State Council	Promoting the green development of the BRI, coordinate the overall ecological and environmental protection work of the 'Belt and Road' initiative for the next five years
May 2017	Guiding Opinions on Promoting 'Green 'Belt and Road' Development; Cooperation Plan for Ecological and Environmental Protection of the 'Belt and Road' Initiative	The former involves the Ministry of Ecology and Environment, the Ministry of Foreign Affairs, the National Development and Reform Commission, and the Ministry of Commerce; the latter involves the Ministry of Ecology and Environment	The former clearly outlines the overall thought for the construction of the 'Green Silk Road'; the latter formulates specific planning goals and six key tasks
December 2017	Action Plan for Standardized Interconnection and Interworking of the 'Belt and Road' (2018–2020)	National Standardization Committee	Focuses on improving the compatibility of the national standard system with the countries related to the BRI, deploy nine key tasks, one of which is to strengthen energy conservation and environmental protection standardization cooperation, serving the building of the 'Green Silk Road'

(continued)

Table 3.1 (continued)

Time	File name	Issuing authority	Main content
April 2019	Jointly Building the 'Belt and Road' Initiative: Progress, Contributions, and Prospects	Office of the Leading Group for Promoting the 'Belt and Road' Initiative	A comprehensive review of the process of jointly building the BRI over the past five years, conducting ecological and environmental protection cooperation with countries along the route, and advocating for the signing of cooperation agreements for the construction of the 'Green Silk Road' with more countries
March 2022	Opinions on Promoting Green Development in the Joint Construction of the 'Belt and Road'	National Development and Reform Commission, Ministry of Foreign Affairs, Ministry of Ecology and Environment, Ministry of Commerce	Strengthen cooperation with countries along the BRI in key fields such as green infrastructure, green energy, green transportation, and green trade

share of global carbon emissions climbed from 44.2% in 1992 to 60.7% in 2020.[4] In 2020, five of the top ten carbon-emitting countries were from countries along the BRI, including China, India, Russia, Iran, and Indonesia, accounting for 75.8% of the region's carbon emissions. Regions with high per capita carbon emissions are concentrated mainly in Western Asian countries; Qatar has the highest per capita carbon emissions at 30.7 tons, followed by Kuwait, the United Arab Emirates, Saudi Arabia, and Kazakhstan, all with per capita carbon emissions exceeding 10 tons, well above the global average of 4.5 tons. Carbon emissions in Southeast Asia, South Asia, and North Africa remain high and continue to grow, while Central Asian countries have relatively small but growing total carbon emissions. It is evident that the rapid growth in carbon emissions has become an significant issue in the BRI region that cannot be ignored.

Economic development is considered the primary factor driving the growth of carbon emissions. Studies have shown that economic growth promotes carbon emissions in both the short and long term (Safi et al., 2021). Research has also revealed a non-linear relationship between economic growth and carbon emissions (Rauf et al., 2018). While some studies indicate an inverted U-shaped relationship, others argue that this relationship only applies to developed economies. In 2019, the total GDP of the 65 countries along the BRI (excluding missing data) was $28.8 trillion, accounting for 32.8% of the world's GDP.[5] China and India together accounted for 59.3% of the total economic output of these countries in 2019. Over the past 20 years, Southeast Asian countries achieved an average GDP growth rate of 5.1%, while Western Asian countries experienced relatively rapid economic development due to oil and gas exports. For most countries, the inflection point of the inverted U-shaped relationship between GDP and carbon emissions has not yet been reached, indicating that carbon emissions are likely to increase.

Energy consumption also positively impacts carbon emissions. The dependence on fossil fuels is a major contributer to the increase in carbon emissions in countries along the BRI (Shakib et al., 2022). Overall, the energy consumption structure of the countries along the BRI is primarily dependent on fossil fuels, which accounted for as much as 86.8% of primary energy in 2018.[6] The top carbon-emitting countries, including China, India, and Russia, all have fossil fuel proportions of over 85%. Countries such as Iran, Iraq, Saudi Arabia, and the United Arab Emirates have fossil fuel consumption rates above 90%. Indonesia, Thailand, Malaysia, and Singapore primarily consume energy from petroleum and natural gas, with renewable energy sources still in the early stages of development, currently meeting only about 15% of energy demand.[7] With the continuous rise in energy demand, the carbon emissions of most countries along the BRI will continue to increase.

Population size and urbanization also directly drive carbon emissions (Fu & Si, 2017). For instance, South Asia and Southeast Asia not only have large population bases, but also maintain high growth rates. The significant increase in population has stimulated the demand for additional energy, further driving carbon emissions. Among the top five carbon-emitting countries along the BRI, four are among the world's top ten in terms of population.[8] Additionally, research by Muhammad et al. found that urbanization leads to the construction and operation of infrastructure, thereby exhibiting an inverted U-shaped relationship with carbon emissions in the BRI region (Muhammad et al., 2020). Apart from certain Western Asian countries (such as Qatar, Kuwait, the United Arab Emirates, and Singapore) with relatively high levels of urbanization, most countries along the BRI are in the stage of accelerated urbanization, especially in South Asia, where the urbanization rate was less than 40% in 2020.[9] The inflection point of the inverted U-shaped relationship between urbanization and carbon emissions has yet to arrive.

3.2.2 Severe Situation of Carbon Leakage

As the global value chain cooperation deepens, increasingly frequent international trade generates a large amount of carbon emissions in the form of embodied carbon, leading to imbalances in both imports and exports. This imbalance leads to importing countries shifting environmental costs onto exporting countries, a phenomenon termed carbon leakage (Lu et al., 2020).

From the perspective of embodied carbon flows within the 'Belt and Road' region, the top three countries with the highest net exports of embodied carbon in 2015 were China, Russia, and India, respectively. Specifically, China's embodied carbon emissions primarily flowed into Southern Asia and Southeast Asia, including countries such as India, Thailand, Singapore, and Vietnam. Russia's embodied carbon emissions mainly flowed into China, Central and Eastern Europe, and the regions of Western Asia and Northern Africa. Meanwhile, India's embodied carbon emissions mainly flowed into Southern Asia and the regions of Western Asia and Northern Africa (Lu et al., 2020). Specifically, Singapore is the largest net importer of embodied carbon emissions, with its embodied carbon emissions primarily originating from countries such as China, Malaysia, Indonesia, and India (Fang et al., 2021a, 2021b, 2021c).

From the perspective of embodied carbon flows between countries along the BRI and countries outside the region, the United States, Western Europe, and Japan and South Korea collectively account for as much as 30% of the consumption-related carbon emissions in countries along the BRI (Han et al., 2018). Among these, China, Southern Asia, and Southeast Asia are the main areas of embodied carbon outflow, while the United States, the United Kingdom, France, Japan, and Germany are the main areas of embodied carbon inflow. Taking China's export trade as an example, the consumption of the United States, the European Union, and Japan accounts for 24%, 25%, and 10%, respectively, of the embodied carbon emissions of China's export trade (Liu et al., 2015). Obviously, a considerable portion of the carbon emissions produced by countries along the BRI are to meet the final consumption demands of developed countries outside the region, making the BRI region a major source of global carbon leakage.

Globalization has deepened economic interdependence among countries, leading to a continuous expansion of international trade, consequently resulting in carbon leakage. Within the BRI region, the trade balance and the structure of import and export industries are essential influencing factors (Liu et al., 2014). Taking China and India as examples, China has become the world's largest exporter of goods since 2009. Machinery and electronic products and labor-intensive products (such as clothing, textiles, toys, etc.) account for as much as 77.1% of the export structure.[10] The export of high-carbon products has made China a major source of carbon leakage. In recent years, India, a significant trading nation, has witnessd a continuous surge in the total value of goods imports and exports. Its imports mainly consist of petroleum, natural gas, iron ore, and other chemical raw materials, while its exports mainly include mineral products, chemical products, and precious metal products, which are high-carbon manufactured goods. Compared to the extraction of raw materials, the processing of these goods generates more carbon emissions, making India another important source of carbon leakage. As one of the world's foremost energy suppliers, Russia's energy product exports have always been an important part of its fiscal revenues,[11] making them another significant source of carbon leakage.

From the perspective of countries along the BRI and countries outside the region, the level of participation in the value chain affects carbon emissions through scale and structural effects. An increase in the level of the value chain will promote a reduction in carbon emissions by reducing the scale of exports and lowering the proportion of manufacturing in GDP (Shi et al., 2022). Developed countries such as the United States and Western Europe, due to their technological and capital advantages, mainly export high-end manufacturing and services, positioning themselves at the mid to high-end of the value chain. In contrast, countries along the BRI mainly export energy-intensive and labor-intensive products, which are at the middle and lower ends of the value chain and often become carbon leakage points. In addition, the transfer of low-end manufacturing to developing countries, influenced by environmental regulations and industrial policies in developed countries, has further aggravated the carbon leakage situation in the BRI region.

3.2.3 Diverse Challenges of Carbon Peaking

Carbon peaking refers to the point when carbon emissions reach their maximum level in a certain region in recent years, and subsequently form a stable trend. During the plateau period following the peak, carbon emissions may rebound, but they should not surpass the peak level (Zhang et al., 2020). According to this criterion, 24 countries along the BRI showed signs of peaking between 1990 and 2019,[12] mainly concentrated in Central and Eastern European countries. Among them, Russia, Azerbaijan, Cyprus, Bulgaria, Romania, and Hungary entered a plateau period after achieving carbon peaking; Georgia, Kyrgyzstan, Armenia, the Czech Republic, and Estonia showed a significant downward trend after carbon peaking. However, nearly two-thirds of the countries along the route have not yet achieved carbon peaking. Among them, China, Pakistan, Vietnam, and other countries are experiencing a rapid economic growth, accompanied by a high demand for energy consumption and a continuous rise in carbon emissions, and have yet to reach their peaking point; Bosnia and Herzegovina, Macedonia, and other countries have shown fluctuating carbon emissions without obvious signs of peaking; Tajikistan's carbon emissions have steadily rebounded after a sharp decline, and it is not yet clear whether it has peaked.

In countries that have already achieved carbon peaking, carbon dioxide emissions and economic growth have shown a decoupling relationship. For example, countries such as Romania, Kyrgyzstan, and Estonia have shown a strong decoupling state, with carbon dioxide emissions decreasing with GDP growth. Russia, Azerbaijan, Georgia, and Armenia have shown a weak decoupling state, where the growth of carbon emissions is lower than that of GDP. Among them, Russia belongs to the natural peaking type, and its peaking path is less affected by emission reduction policies, while Poland, Romania, and other countries belong to the economic recession type, and factors such as the dramatic changes in Eastern Europe and the collapse of the Soviet Union have led to a slowdown or decline in economic growth, resulting in a decrease in carbon emissions and achieving carbon peaking (Wu et al., 2018).

In countries that have not yet achieved carbon peaking, carbon dioxide emissions in countries such as China and Pakistan have shown a continuous growth trend, a weak decoupling relationship with economic growth, and a particular potential for peaking (Wu et al., 2018). Moreover, late-developing countries represented by China belong to the policy peaking type; that is, they aim to achieve carbon peaking as soon as possible through proactive formulation of vital peaking targets and action plans driven by policies (Zhuang et al., 2022). On the other hand, middle- and low-income countries, represented by Tajikistan and Vietnam, are still in the process of rapid industrialization and urbanization, focusing more on economic development rather than greenhouse gas emissions reduction, making the possibility of peaking in the short term relatively low (Muhammad et al., 2020).

3.2.4 Carbon Neutrality Remains to Be Done

China has only 30 years between 2030, when it aims to reach its carbon emission peak, and 2060, when it aims to achieve carbon neutrality. In contrast, the 27 countries of the European Union, as a whole, had already peaked their carbon emissions as early as 1990, but their commitment to carbon neutrality is set for 2050, a gap of 60 years (Fang & Li, 2021). This demonstrates that achieving carbon neutrality is a more daunting task for China (Fang et al., 2021a, 2021b, 2021c). This is also the case for most countries along the BRI.

Nevertheless, within the BRI region, 26 countries have already proposed carbon neutrality targets. These include: 1 country that has achieved carbon neutrality (Bhutan), 1 country that has legislated to ensure carbon neutrality (Hungary), and 3 countries that have declared policies for carbon neutrality (China, Singapore, Slovenia). The carbon neutrality goals of 21 countries are still under discussion and development.[13]

One reason is that most countries along the BRI lack clear constraints on carbon neutrality goals. Writing carbon neutrality targets into law is the most binding form of commitment.[14] While policy declarations represent official actions, their legal binding force is relatively weak. In addition, countries that have legislated or declared carbon neutrality policies do not have consistent definitions of its connotations, using different terms such as climate neutrality, carbon neutrality, net zero carbon emissions, and net zero emissions (Deng et al., 2021). For example, Slovakia describes it as climate neutrality, which not only considers the balance between greenhouse gas emissions and removals, but also the regional or local geophysical effects of human activities; Singapore describes it as net zero emissions, which aims to achieve a balance between greenhouse gas emissions and absorptions.

On the other hand, many countries along the BRI are located in arid and semi-arid areas with low forest coverage and very limited ecological carbon sink capacity. Even in some areas with relatively good vegetation, progress in the forestry carbon sink market has been slow due to the lack of sound commercial development models and policy support. In addition, due to technological and financial constraints, the BRI region has not yet carried out large-scale research and industrial layout for negative emission technologies. Currently, only four countries, including China, Saudi Arabia, the United Arab Emirates, and Qatar, have piloted individual commercial Carbon Capture, Utilization, and Storage (CCUS) projects (Li et al., 2021), with the annual capture volume far below the region's emissions.

3.3 Building Path of the 'Green Silk Road' Towards Carbon Neutrality

This section discusses the building and global context of the 'Green Silk Road' and the BRI region.

3.3.1 At the Chinese Perspective: Deepening Green and Low-Carbon Cooperation with Countries Along the BRI

3.3.1.1 Promote Renewable Energy Cooperation

The development of renewable energy plays an important role in mitigating climate change, improving energy structure, and ensuring energy security. As a major player in renewable energy, China consistently holds the world's leading position in installed capacity for solar, wind, and hydroelectric power generation. It has established a relatively comprehensive renewable energy industry system, boasting leading technologies in hydroelectric power, photovoltaic power, and wind power, and has ranked first in the world in renewable energy investment for ten consecutive years.[15] In 2020, for the first time, the proportion of renewable energy in China's energy investment in countries along the BRI surpassed that of fossil fuels.[16] During the general debate of the 76th session of the United Nations General Assembly in 2021, President Xi Jinping, on behalf of the Chinese government, announced that no new overseas coal-fired power projects would be undertaken.

The BRI region is abundant in renewable energy resources (Wang, 2016), and China, along with countries in the route, have broad prospects for cooperation in the development and utilization of these resources. Examining the different regions, Southeast and South Asian countries possess abundant solar, wind, hydro, and geothermal energy resources. However, due to constraints such as economic, technological, and cultural factors, the utilization of renewable energy remains low. China and this region should engage in practical cooperation focusing on high-proportion renewable energy power systems, innovation in renewable energy technologies, and mutual recognition of standard systems. Central and Western Asian countries have abundant solar and wind energy resources. In recent years, they have successively issued a series of policy incentives that provide opportunities for renewable energy cooperation. For instance, the 100-megawatt wind power project in Zhanatas, the largest in Central Asia and jointly developed by China and Kazakhstan, has been completed and put into operation, generating approximately 350 million kilowatt-hours of electricity annually.[17] Most countries in Central and Eastern Europe possess relatively advanced wind and photovoltaic power generation technologies. In recent years, their energy structures have been continuously optimized, with renewable energy accounting for 24.2% of the total in 2019.[18] China should fully utilize the

'16+1' dialogue mechanism, considering cooperation with Central and Eastern European countries as a new growth point for the building of the 'Green Silk Road', and jointly develop high-quality renewable energy projects.

3.3.1.2 Increase Carbon Sink Cooperation

The concept of 'nature-based solutions' has arouse international attention for addressing climate change since the United Nations New York Summit in September 2019. Natural ecosystems are deeply involved in the Earth's carbon cycle, and their carbon sink is crucial to achieving carbon neutrality. China and countries along the BRI have broad prospects for cooperation on carbon sink. For example, China and the ASEAN (primarily Southeast Asian countries) possess 33% of the global mangroves,[19] which play a significant role in mitigating climate change due to their strong carbon sequestration capabilities.

China should work with ASEAN countries to enhance mangrove resource protection and ecological restoration, increase carbon sink reserves, and improve ecological service functions. China should take the lead in conducting surveys on various ecological carbon sink and their development potentials, as well as researching and formulating internationally compatible monitoring systems and accounting standards for forest, grassland, and marine carbon sinks. At the same time, China should strengthen the research and application of new carbon sink monitoring technologies and facilities, explore the establishment of a regional ecological carbon sink data sharing platform for the BRI countries, and provide basic information for deepening carbon sink monitoring and protection, as well as establishing a sound carbon sink trading system.

CCUS technology is an important means to achieve large-scale carbon emission reduction in the future. As of June 2021, China has invested in 49 operational and under-construction CCUS demonstration projects, with an annual capture capacity of around 3 million tons (Huang et al., 2022). The abundant oil and gas resources of countries along the BRI provide favorable conditions for the promotion of CCUS technology. However, at present, only the above four countries operate small-scale commercial CCUS projects, while Vietnam, the Philippines, Thailand, India, and Egypt are still at the demonstration stage of CCUS projects. Most other countries have not yet invested in CCUS project designs (Sun et al., 2020). China should leverage its comparative advantages in CCUS technology, jointly establish CCUS laboratories and technology industrial parks with special funds such as the Silk Road Fund and the China-Eurasia Cooperation Fund, and provide financial and channel support for the transfer and promotion of CCUS technology cooperation in countries along the route through platforms such as the Asian Infrastructure Investment Bank and the BRI Green Development International Alliance.

3.3.1.3 Deepening Carbon Market Cooperation

The carbon market is an important policy tool that utilizes market mechanisms to control greenhouse gas emissions and promote green and low-carbon development (Fang et al., 2021a, 2021b, 2021c). In 2021, China established the world's largest carbon emissions trading market and initiated a voluntary greenhouse gas emission reduction trading mechanism, taking practical actions to fulfill its international commitments to peak carbon emissions and achieve carbon neutrality (Zhang et al., 2021).

Currently, among the countries along the BRI with the exception of China, India, and Kazakhstan, the carbon markets of the vast majority of countries are still in their infancy or early stages. Research suggests that Russia, as well as Southeast Asian countries such as Singapore, Thailand, Vietnam, Malaysia, and Indonesia, have favorable conditions for developing carbon markets.[20]

China has accumulated considerable experience in carbon market development and can provide experiences and insights for countries along the BRI. To further integrate with countries that have already established carbon market, China should align its carbon emission accounting systems, market regulation and trading rules with those of its partners (Yang et al., 2021). Additionally, China should explore the use of carbon emission reduction projects from relevant countries for domestic enterprises' compliance in the carbon market, and promote mutual recognition of carbon quotas and verified emission reductions within the BRI region.

Cooperation should be carried out in disciplines related to carbon markets, and efforts should be made in talent cultivation. This includes organizing carbon market experience exchanges and inviting government officials, experts, scholars and business representatives from countries along the BRI, to hold in-depth discussions on the establishment of a regionally integrated carbon market. Such initiatives would provide intellectual and talent support to accelerate the establishing of carbon markets in countries along the BRI.

3.3.1.4 Accelerate Green Investment and Financing Cooperation

Strengthening infrastructure construction is important in terms of cooperation between China and countries along the BRI. In the context of carbon neutrality, improving green investment and green finance is of utmost important. China has become the world's largest green credit market and the second largest green bond market (Liu et al., 2021). By 2019, Chinese financial institutions had already provided $440 billion funds to support countries along the BRI.[21] Among them, $6 billion are green financial bonds. Overall, countries along the BRI have relatively low levels of infrastructure construction and a significant proportion of their energy consumption still comes from fossil fuels. Engaging in green investment and financing cooperation can not only provide ample funding sources for infrastructure development in these countries, but also help control and reduce carbon emissions.

To address problems such as small-scale green investments, imperfect green finance standards, and low transparency of environmental information faced by countries along the BRI, China should intensify its efforts in green investment and financing. First, establish a diversified and market-oriented investment and financing system. Currently, China's development finance institutions dominate the investment and financing system of the BRI, leading to a relatively homogenous structure. In the future, the network layout of financial institutions and financial services should be gradually ecpanded, and mutual establishment and financial services integration with these countries should be strengthened (Zhou, 2017). The capital strength of countries along the route should be aggregated to broaden funding sources, and commercial and social capital should be moderately involved.

Second, continuously improve green investment principles and standards. In 2018, the Green Finance Professional Committee of the China Society for Finance and the City of London jointly released the 'Green Investment Principles (GIP) for the BRI, which outlined seven initiatives including corporate governance, project management, and the application of green financial instruments. By 2021, over 40 financial institutions from China, countries along the BRI, and developed countries had signed the GIP, providing guidelines for Chinese and international financial institutions to participate in green financial cooperation. In the future, more institutions should be encouraged to sign and implement the GIP, to guide the flow of funds into green and low-carbon industries from the front end of investment and financing.

Third, continuously improve the environmental information disclosure system. Infrastructure construction and operation are significant sources of carbon emissions in the BRI region. Therefore, efforts should be made to increase the disclosure of environmental information by key enterprises in countries along the route. A database for the green financial development of enterprises should be established to facilitate financial institutions in promptly obtaining data and information on energy consumption and carbon emissions of enterprises. Subsequently, scientific evaluations of their green development capabilities can be conducted. This serves as an important reference for green investment and financing.

3.3.2 BRI Perspective: Strengthening the Building of Green Development System

3.3.2.1 Establishing a Unified and Standardized Carbon Emission Monitoring and Accounting System

Scientifically developed carbon emission inventories are necessary to accurately assess carbon emission trends as well as to effectively implement carbon reduction measures. Therefore, it is urgent to establish a unified and standardized international carbon emission monitoring and accounting system. To this end, it is necessary to establish a BRI regional carbon emission accounting standardization committee, with authoritative experts and scholars from countries along the route serving as members, to discuss and formulate carbon emission monitoring and accounting standards at the regional, industrial, and enterprise levels. Based on this, a BRI regional carbon emission database should be constructed to promote the integration and sharing of data and information among countries along the route.

In addition, the current international focus on monitoring and accounting of producer-side carbon emissions cannot reflect the transfer of responsibility for carbon emissions, the portion that comes from hidden carbon flows. Under the consumer-side accounting system, regions with higher net imports of embodied carbon will have larger carbon emissions based on the consumer-side. Correspondingly, their responsibility for carbon emission reduction will also increase. The United States, Western Europe, and Japan and South Korea, as the main areas of embodied carbon inflow in the BRI region, can better reflect their carbon emission responsibilities through consumer-side accounting, which can embody the principle of environmental fairness under economic globalization.

3.3.2.2 Propose Differentiated Emission Reduction Paths Based on Local Conditions

According to emission intensity and energy structure, countries along the BRI can be divided into four categories. The first category includes countries with high intensity and an optimal structure, such as China, Serbia, and Bulgaria. These countries exhibit high carbon emission intensity but possess a renewable energy proportion higher than the global average. They should continue to promote structural emission reduction, gradually increasing the proportion of renewable energy in their energy consumption structure, and intensify efforts in researching and development technologies for renewable energy extraction, storage, and conversion technologies. This can be accomplished through policy and legal measures that strengthen the standardization and guidance of green and low-carbon development, gradually progressing towards institutional carbon emission reduction.

The second category comprises countries with high intensity and a poor structure, such as Kazakhstan, Turkmenistan, and Iraq. These countries have high carbon emission intensity and a renewable energy proportion lower than the global average. They should further explore their emission reduction potential, particularly through technological advancements, the development of structural emission reduction strategies, the promotion of green technology and clean energy utilization technology, and green energy cooperation, to facilitate green transformation.

The third category consists of countries with low intensity and a poor structure, such as Singapore, Bangladesh, Hungary, and Lithuania. These countries have low emission intensity and a renewable energy proportion lower than the global average. They should focus on structural emission reduction, and research of key technologies for industrial greening and ecological transformation, to support the transformation and upgrading of energy-intensive industries. Special emphasis should be placed on energy conservation and carbon emission reduction in key industries such as transportation, construction, and manufacturing.

The last category encompasses countries with low intensity and an optimal structure, such as Pakistan, Sri Lanka, and Cambodia. These countries have low emission intensity and a renewable energy proportion higher than the global average. They should formulate policy systems for the utilization of renewable energy, the development of circular economy, and strive towards institutionalized carbon emission reduction.

3.3.2.3 Enhance the Capability to Prevent and Mitigate Carbon Leakage Risks

The embodied carbon emissions flow in countries along the BRI have increased the carbon emission pressure on net-exporting countries of goods. It is essential to take effective measures to enhance the monitoring and early warning capabilities for carbon leakage hotspots and industries. First, the incoming enterprises should make comprehensive use of industrial, land, and tax policies to raise the environmental access threshold, reduce the adverse impact brought by the transfer of high-energy-consuming industries on the domestic ecological environment, establish a corporate carbon emission credit system, and strengthen the guidance and regulation of enterprises' low-carbon production behavior.

Second, for 'outward' enterprises, it is necessary to increase support services and regulatory efforts, facilitate enterprises to fully understand the relevant laws, regulations, and green thresholds of the host country. A warning system for the cross-border transfer of carbon-intensive enterprises should be established, and upper limits should be set for the highest emission levels of industries and product categories, to prevent damage to the national image resulting from enterprises blindly pursuing profit maximization.

Third, it is crucial to establish a dynamic hierarchical classification management system for projects, objectively assessing their potential impacts through means such as environmental impact assessments. Based on this assessment, positive and negative project lists should be established, and the environmental impact of projects should be dynamically evaluated based on actual conditions. This will provide scientific guidance for countries along the BRI to effectively prevent and mitigate carbon leakage.[22]

3.3.3 *Global Perspective: Propose the 'Chinese Path Choice' for Climate Governance*

3.3.3.1 Promote the Establishment of a Global Climate Governance System Based on the Concept of 'a Community of Shared Future for Mankind'

Today, as China actively participates in and leads international cooperation to address climate change (Wang, 2016), it is of great significance to promote the building of a fair and equitable, win-win global climate governance system with the concept of a 'community of shared future for mankind'. This should be an indispensable part of the building the 'Green Silk Road' and will help China to grasp international discourse power, while demonstrating the responsibilities and contributions of a major country.

First, it is advocated to embed the concept of 'a community of shared future for mankind' into the building of the global climate governance system. Common interests serve as the inherent driving force for all countries to build 'a community of shared future for mankind' (Liu et al., 2020). Addressing climate change is an important link connecting the destiny of all mankind, and should be one of the core issues with the framework of the concept of 'a community of shared future for mankind'.

Second, China can serve as a bridge between developed and developing countries in international climate negotiations (Han, 2021). On the one hand, it calls on developed countries to provide more financial assistance and support for green technology to developing countries; on the other hand, it sets an example by advocating for developing countries to firmly adhere to the goals, tasks, and principles of the United Nations Framework Convention on Climate Change and the Paris Agreement, actively implement and update their nationally determined contributions.

Third, it is essential to systematically summarize China's contributions and achievements in fulfilling the Paris Agreement and the United Nations 2030 Agenda for Sustainable Development. It is also important to promote China's achievements in ecological civilization and the building of the 'Green Silk Road' to the world. Using a universally understood language, China can propose a 'Chian's path choice' for climate governance (Zhu, 2019).

3.3.3.2 Strengthen the Effective Connection Between the BRI and the Global Development Initiative

In September 2021, President Xi Jinping solemnly proposed the Global Development Initiative during the general debate of the 76th session of the United Nations General Assembly. He called on the international community to accelerate the implementation of the United Nations 2030 Agenda for Sustainable Development and promote a more robust, greener and healthier global development.[23] The Global Development Initiative and the BRI are two important public goods provided by China to the international community. The former provides significant opportunities for the high-quality development of the latter, while the latter offers an important practical platform and accumulated experience for promoting the implementation of the former. Thoroughly advancing the effective connection of the two initiatives can provide strong institutional guarantees for the building of the 'Green Silk Road'.

To achieve this, the primary emphasis should be on the connection regional development strategies, promoting the organic integration of the BRI with other regional development strategies such as the Eurasian Economic Union of Russia and the Juncker Plan of the European Union. Second, based on cooperation in key areas, efforts should be made to expand cross-border investments in new energy with the energy sector, strengthen the development of new energy in South-South cooperation, and promote the research and transfer of green technologies. In terms of trade, it is necessary to strengthen international cooperation in green trade, establish a system of green product standards and certification, and expand the global supply of green and low-carbon products. In the transportation sector, efforts should be intensified in green transportation technologies, new energy vehicles, and mutual recognition of standards. Third, leveraging high-level platforms, a coordinated mechanism for climate governance should be created at the global, regional, and sub-regional levels. Specifically, this involves promoting shared benefits in policies, rules, and standards, exploring more common interest with the framework of the Global Development Initiative for the building of the 'Green Silk Road', and facilitating the implementation of green and low-carbon development and social livelihood projects.

3.4 Conclusion

Adapting to the global carbon neutrality trend and actively building the 'Green Silk Road' is a significant strategic choice in implementing the BRI. However, along the BRI countries, there are widespread practical challenges such as rapid growth in carbon emissions, severe carbon leakage situations, diverse challenges in reaching carbon emission peaks, and significant tasks in achieving carbon neutrality. To address this, efforts should focus on synergistically promoting the building of the 'Green Silk Road' from three levels: China, the BRI, and the global context.

At the national level, China should strengthen cooperation with BRI countries in areas such as renewable energy, carbon sinks, carbon markets, and green investment and financing. At the level of the BRI, the establishing of a green development system should be promoted through measures such as unifying carbon emission monitoring and accounting standards, proposing differentiated emission reduction paths, and improving the ability to prevent and resolve carbon leakage risks. At the global level, the concept of 'a community of shared future for mankind' should guide the building of a global climate governance system, and effective coordination between the BRI and the Global Development Initiative should be strengthened.

In summary, China must take the building of the 'Green Silk Road' as an opportunity to promote the organic integration of the strategies for peak carbon emissions, carbon neutrality, and the global climate governance system so that China's concepts and solutions can better benefit the world.

Notes

1. Source: "Xi Jinping Attends Leaders' Climate Summit and Delivers Important Speech," People's Daily, 1st Edition, April 23, 2021.
2. Source: "How 'Belt and Road' Benefits the Achievement of the '2030 Sustainable Development Agenda'," October 15, 2018, http://world.people.com.cn/n1/2018/1015/c1002-30342362.html.
3. Source: "Working Together to Create a New Splendor on the Silk Road," People's Daily, 2nd Edition, June 23, 2016.
4. Data source: Global Carbon Atlas, same for the following paragraph.
5. Data source: World Bank, same for the following paragraph.
6. Data from "BP Statistical Review of World Energy 2019", same for the following paragraph.
7. Data from "Southeast Asia Energy Outlook 2019" published by the International Energy Agency (IEA).
8. Data from the World Bank.
9. Data from the World Bank.
10. Data from the official website of the General Administration of Customs.
11. "Deepening China-Russia Energy Cooperation," February 7, 2022, https://finance.sina.com.cn/roll/2022-02-07/doc-ikyakumy4699023.shtml
12. Data from the International Energy Agency (IEA) website.
13. Data from Climate News website.
14. Research Team of the Modern Institute of Energy Security, Zhao Hongtu: "International Development Trends and Prospects of Carbon Neutrality", Modern International Relations, 2022, Issue 2.
15. United Nations Environment Programme, Global trends in renewable energy investment 2019, United Nations Environment Programme, 2019.
16. "Renewable energy becomes the main force of energy cooperation along the 'Belt and Road'," China Environment News, 26 August 2021, 3rd edition.
17. "Central Asia's largest wind farm boosts Kazakhstan's new energy layout," 15 June 2021, http://news.china.com.cn/2021-06/15/content_77567692.htm.
18. "China and Central and Eastern Europe have enormous space for clean energy cooperation," China Energy News, 28 September 2020, 2nd edition.
19. "China-ASEAN Mangrove Protection Initiative officially launched", September 28, 2021, http://yn.people.com.cn/n2/2021/0928/c378439-34934754.html.
20. "Belt and Road" Green Development International Alliance: "Research on Carbon Market Mechanism of the 'Belt and Road' Initiative", December 2020.
21. "Financial Institutions Provide Over $440 Billion for 'Belt and Road' Construction", April 26, 2019, http://finance.ce.cn/bank12/scroll/201904/26/t20190426_31945681.shtml.
22. Source: "Belt and Road" Green Development International Alliance: "Belt and Road" Project Green Development Guidelines Baseline Research Report, December 2020.
23. "Xi Jinping Attends the General Debate of the 76th Session of the United Nations General Assembly and Delivers an Important Speech," "People's Daily," September 22, 2021, 1st Edition.

References

Central Asia's Largest Wind Farm Boosts Kazakhstan's New Energy Layout. 2021. http://news.china.com.cn/2021-06/15/content_77567692.htm

China Energy News. (2020). *Huge potential in China-Central and Eastern Europe clean energy cooperation.*

China Environment News. (2021). *Renewable energy becomes the main force in 'Belt and Road' energy cooperation.*

China Overseas Development Alliance for New Energy. (2019). *Research on the pathways and promotion mechanisms of 'Belt and Road' renewable energy development cooperation.*

Deng, X., Xie, J., & Teng, F. (2021). What is carbon neutrality? *Climate Change Research, 17*, 107–113.

Fang, K., & Li, C. L. (2021). Opportunities and pathways for Zhejiang to create the 'important window' in tackling climate change. *Journal of Zhejiang Gong Shang University, 5*, 13–23.

Fang, K., Wang, S., He, J., Song, J., Fang, C., & Jia, X. (2021a). Mapping the environmental footprints of nations partnering the 'Belt and Road' Initiative. *Resources, Conservation and Recycling, 164*, 105068.

Fang, K., Zhang, Q., & Song, J. (2021b). How can national ETS affect carbon emissions and abatement costs? Evidence from the dual goals proposed by China's NDCs. *Resources, Conservation & Recycling, 171*, 105638.

Fang, K., Xu, A. Q., He, J. J., Fang, C. L., & Liu, Q. Y. (2021c). Comprehensive assessment and regional management and control of sustainable development in countries along the 'Belt and Road'. *Science Bulletin, 19.*

Fu, J. Y., & Si, X. M. (2017). Driving factors of carbon emission of the countries along "the 'Belt and Road'", their potential and contribution to the emission reduction. *Tropical Geography, 37*(1), 1–9.

Han, D. R. (2021). Exploration of the interaction between the community of shared future for mankind and global climate governance. *Fudan Review of International Relations, 2.*

Han, M., Yao, Q., Liu, W., & Dunford, M. (2018). Tracking embodied carbon flows in the 'Belt and Road' regions. *Journal of Geographical Sciences, 28*, 1263–1274.

Huang, J., Ma, Q., Shi, M. W., Peng, X., & Zhang, X. (2022). Process and suggestions of CCUS technology development from the perspective of carbon neutrality. *Environmental Impact Assessment, 44*, 42–47.

Jointly Creating a New Splendor of the Silk Road. (2016). *People's Daily*, Edition 2.

Li, N., Zhou, C. Y., Si, J. P., Li, J. H. (2021). Comparative analysis and enlightening suggestions on the development of CCUS at home and abroad. *China Power Enterprise Management, 34.*

Liu, J. L., Wang, K., & Zou, J. (2014). Analysis of the net flow of carbon emissions embodied in trade of China. *Resources Science, 36–5*, 979–987.

Liu, Z., Ciais, P., Deng, Z., Lei, R., Davis, S. J., Feng, S., Zheng, B., Cui, D., Dou, X., Zhu, B., & Guo, R. (2020). Near-real-time monitoring of global CO2 emissions reveals the effects of the COVID-19 pandemic. *Nature Communications, 11*, 5172.

Liu, Z., Davis, S., Feng, K., Hubacek, K., Liang, S., Anadon, L. D., Chen, B., Liu, J., Yan, J., & Guan, D. (2015). Targeted opportunities to address the climate-trade dilemma in China. *Nature Climate Change, 6*, 201–206.

Lu, Q., Fang, K., Heijungs, R., Feng, K., Li, J., Wen, Q., Li, Y., & Huang, X. (2020). Imbalance and drivers of carbon emissions embodied in trade along the 'Belt and Road' Initiative. *Applied Energy, 280*, 115934.

Muhammad, S., Long, X., Salman, M., & Dauda, L. (2020). Effect of urbanization and international trade on CO_2 emissions across 65 belt and road initiative countries. *Energy, 196*, 117102.

Rauf, A., Liu, X., Amin, W., Ozturk, I., Rehman, O. U., & Hafeez, M. (2018). Testing EKC hypothesis with energy and sustainable development challenges: A fresh evidence from belt and road initiative economies. *Environmental Science and Pollution Research, 25*, 32066–32080.

Research, Center, for Modern Court Energy Security Project Team, & Hongtu, Z. (2022). International carbon neutrality development trends and prospects. *Contemporary International Relations, 2*, 20–23.

Research Group of the International Department of the People's Bank of China. (2021). Supporting 'Belt and Road' construction with green financial cooperation. *China Finance, 22*.

Ridzuan, N. H. A. M., Marwan, N. F., Khalid, N., Ali, M. H., & Tseng, M. L. (2020). Effects of agriculture, renewable energy, and economic growth on carbon dioxide emissions: Evidence of the environmental Kuznets curve. *Resources, Conservation & Recycling, 160*, 104879.

Safi, A., Chen, Y., & Wahab, S. (2021). Financial instability and consumption-based carbon emission in E-7 countries: The role of trade and economic growth. *Sustainable Production and Consumption, 27*, 383–391.

Shakib, M., Hou, Y., & Rauf, A. (2022). Revisiting the energy-economy-environment relationships for attaining environmental sustainability: Evidence from 'Belt and Road' Initiative countries. *Environmental Science and Pollution Research, 29*, 3808–3825.

Shi, Q., Zhao, Y., & Qian, Z. (2022). Global value chains participation and carbon emissions: Evidence from 'Belt and Road' countries. *Applied Energy, 310*, 118505.

Sun, L. L., Cui, H. J., & Ge, Q. S. (2020). Potential and prospect of carbon capture, utilization and storage CCUS in the main 'Belt and Road' Initiative countries. *Climate Change Research, 16*, 609–616.

The 'Belt and Road' Initiative Facilitates the Achievement of the 2030 Agenda for Sustainable Development. http://world.people.com.cn/n1/2018/1015/c1002-30342362.html. Accessed 15 October 2018.

Wang, M. (2016). Research on energy strategic cooperation under the 'Belt and Road' initiative. *Review of Economic Research, 22*, 34–44.

Wu, N., Fu, Z. Q., & Wang, Y. H. (2018). EKC test and decoupling analysis of carbon emissions in countries along the "One Belt and One Road." *Journal of Environmental Engineering Technology, 8*, 671–678.

Yang, D. P., Wang, S. T., & Li, Y. H. (2021). Assumptions and prospects of developing carbon market links in countries and regions along the Belt and Road. *China Environment, 12*, 32-35.

Zhang, L., Xie, Z. X., & Cao, L. B. (2020). Discussion on evaluation method on carbon dioxide emissions peaking for Chinese cities. *Environmental Engineering, 38*(11), 1–5.

Zhang, X. L., Zhang, D., & Yu, R. X. (2021). Theory and practice of China's national carbon emissions trading system. *Journal of Management World, 37*, 80–95.

Zhou, X. C. (2017). Jointly build a financing and investment cooperation system for the Belt and Road Initiative. *China Finance, 9*: 6-8.

Zhu, D. J. (2019). Interpreting ecological civilization with new achievements in international sustainable development research and a universal language. *China Environmental Management, 3*.

Zhuang, G. Y., Dou, X. M., & Wei, M. X. (2022). Theoretical interpretation and path analysis of 'Peak Carbon Dioxide Emission' and 'Carbon Neutrality.' *Journal of Lanzhou University Social Sciences, 50*, 57–68.

Part III
Issues and Challenges of China's Dual-Carbon Transition

Chapter 4
Risk Challenges and Path Options for Realizing the Dual-Carbon Goal in the Context of High-Quality Development in China

Xinkai Zhu and Binlei Gong

Abstract Achieving the goals of carbon peaking and climate neutrality is a significant strategic decision made by the Central Committee of the Communist Party of China, reflecting a comprehensive understanding of the domestic and international landscape. Currently, structural imbalances within China's population, investment efficiency, and energy supply and demand pose major challenges to achieving those goals. China's target to transition from "carbon peaking" to "climate neutrality" within three decades, from 2030 to 2060, presents a tighter timeframe than that of most developed countries, leading to greater challenges across technical, economic, social and even political aspects. This transition necessitates a series of economic, financial and social risks, particularly in balancing economic growth with carbon reduction. In order to successfully achieve the carbon peaking and climate neutrality goals, China should establish a "1+N" policy system, foster the low-carbon industries, cultivate a low-carbon investment market, increase R&D investment in low-carbon technologies, and promote integrated air pollution control alongside low-carbon control.

Keywords Carbon peaking and climate neutrality · High-quality development · Transformation risk

---

X. Zhu
Renmin University of China, Beijing, China

B. Gong (✉)
School of Public Affairs, China Academy for Rural Development, Zhejiang University, Hangzhou, China
e-mail: gongbinlei@zju.edu.cn

B. Gong et al. (eds.), *Chinese Governance and Transformation Towards Carbon Neutrality*, Resources, Environment and Agricultural Development,
https://doi.org/10.1007/978-981-97-9996-1_4

4.1 Promoting "Dual Carbon" Work: An Integral Element of High-Quality Development

The global community recognizes the urgency of addressing environmental challenges. The increasing prominence of resource and environmental issues stemming from industrialization and modernization underscores the need for a collective shift towards green development. China, acknowledging the significance of this global imperative, has incorporated the concept of "green development" into its new development philosophy of "innovative, coordinated, green, open and shared development". This concept, embraced since the 18th National Congress of the Communist Party of China, reflects a commitment not only to current economic progress but also to the well-being of future generations.

Solid progress towards "carbon peaking and carbon neutrality" aligns with this commitment and forms a critical component of China's efforts to build an ecological civilization. President Xi Jinping's articulation of the "3060 goal" (also known as "dual carbon" goals)—striving to peak carbon dioxide emissions by 2030 and achieve carbon neutrality by 2060—at the 75th United Nations General Assembly reflects China's determination to contribute to a shared future for mankind. Achieving "dual carbon" goals goes beyond environmental stewardship; it represents a strategic decision to promote economic restructuring, bolster energy security, further achieve high-quality economic development, and amplify China's international voice (Liu, 2021).

Since "3060 goal" has been proposed, considerable progress has been made in advancing the agenda, from the central to local governments, from industrial layout and planning to technological innovation and other fields. However, there remain challenges in achieving a comprehensive understanding of the economic implications, potential risks, and optimal pathways for realizing these goals. Therefore, analyzing the situation and conditions under which China achieves carbon neutrality and carbon peaking, dissecting the path to promote high-quality economic development by achieving the "dual carbon" goal, and proposing potential risks in the "dual carbon" transition process have important theoretical and practical significance.

4.2 Navigating the Landscape: Opportunities and Challenges in Achieving the "Dual Carbon" Goals

China's economy has demonstrated remarkable resilience in the face of recent global challenges, exemplified by its rapid recovery from the impact of the COVID-19 pandemic. The 8.1% GDP growth in 2021 underscores the enduring strength of the Chinese economy (Fig. 4.1). Nevertheless, this period of economic transition also presents a set of opportunities and challenges, particularly as China shifts its focus from high-speed growth to high-quality development.

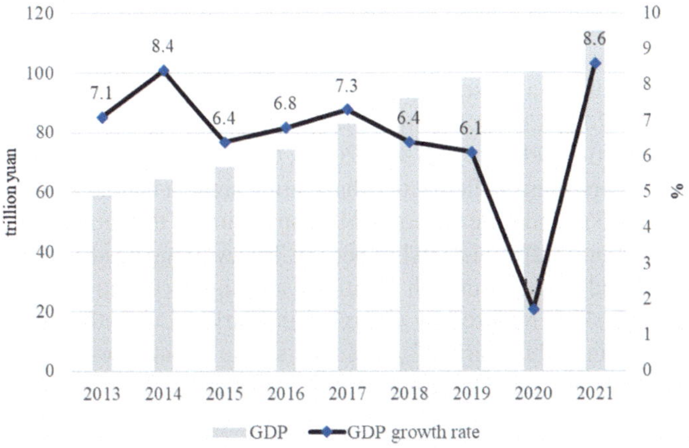

Fig. 4.1 China's GDP and its growth rate, 2016–2021. *Source* National Statistical Office

Recognizing that high-quality development extends beyond the purely economic realm, President Xi Jinping has emphasized the importance of innovation-driven growth in enhancing total factor productivity (Liu & Ling, 2020; Tang et al., 2020). While the robust performance of the Chinese economy provides a solid foundation for achieving the "dual carbon" goals, structural imbalances within the economy also bring certain challenges and new requirements, which reflects in the following three aspects.

4.2.1 Addressing Imbalance in Human Capital

The emergence of new models and formats, such as urban low-carbon industries and digital economy, necessitates new requirements for the dynamic balance of human capital represented by labor and intelligence between urban and rural areas, regions, and industries. With the development of the market economy, the flow of factors between urban and rural areas, regions, and industries in China is constantly accelerating. Although urbanization has brought significant labor flows from rural to urban areas and education advancement have contributed to a more skilled workforce, imbalances persist.

Low-carbon and digital industries naturally gravitate towards modern cities. On the demand side, high initial fixed inputs require large consumer markets, and the concentration of population in urban centers creates economies of scale, particularly for the digital economy. On the supply side, urban areas with higher population densities and generally higher levels of education can provide the skilled talent pool required for these industries. Consequently, ongoing urbanization and the continuous improvement in the quality of the urban workforce have laid a good foundation for the growth of "dual carbon" friendly industries.

However, uneven development of labor factors between urban and rural areas, regions, and industries poses a potential threat. Despite urbanization, the agricultural sector still accounts for a substantial portion of China's workforce (25.2% in 2019, according to the 2020 China Statistical Yearbook), while its contribution to GDP remains disproportionately low (7.1% in 2019). Objectively speaking, this disparity underscores the persistent challenge of urbanization lagging behind industrialization (Huang et al., 2013), hindering the equitable distribution of the benefits of economic growth. Furthermore, skills mismatches persist. The evolving needs of a low-carbon economy require adjustments in both vocational and higher education to ensure graduates possess the skills required by emerging industries. Currently, certain sectors crucial for achieving "dual carbon" goals face severe talent shortage, highlighting the need to address the imbalance in the talent structure.

4.2.2 Optimizing Infrastructure Investment for a Low-Carbon Future

Despite considerable progress, China's per capita capital stock remains significantly lower than that of developed countries represented by the G7, making effective investment a key driver of continued economic growth. However, since 2009, the driving force of China's total capital formation on GDP growth has continued to decline (Bai & Zhang, 2014) (Fig. 4.2). The weakening investment engine poses a potential risk to China's high-quality growth.

As the pioneer of economic development, infrastructure plays an important role in driving economic growth (Zhang, 2012). Accelerating the construction of new,

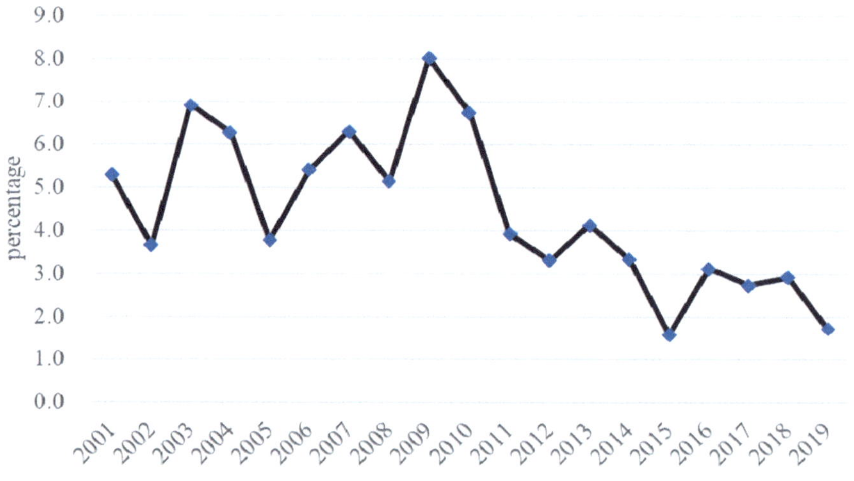

Fig. 4.2 Gross capital formation's contribution to China's GDP growth, 2001–2019. *Source* China Statistics Yearbook 2020

"dual-carbon" oriented infrastructure is not only a short-term measure to cope with economic downturn and stabilize economic growth (Li, 2020), but also a forward-looking strategy to create new productivity and open up broad space for advanced manufacturing, digital services, and sustainable consumption (Jia, 2020).

Under the "dual carbon" background, the huge demand for intelligent and digital upgrades to existing infrastructure, alongside the construction of new assets like energy vehicle charging networks, 5G infrastructure, and big data centers, represents a significant avenue for expanding effective investment (Cao, 2022). Previous studies have shown that, compared to traditional infrastructure, investments in new infrastructure yield higher economic and employment multipliers while offering greater energy efficiency and emissions reduction potential, with an emission reduction rate of 7.24%, and there is still room for further optimization (Wang et al., 2021). Therefore, the convergence of economic and environmental benefits makes "dual carbon-oriented" new infrastructure a powerful tool for achieving sustainable and inclusive growth.

4.2.3 Transitioning Towards a Sustainable Energy Structure

As the world's largest energy producer and consumer, China faces a critical challenge in decoupling economic growth from its heavy reliance on energy and resources. This challenge is amplified by the country's energy consumption structure, which remains dominated by coal (Lin et al., 2010), creating a significant obstacle to achieving energy conservation, emission reduction, and high-quality growth.

Specifically, on the one hand, China's "rich coal, poor oil, and little gas" energy endowment has led to a heavy dependence on coal, accounting for more than half of its energy consumption. With an external dependence on oil exceeding 70%, and a relatively small share of non-fossil fuels in energy supply (Gong, 2020), transitioning away from fossil fuels will require a concerted and potentially disruptive effort. On the other hand, while China has made strides in improving energy processing and conversion increasing from 69.7% in 2001 to 72.3% in 2019 (according to the 2020 China Energy Statistical Yearbook), both energy consumption and total carbon dioxide emissions have continued to rise (Fig. 4.3), reaching approximately one-third of the global total in 2020. This translates to per capita carbon emissions of around 7 tons, putting China under considerable international pressure.

In summary, China has not yet achieved an effective decoupling between GDP growth and energy consumption emissions. Therefore, under the "dual carbon" goal, it is necessary to control the total amount and intensity of energy use in various fields, further adjust the energy consumption structure (Lin & Liu, 2010), reduce the use of fossil fuels, increase the proportion of non-fossil fuels, improve the conversion efficiency of energy processing, enhance the economic output of unit energy consumption, and drive the achievement of the "dual carbon" goal through energy transformation.

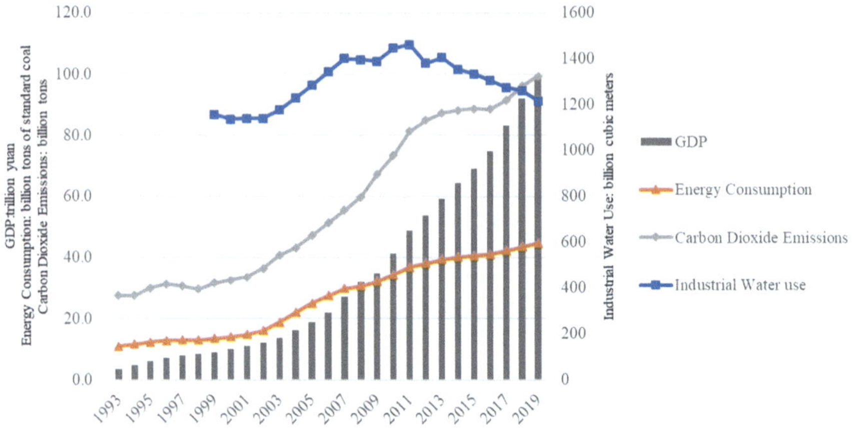

Fig. 4.3 China's GDP, CO_2 emissions, energy consumption and industrial water use since 1993. *Data source* China Statistical Yearbook 2020, China Energy Statistical Yearbook 2020, China Environmental Statistical Yearbook 2019

From the above analysis, it can be seen that the structural optimization required in human capital, effective investment, and the energy structure constitute important conditions for achieving carbon neutrality and peaking. In the above context, China's announcement to strive for carbon dioxide peaking before 2030 and carbon neutrality before 2060 reflects not only China's commitment to global climate action, but also an inherent need to transform its development pattern. The "dual carbon" construction and China's population, investment, and energy consumption transformation complement each other, and are mutually causal. As a broad and profound systemic change in the economic and social system, peaking carbon emissions and achieving carbon neutrality will actively promote industrial, technological, and energy revolutions. This will not only effectively promote high-quality economic development in China, but also conform to the international situation and enhance international discourse power.

4.3 Managing Transition Risks: A Precondition for Sustainable Development

From the perspective of carbon emission paths in developed countries, achieving "carbon peaking" and "carbon neutrality" requires a relatively long process. These countries generally experienced a natural peaking in the 1970s and 1980s, followed by a long period of carbon emission plateau before entering a gradual decline. This suggests a 50–60 year timeframe for the transition from carbon peaking to carbon neutrality.

China, however, is pursuing a more compressed timeline. Committing to peaking carbon dioxide emissions before 2030 requires achieving this milestone at a lower level of economic development, with a per capita GDP of less than 15,000 US dollars, and per capita carbon emissions not exceeding 8 tons. This accelerated trajectory, with a lower peak level of carbon emissions and a shorter timeframe, means more transformation pressure compared to the experience of developed countries (Hu, 2021).

As President Xi Jinping has emphasized, China, despite being the world's largest developing country, is committed to achieving the steepest decline in carbon intensity and the fastest transition from carbon peaking to carbon neutrality in history. This underscores both the leadership's unwavering commitment and the sheer scale of the undertaking. While China aims for an earlier and lower carbon peaking than developed countries, its developing country status, coupled with persistent imbalances in population, investment, and energy consumption, presents a unique set of challenges. Achieving both rapid decarbonization and high-quality economic growth will require navigating a complex landscape of trade-offs and potential risks.

4.3.1 Understanding of Systemic Risks in the Process of "Dual Carbon"

This paper believes that "carbon peaking" and "carbon neutrality" will bring about a comprehensive transformation of the energy system and infrastructure across all sectors, which will have profound implications, impacting asset values, industry structures, and stakeholder interests, creating challenges across technological, economic, and social dimensions.

China's ambition to achieve "carbon peaking" to "carbon neutrality" faster than any countries in history introduces a unique set of economic, financial, social, and political risks. These risks may cascade through interconnected systems, triggering cross-regional and cross-sectoral disruptions that threaten the overall stability of the economy and society (Lin & Zhu, 2021).

Figure 4.4 shows the potential risks that may arise from adopting energy-saving and carbon reduction measures, with the micro subject as the analysis object. Firstly, aggressive decarbonization of high-emission industries could significantly increase operating costs for businesses. In extreme scenarios, this could lead to production shutdowns, supply shortages, and price spikes. The resulting revenue losses and increased input costs would squeeze profit margins, potentially triggering bankruptcies and creating ripple effects throughout supply chains.

Secondly, financial systems are also vulnerable. Declining corporate profits reduces the repayment ability of the enterprise, leading to an increase in debt risk. This risk is easily transmitted through the upstream and downstream industrial chains, ultimately entering the financial system and transmitting between financial industry subsystems such as banks, insurance, and capital markets. For example, it leads to

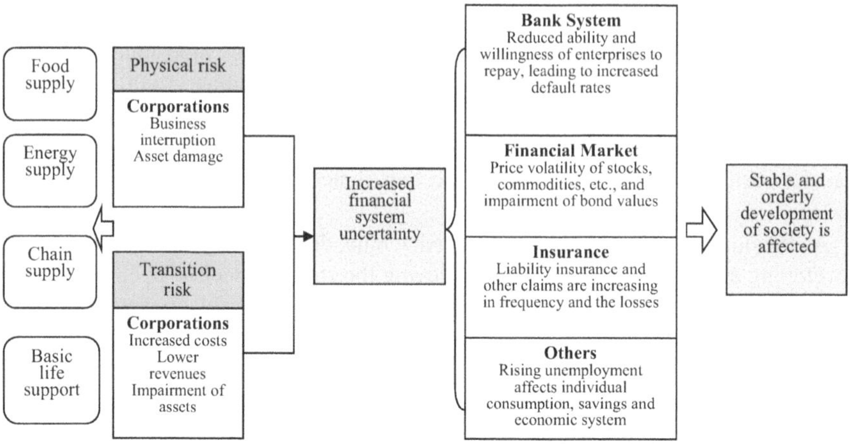

Fig. 4.4 Transmission of climate risks in socio-economic systems

an increase in non-performing assets in banks, fluctuations in stock and commodity prices, impairment of bond values, and an increase in insurance claims, inducing systemic financial risks.

Moreover, rapid decarbonization can disrupt labor markets. Difficulties in business operations will directly lead to the inability of the employment stabilizer to function properly. The increase in unemployment will affect individual consumption and savings behavior, which in turn will affect the process of the economic system continuously expanding its "cake". In summary, the artificial obstruction of logistics and capital flow can have an impact on normal production and living order, thereby affecting the stable and orderly development of society, affecting people's livelihood security, and even causing serious social problems.

Therefore, recognizing these complexities, the Chinese government has emphasized that the transition process needs to handle all the relationships in the process of energy conservation, pollution reduction, and carbon reduction, effectively respond to the economic, financial, and social risks, prevent overreaction, and safely reduce carbon emissions. It is necessary to first establish and then break through. This requires a deep understanding of the interdependencies between energy systems, economic activity, and social well-being (Yang, 2021).

China's current energy consumption and industrial structure necessitate a continued reliance on significant energy consumption and carbon emissions to sustain GDP growth for the foreseeable future. The gradual pace of low-carbon technology research and development, coupled with the time required for business to adopt these technologies and retrofit existing infrastructure, creates a tension between maintaining economic growth and pursuing decarbonization goals. This presents a delicate balancing act for policymakers. While prioritizing economic growth at the expense of environmental sustainability is untenable, pursuing aggressive decarbonization without considering the economic consequences could be equally detrimental. The key lies in carefully managing the pace of transition. By leveraging technological advancements and institutional innovations, China can strive to smooth economic growth in the process of achieving the "dual carbon" goals, ensuring that the pace of decarbonization aligns with both technological progress and economic development status.

4.3.2 Risk Management in the Process of Achieving the "Dual Carbon" Goals: A Case Study in Coal-Power Industry

Having established the inherent risks and challenges associated with China's "dual carbon" goals, and recognizing the complex interplay between economic growth and decarbonization, the focus shifts to identifying pathways that can mitigate these risks. The transition of the coal-fired power sector provides a compelling case study.

Currently, the power sector is still the main sector for coal consumption in China, with coal-fired power plants accounting for roughly 40% of the national carbon emissions. In order to achieve carbon neutrality goals, various sectors will decarbonization through electrification, shifting the burden of emission reduction onto the power sector. This makes the transformation of the power sector a critical priority. At the same time, China possesses roughly half of the world's coal-fired power capacity, with an average plant age of less than 12 years—half the global average. Therefore, it is necessary to find the right positioning, handle the relationship between short-term and long-term, and achieve a smooth transformation. From the perspective of coal-fired power positioning, coal-fired power remains the main power source to ensure a stable power supply in the short and medium term. China has clearly set the goal of exceeding 80% of non- fossil energy sources by 2060. As renewable energy technologies advance and costs decline, the foundation and conditions for the transformation of the power system will become more complete. Coal power will gradually shift from a dominant power source to a flexible power source, supporting the integration of greater renewable energy capacity.

At present, the influencing factors that lead to the transformation risks of China's coal-fired power industry mainly include two parts. On the one hand, Measures aimed at decarbonizing the power sector, such as flexible transformation measures, carbon emission trading schemes, carbon pricing, and other restrictive policies, will increase operating costs for coal-fired power plants, directly impacting their profits. On the other hand, the technological progress of renewable energy has led to a decrease in production costs, which will increasingly compete with and displace coal-fired power, further squeezing profit margins and posing an existential threat to the sector's long-term viability. These internal and external pressures on the coal-fired power sector create cascading risks for the broader economy, thereby potentially triggering a series of economic, financial, and social risks as mentioned above. Essentially, these risks are still derived from the relationship between economic growth and energy conservation and carbon reduction, and the degree of conflict that arises generally depends on the duration of the process. It is necessary to orderly promote the transformation of coal-fired power, achieve a smooth transition, and be vigilant against issues such as power supply security, financial losses, stranded assets, economic shocks, financial instability, and even social unrest.

As the coal power industry grapples with significant financial losses, the transition to a low-carbon economy will exacerbate this strain, further diminishing profitability and impacting the value of assets held by these companies. As shown in Table 4.1, both flexible transformation and early retirement scenarios could result in trillions of yuan in stranded assets (Wang et al., 2022). Provinces and regions highly dependent on traditional coal-fired power resources, such as Shandong, Xinjiang, and Inner Mongolia, may suffer significant economic losses as a result. At present, the coal-fired power sector, including its upstream and downstream enterprises, supports over 3 million jobs. In the context of coal-fired power transformation, careful consideration must be given to mitigating potential job displacement and ensuring adequate social security measures for affected workers. By calculating 3730 coal-fired power generation units across the country, it was found that most of the funds for coal-fired power construction come from bank loans. Coal-heavy provinces like Xinjiang, Inner Mongolia, and Shandong carry particularly large outstanding loan balances, exceeding 100 billion yuan each. If the transformation is not carefully managed, the asset value will decrease, which could create a surge in non-performing loans, jeopardizing the asset quality of banks and potentially undermining the stability of the financial system.

To achieve the goal of carbon neutrality, China's power sector must clarify the positioning of coal-fired power and prioritize an orderly phase-out of coal-fired power.

Table 4.1 Distribution of stranded assets of existing coal-fired power units in different scenarios

	Flexibility transformation scenario (100 million RMB)	Early retirement scenario (100 million RMB)
Total nationwide	36,277.90	17,774.46
Shandong	4374.62	1738.95
Inner Mongolia	4734.09	1724.51
Jiangsu	2406.34	1926.23
Guangdong	2257.96	1692.70
Henan	2200.80	1222.03
Xinjiang	2379.63	152.39
Shanxi	2885.40	1176.04
Anhui	2073.35	1118.56
Hebei	2333.95	1139.21
Shanxi	2214.63	935.55
Zhejiang	1125.73	1109.82

This requires transitioning it from a dominant baseload source to a more limited, flexible capacity, while simultaneously accelerating the deployment of cleaner alternatives to minimize locked-in carbon emissions. A successful transition requires a stable approach.

1. Strategic Planning: Developing a national and regional roadmap for phasing out coal-fired power, tailored to local conditions and avoiding a "one-size-fits-all" approach. This includes conducting plant-by-plant evaluation of existing coal-fired power units and develop customized transition plans ("one plant, one policy"). Coal power units with advanced technology and shorter operating years can leverage their comparative advantages and establish a combination of technologies such as "coal-fired power + CCUS".
2. Prudent Investment on new coal-fired power projects: Being particularly cautious about the expectations for the future development of coal-fired power. Strict approval should be given to the demand for ultra-high voltage supporting facilities and units such as "increasing large and suppressing small" to avoid the burden of new coal-fired power projects on emission reduction work.
3. Targeted Support: Providing guidance and support to regions heavily reliant on coal, mitigating economic and social impacts while minimizing the systemic financial risks in process. This includes strategies to ensure local employment stability, and prevent the social unrest.
4. Accelerated Renewable Energy Deployment: Planning and building out a renewable energy supply system, ensuring sufficient capacity to meet future demand. This includes strategic investment in renewable energy infrastructure in key areas, creating hubs for clean energy production.

4.4 Towards a Low-Carbon, High-Quality Development Pathway

China is at a critical period of transitioning its development mode, optimizing its economic structure, and transforming new divers of growth. Achieving high-quality development has become the center theme of economic and social agenda, crucial for overall socialist modernization construction, as outlined in the 14th Five-Year Plan and even longer. The pursuit of high-quality development necessitates a focus on quality over quantity, prioritizing efficiency and innovation to drive improvements in total factor productivity and enhance China's economic competitiveness.

In this context, the "dual carbon" goals have been integrated into the broader framework of ecological civilization construction, becoming a core element of the socialist modernization pathway. The goals of carbon peaking and carbon neutrality are highly consistent with the goal of socialist modernization. By pursuing these goals, China can leverage them as catalysts for economic transformation, driving innovations across industries, technologies, and energy systems. This will not only enhance the quality and efficiency of economic growth but also serve as a powerful engine for upgrading China's economy. It is also a major responsibility to promote the construction of a community with a shared future for mankind.

While "carbon peaking and carbon neutrality" are often framed as temporal targets, their essence lies in achieving fundamental transformations across multiple dimensions: raising incomes, restructuring the economy, and enhancing economic efficiency. These transformations are intrinsic to China's pursuit of socialist modernization and high-quality development. To achieve the "dual carbon" goal, it is necessary to follow the five principles of "national coordination, prioritization of resource conservation, leveraging synergistic government and market forces, promoting open domestic and international collaboration (of goods, capital, and technology), and risk prevention". This paper proposes five approaches to achieving "dual carbon" goals: establishing a comprehensive policy framework, fostering the growth of "dual carbon" industries according to local conditions, cultivating a "dual carbon" investment market, driving innovation in "dual carbon" technologies, and integrating environmental governance for synergistic benefits.

4.4.1 *Establishing a Comprehensive Policy Framework ("1+N" Policy System)*

A comprehensive policy framework is essential for effectively advancing China's "dual carbon" goals. This framework must be grounded in China's current development stage and national circumstances, encompassing both top-level design and sector-specific implementation guidelines tailored to regional variations.

In September 2021, the Communist Party of China Central Committee and the State Council jointly issued the "Opinions on Fully and Accurately Implementing the New Development Concept and Doing a Good Job in Carbon Peaking and Carbon Neutrality". This document provides a blueprint, outlining key milestones for 2025, 2030, and 2060, and articulating a comprehensive strategy across 11 key areas:

- Promoting a green transformation of economic and social development;
- Deeply adjusting the industrial structures;
- Accelerating the development of a clean, low-carbon, safe and efficient energy system;
- Advancing the development of a low-carbon transportation system;
- Enhancing the quality of green and low-carbon development in urban and rural areas;
- Strengthening major scientific and technological breakthroughs in green and low-carbon technologies and promoting their application;
- Continuously consolidating and improving carbon sink capacity;
- Increasing the level of green and low-carbon development international collaboration
- Improving laws, regulations, standards, and statistical monitoring systems;
- Improving policy mechanisms;

- Effectively strengthening organizational implementation.

Further strengthening this framework, the Action Plan for Carbon Peaking before 2030 (Guo Fa [2021] No. 23) further outlines ten major actions and three major supporting measures, emphasizing the importance of a phased and coordinated approach to carbon peaking across different regions. It provides guidance and enhances the practicality and effectiveness of China's carbon reduction efforts.

Under the guidance of top-level design, individual sectors and industries should develop more detailed implementation plans and supporting measures. Key sectors such as energy, industry, transportation, and urban-rural construction require particular attention. Simultaneously, policy areas like technological innovation, energy security, carbon sequestration capacity, fiscal and financial policies, standards and measurement systems, and monitoring and evaluation mechanisms must be strengthened and accelerated. This multi-layered "1+N" policy system, characterized by clear targets, well-defined responsibilities, effective measures, and orderly linkage, is crucial for achieving China's "dual carbon" goals and driving a comprehensive and systemic transformation of the economy and society.

4.4.2 Fostering the Growth of "Dual Carbon" Industries According to Local Conditions

Achieving nationwide carbon neutrality requires a holistic approach, beginning with a coordinated effort to reach peak carbon emissions before 2030. This entails maximizing emissions reductions in energy, industry, transportation, construction and other sectors. Through a combination of enhanced energy efficiency and the deployment of low-carbon energy sources, China aims to progressively reduce carbon dioxide emissions toward near-zero levels, ultimately achieving a transition from near-zero to net-zero emissions.

Some studies have highlighted the close relationship between carbon emissions and economic growth, but also emphasize the potential for strategic industrial restructuring to weaken this linkage and create greater opportunities for decarbonization (Tu, 2012). The industrial foundation is also crucial for facilitating China's energy transformation (Ma et al., 2018). Therefore, achieving these goals urgently necessitates a comprehensive, cross-sectoral strategy that promotes industrial transformation and upgrading, unlocking new opportunities for industrial transformation and upgrading. This paper suggests that developing "dual carbon" industries according to local conditions should mainly follow the following ideas:

1. Promote Sustainable Consumption: All end-use sectors must prioritize sustainable consumption patterns and accelerate the development of circular economy practices, energy conservation measures, and green production and lifestyles. On this basis, the electrification of end-use sectors and the low-carbon of the power sector should be regarded as a combination of interrelated punches in industry. Efforts should be intensified in industries, transportation, construction.

This includes cultivating low-carbon products, strengthening and extending the low-carbon industry chain, such as promoting the adoption of electric vehicles in the transportation sector, developing associated industries like battery production and recycling, increasing the electrification of central heating systems in northern regions and rural areas, and promoting digital transformation and electric kiln transformation in the industrial field.

2. Transition to Renewable Energy Sources: Shifting away from traditional fossil fuels is fundamental to achieving a low-carbon economy. Electrifying end-use sectors alone is insufficient, as this merely shifts emissions upstream to the power generation sector and puts greater pressure on emissions reduction. Therefore, a comprehensive approach is needed, combining electrification with a fundamental transformation of the power system. This involves building a new power system centered around renewable energy sources, developing industries related to solar photovoltaic power generation, energy storage, and microgrids to accelerate the achievement of the goal of China's non-fossil energy consumption reaching about 20% by 2025, and the goal of increasing the proportion of non-fossil energy consumption to 25% and 80% by 2030 and 2060 respectively.
3. Explore Low-Carbon Fuel Alternatives: Recognizing that full electrification is not feasible across all sectors, China must also explore alternative low-carbon fuels for hard-to-abate sectors like aviation, shipping, and certain industrial processes. In China's future industrial sector, industrial hydrogen has great market potential, and biomass energy will be in a development boom. These alternative energy sources hold considerable promise for further reducing China's reliance on fossil fuels.

4.4.3 Cultivating a "Dual Carbon" Investment Market

The goals of achieving "carbon peaking and carbon neutrality" will give rise to huge industries and markets, bringing huge investment opportunities. Especially for China's energy, industry, construction, and transportation sectors, they face a dual challenge: meeting the demands of a rapidly growing economy driven by urbanization and industrialization, while simultaneously undertaking a massive transformation of existing infrastructure towards low-carbon alternatives. This encompasses retrofitting traditional equipment, electrifying existing systems, and transitioning to clean energy sources for power generation. Consequently, there is a huge demand for low-carbon, zero-carbon, and even carbon-negative technologies and products.

Many research institutions have estimated the investment required for China's "carbon peaking and carbon neutrality" goals (see Table 4.2). While methodologies vary, there is a consensus that China's carbon neutrality goals will leverage billions of investments across a wide range of sectors, including digital energy conservation, renewable energy, energy storage, and advanced manufacturing (Wang et al., 2021).

Therefore, it is necessary to establish a robust "dual carbon" investment ecosystem. This requires:

Table 4.2 Estimation results of low-carbon investment demand under carbon neutrality scenarios

Research institutions	Scenario assumptions	Time	Total investment scale (trillion yuan)	Annual investment scale (trillion yuan)	
				2021–2030	2031–2060
Tsinghua University	2 °C scenario	2021–2050	127.24	4.2	
	1.5 °C scenario	2021–2050	174.38	5.8	
China Investment Association	Carbon neutrality	2021–2050	70	2.3	
Green Gold Commission	Carbon neutrality	2021–2050	487	16.2	
Price Monitoring Center of National Development and Reform Commission of the People's Republic of China	Carbon neutrality	2021–2060	139	3.1–3.6	3.4–3.6
CICC Research Institute	Carbon neutrality	2021–2060	139	2.2	3.9

Note The results are organized based on reports from Caixin Research Institute and Green Gold Commission

Multi-layered and gradient investment policies: Implementing a comprehensive suite of investment policies with varying levels of incentives and support, tailored to specific sectors and technologies.

Strategic government guidance: Leveraging public investment to catalyze private sector investment, particularly in early-stage technologies and critical infrastructure.

Tailored investment and financing system: Developing an investment and financing framework that aligns with the needs of the "dual carbon" transition, facilitating access to capital for both large-scale projects and smaller, innovative ventures.

Rapid development of green finance: Scaling up green finance instruments and mechanisms to direct capital flows toward sustainable investments.

Preferential policies for key actors: Providing targeted support, including financial incentives, tax breaks, and streamlined regulatory processes, to businesses engaged in developing and deploying low-carbon technologies and solutions.

4.4.4 Driving Innovation in "Dual Carbon" Technologies

According to the research by the International Energy Agency (IEA), existing mature technologies can satisfy 90% of the emission reduction requirements under the carbon peak target, but only address 50% of the needs for achieving carbon neutrality target. This gap underscores the need to accelerate the development and deployment of more advanced low-carbon technologies. In addition, many promising emission reduction technologies remain costly and have yet to reach commercial viability. Some are still in the early stages of development. The development of low-carbon technologies aimed at carbon neutrality requires identifying and evaluating the cost, emissions reduction potential, and scalability of various low-carbon technologies, which puts higher demands on China's low-carbon technology R&D strategy and policy support.

Accelerating the demonstration, commercialization, and adoption of key low-carbon technologies remains a top priority for China's scientific and technological development (He, 2015). In July 2021, the Ministry of Education specifically issued the "Carbon Neutrality Science and Technology Action Plan for Higher Education Institutions", outlining the R&D requirements for technologies such as carbon emission reduction, zero-carbon, and carbon-negative technologies. The "Opinion on Fully Implementing the New Development Concept and Doing a Good Job in Carbon Peaking and Carbon Neutrality", issued in September 2021, further emphasized the need to strengthen both fundamental research and cutting-edge technology development, alongside the scaling up of advanced and applicable technologies.

Universities are expected to play a leading role in this endeavor, forming a collaborative of "dual carbon" technology R&D ecosystem alongside businesses and research institutions. By developing key technologies such as carbon reduction, zero-carbon, and carbon-negative technologies, China can enhance its global competitiveness in low-carbon technological revolution, unlock new drivers of economic growth, and accelerate the construction of an innovative country.

4.4.5 Integrating Environmental Governance for Synergistic Benefits

The achievement of the "dual carbon" goal and the promotion of atmospheric environmental governance are mutually beneficial. Coordinating the reduction of both air pollutants and greenhouse gases is not only essential for a successful green and low-carbon transition, but also crucial for modernizing China's environmental and climate governance system. This integrated approach represents a strategic choice for achieving high-quality economic development, protecting the ecological environment, and realizing carbon peaking goals.

Since carbon dioxide and many air pollutants share common source, efforts to reduce air pollution often contribute directly to reducing carbon emissions. Research suggests that shifting energy structures to prioritize environmental improvement does not necessarily hinder economic growth (Lin & Li, 2015). To further enhance these synergistic benefits, China must continue to strengthen its carbon sink capacity.

While reducing emissions at the source is paramount, even after achieving widespread electrification and energy substitution across industries, some sectors and processes will remain difficult to fully decarbonize. Therefore, in addition to leveraging natural carbon sinks like forests and oceans (Yu et al., 2021), it is also necessary to develop technologies and industries to address these residual emissions. This includes fostering the growth of a "last mile" carbon removal industry focused on deploying negative emissions technologies, such as Direct Air Capture method (DAC), to capture and sequester carbon dioxide from the atmosphere. These innovations will be essential for achieving near-zero carbon emissions and realizing China's climate goals.

4.5 Conclusion

China's pursuit of "carbon peaking and carbon neutrality" represents a strategic, forward-looking decision by the Communist Party of China Central Committee, reflecting a deep understanding of the country's current economic and social development needs. Achieving these "dual carbon" goals holds immense significance, not only for improving resource and environmental management, ensuring people's well-being, but also for driving industrial upgrading, economic transformation, and high-quality development, ultimately contributing to the long-term sustainable development of China. Furthermore, this undertaking strengthens China's international standing, enhancing its voice and influence on the global stage, and building a community with a shared future for mankind.

Since the COVID-19 pandemic, China's economy has demonstrated strong resilience, rebounding rapidly from the initial shock. However, challenges persist, particularly the unbalanced and insufficient development across different regions and sectors. Achieving the "dual carbon" goals requires a solid foundation of economic and social progress. Therefore, these problems may become obstacles.

Structural contradictions in China's population structure, investment efficiency, and energy supply and demand are the main social contradictions in promoting the "dual carbon" construction. China needs to accelerate urbanization, enhance education reform, improve investment efficiency, and optimize energy structure in a comprehensive effort to address these imbalances. These efforts constitute a systematic social engineering project essential for laying a strong foundation for achieving the "dual carbon" goals.

China's target of moving from "carbon peaking" to "carbon neutrality" within 30 years, a shorter timeframe than most developed countries, presents significant challenges across technological, economic, and social aspects. Managing the inherent risks and navigating the complex interplay between decarbonization and economic growth will be crucial for preventing unintended consequences such as increased operating costs for businesses, heightened financial risks, and job losses.

Therefore, China must adopt a balanced approach that recognizes the inherent tension between economic growth and decarbonization, avoiding both overly aggressive policies and complacency. On the one hand, China should strengthen technological research and promotion. This necessitates a clear understanding that decoupling economic growth from carbon emissions will be a gradual process. On the other hand, by promoting the adoption of advanced low-carbon technologies while respecting the realities of technological progress and equipment lifecycles, China can smooth its economic growth trajectory, minimize disruptions for businesses, and prevent economic, financial, and social risks caused by "sports style" energy conservation and carbon reduction.

Achieving the "dual carbon" goal is an irreversible commitment that demands a clear understanding of current opportunities, challenges, and risks, coupled with a comprehensive policy framework. This entails establishing a multi-layered "1 + N" policy system that combines top-level national strategies with detailed implementation guidelines tailored to local conditions. China must actively promote the development of "dual carbon" industries, create a thriving investment environment for low-carbon technologies, and accelerate technological innovation through collaboration between universities, research institutions, and businesses. Furthermore, integrating "dual carbon" goals with existing resource conservation and environmental protection policies will create synergistic benefits and ensure a more sustainable transition. Ultimately, achieving these goals requires a collective effort, fostering a shared understanding across society and prioritizing both economic stability and a low-carbon future.

References

Bai, C. E., & Zhang, Q. (2014). Analysis of China's return on capital and its influencing factors. *World Economy, 10*, 3–30.

Cao, H. Y. (2022, January 17). Accelerating greenization of new infrastructure under the "Dual Carbon "Goal". *Economic Daily*. http://fashion.ce.cn/news/202201/17/t20220117_37261678.shtml

Gong, B. L. (2020). *Shale energy revolution: The rise and fall and changes of the global oil and gas industry*. Zhejiang University Press.

He, J. K. (2015). The strategic choice of China's energy revolution and low-carbon development. *Journal of Wuhan University: Philosophy and Social Sciences Edition, 1*, 5–12.

Hu, A. G. (2021). China's goal of peaking carbon emissions before 2030 and its main pathways. *Journal of Beijing Institute of Technology (Social Sciences Edition), 21*(3), 1–15.

Huang, Z. H., Shao, F., & Peng, W. H. (2013). Promote coordinated development of industrialization, urbanization, and agricultural modernization. *China's Rural Economy, 1*, 8–14.

Jia, K. (2020). New infrastructure: It is both an urgent task and a long-term support. *Party and Government Research, 4*, 11–16.

Li, X. H. (2020). "New infrastructure" and its policy orientation for a smart society. *Reform, 5*, 34–48.

Lin, B. Q., & Li, J. L. (2015). The transformation of China's energy structure under environmental governance constraints—Analysis based on coal and carbon dioxide peaks. *Chinese Social Sciences, 9*, 84–107.

Lin, B. Q., & Liu, X. Y. (2010). Carbon emissions during China's urbanization stage: Influencing factors and emission reduction strategies. *Economic Research, 8*(1), 66–78.

Lin, B. Q., Yao, X., & Liu, X. Y. (2010). Strategic adjustment of China's energy structure under energy conservation and carbon emission constraints. *Chinese Social Sciences, 1*, 58–71.

Lin, W. B., & Zhu, T. (2021). To achieve carbon peak and carbon neutrality, attention should be paid to three "overall planning." *Price Theory and Practice, 1*, 17–19.

Liu, M. P. (2021). Twelve policy recommendations for achieving carbon neutrality in China. *Power Equipment Management, 2*, 23–25.

Liu, Z. B., & Ling, Y. H. (2020). Structural transformation, total factor productivity, and high-quality development. *Managing the World, 36*(7), 15–28.

Ma, L. M., Shi, D., & Pei, Q. B. (2018). China's low carbon energy transformation (2015–2050): Renewable energy development and feasible paths. *Chinese Population, Resources and Environment, 28*(2), 8–18.

Tang, D. D., Liu, X. L., Ni, H. F., Yang, Y. W., Huang, Q. H., & Zhang, X. J. (2020). The global economic upheaval, China's potential growth rate, and high-quality development in the post pandemic period. *Economic Research, 55*(8), 4–23.

Tu, Z. G. (2012). China's carbon emission reduction path and strategic choice-based on index decomposition analysis of carbon emissions from eight major industry sectors. *Chinese Social Sciences, 3*, 78–94.

Wang, K., Zhang, Y. N., Yang, X. R., & Xu, J. Y. (2021). The real impact of new infrastructure investment: Comprehensive benefit evaluation and analysis based on green and inclusive recovery framework.

Wang, Y. H., Wang, K., Liu, J. L., & Zou, J. (2022). Risk assessment of stranded assets in China's coal-fired power industry under carbon emission constraints. *Chinese Environmental Science, 42*(3), 1427–1434.

Yang, B. W. (2021). Systematic thinking, economic theory and scientific path to achieve carbon neutrality goal strategy under Xi Jinping's new development concept. *The Economist, 1*(9), 5–12.

Yu, B. Y., Zhao, G. P., An, R. Y., Chen, J. M., Tan, J. X., & Li, X. Y. (2021). Research on China's carbon emission path under carbon neutrality goals. *Beijing Institute of Technology (Social Sciences Edition), 23*(2), 17–24.

Zhang, X. L. (2012). Does China's transportation infrastructure promote regional economic growth? Also on the spatial spillover effect of transportation infrastructure. *Chinese Social Sciences, 3*, 60–77.

Chapter 5
Emission Reduction Tournament Would Postpone Carbon Peaking in China

Ming Chen, Dan Yu, Xunpeng Shi, and Ke Wang

Abstract The mitigation of climate change is one of the most serious issues in global public governance. To address the climate crisis, Chinese government has proposed a clear target of carbon peaking and carbon neutrality. Regional efforts are expected to play a key role in delivering China's pledge to peak CO_2 emissions before 2030. However, the emission reduction tournament would result in rapid increases in emission transfers among provinces in China. If the current trend of provincial economic development and associated emission transfer mode remains unchanged, we forecast that 24 progressive provinces in China would peak their CO_2 emissions before 2030, while 6 lagged provinces would peak later than 2030. However, if emission transfers were not existed, the nationwide carbon peaking time would be one year earlier and the corresponding carbon peaking level would be 13% lower. Furthermore, compared to the situation in 2012, the emission transfer mode in 2017 would lead to a higher carbon peaking level, indicating that the switch

M. Chen · K. Wang (✉)
Center for Energy and Environmental Policy Research, Beijing Institute of Technology, Beijing 100081, People's Republic of China
e-mail: wangkebit@bit.edu.cn

School of Management and Economics, Beijing Institute of Technology, Beijing 100081, People's Republic of China

D. Yu
Zhejiang Huayun Electric Power Engineering Design and Consultation Company, Hangzhou 310000, China

X. Shi
Australia-China Relations Institute, University of Technology Sydney, Ultimo, NSW 2007, Australia

K. Wang
Sustainable Development Research Institute for Economy and Society of Beijing, Beijing 100081, People's Republic of China

Beijing Key Lab of Energy Economics and Environmental Management, Beijing 100081, People's Republic of China

Collaborative Innovation Center of Electric Vehicles in Beijing, Beijing, China

B. Gong et al. (eds.), *Chinese Governance and Transformation Towards Carbon Neutrality*, Resources, Environment and Agricultural Development,
https://doi.org/10.1007/978-981-97-9996-1_5

to the emission transfer mode from 2012 to 2017 had increased the difficulty of carbon peaking in China. We suggest that the principle of common but differentiated responsibilities should be applied when decomposing the national carbon peaking targets into provinces, and China must avoid a tournament among local governments on carbon peaking.

Keywords Carbon peaking · Climate governance · Counterfactual analysis · Emission reduction · Emission transfer · Forecast · Input–output analysis

5.1 Introduction

China has pledged to peak CO_2 emissions before 2030 and achieve carbon neutrality before 2060. To achieve the carbon peak target as early as possible, the Chinese government has introduced a series of policies to reduce CO_2 emissions (Bondes, 2022; Joseph, 2023; Shapiro, 2021). However, some existing phenomena may be harmful to the achievement of the carbon peak target nationwide, and one of them is the emission reduction tournament among China's provinces. Although the central government of China has released a nationwide schedule for carbon peaking, its implementation depends on the regional governments of China. China has 34 provincial regions, each of which has its own regional CO_2 emission reduction governance. Since China pledged to strive to peak CO_2 emissions before 2030, emission reduction becomes an important performance index for regional governments. Recently, there is an emission reduction tournament among provinces in China, as some regional governments have proposed advanced schedules of carbon peaking, leading to an over ambitious energy transition (Kuhn, 2018; Liu et al., 2022; Shi et al., 2021). For example, among the 16 provinces that have announced carbon peak targets, 14 provinces, with Fujian and Ningxia as exceptions, had promised to achieve carbon peaking target by 2030 or to peak their CO_2 emissions earlier than other provinces. The carbon peak targets of these 16 provinces are shown in Table 5.1.

Radical carbon reduction goals may defeat long-term environmental goals (Liu et al., 2020). Recently, the China National Development and Reform Commission (NDRC) has pointed out that there are some inefficient carbon reduction policies in some provinces, which could be called 'campaign-style' carbon reduction (Zheng, 2021). Some provinces have set unrealistic and overly ambitious goals without making solid energy savings efforts, which are not beneficial for the nationwide carbon peaking. If all current policies could be implemented effectively, China is likely to peak CO_2 emissions before 2030 (Gallagher et al., 2019). However, this does not mean that all provinces and regions will peak before 2030. Due to the remarkable differences in the characteristics of energy consumption (Wang et al., 2020c; Zhang et al., 2018) and the difficulty of balancing the target of emissions reduction and economic development (Ning et al., 2020), each province in China may not reach carbon peak value at the same time (Zhang et al., 2021). For some provinces, peaking carbon as early as possible may not be the best opinion (Fang et al., 2019). To propose a reasonable

Table 5.1 Carbon peaking targets of some provinces

Province	Release time	Emission reduction target
Beijing	Oct. 2021	To be the 'bellwether' of nationwide peaking carbon
Hebei	Jan. 2022	Ensuring peaking carbon by 2030
Jilin	Nov. 2021	By 2030, CO_2emissions will have reached a peak and will have decreased steadily
Shanghai	Sep. 2021	Taking the lead in reaching carbon peak in 2025
Jiangsu	May 2021	The carbon peaking time will be earlier than 2030, as proposed by the nation
Zhejiang	Dec. 2021	Peaking carbon with high quality by 2030
Fujian	Apr. 2022	By 2035, CO_2emissions will gradually decrease after reaching the peak
Jiangxi	Apr. 2022	By 2030, CO_2emissions will have reached a peak and will have decreased steadily
Henan	Feb. 2022	CO_2emissions have reached a peak by 2030, and have decreased steadily by 2035
Hunan	Mar. 2022	By 2030, CO_2emissions will have reached a peak and will have decreased steadily
Guangdong	Feb. 2021	Leading to peak carbon
Hainan	Feb. 2021	Striking to achieve a "carbon peak" by 2025
Chongqing	Apr. 2022	Taking effective measures to promote the achievement of the goal of peaking CO_2emissions by 2030
Sichuan	Dec. 2021	By 2030, CO_2emissions will have reached a peak and will have decreased steadily
Shaanxi	Oct. 2021	Ensuring that the carbon peak target by 2030 is achieved on schedule
Ningxia	Jan. 2022	By 2030, CO_2emissions will reach a peak smoothly

carbon peaking schedule, each province must consider many factors, such as the potential energy intensity and effects of carbon factor effects (Chen et al., 2019a), the industrial structure (Nie et al., 2020), and the structure of the population and income level (Deng et al., 2021). The emission reduction tournament would promote unreasonable carbon peaking schedules in provinces.

Environmental integrity is a key principle in achieving climate mitigation throughout the world (Keohane, 2019; Schneider & Theuer, 2019). On the one hand, global time flexibility in reducing GHG emissions is justifiable. However, international trade may cause adverse effects on emission reductions in developing countries (Babiker et al., 2000). Globalization of supply chains has resulted in rapid increases in emission transfers. Developed countries have been able to decarbonize domestically, at the expense of increased emissions in developing countries (Glemarec, 2019; Wood et al., 2020).

To achieve a common emission reduction target, there are two types of reduction regime, universal regime and fragmented regime. The universal regime involves a single comprehensive climate regime in which all countries participate, and the fragmented regime involves either multiple treaties or a single treaty in which not all countries participate (Hof et al., 2009). Although global time flexibility is justifiable to some extent, this equity-orientated argument may be robust against time and spatial efficiency consideration (Sugiyama & Liu, 2004). However, establishing a universal regime will be challenging due to cost differences among regions (Hof et al., 2009). It is necessary to consider environmental integrity and the regional differences while setting carbon peaking targets.

Furthermore, emissions transfers have been suggested to integrate climate policy (Scott & Barrett, 2015). Combined with foreign direct investment, CO_2 emissions decreased in high-income countries and increased in middle-income countries in the short term (Marques & Caetano, 2020). Therefore, developed regions should implement stricter emissions regulations in almost all scenarios based on current research (Tamaki et al., 2019).

Currently, almost all provinces in China have been deeply involved in domestic supply chains by economic flows (Feng et al., 2020; Wang et al., 2020b), and economic flows are always accompanied by CO_2 emissions flows (Steininger et al., 2016; Yang et al., 2020). To reduce their own CO_2 emissions and peak carbon earlier, some regional governments had been transferring CO_2 emissions to other provinces through supply chains for years. These emission transfers exist both within well-developed and less-developed regions and among them (Pan et al., 2018). In particular, 64 and 35% of China's emissions are transferred between provinces driven by final demands and primary inputs, respectively (Chen et al., 2019a, 2019b). Some economically underdeveloped provinces always receive CO_2 emissions from economically developed provinces (Han et al., 2020; Wang et al., 2018); and some developed provinces with enough self-sufficiency abilities still transfer more CO_2 to other provinces to promote their own development (Zhai et al., 2020). Based on the multi-regional input–output (MRIO) table, we could estimate the effect of emission transfers among provinces by input–output analysis, which is a common method in many similar studies (Ji et al., 2020; Long et al., 2020; Mi et al., 2020).

Given the likelihood of heterogeneous carbon peak timelines, it is important to set fair targets for different provinces. It is an important but difficult task for the Chinese government to balance the CO_2 emissions in provinces reasonably (Chen & Huang, 2021; Wang et al., 2020a). This target setting will involve all the debates on common but differential responsibility (CBDR) that has been popular in the international carbon negotiations. Additionally, heterogeneity would allow industry transfer (or relocation) among provinces and thus create domestic carbon leakage similar to that between countries. Therefore, this circumstance creates two research questions. First, what is the consequence of the emission reduction tournament? Second, how will industry transfer affect national emission peak targets?

Emission transfers caused by emission reduction tournament play an important role in China's CO_2 emissions and may be beneficial or detrimental to the achievement of the carbon peak target. Nevertheless, very few studies have attempted to examine the effects of interprovincial trade on the carbon peaking target of China.

Here, we try to reveal the role of emission reduction tournament in the carbon peaking target and estimate the consequence by counterfactual analysis. In this study, we estimate three groups of carbon peaking times and levels for each province. First, we use an econometric model to forecast future CO_2 emissions of each province and, on this, we could find out each province's carbon peaking time and carbon peaking level under the benchmark scenario. Then, supposing that there were no emission transfers, we establish two counterfactual scenarios based on the MRIO table in 2017 and 2012, respectively. In the counterfactual scenario (2017), we adjusted the CO_2 emissions of each province by MRIO table in 2017, and found a new group of carbon peaking times and carbon peaking levels. The difference between the benchmark scenario and the counterfactual scenario (2017) can be used to assess whether emission transfer mode in China would affect the national carbon peaking time or carbon peaking level. Then, we replace the MRIO table in 2017 with the MRIO table in 2012, and get the counterfactual scenario (2012). The differences between the two counterfactual scenarios would release the effects of the change in emission transfer modes on carbon peaking.

Our contributions are threefold. First, we adjust the carbon peaking time and carbon peaking level based on emission transfer mode and identify the relationship between emission transfer mode and carbon peaking target. Second, we release the phenomenon that the emission reduction tournament among provinces would affect the achievement of the carbon peaking target by changing the emission transfer mode. Lastly, we discuss the reasons for this phenomenon and derive some purposeful policy implications to avoid the emission reduction tournament and peak CO_2 emissions efficiently.

We find that China has the ability to achieve the national carbon peaking target before 2030, but not all provinces would peak CO_2 emissions by 2030. Current carbon peaking proposals at the provincial level show that there is an emission reduction tournament among provinces in China. The emission reduction tournament would postpone the nationwide carbon peaking and increase the nationwide carbon peaking level. Therefore, we suggest that the principle of common but differentiated responsibilities should be applied when decomposing the national carbon peaking targets into provinces. Decreasing emission intensities is the main measure to reduce CO_2 emissions, and the progressive provinces have responsibilities and obligations to help achieve emission reduction targets in lagged provinces.

The remainder of this article is organized as follows. Section 5.2 describes the econometric model to forecast the CO_2 emissions, the input–output method to adjust the prediction results, and the data used in this paper. Section 5.3 explains and compares the estimation results under the benchmark and counterfactual scenarios. Based on discussing the estimating results, Sect. 5.4 presents some policy implications. Section 5.5 concludes this paper.

5.2 Method

5.2.1 Forecast of Carbon Peaking

We establish an econometric model to forecast the CO_2 emissions. Firstly, the CO_2 emissions could be decomposed into two variables, which are the outputs and the emission factors (Du et al., 2019). In this paper, we choose GDP as the variable output and the emission intensity (EI) as the variable emission factor. While the GDP and emission intensity have been forecast, it will be easy to forecast the CO_2 emissions for each province:

$$emission_{i,t} = GDP_{i,t} \times EI_{i,t} \tag{5.1}$$

In Eq. (5.1), i denotes the province and t denotes the year. In order to simplify the calculation, this research defines t = 1 when the variable is for 1997, t = 2 when the variable is for 1998, etc.

To forecast GDP, we established the ARIMA model[1] for each province, which is one of the most popular models for time series forecasting analysis (Ediger & Akar, 2007). The ARIMA (p, d, q) model is

$$y_{i,t} = Q_0 + \sum_{j=1}^{p} \varphi_j y_{i,t-j} + \sum_{k=1}^{q} \theta_k e_{i,t-k} + e_{i,t}$$

in which, $y_{i,t}$ is the data series after d th-order difference, $e_{i,t}$ denotes the random error term, and Q_0 denotes the constant term. Parameters p, d, and q of ARIMA are determined by the Unit Root Test and Akaike Information Criterion (AIC). The parameters and AIC for each province are shown in Appendix.

In recent years, along with the implementation of emission reduction policies and the improvement of the technical level, the emission intensity in China declined steadily. We suppose that the emission intensity would be reduced by a fixed proportion in the coming years, and the index EI could be forecast by the regression Eq. (5.2):

$$EI_{i,t} = \alpha_i \, e^{-\beta_i t} \tag{5.2}$$

in which, α_i and β_i are the regression coefficient for province i. Taking logarithms on both sides of the equation, it could be easily obtained by the OLS method. The regression results are shown in Appendix.

While the GDP and emission intensity have been forecast, the product of these two indexes is the predictive value of CO2 emissions. Then, we could find out the carbon peaking time and carbon peaking level of each province.

5.2.2 Input–Output Analysis for Measuring Emission Transfers

In this section, we aim to obtain the avoid emission coefficient ($AEC_{i1,i2}$) between provinces. Along with the economic flow from province $i1$ to province $i2$, province $i2$ could avoid its own CO_2 emissions by increase CO_2 emissions in province $i1$. The ratio that the avoided CO_2 emissions in province $i2$ to the CO_2 emissions in province $i1$ will be defined as $AEC_{i1,i2}$. In other words, $AEC_{i1,i2}$ can be considered as how much CO_2 emissions in province $i2$ will be reduced when province $i1$ adds a unit of CO_2 emissions under the current emission transfer mode.

In this section, all data are for the same year (2017 or 2012). For simplicity, the year subscript is omitted. First, the direct consumption coefficient matrix (A) and the Leontief inverse matrix (L) could be calculated using the MRIO table as follows

$$A = \begin{bmatrix} A_{1,1,1,1} & A_{1,1,1,2} & \cdots & A_{1,1,1,29} & A_{1,1,2,1} & A_{1,1,2,2} & \cdots\cdots & A_{1,1,30,29} \\ A_{1,2,1,1} & A_{1,2,1,2} & \cdots & A_{1,2,1,29} & A_{1,2,2,1} & A_{1,2,2,2} & \cdots\cdots & A_{1,2,30,29} \\ \vdots & \vdots & \ddots & \vdots & \vdots & \vdots & \ddots & \vdots \\ A_{1,29,1,1} & A_{1,29,1,2} & \cdots & A_{1,29,1,29} & A_{1,29,2,1} & A_{1,29,2,2} & \cdots\cdots & A_{1,29,30,29} \\ A_{2,1,1,1} & A_{2,1,1,2} & \cdots & A_{2,1,1,29} & A_{2,1,2,1} & A_{2,1,2,2} & \cdots\cdots & A_{2,1,30,29} \\ A_{2,2,1,1} & A_{2,2,1,2} & \cdots & A_{2,2,1,29} & A_{2,2,2,1} & A_{2,2,2,2} & \cdots\cdots & A_{2,2,30,29} \\ \vdots & \vdots & \ddots & \vdots & \vdots & \vdots & \ddots & \vdots \\ \vdots & \vdots & & \vdots & \vdots & \vdots & & \vdots \\ A_{30,29,1,1} & A_{30,29,1,2} & \cdots & A_{30,29,1,29} & A_{30,29,2,1} & A_{30,29,2,2} & \cdots\cdots & A_{30,29,30,29} \end{bmatrix} \tag{5.3}$$

$$A_{i1,j1,i2,j2} = \begin{cases} \frac{a_{i1,j1,i2,j2}}{total_{i2,j2}}, & total_{i2,j2} \neq 0 \\ 0, & total_{i2,j2} = 0 \end{cases} \tag{5.4}$$

$$L = (I - A)^{-1} \tag{5.5}$$

In Eqs. (5.3) to (5.5), $a_{i1,j1,i2,j2}$ denotes the economic flow from province $i1$ sector $j1$ to province $i2$ sector $j2$; $total_{i2,j2}$ denotes the total input (which is equal to total output in input–output table) of province $i2$ sector $j2$; I is an identity matrix.

Then, the complete economic flow (CEF) from the province $i1$ sector $j1$ to the province $i2$ sector $j2$ is calculated as in Eq. (5.6):

$$CEF_{i1,j1,i2,j2} = L_{i1,j1,i2,j2} * F_{i2,j2} \tag{5.6}$$

in which, F denotes the final use in MRIO table.

The production technology and the production environment are obviously different among provinces. For this reason, the CO_2 emissions may not be the same when the same amount of the same products are produced in different provinces. For the province i sector j, we define the emission intensity ($EI_{i,j}$) as the ratio of CO_2 emissions to the economic value added (EVA). The variable economic value added for each province and sector, which is equal to the GDP in macroeconomics, could be obtained from the input–output table. Some sectors do not exist in all provinces. The $EI_{i,j}$ could not be directly calculated if province i does not have any economic activity in sector j. For this reason, if $EVA_{i,j} = 0$, we assume that the $EI_{i,j}$ is equal to the weighted average of the intensity of the emission of all provinces for sector j. The math is shown in Eq. (5.7):

$$EI_{i,j} = \begin{cases} \frac{emission_{i,j}}{EVA_{i,j}}, EVA_{i,j} > 0 \\ \frac{\sum_i emission_{i,j}}{\sum_i EVA_{i,j}}, EVA_{i,j} = 0 \end{cases} \tag{5.7}$$

Due to the economic flow from province $i1$ sector $j1$ to the province $i2$ sector $j2$, province $i2$ could avoid some CO_2 emissions. CO_2 emissions avoided in province $i2$ are defined as import-free emissions avoided by import ($EAI_{i1,j1,i2,j2}$). The definition is similar to the studies in López et al. (2013) and Feng et al. (2020). If the products in the province $i1$ sector $j1$ are demanded by the provinces $i2$ sector $j2$, we suppose that the province $i2$ sector $j1$ would produce them. To produce these products, the additional CO_2 emissions in province $i2$ are the $EAI_{i1,j1,i2,j2}$ which calculated in Eq. (5.8).

$$EAI_{i1,j1,i2,j2} = CEF_{i1,j1,i2,j2} * EI_{i2,j1} \tag{5.8}$$

Lastly, the above-mentioned avoid emission coefficient (AEC) can be calculated as:

$$AEC_{i1,i2} = \frac{\sum_{j1,j2} EAI_{i1,j1,i2,j2}}{emission_{i1}} \tag{5.9}$$

Using the avoid emission coefficient, we could adjust each province's CO_2 emissions to the counterfactual scenario, under which we could assume that there were no emission transfers among provinces in China.

5.2.3 Adjustment of Carbon Peaking Forecast

After forecasting CO_2 emissions and calculating the AECs, we could establish a counterfactual scenario. For this scenario, we assume that all the production demanded by a province would be produced in this province, and there are no economic flows among provinces. Under this scenario, all the CO_2 emissions in a province can be entirely blamed for the demand of this own province.

To calculate the CO_2 emissions of each province in each year under the counterfactual scenario, the estimation results under the benchmark scenario should be adjusted by AECs as follows:

$$emission_{i2,t}^{after} = \sum_{i1} AEC_{i1,i2} emission_{i1} \quad (5.10)$$

In Eq. (5.10), $emission_{i2,t}^{after}$ represents the CO_2 emissions of province $i2$ in year t under the counterfactual scenario. After the adjustment, we could find out the counterfactual estimation results of carbon peaking time and carbon peaking level for each province and the entire country.

5.2.4 Data Sources

The GDP data for 1997 to 2017 is published by the China National Bureau of Statistics. The CO_2 emissions data from 1997 to 2017 is obtained from the table "Emission Inventories for 30 Provinces" in Carbon Emission Accounts & Datasets (CEADs) (Shan et al., 2016, 2018, 2020), which covers 47 socioeconomic sectors (45 production sectors and 2 consumption sectors). And the MRIO tables of China are obtained from the tables "China multi-regional input–output table for 2012" and "China multi-regional input–output table for 2017" in CEADs (Zheng et al., 2020), which cover 42 socioeconomic sectors. All data cover 30 provinces in China. Other Chinese provincial regions of Tibet, Hong Kong, Macao, and Taiwan are not estimated due to the lack of data. There are 45 sectors in the CO_2 emissions and 42 sectors in the MRIO tables, and the sectors in the MRIO tables for 2012 and 2017 are not the same. Therefore, we combine the data into 29 sectors by Appendix.

5.3 Results

5.3.1 Most Provinces Could Achieve Carbon Peaking Before 2030 Under Current Trend of Emission Transfer Mode

As described above, working with the econometric model, we are able to forecast the CO_2 emissions of each province. Then, we can find out each province's carbon peaking time and carbon peaking level. The carbon peaking times and carbon peaking levels are shown in Fig. 5.1, and the estimation results are shown in Appendix in detail.

Based on the prediction results, the 30 provinces are divided into 3 groups. As shown in Fig. 5.5.1, 8 provinces have been carbon peaking during the data collection period, which are Beijing, Jilin, Hubei, Heilongjiang, Shanghai, Shanxi, Gansu, and Liaoning; 16 other provinces would peak their CO_2 emissions between 2020 to 2030, which are Tianjin, Chongqing, Guizhou, Hunan, Guangdong, Jiangxi, Shaanxi, Sichuan, Anhui, Zhejiang, Henan, Jiangsu, Qinghai, Hebei, Shandong, and Yunnan; and 6 provinces would peak their CO_2 emissions after 2030, which are Guangxi, Hainan, Fujian, Inner Mongolia, Ningxia, and Xinjiang.

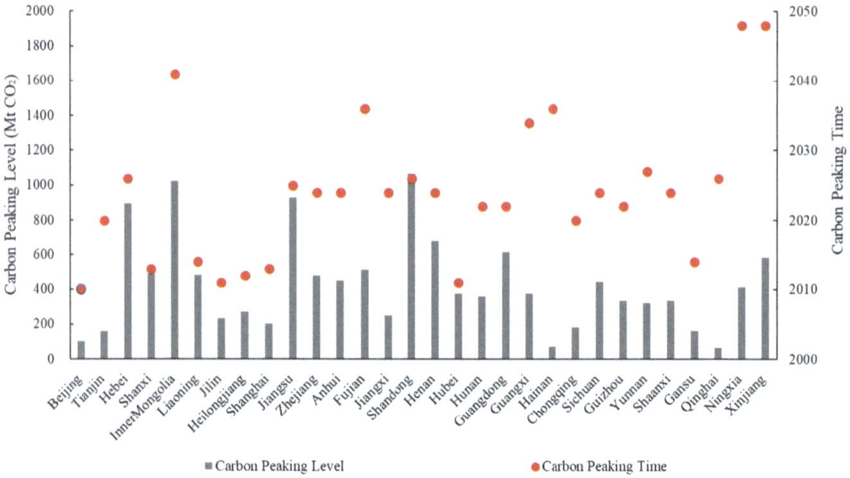

Fig. 5.1 The times and levels of carbon peaking

During the past decades, China has made significant efforts to reduce carbon. From our prediction results, 24 of the 30 provinces are able to peak their CO_2 emissions before 2030, which could be considered as the progressive provinces. Moreover, to obtain the prediction results, we assume that the current trend of provincial economic development and associated emission transfer mode remain unchanged, and the provincial emission reduction policies could be implemented effectively. Therefore, it is important for these progressive provinces to ensure that all current provincial economic development and associated emission transfer mode remains unchanged, and that provincial emission reduction policies would be implemented effectively.

But for the other 6 provinces in China, it is difficult to peak carbon before 2030 according to our prediction results, which could be considered as lagged provinces. These provinces are all in the northwest (Inner Mongolia, Ningxia, and Xinjiang) or southern (Fujian, Guangxi, and Hainan) of China. To peak carbon earlier than 2030, these lagged provinces need to take more additional policies or measures to reduce CO_2 emissions.

According to our estimate, China will get nationwide CO_2 emissions in 2025. In this year, the total CO_2 emissions in China may be 12.02Bt. If all provinces could maintain economic development and technological development steady, China is possibly to achieve the nationwide carbon peak target before 2030. But for some provinces, the carbon peaking time may be later.

5.3.2 *Nationwide Carbon Peaking Time Would Be Advanced Supposing No Emissions Transfers*

In this section, we calculate all the AECs among 30 provinces in 2017 by input–output analysis. Figure 5.2 shows the avoid emission coefficient matrix. In Fig. 5.2, each row represents a province that causes export emission transfer, and each column represents a province which cause emission transfer. The color of each square denotes the number of AEC.

There is obvious difference in AECs among provinces, which could be explained by the differences of trade structure and emission intensity. Summing the avoid emission coefficient matrix by row, we could obtain the sum of AECs induced by export for each province. The results are shown in Table 5.2.

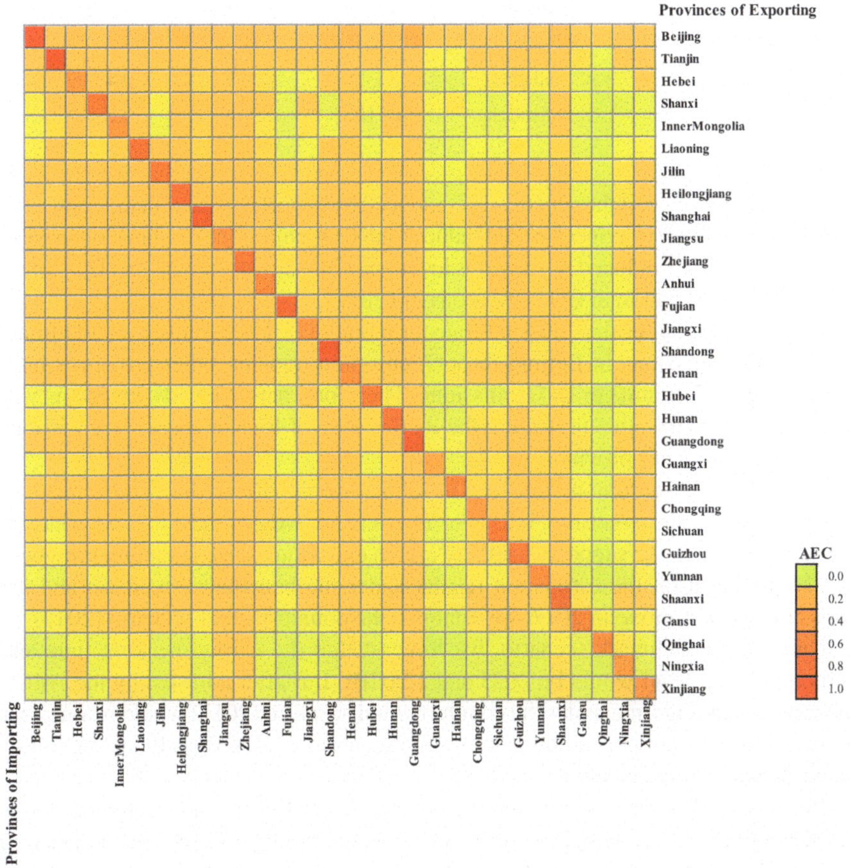

Fig. 5.2 The avoid emission coefficient matrix

Table 5.2 The sum of AECs induced by export

Province	Sum of AECs	Province	Sum of AECs
Beijing	2.5346	Henan	0.7825
Tianjin	1.5902	Hubei	0.7579
Hebei	0.5205	Hunan	0.9017
Shanxi	0.9685	Guangdong	1.2696
Inner Mongolia	0.5486	Guangxi	0.3783
Liaoning	0.9388	Hainan	0.8015
Jilin	0.9395	Chongqing	0.6585
Heilongjiang	1.0038	Sichuan	0.8371
Shanghai	1.5293	Guizhou	0.8821
Jiangsu	0.6337	Yunnan	0.6242
Zhejiang	0.9413	Shaanxi	1.1140
Anhui	0.7317	Gansu	0.7330
Fujian	1.1047	Qinghai	0.6046
Jiangxi	0.6398	Ningxia	0.4835
Shandong	1.5105	Xinjiang	0.5332

For each province, if the sum of AECs induced by export is greater than 1, emission transfers from other provinces would reduce total CO_2 emissions in China; otherwise, if the sum of AECs induced by export is less than 1, the emission transfers from other provinces would add total CO_2 emissions in China.

For example, under the emission transfer mode in 2017, to reduce an additional unit of CO_2 emissions in Beijing through emission transfer, other provinces have to increase 2.5346 units of CO_2 emissions. Therefore, national CO_2 emissions will increase by 1.5346 units, indicating the inefficiency of transferring CO_2 emissions from Beijing to other provinces.

Therefore, the emission transfers in China would affect the achievement of the carbon peaking target in China. For this reason, we establish a counterfactual scenario, in which we suppose that there are no emission transfers among provinces in China. Based on the estimation results under the benchmark scenario and the emission transfer mode in 2017, we establish the counterfactual scenario (2017).

Under the benchmark scenario, we forecast that the carbon peaking time and carbon peaking level would be 2025 and 12.02Bt. But after adjusted by the AECs, the carbon peaking time under the counterfactual scenario (2017) would be one year earlier; and the carbon peaking level in this scenario is 10.46Bt, about 13% lower than the benchmark scenario.

Because of the vast territory and the notable disparities in socioeconomic development and energy system, provinces in China are unlikely to keep pace in peaking carbon.[1] However, since the carbon peak target has been proposed, some developed provinces have been urged to transfer high-emission industries to underdeveloped provinces in order to peak CO_2 emissions locally earlier. Therefore, the underdeveloped provinces achieve economic growth and the developed provinces achieve emission reduction. However, the emission intensities in underdeveloped provinces are usually higher than those in developed provinces. For this reason, the emissions transfers may increase the total CO_2 emissions in China.

Compared to the estimating results under benchmark scenario, we estimate that the emission transfer mode in 2017 would postpone the carbon peaking time and increase the carbon peaking level nationwide. Therefore, China should avoid a tournament among local governments on carbon peaking. Reducing CO_2 emissions by emission transfers is not an effective and efficient measure in China.

5.3.3 The Progressive Provinces Could Further Advance Their Carbon Peaking Time at the Expense of Postponing the Lagged Provinces' Carbon Peaking Time

For each province, the estimating results could be adjusted by AECs as well. Then, we find another group of carbon peaking times and carbon peaking levels of provinces. The detailed results under the counterfactual scenario (2017) are shown in Appendix. Under the benchmark scenario and the counterfactual scenario (2017), the carbon peaking times may be different in some provinces. We compare the carbon peaking time under the two scenarios in Fig. 5.3.

The horizontal axis represents the carbon peaking time under the benchmark scenario discussed in Sect. 5.3.1. And the longitudinal axis represents the carbon peaking time under the counterfactual scenario (2017), which could be also considered as the carbon peaking time without any emission transfers among provinces in China. The area of each dot represents the carbon peaking level under the counterfactual scenario (2017).

In Fig. 5.3, most of the progressive provinces are above the diagonal line, especially Heilongjiang, Hubei, Liaoning, Shanghai, and Shanxi. Without any emission transfers, these progressive provinces could peak CO_2 emissions earlier than 2030 as well. The emission transfer mode makes the carbon peaking time even earlier, at the expense of transferring emissions to other provinces.

Furthermore, the lagged provinces that may peak CO_2 emissions after 2030, such as Fujian, Guangxi, Hainan, Inner Mongolia, Ningxia, and Xinjiang, are all below the diagonal line. The emission transfer mode in China is not beneficial for the achievement of the carbon peaking target in these provinces. According to our estimation above, these provinces would peak their CO_2 emissions later than 2030. It could be partly attributed to emission transfers from other provinces. Without any emission transfers, these lagged provinces could be peaking carbon earlier.

Under current emission transfer mode, the progressive provinces could further advance their carbon peaking time at the expense of postponing the lagged provinces' carbon peaking time. Some progressive provinces (above the diagonal line in Fig. 5.3) that have enough abilities to peak their CO_2 emissions before 2030, could achieve

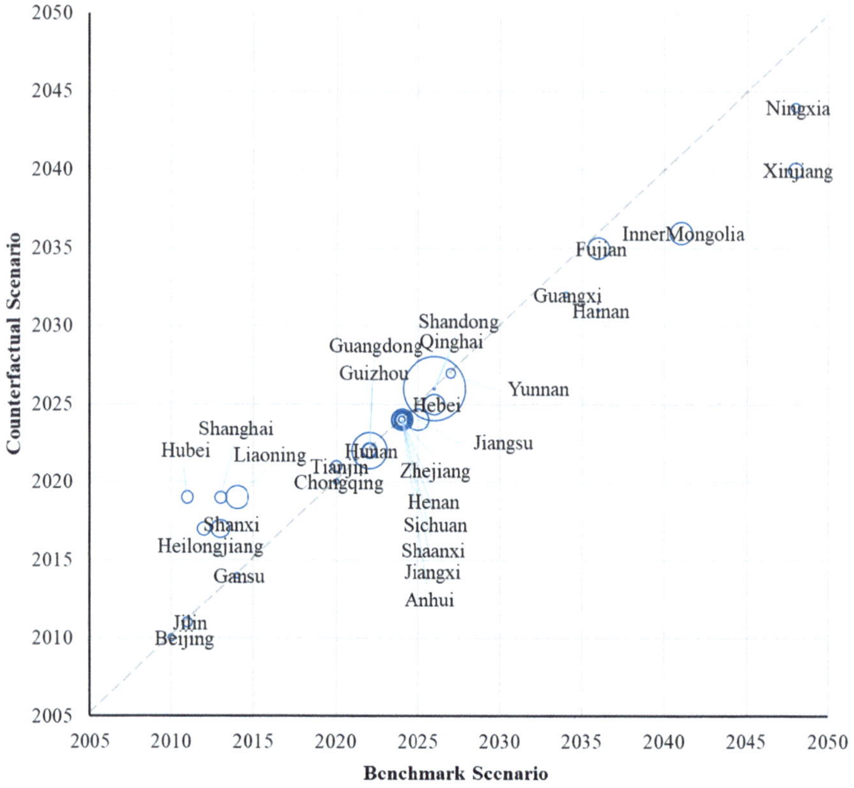

Fig. 5.3 Comparison of the carbon peaking time under the two scenarios

the carbon peaking target even earlier by emission transfers. But for the lagged provinces (below the diagonal line in Fig. 5.3) that have difficulty to peak their CO_2 emissions before 2030, the emission transfer mode is not beneficial for achieving the carbon peaking targets in these provinces. Without any emission transfers, some of the progressive provinces would peak CO_2 emissions 1–8 years later, but the carbon peaking times of these provinces may not later than 2030 under the counterfactual scenario (2017). For some lagged provinces, the carbon peaking time would advance 1–8 years without any emission transfers, but not earlier than 2030.

Radical carbon reduction targets are harmful (Lu et al., 2019), and therefore a gradual and regional-specific roadmap is required. Therefore, the Chinese government should take measures in the incoming national emission reduction roadmaps to account for the regional heterogeneity.

In addition, the developed provinces have the responsibility and obligations to provide funds and technology for emission reduction in the underdeveloped provinces. Along with the proper financial transfer, technology transfer, as well as enterprise re-location, the negative effect of emission reduction tournament would be weakened, which is beneficial to the achievement of nationwide carbon peaking target.

5.3.4 *Change in Emission Transfer Mode is Detrimental to Achieving the Carbon Peaking Target*

The emission transfer mode in China plays an important role in China's CO_2 emissions. However, there are obvious differences between emission transfer modes in 2017 and 2012. Therefore, in this section, we establish the counterfactual scenario (2012) based on the MRIO table in 2012. We replace the MRIO table for 2017 with the MRIO table for 2012, then repeat the steps mentioned above. Comparing the results under the two counterfactual scenarios, we could reveal the effect of the change in emission transfer mode on the carbon peaking target in China.

Figure 5.4 compares the AECs calculated by the MRIO table in 2012 and 2017. The sum of AECs induced by exported from each province is shown above the horizontal axis. For each province, the length of the left bar represents the sum of AECs in 2017, and the length of the right bar represents the sum of AECs in 2012.

For most provinces, the sums of AECs induced by exported are close between 2012 and 2017. However, it is more valuable to pay attention to the provinces whose AECs are greatly different in 2012 and in 2017. The differences reveal the effect of the change in emission transfer mode on the change in CO2 emissions. During the 30 provinces, the AECs of 8 provinces are increase from 2012 to 2017, which are Shaanxi, Guangdong, Qinghai, Beijing, Fujian, Jilin, Anhui, and Zhejiang. Other 22 provinces' AECs is lower in 2017 than in 2012.

Based on the AECs in 2012, the carbon peaking time and the carbon peaking level of each province could be adjusted into the counterfactual scenario (2012). The estimation results after adjustment are shown in Appendix.

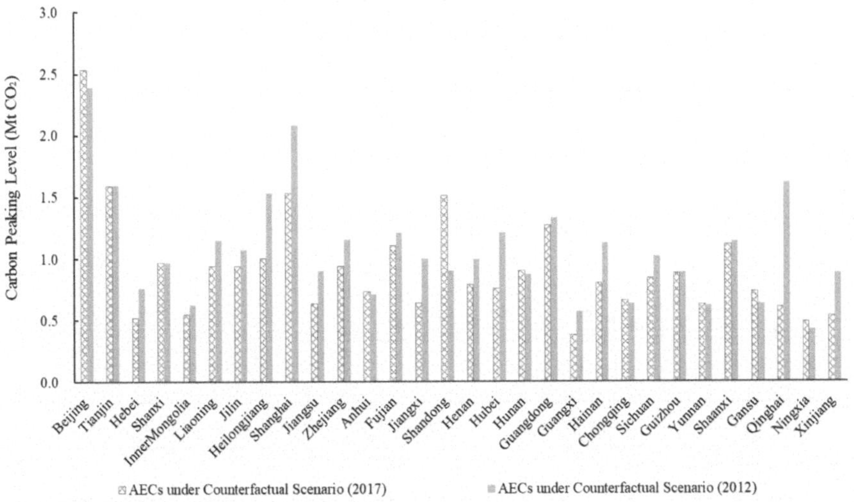

Fig. 5.4 Comparison of AECs in 2012 and 2017

Under the counterfactual scenario (2012), the nationwide carbon peaking time would be the same as in the counterfactual scenario (2017). However, the national carbon peaking level is 11.55Bt under this scenario, a little higher than the counterfactual scenario (2017). For these two counterfactual scenarios, we both assume that there are no emission transfers among provinces in China. Hence, the carbon peaking levels in these two scenarios could be considered as the carbon peaking levels, which have excluded the effect of emission transfer mode. Therefore, we can explain the carbon peaking levels as follows: the emission transfer mode in 2017 may increase 1.56Bt CO_2 emissions on nationwide carbon peaking level; and the emission transfer mode in 2012 may increase just 0.47Bt CO_2 emissions on nationwide carbon peaking level. The emission transfer mode in 2017 is more detrimental for peaking carbon level than the emission transfer mode in 2012.

We compare the carbon peaking level and carbon peaking time of each province under the three scenarios (one benchmark scenario and two counterfactual scenarios) in Fig. 5.5. Compared with the benchmark scenario, if the emission transfer mode is more beneficial or less detrimental to the achievement of carbon peaking target in China, the carbon peaking time would be later, and the carbon peaking level would be larger under the counterfactual scenarios.

Among the 30 provinces, the carbon peaking times of 14 provinces are totally same under the three scenarios. However, for the other provinces, most of the carbon peaking times under the counterfactual scenario (2012) are later than the carbon peaking times under the counterfactual scenario (2017). Moreover, the carbon peaking levels under the counterfactual scenario (2012) are mostly larger than the carbon peaking levels under the counterfactual scenario (2017) as well. For most provinces, it is more difficult to achieve the carbon peaking targets under the emission transfer mode in 2017 than under the emission transfer mode in 2012.

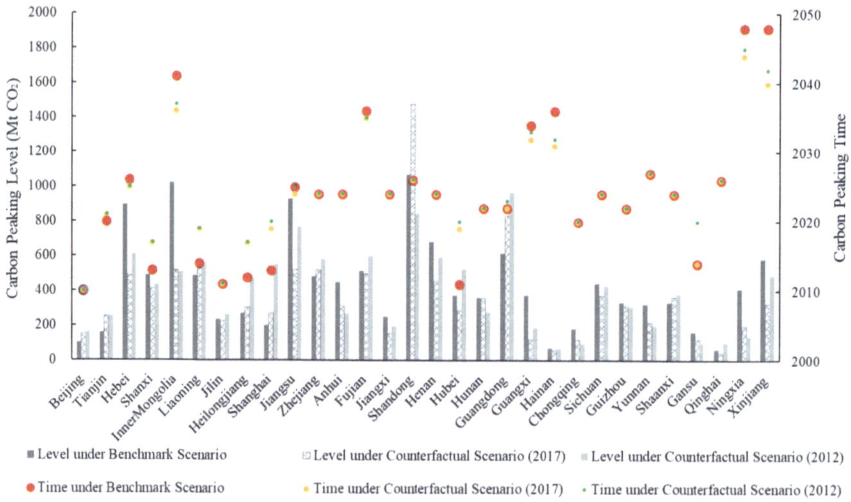

Fig. 5.5 Comparison of carbon peaking time and carbon peaking level

As a result of the emission reduction tournament among provinces, local governments may be urged to transfer CO_2 emissions to other provinces. The additional emission transfers could be reflected in the change in emission transfer modes. By comparing the estimation results between two counterfactual scenarios, the 'campaign-style' carbon reduction may be more detrimental in 2017 than in 2012. To peak CO_2 emissions more efficient, the Chinese government should transform the trend of emission transfer mode.

5.4 Discussions and Policy Implications

As we forecast, most provinces have enough abilities to peak CO_2 emissions before 2030. However, if there were not any emission transfers between provinces, the nationwide carbon peaking time would be one year earlier and the nationwide carbon peaking level would be a little lower. Both emission transfer modes in 2017 and 2012 are not beneficial to achieving the carbon peaking target in China. The emission transfer mode in 2017 is more detrimental than the emission transfer mode in 2012.

Without any emission transfers, most progressive provinces would peak CO_2 emissions later, and most of the lagged provinces would peak CO_2 emissions earlier. The emission transfer mode in China is beneficial for the progressive provinces, and detrimental for the lagged provinces.

To achieve the target of carbon peaking, China need make more effects on it. We suggest some policy implications to ensure that China could peak CO_2 emissions before 2030 effectively and efficiently.

(1) The principle of common but differentiated responsibilities should be applied when decomposing the national carbon peak targets into provinces when setting the initial targets for each province. In order to coordinate the nationwide carbon peaking target and local carbon peaking schedule, it is an important issue to determine how to reasonably allocate carbon emission rights among provinces and industries. Our estimation shows that some economically effective emission transfers are, however, not environmentally effective. This initial allocation of targets should allow those less-developed provinces to continuously increase their emissions after 2030. As mentioned before, most of the provinces in China could be divided into two groups. Progressive provinces are mostly economically developed, and lagged provinces are mostly economically backward. In the recent future, the progressive provinces could make more contributions to the national emission reduction targets, and provide services to lagged provinces. And lagged provinces need pay more attention to economic targets, while introducing financial transfers and technology transfers to reduce CO_2 emissions.

(2) The central government should avoid a tournament among local governments on carbon peaking. The central government and the public should not commend those who have peaked and condemn those who have not. The assessment should

instead focus on the progress toward their individual goals. For lagged provinces, peaking CO_2 emissions may not be the most important policy objectives today. As shown above, most of the provinces that have abilities to peak CO_2 emissions before 2030 are progressive. The achievement of the carbon target mainly depends on the decrease in emission intensity, not the decrease of economic output. Emission reduction tournament is not beneficial in long-run, especially for lagged provinces. These provinces need take more efficient measures to reduce CO_2 emissions in long-run, but not strive to peak CO_2 emissions as early as possible.

(3) The central government should facilitate cooperation among regional governments. Progressive provinces whose carbon peaking time is early, such as Beijing, Jilin, Heilongjiang, and Shanghai, might also have also transferred emissions to other provinces. These provinces have responsibilities and obligations to provide funds and technology for the reduction in the provinces that would peak carbon later than 2030. Because the emission intensities in lagged provinces are significantly higher than in progressive provinces, there must be some low-carbon technologies in progressive provinces. These low-carbon technologies could be helpful in decreasing the intensity of emission in lagged provinces. The lagged provinces could introduce these low-carbon technologies. As current studies show, financial transfers from developed countries to developing countries would enhance pro-poor growth and help the effectiveness of poor countries in reducing emissions (Cantore et al., 2014). No financial transfers would lead to great efficiency losses (Bauer et al., 2020). Transfers between progressive provinces and lagged provinces will likely have the same effects.

(4) CO_2 emission reduction strategies need to reduce emission intensity and increase energy efficiency, but not transfer high-emission enterprises to other provinces. Although emission transfers could quickly reduce CO_2 emissions quickly, it may not be beneficial to the nationwide reduction of emissions. Due to the difference on emission intensity of emissions between provinces before and after the transfer, these enterprises may increase their CO_2 emissions after moving. Therefore, emission transfers would increase CO_2 emissions in the provinces to which companies have been relocated, and the increased CO_2 emissions may be more than reduced CO_2 emissions in the provinces of enterprises moving out.

(5) To improve the structure of energy consumption, China should promote the use of clean energy as a whole. It is also a key measure to decrease emission intensities while keeping economic growth. Replacing high-emission energy with clean energy, which could reduce CO_2 emissions while ensuring economic production. However, improving the structure of energy consumption often requires large initial investment, which is used to develop clean energy production, use technologies and establish a clean energy market. The initial investment is huge and has significant externalities for local governments. Therefore, it is beneficial to promote the use of clean energy at the national level (Altiparmak, 2022). Progressive provinces could invest more in clean energy use technologies, and lagged provinces should actively introduce these technologies. Consumers could

also play an important role by changing their consumption structure to avoid products with much embodied carbon. In China, most of the economic production is driven by demand. While consumers tend to purchase cleaner products, the producers would reduce the products with much embodied carbon. It could effectively reduce CO_2 emissions by the 'invisible hand' of the market.

(6) Promoting the construction of the national carbon emission trading market would be helpful in transfer carbon emission rights to more efficient places and industries. Other market instruments, such as energy consumption permit trading, can be applied at the regional level to minimize emission reduction costs (Wang et al., 2016; Xian et al., 2019). Companies should pay more attention to adapting the carbon market. Considering the change in carbon price while developing business strategies would be effective in reducing production costs and reducing CO_2 emissions.

5.5 Conclusions

In this paper, we forecast the future CO_2 emissions and estimate the carbon peaking time and carbon peaking level for China's each province. Then, we adjust the estimation results by AECs, which are calculated based on two MRIO tables. Comparing the estimation results under the benchmark scenario and two counterfactual scenarios, we discuss the possible effect of the emission reduction tournament among provinces on the achievement of the carbon peaking target in China. First, if the current trend of provincial economic development and the associated emission transfer mode remain unchanged and the provincial emission reduction policies could be implemented effectively, most provinces could reach carbon earlier than 2030. Second, assuming that there were no emission transfers among provinces in China, the national carbon peaking time would be one year earlier than in the benchmark scenario, and the corresponding carbon peaking level would reduce 13%. Third, in the current emission transfer mode, progressive provinces could further advance their carbon peaking time at the expense of postponing the carbon peaking time. Fourth, compared with 2012, the emission transfer mode in 2017 may be more detrimental to the achievement of the carbon peaking target in China.

On the basis of the analysis, we first suggest that the principle of common but differentiated responsibilities should be applied when decomposing the national carbon peaking targets into provinces. Less developed provinces should have less responsibility of emission control. In addition, China needs to avoid a tournament among local governments on carbon peaking. Each province should be assessed against their goals, which should be different among provinces. Lastly, the Chinese central government should facilitate cooperation among regional governments to achieve just and cost-effective emission reductions throughout the country. Once the goals are set, the cap in emissions or energy consumption can be traded among provinces so that the national total compliance costs can be minimized.

There are some limitations to this study. First, due to the lack of more samples and data, the forecast of CO_2 emissions is not accurate enough. Based on research on impact factors of CO_2 emissions, a detailed forecast of each sector and each province may be more convincing. Secondly, we do not consider the possible effect of COVID-19, which can change the economic development trend in China. Third, due to the limitation of data, we were unable to analyze the uncertainties of the results.

Notes

1. Autoregressive Integrated Moving Average model.

Appendix

Appendix Table 5.3

Appendix Table 5.6

There are peaking carbon levels in parentheses.

The CO_2 emissions for 1997–2017 are obtained from the CEADs, and the CO_2 emissions for 2018–2050 are the forecast results of this research.

Appendix Table 5.7

There are peaking carbon levels in parentheses.

Appendix Table 5.8

There are peaking carbon levels in parentheses.

Table 5.3 The parameters and AIC for each province

Beijing	Tianjin	Hebei	Shanxi
ARIMA (2,2,2): 237.7834 ARIMA (0,2,0): 230.0679 ARIMA (1,2,0): 232.0501 ARIMA (0,2,1): 232.0476 ARIMA (1,2,1): 234.8691 Best model: ARIMA (0,2,0)	ARIMA (2,2,2): Inf ARIMA (0,2,0): 248.1177 ARIMA (1,2,0): 250.2729 ARIMA (0,2,1): Inf ARIMA (1,2,1): 252.6152 Best model: ARIMA (0,2,0)	ARIMA (2,2,2): Inf ARIMA (0,2,0): 242.9575 ARIMA (1,2,0): 242.7886 ARIMA (0,2,1): 240.7958 ARIMA (1,2,1): 242.6464 ARIMA (0,2,2): 242.7950 ARIMA (1,2,2): 245.8933 Best model: ARIMA (0,2,1)	ARIMA (2,2,2): Inf ARIMA (0,2,0): 247.3299 ARIMA (1,2,0): 249.7479 ARIMA (0,2,1): Inf ARIMA (1,2,1): Inf Best model: ARIMA (0,2,0)
Inner Mongolia	Liaoning	Jilin	Heilongjiang
ARIMA (2,2,2): Inf ARIMA (0,2,0): 237.8057 ARIMA (1,2,0): 238.0363 ARIMA (0,2,1): 238.7339 ARIMA (1,2,1): 240.4667 Best model: ARIMA (0,2,0)	ARIMA (2,1,2): Inf ARIMA (0,1,0): 317.5271 ARIMA (1,1,0): 307.8521 ARIMA (0,1,1): 311.0926 ARIMA (0,1,0): 339.4543 ARIMA (2,1,0): 311.0181 ARIMA (1,1,1): 311.0184 ARIMA (2,1,1): Inf ARIMA (1,1,0): 308.3855 Best model: ARIMA (1,1,0)	ARIMA (2,2,2): Inf ARIMA (0,2,0): 222.4157 ARIMA (1,2,0): 221.8090 ARIMA (0,2,1): 221.2419 ARIMA (1,2,1): 223.8388 ARIMA (0,2,2): Inf ARIMA (1,2,2): Inf Best model: ARIMA (0,2,1)	ARIMA (2,2,2): Inf ARIMA (0,2,0): 227.1688 ARIMA (1,2,0): 223.1002 ARIMA (0,2,1): 223.7028 ARIMA (2,2,0): 224.8558 ARIMA (1,2,1): 225.3829 ARIMA (2,2,1): 227.7266 Best model: ARIMA (1,2,0)
Shanghai	Jiangsu	Zhejiang	Anhui
ARIMA (2,2,2): 253.3838 ARIMA (0,2,0): 250.0955 ARIMA (1,2,0): 252.0739 ARIMA (0,2,1): 251.7710 ARIMA (1,2,1): 254.6176 Best model: ARIMA (0,2,0)	ARIMA (2,2,2): Inf ARIMA (0,2,0): 262.6673 ARIMA (1,2,0): 260.1996 ARIMA (0,2,1): 260.3230 ARIMA (2,2,0): 262.1263 ARIMA (1,2,1): 262.5790 ARIMA (2,2,1): 264.9575 Best model: ARIMA (1,2,0)	ARIMA (2,2,2): 273.6264 ARIMA (0,2,0): 266.3017 ARIMA (1,2,0): 268.6577 ARIMA (0,2,1): 268.5837 ARIMA (1,2,1): 271.4178 Best model: ARIMA (0,2,0)	ARIMA (2,2,2): Inf ARIMA (0,2,0): 231.8909 ARIMA (1,2,0): 228.8699 ARIMA (0,2,1): 230.3330 ARIMA (2,2,0): 231.0889 ARIMA (1,2,1): Inf ARIMA (2,2,1): Inf Best model: ARIMA (1,2,0)

(continued)

Table 5.3 (continued)

Fujian	Jiangxi	Shandong	Henan
ARIMA (2,2,2): Inf ARIMA (0,2,0): 236.9505 ARIMA (1,2,0): 235.2459 ARIMA (0,2,1): 234.8543 ARIMA (1,2,1): 237.7040 ARIMA (0,2,2): 237.7041 ARIMA (1,2,2): Inf Best model: ARIMA (0,2,1)	ARIMA (2,2,2): Inf ARIMA (0,2,0): 210.4173 ARIMA (1,2,0): 197.4867 ARIMA (0,2,1): 202.0680 ARIMA (2,2,0): 200.3064 ARIMA (1,2,1): Inf ARIMA (2,2,1): Inf Best model: ARIMA (1,2,0)	ARIMA (2,2,2): 258.7286 ARIMA (0,2,0): 259.1599 ARIMA (1,2,0): 253.0570 ARIMA (0,2,1): 253.9658 ARIMA (2,2,0): 255.5260 ARIMA (1,2,1): 253.6007 ARIMA (2,2,1): Inf Best model: ARIMA (1,2,0)	ARIMA (2,2,2): Inf ARIMA (0,2,0): 245.7682 ARIMA (1,2,0): 243.8675 ARIMA (0,2,1): 242.3129 ARIMA (1,2,1): 245.1626 ARIMA (0,2,2): 245.1626 ARIMA (1,2,2): Inf Best model: ARIMA (0,2,1)
Hubei	Hunan	Guangdong	Guangxi
ARIMA (2,2,2): Inf ARIMA (0,2,0): 233.6551 ARIMA (1,2,0): 226.5905 ARIMA (0,2,1): Inf ARIMA (2,2,0): 229.1289 ARIMA (1,2,1): Inf ARIMA (2,2,1): Inf Best model: ARIMA (1,2,0)	ARIMA (2,2,2): Inf ARIMA (0,2,0): 233.4328 ARIMA (1,2,0): 230.8494 ARIMA (0,2,1): Inf ARIMA (2,2,0): 232.9109 ARIMA (1,2,1): 231.1715 ARIMA (2,2,1): Inf Best model: ARIMA (1,2,0)	ARIMA (2,2,2): Inf ARIMA (0,2,0): 286.4972 ARIMA (1,2,0): 289.0100 ARIMA (0,2,1): 289.0077 ARIMA (1,2,1): Inf Best model: ARIMA (0,2,0)	ARIMA (2,2,2): 217.6841 ARIMA (0,2,0): 213.6292 ARIMA (1,2,0): 212.9985 ARIMA (0,2,1): 214.2546 ARIMA (2,2,0): 212.8916 ARIMA (3,2,0): 213.7768 ARIMA (2,2,1): 215.1232 ARIMA (1,2,1): 212.9180 ARIMA (3,2,1): 216.6917 Best model: ARIMA (2,2,0)
Hainan	Chongqing	Sichuan	Guizhou
ARIMA (2,2,2): Inf ARIMA (0,2,0): 179.8303 ARIMA (1,2,0): 182.2507 ARIMA (0,2,1): 182.0869 ARIMA (1,2,1): 184.8079 Best model: ARIMA (0,2,0)	ARIMA (2,2,2): 227.5303 ARIMA (0,2,0): 224.4398 ARIMA (1,2,0): 220.4253 ARIMA (0,2,1): 220.2983 ARIMA (1,2,1): 222.9241 ARIMA (0,2,2): 223.0037 ARIMA (1,2,2): Inf Best model: ARIMA (0,2,1)	ARIMA (2,2,2): 266.2091 ARIMA (0,2,0): 255.8373 ARIMA (1,2,0): 257.6613 ARIMA (0,2,1): 257.8419 ARIMA (1,2,1): 260.3397 Best model: ARIMA (0,2,0)	ARIMA (2,2,2): 202.9688 ARIMA (0,2,0): 197.9360 ARIMA (1,2,0): 196.1244 ARIMA (0,2,1): 197.9899 ARIMA (2,2,0): 197.5228 ARIMA (1,2,1): Inf ARIMA (2,2,1): 199.3491 Best model: ARIMA (1,2,0)
Yunnan	Shaanxi	Gansu	Qinghai
ARIMA (2,2,2): Inf ARIMA (0,2,0): 227.2157 ARIMA (1,2,0): 229.4815 ARIMA (0,2,1): 229.5703 ARIMA (1,2,1): Inf Best model: ARIMA (0,2,0)	ARIMA (2,2,2): Inf ARIMA (0,2,0): 216.1266 ARIMA (1,2,0): 212.8080 ARIMA (0,2,1): 214.8371 ARIMA (2,2,0): 215.2872 ARIMA (1,2,1): 215.2725 ARIMA (2,2,1): Inf Best model: ARIMA (1,2,0)	ARIMA (2,2,2): Inf ARIMA (0,2,0): 206.1899 ARIMA (1,2,0): 207.1689 ARIMA (0,2,1): 207.0816 ARIMA (1,2,1): 209.9021 Best model: ARIMA (0,2,0)	ARIMA (2,2,2): 159.5478 ARIMA (0,2,0): 149.3025 ARIMA (1,2,0): 151.8165 ARIMA (0,2,1): 151.8167 ARIMA (1,2,1): 154.4945 Best model: ARIMA (0,2,0)
Ningxia	Xinjiang		
ARIMA (2,2,2): Inf ARIMA (0,2,0): 138.9798 ARIMA (1,2,0): 138.0686 ARIMA (0,2,1): 138.6844 ARIMA (2,2,0): 140.7058 ARIMA (1,2,1): Inf ARIMA (2,2,1): Inf Best model: ARIMA (1,2,0)	ARIMA (2,2,2): Inf ARIMA (0,2,0): 199.0304 ARIMA (1,2,0): 199.1597 ARIMA (0,2,1): 198.4839 ARIMA (1,2,1): Inf ARIMA (0,2,2): 201.2544 ARIMA (1,2,2): Inf Best model: ARIMA (0,2,1)		

Appendix Table 5.4

Table 5.4 The regression results of emission intensities

	Beijing	Tianjin	Hebei	Shanxi	Inner Mongolia	Liaoning
lnt	−0.0791*** (−37.38)	−0.0645*** (−23.80)	−0.0250*** (−7.49)	−0.0319*** (−11.53)	−0.0221*** (−6.01)	−0.0452*** (−27.73)
Cons	−3.4959*** (−131.50)	−3.0349*** (−89.24)	−2.7740*** (−66.30)	−22,305*** (−64.20)	−2.5019*** (−54.24)	−2.9344*** (−163.33)
	Jilin	Heilongjiang	Shanghai	Jiangsu	Zhejiang	Anhui
lnt	−0.0533*** (−12.24)	−0.0473*** (−21.71)	−0.0629*** (−57.12)	−0.0285*** (−8.78)	−0.0341*** (−8.87)	−0.0361*** (−14.96)
Cons	−2.6694*** (−48.79)	−2.9535*** (−107.99)	−3.4477*** (−249.20)	−3.5756*** (−87.81)	−3.6198*** (−74.92)	−3.1118*** (−102.67)
	Fujian	Jiangxi	Shandong	Henan	Hubei	Hunan
lnt	−0.0162* (−2.55)	−0.0238*** (−9.01)	−0.0264*** (−4.23)	−0.0326*** (−6.03)	−0.0518*** (−12.34)	−0.0302*** (−4.72)
Cons	−4.0000*** (−50.13)	−3.4337*** (−103.60)	−3.3675*** (−43.00)	−3.1475*** (−46.38)	−2.9635*** (−56.23)	−3.4412*** (−42.82)
	Guangdong	Guangxi	Hainan	Chongqing	Sichuan	Guizhou
lnt	−0.0441*** (−16.14)	−0.0165*** (−4.37)	−0.0060 (−1.32)	−0.0576*** (−14.33)	−0.0431*** (−10.88)	−0.0371*** (−7.90)
Cons	−3.7728*** (−109.97)	−3.5025*** (−73.93)	−3.9118*** (−67.33)	−3.0781*** (−61.00)	−3.2766*** (−65.91)	−2.2842*** (−38.74)
	Yunnan	Shaanxi	Gansu	Qinghai	Ningxia	Xinjiang
lnt	−0.0211* (−2.30)	−0.0243*** (−5.76)	−0.0324*** (−12.87)	−0.0215*** (−9.97)	0.0140 (1.73)	0.0096* (2.27)
Cons	−3.2923*** (−28.58)	−3.1114*** (−58.76)	−2.7889*** (−88.30)	−2.8899*** (−106.54)	−2.4416*** (−22.63)	−3.1111*** (−58.55)

***, **, and * denote statistical significance at the 1%, 5%, and 10% levels

Appendix Table 5.5

Table 5.5 Sector classification for the CO_2 emissions and the MRIO table

Sector code	CO_2emissions	MRIO for 2012	MRIO for 2017
1	Farming, forestry, animal husbandry, fishery and water conservancy	Agriculture, forestry, animal husbandry and fishery	Agriculture, forestry, animal husbandry and fishery
2	Coal mining and dressing	Mining and washing of coal	Mining and washing of coal
3	Petroleum and natural gas extraction	Extraction of petroleum and natural gas	Extraction of petroleum and natural gas
4	Ferrous metals mining and dressing	Mining and processing of metal ores	Mining and processing of metal ores
	Nonferrous metals mining and dressing		
5	Nonmetal minerals mining and dressing	Mining and processing of nonmetal and other ores	Mining and processing of nonmetal and other ores
	Other minerals mining and dressing		
6	Food processing	Food and tobacco processing	Food and tobacco processing
	Food production		
	Beverage production		
	Tobacco processing		
7	Textile industry	Textile industry	Textile industry
8	Garments and other fiber products	Manufacture of leather, fur, feather and related products	Manufacture of leather, fur, feather and related products
	Leather, furs, down and related products		
9	Logging and transport of wood and bamboo	Processing of timber and furniture	Processing of timber and furniture
	Timber processing, bamboo, cane, palm fiber & straw products		
	Furniture manufacturing		

(continued)

Table 5.5 (continued)

Sector code	CO_2emissions	MRIO for 2012	MRIO for 2017
10	Papermaking and paper products	Manufacture of paper, printing and articles for culture, education and sport activity	Manufacture of paper, printing and articles for culture, education and sport activity
	Printing and record medium reproduction		
	Cultural, educational and sports articles		
11	Petroleum processing and coking	Processing of petroleum, coking, processing of nuclear fuel	Processing of petroleum, coking, processing of nuclear fuel
12	Raw chemical materials and chemical products	Manufacture of chemical products	Manufacture of chemical products
	Medical and pharmaceutical products		
	Chemical fiber		
	Rubber products		
	Plastic products		
13	Nonmetal mineral products	Manuf. Of non -metallic mineral products	Manuf. Of non -metallic mineral products
14	Smelting and pressing of ferrous metals	Smelting and processing of metals	Smelting and processing of metals
	Smelting and pressing of nonferrous metals		
15	Metal products	Manufacture of metal products	Manufacture of metal products
16	Ordinary machinery	Manufacture of general purpose machinery	Manufacture of general purpose machinery
17	Equipment for special purposes	Manufacture of special purpose machinery	Manufacture of special purpose machinery
18	Transportation equipment	Manufacture of transport equipment	Manufacture of transport equipment
19	Electric equipment and machinery	Manufacture of electrical machinery and equipment	Manufacture of electrical machinery and equipment
20	Electronic and telecommunications equipment	Manufacture of communication equipment, computers and other electronic equipment	Manufacture of communication equipment, computers and other electronic equipment

(continued)

Table 5.5 (continued)

Sector code	CO_2emissions	MRIO for 2012	MRIO for 2017
21	Instruments, meters, cultural and office machinery	Manufacture of measuring instruments	Manufacture of measuring instruments
22	Other manufacturing industry	Other manufacturing	Other manufacturing and waste resources
	Scrap and waste	Comprehensive use of waste resources	
		Repair of metal products, machinery and equipment	Repair of metal products, machinery and equipment
23	Production and supply of electric power, steam and hot water	Production and distribution of electric power and heat power	Production and distribution of electric power and heat power
24	Production and supply of gas	Production and distribution of gas	Production and distribution of gas
25	Production and supply of tap water	Production and distribution of tap water	Production and distribution of tap water
26	Construction	Construction	Construction
27	Wholesale, retail trade and catering services	Wholesale and retail trades	Wholesale and retail trades
		Accommodation and catering	Accommodation and catering
28	Transportation, storage, post and telecommunication services	Transport, storage, and postal services	Transport, storage, and postal services
		Information transfer, software and information technology services	Information transfer, software and information technology services
29	Others	Finance	Finance
		Real estate	Real estate
		Leasing and commercial services	Leasing and commercial services
		Scientific research and polytechnic services	Scientific research
			Polytechnic services
		Administration of water, environment, and public facilities	Administration of water, environment, and public facilities

(continued)

Table 5.5 (continued)

Sector code	CO_2emissions	MRIO for 2012	MRIO for 2017
		Resident, repair and other services	Resident, repair and other services
		Education	Education
		Health care and social work	Health care and social work
		Culture, sports, and entertainment	Culture, sports, and entertainment
		Public administration, social insurance, and social organizations	Public administration, social insurance, and social organizations

Table 5.6 The forecast of carbon peaking

Year	Carbon peaking provinces
2010	Beijing (103.00 Mt)
2011	Jilin (233.90 Mt), Hubei (373.60 Mt)
2012	Heilongjiang (269.20 Mt)
2013	Shanghai (201.20 Mt), Shanxi (488.20 Mt)
2014	Gansu (163.50 Mt), Liaoning (484.5 Mt)
2020	Tianjin (158.21 Mt), Chongqing (184.03 Mt)
2022	Guizhou (334.32 Mt), Hunan (359.41 Mt), Guangdong (614.54 Mt)
2024	Jiangxi (249.78 Mt), Shaanxi (333.35 Mt), Sichuan (441.91Mt), Anhui (447.75 Mt), Zhejiang (481.06 Mt), Henan (681.68 Mt)
2025	Jiangsu (928.25 Mt)
2026	Qinghai (63.75 Mt), Hebei (893.99 Mt), Shandong (1067.32 Mt)
2027	Yunnan (322.25 Mt)
2034	Guangxi (374.19 Mt)
2036	Hainan (71.64 Mt), Fujian (511.83 Mt)
2041	Inner Mongolia (1021.40 Mt)
2048	Ningxia (411.41 Mt), Xinjiang (583.15 Mt)

Unit: CO_2

Table 5.7 The carbon peaking under the counterfactual scenario (2017)

Year	Carbon peaking provinces
2010	Beijing (151.93 Mt)
2011	Jilin (224.96 Mt)
2014	Gansu (124.67 Mt)
2017	Heilongjiang (302.99 Mt), Shanxi (413.90 Mt)

(continued)

Table 5.7 (continued)

Year	Carbon peaking provinces
2019	Shanghai (268.90 Mt), Hubei (287.40 Mt), Liaoning (529.14 Mt)
2020	Chongqing (120.31 Mt)
2021	Tianjin (252.75 Mt)
2022	Guizhou (315.24 Mt), Hunan (358.50 Mt), Guangdong (831.94 Mt)
2024	Jiangxi (153.90 Mt), Anhui (314.61 Mt), Shaanxi (364.93 Mt), Sichuan (372.06 Mt), Henan (457.45 Mt), Zhejiang (520.30 Mt), Jiangsu (521.84 Mt)
2025	Hebei (485.35 Mt)
2026	Qinghai (44.99 Mt), Shandong (1478.42 Mt)
2027	Yunnan (219.35 Mt)
2031	Hainan (59.25 Mt)
2032	Guangxi (121.22 Mt)
2035	Fujian (498.11 Mt)
2036	Inner Mongolia (517.11 Mt)
2040	Xinjiang (328.92 Mt)
2048	Ningxia (199.33 Mt)

Unit: CO_2

Table 5.8 The carbon peaking under the counterfactual scenario (2012)

Year	Carbon peaking provinces
2010	Beijing (163.04 Mt)
2011	Jilin (264.59 Mt)
2017	Heilongjiang (475.96 Mt), Shanxi (433.84 Mt)
2019	Liaoning (565.91 Mt)
2020	Chongqing (97.74 Mt), Gansu (103.63 Mt), Hubei (524.44 Mt), Shanghai (554.21 Mt)
2021	Tianjin (254.97 Mt)
2022	Hunan (279.96 Mt), Guizhou (308.09 Mt)
2023	Guangdong (969.16 Mt)
2024	Jiangxi (198.33 Mt), Anhui (266.87 Mt), Shaanxi (384.33 Mt), Sichuan (426.50 Mt), Zhejiang (585.07 Mt), Henan (594.97 Mt)
2025	Hebei (609.92 Mt), Jiangsu (769.40 Mt)

(continued)

References

Altiparmak, S. O. (2022). China and lithium geopolitics in a changing global market. *Chinese Political Science Review*.

Babiker, M., Reilly, J. M., & Jacoby, H. D. (2000). The Kyoto Protocol and developing countries. *Energy Policy, 28*(8), 525–536.

Table 5.8 (continued)

Year	Carbon peaking provinces
2026	Qinghai (107.04 Mt), Shandong (847.32 Mt)
2027	Yunnan (199.59 Mt)
2032	Hainan (70.15 Mt)
2033	Guangxi (188.89 Mt)
2035	Fujian (599.96 Mt)
2037	Inner Mongolia (509.05 Mt)
2042	Xinjiang (489.49 Mt)
2045	Ningxia (137.93 Mt)

Unit: CO_2

Bauer, N., Bertram, C., Schultes, A., Klein, D., Luderer, G., Kriegler, E., Popp, A., & Edenhofer, O. (2020). Quantification of an efficiency-sovereignty trade-off in climate policy. *Nature, 588*(7837), 261.

Bondes, M. (2022). Yanzhong Huang, toxic politics: China's environmental health crisis and its challenge to the Chinese state. *Journal of Chinese Political Science, 27*(3), 415–417.

Cantore, N., te Velde, D. W., & Peskett, L. (2014). How can low-income countries gain from a framework agreement on climate change? An analysis with integrated assessment modelling. *Development Policy Review, 32*(3), 313–326.

Chen, W. M., Lei, Y. L., Feng, K. S., Wu, S. M., & Li, L. (2019b). Provincial emission accounting for CO_2 mitigation in China: Insights from production, consumption and income perspectives. *Applied Energy, 255.*

Chen, J., & Huang, C. (2021). Policy reinvention and diffusion: Evidence from Chinese provincial governments. *Journal of Chinese Political Science, 26*(4), 723–741.

Chen, J. D., Xu, C., Cui, L. B., Huang, S., & Song, M. L. (2019a). Driving factors of CO_2 emissions and inequality characteristics in China: A combined decomposition approach. *Energy Economics, 78*, 589–597.

Deng, Y., Sarkar, A., Yu, C., Lu, Q., Zhao, M., & Das, J. C. (2021). Ecological compensation of grain trade within urban, rural areas and provinces in China: A prospect of a carbon transfer mechanism. *Environment Development and Sustainability.*

Du, Z. W., Wei, J. X., & Cen, K. (2019). China's carbon dioxide emissions from cement production toward 2030 and multivariate statistical analysis of cement consumption and peaking time at provincial levels. *Environmental Science and Pollution Research, 26*(27), 28372–28383.

Ediger, V. S., & Akar, S. (2007). ARIMA forecasting of primary energy demand by fuel in Turkey. *Energy Policy, 35*(3), 1701–1708.

Fang, K., Tang, Y. Q., Zhang, Q. F., Song, J. N., Wen, Q., Sun, H. P., et al. (2019). Will China peak its energy-related carbon emissions by 2030? Lessons from 30 Chinese provinces. *Applied Energy, 255.*

Feng, T., Du, H. B., Zhang, Z. K., Mi, Z. F., Guan, D. B., & Zuo, J. (2020). Carbon transfer within China: Insights from production fragmentation. *Energy Economics, 86.*

Gallagher, K. S., Zhang, F., Orvis, R., Rissman, J., & Liu, Q. (2019). Assessing the Policy gaps for achieving China's climate targets in the Paris agreement. *Nature Communications, 10*(1), 1256.

Glemarec, Y. (2019). Aligning national interests and global climate justice: the role of human rights in enhancing the ambition of nationally determined contributions to combat climate change. *Fudan Journal of the Humanities and Social Sciences, 12*, 309–327.

Han, M. Y., Yao, Q. H., Lao, J. M., Tang, Z. P., & Liu, W. D. (2020). China's intra- and inter-national carbon emission transfers by province: A nested network perspective. *Science China-Earth Sciences, 63*(6), 852–864.

Hof, A. F., den Elzen, M. G. J., & van Vuuren, D. P. (2009). Environmental effectiveness and economic consequences of fragmented versus universal regimes: What can we learn from model studies? *International Environmental Agreements-Politics Law and Economics, 9*(1), 39–62.

Ji, X., Liu, Y. F., Han, M. Y., & Meng, J. (2020). The mutual benefits from Sino-Africa trade: Evidence on emission transfer along the global supply chain. *Journal of Environmental Management, 263*, 110332.

Joseph, J. (2023). State, society and environmental security in international relations theory. *Fudan Journal of the Humanities and Social Sciences.*

Keohane, R. O. (2019). Institutions for a world of climate injustice. *Fudan Journal of the Humanities and Social Sciences, 12*, 293–307.

Kuhn, B. M. (2018). China's commitment to the sustainable development goals: an analysis of push and pull factors and implementation challenges. *Chinese Political Science Review, 3*, 359–388.

Liu, D., Wang, R., & Thompson, J. (2020). Don't cheat Chinese environment laws. *Nature, 578*(7793), 37–37.

Liu, H. Y., Zhang, Z. Q., Wang, Y., Zhang, C. H., & Wang, D. W. (2022). Testing the correlation between eco-environmental performance and provincial official promotion in China. *Journal of Chinese Political Science, 28*, 375–399.

Long, Y., Yoshida, Y., Liu, Q. L., Zhang, H. R., Wang, S. Q., & Fang, K. (2020). Comparison of city-level carbon footprint evaluation by applying single- and multi-regional input-output tables. *Journal of Environmental Management, 260*, 110108.

López, L. A., Arce, G., & Zafrilla, J. E. (2013). Parcelling virtual carbon in the pollution haven hypothesis. *Energy Economics, 39*, 177–186.

Lu, X. Q., Vogt, R. D., Li, H., Han, S. Q., Mo, X. Q., Zhang, Y. F., Ullah, S., Chen, C., Han, X. X., Li, H. Y., & Seip, H. M. (2019). China's ineffective plastic solution to haze. *Science, 364*(6446), 1145–1145.

Marques, A. C., & Caetano, R. (2020). The impact of foreign direct investment on emission reduction targets: Evidence from high- and middle-income countries. *Structural Change and Economic Dynamics, 55*, 107–118.

Mi, Z. F., Zheng, J. L., Meng, J., Ou, J. M., Hubacek, K., Liu, Z., Coffman, D., Stern, N., Liang, S., & Wei, Y. M. (2020). Economic development and converging household carbon footprints in China. *Nature Sustainability, 3*(7), 529–537.

Nie, Y. Y., Tian, H., Zhang, P., Wang, E. C., Zhang, T. Y., & Guo, Q. X. (2020). A study of the stability of China's carbon dioxide emissions. *Emerging Markets Finance and Trade, 56*(13), 3193–3204.

Ning, Y. D., Chen, K. K., Zhang, B. Y., Ding, T., Guo, F., & Zhang, M. (2020). Energy conservation and emission reduction path selection in China: A simulation based on Bi-Level multi-objective optimization model. *Energy Policy, 137*.

Pan, C., Peters, G. P., Andrew, R. M., Korsbakken, J. I., Li, S. T., Zhou, P., & Zhou, D. Q. (2018). Structural changes in provincial emission transfers within China. *Environmental Science & Technology, 52*(22), 12958–12967.

Schneider, L., & Theuer, S. L. (2019). Environmental integrity of international carbon market mechanisms under the Paris agreement. *Climate Policy, 19*(3), 386–400.

Scott, K., & Barrett, J. (2015). An integration of net imported emissions into climate change targets. *Environmental Science & Policy, 52*, 150–157.

Shan, Y. L., Guan, D. B., Zheng, H. R., Ou, J. M., Li, Y., Meng, J., Mi, Z. F., Liu, Z., & Zhang, Q. (2018). Data descriptor: China CO2 emission accounts 1997–2015. *Scientific Data, 5*, 170201.

Shan, Y. L., Huang, Q., Guan, D. B., & Hubacek, K. (2020). China CO2 emission accounts 2016–2017. *Scientific Data, 7*(1), 54.

Shan, Y. L., Liu, J. H., Liu, Z., Xu, X., Wang, H., Shao, S., Wang, P., & Guan, D. B. (2016). New provincial CO_2 emission inventories in China based on apparent energy consumption data and updated emission factors. *Applied Energy, 184*, 742–750.

Shapiro, J. (2021). Ashley Esarey, Mary Alice Haddad, Joanna I. Lewis, and Stevan Harrell, eds., Greening East Asia: the Rise of the Eco-developmental State. *Journal of Chinese Political Science, 26*(2), 433–435.

Shi, X., Sun, Y., & Shen, Y. (2021). China's ambitious energy transition plans. *Science, 373*(6551), 170–170.

Steininger, K., Lininger, C., Meyer, L., Munoz, P., & Schinko, T. (2016). Multiple carbon accounting to support just and effective climate policies. *Nature Climate Change, 6*(1), 35–41.

Sugiyama, T., & Liu, D. S. (2004). Must developing countries commit quantified targets? Time flexibility and equity in climate change mitigation. *Energy Policy, 32*(5), 697–704.

Tamaki, T., Nozawa, W., & Managi, S. (2019). Controlling CO2 emissions for each area in a region: The case of Japan. *Carbon Balance and Management, 14*(1), 19.

Wang, C., Guo, Y., Shao, S., Fan, M. T., & Chen, S. Y. (2020a). Regional carbon imbalance within China: An application of the Kaya-Zenga index. *Journal of Environmental Management, 262*, 110378.

Wang, J. Y., Wang, K., & Wei, Y. M. (2020b). How to balance China's sustainable development goals through industrial restructuring: A multi-regional input–output optimization of the employment–energy–water–emissions nexus. *Environmental Research Letters, 15*(3), 034018.

Wang, K., Xian, Y., Zhang, J., Li, Y., & Che, L. (2016). Potential carbon emission abatement cost recovery from carbon emission trading in China: An estimation of industry sector. *Journal of Modelling in Management, 11*(3), 842–854.

Wang, Q. Q., Lu, M., Bai, Z. M., & Wang, K. (2020c). Coronavirus pandemic reduced China's CO_2 emissions in short-term, while stimulus packages may lead to emissions growth in medium- and long-term. *Applied Energy, 278*, 115735.

Wang, Z. H., Yang, Y. T., & Wang, B. (2018). Carbon footprints and embodied CO2 transfers among provinces in China. *Renewable & Sustainable Energy Reviews, 82*, 1068–1078.

Wood, R., Grubb, M., Anger-Kraavi, A., Pollitt, H., Rizzo, B., Alexandri, E., Stadler, K., Moran, D., Hertwich, E., & Tukker, A. (2020). Beyond peak emission transfers: Historical impacts of globalization and future impacts of climate policies on international emission transfers. *Climate Policy, 20*(sup1), S14–S27.

Xian, Y., Wang, K., Wei, Y. M., & Huang, Z. (2019). Would China's power industry benefit from nationwide carbon emission permit trading? An optimization model-based ex post analysis on abatement cost savings. *Applied Energy, 235*, 978–986.

Yang, Y. T., Qu, S., Cai, B. F., Liang, S., Wang, Z. H., Wang, J. N., & Xu, M. (2020). Mapping global carbon footprint in China. *Nature Communications, 11*(1), 2237.

Zhai, M. Y., Huang, G. H., Liu, L. R., Zheng, B. Y., & Guan, Y. R. (2020). Inter-regional carbon flows embodied in electricity transmission: network simulation for energy-carbon nexus. *Renewable & Sustainable Energy Reviews, 118*.

Zhang, F., Deng, X. Z., Xie, L., & Xu, N. (2021). China's energy-related carbon emissions projections for the shared socioeconomic pathways. *Resources Conservation and Recycling, 168*.

Zhang, Q. X., Liao, H., & Hao, Y. (2018). Does one path fit all? An empirical study on the relationship between energy consumption and economic development for individual Chinese provinces. *Energy, 150*, 527–543.

Zheng, H. R., Zhang, Z. K., Wei, W. D., Song, M. L., Dietzenbacher, E., Wang, X. Y., et al. (2020). Regional determinants of China's consumption-based emissions in the economic transition. *Environmental Research Letters, 15*(7).

Zheng, Z. (2021). China to rectify 'campaign-style' carbon reduction: NDRC. Xinhua News Agency.

Chapter 6
A Study of the Coordinated Development of Energy Supplies and the Demand for Carbon Neutrality

Boqiang Lin, Yanhong Zhan, and Chuanwang Sun

Abstract Building a clean, low-carbon, and efficient energy system is of paramount importance for China to achieve its carbon neutrality goal. The long-term requirement of green development has injected new connotations into the coordinated development of the energy system in the traditional sense. The coordinated development of energy supplies and the demand for carbon neutrality consists of five aspects: the deep integration of the energy industrial chain, the spatial equilibrium of energy production and consumption, the development of energy technology, the interaction of energy markets, and the coordination of energy policy systems. In the face of the challenges China currently faces in promoting the coordinated transformation of energy supply and demand, the future relationship between energy supply and demand needs to evolve from "passive" coordination to "active" coordination, from "weak" coordination to "strong" coordination, and from "static" coordination to "dynamic" coordination, forming a two-way driving method of "demand-driven supply, supply adapts to demand". The in-depth transformation of the energy system should not only solve the problems of energy misallocation in quantity but also promote the deep coupling of energy supply and demand in industry, region, technology, markets, and policy systems.

Keywords Carbon neutrality · Energy supply and demand balance · Policy coordination · Green low-carbon development

B. Lin
China Institute for Studies in Energy Policy, School of Management, Xiamen University, Xiamen, China

Y. Zhan · C. Sun (✉)
China Center for Energy Economics Research, School of Economics, Xiamen University, Xiamen, China
e-mail: cw_sun@foxmail.com

Present Address:
Y. Zhan
School of Economics and Management, Southeast University, Nanjing, China

B. Gong et al. (eds.), *Chinese Governance and Transformation Towards Carbon Neutrality*, Resources, Environment and Agricultural Development,
https://doi.org/10.1007/978-981-97-9996-1_6

6.1 Introduction

As the largest developing country in the world, China proposed the low-carbon development goal of "striving to peak carbon dioxide emissions by 2030 and striving to achieve carbon neutrality by 2060" in September 2020. However, from the perspective of the overall emission situation, China's carbon emissions are still in the historical stage of "high total amount and high increment", of which the carbon emissions caused by energy activities are more than 85%. By the end of 2020, the proportion of non-fossil energy in China was about 15%, while fossil energy still accounted for a high proportion. Transforming the high-carbon energy structure has become the fundamental path and inevitable requirement for green and low-carbon development of the economy and society. In September 2021, the Central Committee of the Communist Party of China and the State Council issued the "Opinions on the complete, accurate and comprehensive implementation of the new development concept to do a good job in carbon peak and carbon neutrality" (Zhongfa (2021) No.36). It is proposed that the proportion of non-fossil energy consumption should reach 25% and 80% by 2030 and 2060, respectively, drawing a grand blueprint for the structural transformation of the energy system.

The widespread use of energy and its fundamental support to the economy and society determine the complexity of the energy system transformation. From the supply side, the low-carbon transformation of energy means increasing the supply of clean energy and gradually changing the coal-dominated supply structure. Therefore, it requires a series of adjustments, such as energy production technology innovation, industrial structure transition, and optimization of energy production spatial layout. From the demand side, in the face of the long-term goal of green development, energy-saving management, clean consumption, and electrification transformation must also be put in place in time to promote the effective connection between low-carbon energy consumption and clean energy production. This puts forward higher requirements for relevant market incentives, institutional construction, and policy guidance. At the same time, different from the previous research on the bilateral reform of energy supply and demand, which mainly focuses on the total balance of energy supply and demand (Wu et al., 2014) or a single structural balance (Zhang et al., 2011), the energy transformation oriented toward the goal of carbon neutrality also needs to further consider whether the carbon reduction targets on both sides of energy supply and demand match the pace of action. Fundamentally, whether the energy system can complete deep structural adjustments and clean transformation depends on whether the green low-carbon development of energy supply and demand sides can effectively coordinate.

Therefore, this article, based on the requirements of energy low-carbon transformation in the context of carbon neutrality, first thoroughly analyzes the theoretical connotations of the coordinated development of the energy supply and demand sides. Secondly, it reviews and analyzes existing research on low-carbon development of the energy system and proposes an overall research framework for coordinated development of energy supply and demand sides in line with the requirements of the times and the connotation of coordinated development. Thirdly, considering the characteristics of current development, it systematically dissects the challenges faced by the energy supply and demand system in achieving low-carbon transformation. Fourthly, it studies and demonstrates the evolutionary goals and driving mechanisms of coordinated development on both the supply and demand sides of energy under the requirements of green and low-carbon development. Finally, it proposes a path plan for the coordinated development of energy supply and demand sides under low-carbon constraints to provide a valuable reference for strengthening the coordinated management of energy supply and demand sides and consolidating the foundation of resilient development of the energy economy system.

6.2 Carbon Neutrality Endows New Connotations to the Coordinated Development of Energy Supply and Demand

The era of low-carbon development not only puts new pressure on the system reconstruction of the energy economy but also endowed the coordinated development of energy supply and demand with new connotations. According to synergy theory, various subsystems in a complex open system can generate synergy effects through mutual interactions (Wang et al., 2013). Therefore, the coordinated development of energy supply and demand can be summarized as leveraging the interactions and cooperation between relevant subsystems on the energy supply and demand sides, ultimately unleashing the synergy effects of the energy system. Among them, the development system of the energy industry, the layout network of energy production and consumption, energy technology innovation, market allocation of energy resources, and related policy systems are key factors affecting the coordination degree of the energy system. Under the "carbon peak" and "carbon neutrality" goals, a comprehensive understanding of the coordinated development of energy supply and demand requires further integration with green and low-carbon requirements. Based on multiple synergy perspectives, it is essential to re-examine the low-carbon transformation issues of subsystems such as industrial development, spatial layout, technological progress, market allocation, and institutional construction, as well as the effective connections, cooperation, and dynamic matching issues among these subsystems. Based on the above analysis, the coordinated development of energy supply and demand under the backdrop of carbon neutrality should encompass at least the following five aspects:

The first aspect involves the synergistic and integrated development of the low-carbon energy industry chain. Currently, the main problem of energy supply and demand in China is the contradiction between the coal-dominated energy supply structure and the rapidly growing energy consumption demand. In the absence of a clean energy system, the enormous energy demand can only be satisfied through a high-carbon energy supply. Therefore, promoting the clean development of the energy industry system has become a top priority for China's low-carbon transformation under the goal of carbon neutrality. However, a high proportion of renewable energy systems also face many challenges, such as the probabilistic nature of power balance, the scarcity of flexible resources, and the blurred boundaries between sources and loads (Lu et al., 2017). Therefore, it is necessary to pay more attention to the connection between the upstream and downstream industry chains, the matching between the energy supply and the demand sides, and the bidirectional feedback between energy flow and information flow. This will achieve the integration and balance of the energy industry chain in the development of traditional energy transformation and the utilization of clean energy at scale.

The second aspect involves regional coordination and spatial equilibrium in the production and consumption of clean energy. The spatial imbalance between energy production and consumption leads to low energy allocation efficiency. From a national perspective, China's clean energy endowment is inversely distributed relative to electricity demand, with over 60% of clean resources such as wind, solar, and hydro concentrated in the "Three North" and Southwest regions. However, the eastern and central regions account for over 75% of the national electricity consumption. It is urgent to coordinate the planning of power bases and transmission channels to achieve the overall optimization of new energy electricity allocation and the coordinated development of supply and demand. At the regional level, the layout of distributed clean energy imposes higher requirements on the synergistic optimization of various energies such as electricity, heat, and gas within the region, as well as the comprehensive development of energy in local spaces. With the deepening of the carbon–neutral goal, the penetration rate of clean electricity in the energy supply and demand system will continue to increase. Improving the spatial network layout of energy regions and promoting the spatial balance of energy resource endowment and demand load, have become important bases for promoting the coordinated green and low-carbon development of energy supply and demand.

The third aspect is the effective driving of new energy system coupling through energy technology innovation. China's energy transformation will be a leapfrogging and iterative development directly from the coal era to the renewable energy era. Breaking through core technology is not only the fundamental way to subvert the energy structure dominated by coal and reconstruct a clean and efficient energy system but also the basic support for the orderly development of the energy system. In the era of low-carbon transformation, the coordinated development of the energy system requires comprehensive application of energy technology in resource optimization and utilization on both the supply and demand sides, system planning and design (Liu & Hu, 2014), as well as information assurance, operational optimization, and resilience enhancement (Yang et al., 2020). This will achieve comprehensive cooperation in the vertical collaborative vision of "integration of source, grid, load, and storage" and the horizontal linkage perspective of "multi-energy complementarity". It will promote the formation of bidirectional interaction between energy supply and demand and ultimately facilitate the coupling and coordination of various subsystems in the energy system.

The fourth aspect is the effective enhancement of energy resource allocation efficiency through market mechanisms. The key path to the integration of energy production and consumption is to achieve balance through the market. Economic theory suggests that the market, as the "invisible hand", can coordinate the supply–demand relationship through price mechanisms, thus achieving efficient utilization and effective allocation of resources at lower economic costs. Solving the externality of carbon will inevitably bring about certain transformation costs and expenses. Achieving competitive substitution of high-carbon and low-carbon energy through market means is an important way to alleviate the costs and expenses of low-carbon transformation. The deepening of carbon neutrality, the reform of the national electricity market, and the construction of the carbon market mean that the promotion of the power market and the carbon market are interlinked and deeply coupled, and will become a key link in promoting the coordinated development of green and low-carbon energy supply and demand.

The fifth aspect is the scientific guidance of policy systems for the coordinated carbon reduction of energy supply and demand. The green and low-carbon development of the energy supply and demand system is a complex systematic project involving economic transformation, industrial upgrading, energy system reform, changes in individual and organizational behavior, and innovation in environmental governance systems. It faces many challenges and uncertainties, requiring timely guidance and promotion from institutional design and policy systems. The reform of the energy system mechanism to alleviate market access and competition conflicts, the sound legal system promoting the integrated development of energy supply and demand, the guidance of funds to accurately flow into the low-carbon field through green finance and fiscal policies, and the demand feedback mechanism promoting public participation in green and low-carbon development must be put in place promptly. These policy systems will provide a solid guarantee and strong support for the coordinated low-carbon transformation and green development of energy supply and demand.

6.3 The Theoretical Exploration of Advancing the Low-Carbon Development of the Energy Supply and Demand System

Research and argumentation on the green development of the energy system cannot be separated from theoretical foundations such as low-carbon economic growth and sustainable development. Over the past decades, continuous progress in theories related to green and low-carbon development, market equilibrium, sustainable development, and ecological civilization construction has significantly promoted the development of green and low-carbon initiatives in the energy sector. As a development method that maintains the foundation of human development and achieves harmonious prosperity between the economy and the environment (Fan & Yi, 2021), green development has become a consensus among scholars as the inevitable direction for future energy transformation (He, 2014). The fundamental solution to achieving green and low-carbon energy development lies in the cleanliness of the energy structure, the efficiency of energy use, and the carbonization of energy technology (Han, 2016). Meanwhile, increasing attention to low-carbon economics, sustainable development, and ecological civilization has prompted scholars to actively explore issues such as energy conservation, emission reduction, efficiency improvement, energy environmental pollution control, and sustainable development assessments (Duan & Wang, 2019). Scholars generally agree that changing the dominant position of coal in China's energy structure is imperative. However, in the specific research and analysis of energy low-carbon transformation, there exist different perspectives. The supply-side school believes that energy supply is the practical foundation determining the development of the energy industry. The total amount, capacity, structure, and security of clean energy supply are key factors influencing a country's low-carbon sustainable development (Tu et al., 2020). The low-carbon transformation of the energy system needs to prioritize supply-side reforms. On the other hand, the demand-side school argues that demand drives supply, and the low-carbon transformation of energy demand is conducive to compelling clean energy supply. Additionally, regional differences in energy demand determine that energy supply must adapt to energy demand. Therefore, adjusting the capacity of the energy consumption market, curbing unreasonable energy demand, and guiding clean energy utilization are more effective demand-side management measures (Bi et al., 2013).

In terms of the synergy between energy supply and demand, although there is no systematic argument for the coordinated development of energy supply and demand, the structural balance of economic and social development has also triggered scholars' thinking about the balance of energy supply and demand and the coordinated development of the energy system. Among them, the issue of balance of overall energy supply and demand is considered one of the most critical factors affecting the coordinated development of the energy system (Li & Zhang, 2017). This has led to a series of studies focused on promoting the balance of overall energy supply and demand, including research on energy structure adjustment (Lin & Li, 2015), optimization of energy allocation efficiency (Aldieri et al., 2021), and design of energy and environmental policies (Lin, 2018). For instance, from the perspective of coordinated allocation of factors, researchers have characterized the degree of mismatch in China's energy factors and proposed corrective measures such as facilitating the transfer and flow of energy factors between industries with different efficiencies and accelerating the establishment of a more market-oriented energy pricing mechanism (Ouyang & Sun, 2015). Another example is the research and analysis of regional coordination and collaborative governance in the energy economic system, addressing issues such as energy infrastructure construction, environmental impacts, and regional coordination of energy economic policies. These studies reveal the importance of balanced investment in energy infrastructure, inclusive economic growth in energy regions, and regional coordination of energy and environmental policies in promoting the balanced development of the energy economic system

(Yao et al., 2017). The importance of the coordinated development of energy supply and demand as a key driving force for the future energy system is self-evident.

The explorations of the scholars mentioned above provide significant references for the in-depth investigation in this article into the coordinated development path of energy supply and demand under the backdrop of green and low-carbon initiatives. However, further systematic integration and summarization of relevant literature revealed that most existing studies mainly discuss issues such as energy supply and demand characteristics, low-carbon development paths on the supply or demand side, and factors influencing energy supply and demand coordination under the soft constraints of green and low-carbon. There is a lack of comprehensive consideration across various aspects affecting the coordinated operation of the energy system, including industry and region, technology and market, policy, and legal aspects. Additionally, there is no theoretical exploration into the ways and mechanisms of energy supply and demand coordination. On the one hand, the carbon peak and carbon neutrality impose strict constraints on green and low-carbon development, marking a fundamental shift in the development environment of the energy system.

Under the original low-carbon conditions, the research path focusing on the coordination of energy supply and demand no longer adequately meets the practical requirements of the disruptive restructuring of the energy system. The transition of the energy system to carbon neutrality and low carbon, and the synergistic development of energy supply and demand require new theoretical foundations and research frameworks. With the increasing demand for greening, low-carbonization, and electrification, the importance of cooperation and coordination of energy subsystems is becoming more prominent. Studies on the green and low-carbon development of energy should no longer be limited to separate analyses of the energy supply or demand side. Instead, they should be guided by coordination theory, conducting multidimensional comprehensive analyses of the internal development characteristics and issues within energy subsystems, the mutual influence among subsystems, and the impact of each subsystem on the overall system. Especially in the current stage, where the level of coordinated development of the green and low-carbon energy supply and demand structure in China remains relatively low, and the uncertainty of the imbalance in the total energy supply and demand continues to rise, a reassessment and systematic interpretation of the coordinated development of the energy system under the constraints of carbon neutrality is crucial. This will provide valuable references for addressing the practical challenges of energy system transformation.

Based on this, this article grounded in the new connotations of energy supply and demand coordination development under the context of carbon neutrality, constructs a systematic research framework with industry synergy, spatial coordination, technological driving, market allocation, and policy guidance as its main components. It comprehensively analyzes the current challenges of coordinated carbon reduction in China's energy supply and demand. The focus is researching how to effectively promote the coordinated low-carbon development of energy supply and demand, under the transformation of coordination methods and the driving mode of "demand-driven supply and supply adapting to demand". This will provide theoretical support for finding efficient and rational mechanisms and paths for energy low-carbon transformation.

6.4 Challenges in the Coordinated Low-Carbon Transformation of Energy Supply and Demand

From the overall characteristics of China's energy supply and demand relationship, the current energy supply and demand structure in China still faces significant uncertainty. On one hand, the continuous advancement of economic growth and societal electrification will continue to increase the overall energy and electricity demand. On the other hand, the decline in traditional energy sources such as coal in recent years, coupled with the extended planning and construction periods of new energy sources like wind and solar, has led to a nationwide overall tightness in energy supply. Under the new connotations of the coordinated development of energy supply and demand, there exist various challenges in the green and low-carbon transformation of the energy system. These challenges include bottlenecks in the development of the energy industry, imbalances in regional economic and energy development, the urgent need for energy technology innovation, the lack of coordination in energy market mechanisms, and the imperfection of related policy systems.

6.4.1 Unclear Coupling Mechanism in the Green and Low-Carbon Energy Industry Value Chain

Total energy consumption is not only affected by the scale of economic development but is also closely related to economic and industrial structures. From a low-carbon development perspective, the clean transformation of the energy industry chain is the starting point for the coordinated green development of energy supply and demand, and the fundamental support for the low-carbon transformation of the energy structure. To achieve carbon neutrality goals, industrial coupling based on the value chain requires an optimized configuration of factors, energies, products, and waste flows. This optimization should meet the performance indicators of various stakeholders in the industrial chain while ensuring the sustainable development of natural ecosystems (Liang & Liu, 2017). However, challenges exist in the current energy industry chain:

(a) In the upstream sector of energy exploration and development, the paces of gradual withdrawal of traditional energy and the safe and reliable substitution of new energy have not yet matched. The decline in energy supply capacity caused by the low-carbon transformation of the fossil energy industry coexists with the difficulty of grid integration brought about by the large-scale development of clean energy. The contradiction of energy supply and demand imbalance is further intensified in the absence of a smooth transition between old and new energy industries.

(b) In the downstream sector of energy consumption, energy consumption has long been concentrated in industries with high energy consumption and pollution, such as the industrial and transportation sectors. For example, the development of industries like steel and cement not only relies on significant energy inputs but also involves the production processes of other industries as crucial input factors. The energy industry's complex interdependence exacerbates the difficulty of coordinating the development of energy supply and demand and poses significant challenges to the overall green development of the energy industry.

6.4.2 Difficulty in Coordinating the Breadth of Energy Network System and Spatial Layout

From a spatial dimension, re-evaluating the main contradictions in the coordinated development of energy supply and demand, the green and low-carbon development under the traditional energy supply reform often prioritizes scale efficiency, leading to spatial separation of supply and demand. In the imperfectly developed market scenario, this results in inefficient resource allocation and regional mismatch in the supply and demand structure. Examining the spatial characteristics of energy supply and demand distribution reveals three challenges in promoting the coordinated green development of energy supply and demand in China:

(a) Clean energy resource areas and demand load centers show a clear reverse distribution. The Northwest and Southwest regions, relying on abundant clean energy reserves, become major energy suppliers, while regions with advantageous conditions, like East China, serve as major energy consumers. Long-distance energy transport becomes a primary means to balance energy supply and demand.

(b) The uneven distribution of clean energy sources such as wind, solar, and water is notable. Non-fossil energy sources like wind and solar are mainly concentrated in the Northwest; Water resources are concentrated in the Southwest, and the eastern coastal areas have more offshore wind energy. Adapting to the demand for clean energy in different regions requires "spatial transfer" of energy; However, the widespread distribution complicates regional energy coordination and complementarity (Ai & Hao, 2018).

(c) Significant differences in energy consumption types and energy infrastructure configuration exist between urban and rural areas. Compared to the rapid electrification development in urban areas, rural energy consumption still relies mainly on solid fuels such as coal. The imbalance in the construction of energy infrastructure between urban and rural areas results in low adoption of clean energy sources such as natural gas, photovoltaics, and wind power in rural regions.

6.4.3 Constraints in Green and Low-Carbon Energy Technology Innovations and Their Coupling Paths

Promoting the coordinated transformation of energy supply and demand is a systematic project that fundamentally solves the innovation and coupling problems of energy technology. However, meeting the requirements of green and low-carbon development poses two major challenges for energy technology innovation and system coupling. On the one hand, the gradual decline in generation from traditional fossil energy sources and the intermittent nature of large-scale new energy grid integration will lead to increasingly unpredictable and fluctuating electricity generation. On the other hand, although China has implemented a number of energy demand management and demand response pilot projects in recent years, the random nature of power demand has not changed. The development model relying on traditional increases in supply-side resources to meet electricity demand is no longer sustainable. However, there are still bottlenecks in current energy technology innovation:

(a) In the field of clean alternative technologies, wind and solar power generation technologies in extreme weather conditions have not been systematically mastered. The instability of clean electricity supply, coupled with the challenges of wind, solar, and hydropower grid integration, has not been fundamentally reversed.
(b) In the field of energy interconnection technology, traditional power infrastructure struggles to achieve interactive source-grid-load-storage, multi-energy synergy, and spatial-temporal scheduling mutual aid. Insufficient capacity to optimize the allocation of clean energy, on a large scale, clean energy grid integration, and large-scale energy storage technologies need to be urgently developed. Advanced transmission technologies such as ultra-high-voltage DC transmission also need to progress toward low-cost and intelligent directions.
(c) In the field of electricity substitution technologies, electric heating and electric mechanical power technologies in the industrial sector, intelligent connected vehicles, and fuel cell technologies in the transportation sector, and electric heating, heat pump, and electric fuel production technologies in the construction sector still face issues of high costs and lack the conditions to achieve economies of scale.

6.4.4 Incomplete Comprehensive Energy Market System to Promote Efficient Operation of the Energy System

The key path to achieving the integration of energy production and consumption is through the balanced mechanism of market mechanisms. As the "invisible hand" regulating resource allocation, effective markets can achieve efficient resource allocation at a lower economic cost through price discovery functions. With the increasing contradictions between outdated energy utilization methods and the natural ecological environment, breaking down existing industry barriers and market barriers in the energy system, and constructing a unified, open, and competitively orderly comprehensive energy market system, is crucial for achieving the coordinated green and low-carbon development of energy supply and demand. The electricity trading market, carbon emission rights trading market, and the electricity-carbon coordination market are vital components of the comprehensive energy market. However, there are clear deficiencies in various markets at present, hindering the coordinated low-carbon development of energy supply and demand:

(a) In the electricity trading market, the competitive segment of electricity prices has not yet been fully liberalized (Zheng, 2017), leading to a contradiction between the continuously decreasing costs of industrial and commercial electricity consumption and the rising costs of power generation fuel. Particularly, the market supply chain for coal and thermal power has not been completely streamlined, posing risks of market price fluctuations and industry chain leveraging for the coal power industry in the process of transitioning to a low-carbon energy structure (Lin, 2021).
(b) In the carbon emission rights trading market, the free single-quota method and the limited market coverage make it difficult to balance price stability and market liquidity. This approach is insufficient to provide effective incentives for the clean energy industry and a constraint mechanism for the fossil energy industry.
(c) In the electricity-carbon coordination market, the policy functions, such as excess renewable energy consumption trading, green certificate trading, and carbon emission rights trading, are highly redundant and overlapping. With additional barriers, such as single-product market transactions and insufficient market liquidity, it is challenging for energy supply and demand entities to achieve synergistic conduction and organic integration in terms of price, resources, and production factors in the market.

6.4.5 Increasing Complexity in Energy Transformation Enhance the Difficulty in Top-Level Design and Policy Research

The coordinated green and low-carbon development of energy supply and demand is a long-term and complex undertaking, requiring the coordination of institutional reforms, financial and taxation support, financial guidance, legal construction, and public participation across various sectors of the energy field. Future reforms in energy development policies face challenges in traditional energy market reforms, the in-depth development of renewable energy, electricity substitution, and flexible dispatch of electricity from the supply side. From the demand side, challenges include reducing the cost of energy low-carbon transformation, coordinating legal construction to meet the needs of energy supply and demand, and promoting public participation in the green development process. The complexity of systemic transformation and the inadequacies in related institutional construction pose greater difficulties in establishing a policy system for energy transformation under the background of carbon neutrality. Specific challenges include:

(a) In the existing institutional reform on the green and low-carbon development of energy, there is an imbalance between the government's macro-regulation and the coordinated mechanism between energy supply and demand. The energy supervision system urgently needs to be adjusted.
(b) The funding support and financing tools for supporting the green and low-carbon development of energy are single and lack a favorable market environment. Environmental violation information disclosure mechanisms are still incomplete, and strategic arrangements and supporting policies for green finance and green taxation need urgent improvement.
(c) With weak connectivity, uniformity, implementation, and authority between national and local special energy plans, there is a lack of legal construction to ensure the integration of energy supply and demand. Regulatory agencies have insufficient regulatory measures and administrative penalties, and the boundaries of legal management responsibilities are unclear (Zhang, 2021).
(d) Public participation is limited in the practice of green and low-carbon development of energy supply and demand. In addition to choosing energy-saving low-carbon products and frugal lifestyles, individuals who seek to exercise their rights and means of environmental monitoring and environmental public interest litigation, face constraints such as cumbersome approval procedures and untimely information feedback.

6.5 Evolutionary Goals and Driving Mechanisms of Coordinated Development of Energy Supply and Demand

6.5.1 Evolutionary Goals of the Collaborative Relationship Between Energy Supply and Demand

Facing the transformation of national economic development strategies, the green and low-carbon development of the energy system not only implies promoting reforms on the supply side of energy and management on the demand side, but also requires more coordinated development and dynamic balance between energy supply and demand. In terms of coordination methods, environmental elements, and their associated products need to be regarded as endogenous driving forces to promote the coordinated and low-carbon development of energy supply and demand. Ultimately, the evolution needs to progress from "passive" coordination to "active" coordination, from "weak" coordination to "strong" coordination, and from "static" coordination to "dynamic" coordination. Specifically:

6.5.1.1 Evolution from "Passive" Coordination to "Active" Coordination

Traditionally, most considerations of energy supply and demand development have focused on the supply side (Yao & Kong, 2010) or the demand side (Li & Yang, 2021). Discussions have mainly centered on economic coordination mechanisms and development pathways in the context of unilateral energy reforms. As green and low carbon are constraints, the discussion focuses on energy supply-side or demand-side adjustments and reforms, and the coordination between energy supply and demand shows a "passive" relationship in terms of green and low carbon development. The passive way fails to meet the inherent requirements of a carbon–neutral vision for sustainable economic growth. The traditional "passive" coordination relationship between energy supply and demand needs to be urgently evolved into an "active" one, so that green and low carbon, from being mere constraints, can be transformed into endogenous drivers of sustainable economic growth. Similar to the factors of capital and labor, the green natural environment and ecological resources can also be regarded as factors that enter the economic production function. In the era of low carbon development, the improvement of environmental factors should not only be treated as external constraint targets. Green and low-carbon factors can form part of product costs and market prices. Pollutants and carbon emissions, as negative externalities, should also be involved in market resource allocation and the regulation of supply and demand. Taking green and low-carbon factors as endogenous driving forces can inject sustained impetus into the coordinated development of energy supply and demand, and fundamentally meet the long-term needs of economic development and the better needs of sustainable social development.

6.5.1.2 Evolution from "Weak" Coordination to "Strong" Coordination

The term "weak" coordination refers to the balance of energy supply and demand at the overall level. A purely "weak" coordination cannot resolve such real-life contradictions as cross-provincial electricity consumption and inter-provincial barriers, lagging power grid planning and construction, and the expansion of renewable energy power generation. At the same time, it is also unable to solve the problems of aggravated upstream and downstream conflicts in the energy industry, rapid growth in energy consumption, and distorted prices in the energy market, as well as fundamentally alleviating the structural mismatch between energy supply and demand in different regions. Therefore, it is challenging to guide the coordinated development of energy supply and demand under the requirements of green and low-carbon transformation. The goal of "strong" coordination is to consider balance based on "weak" coordination, taking into account all aspects of the aggregate, industrial, spatial, technological, and market structure of energy supply and demand. Compared with "weak" coordination, "strong" coordination emphasizes more on the structural balance within and between subsystems while achieving the balance of total energy. It considers the overall green development of the energy industry chain, focuses on the spatial balance of energy supply and demand, and takes into account technological innovation and market transformation in the context of green and low-carbon requirements. As a result, the energy system formed under "strong" coordination has a stronger ability to resist risks and shocks. It can guide the resilient construction of the energy system through the effective coordination and adaptive linkage of energy supply and demand, and address the major points and difficulties in the coordinated development of energy supply and demand.

6.5.1.3 Evolution from "Static" Coordination to "Dynamic" Coordination

Theoretically, the goal of energy supply-side reform relies on green innovation, low-carbon technology, and institutional driving forces to achieve the optimal allocation of factors and output structure by the evolution pattern of demand. And the goal of energy demand-side management is to adapt to changes, brought about by supply-side adjustments, in terms of domestic and foreign consumption or investment demand, and to seek an optimal overall demand and its structural configuration to achieve the goal of green and low-carbon development. However, the optimal allocation of energy supply and demand depends on whether the market mechanism can play a decisive role in resource allocation and whether market prices can accurately reflect the costs of supply and demand. In this context, "static" coordination refers to a single and fragmented relationship between energy supply and demand, with market prices unable to play a resource allocation role among various energy sources simultaneously. Taking the electricity market as an example, in the previous studies on the reform path of the electricity supply side, the focus was on increasing the supply of clean electricity through infrastructure investment and technological upgrades. In situations where the electricity market is not fully liberalized, and prices cannot accurately reflect supply and demand information, phenomena such as abandoning wind and solar energy and energy shortages coexist in the short term. The long-term green development of the energy system requires the evolution from "static" coordination to "dynamic" coordination. "Dynamic" coordination involves opening up market prices, allowing energy prices to flexibly adjust the supply and demand relationship. This transformation shifts the fragmented demand for energy into comprehensive energy demands that are mutually complementary and diverse in terms of types, time, and space. Consequently, it enables real-time adjustment and dynamic balance in the energy supply and demand relationship.

6.5.2 Driving Methods for Effective Coordination Between Energy Supply and Demand in the Green and Low-Carbon Context

The driving force for the coordinated and low-carbon development of energy supply and demand can be summarized as "demand leading supply, and supply adapting to demand". The reform of the energy supply side is driven by the goal of improving the adaptability of supply to meet demand. At the same time, demand-side management operates as a "demand leading supply" driving force. In the context of green and low-carbon development, the bidirectional interaction and coordinated carbon reduction between energy supply and demand will drive the energy system to achieve a higher level of dynamic balance.

6.5.2.1 Energy Supply-Side Reform: Improving the Demand Adaptability

Currently, the adaptability of China's energy supply system to energy demand is relatively low. On the supply side, there is a trend of inertia growth in electricity supply in terms of total quantity. However, the energy supply structure still faces problems such as a small proportion of clean energy sources, uneven distribution of energy layout, and imbalances in the construction of urban and rural distribution grids. On the demand side, there is a general slowdown in the overall growth rate of electricity consumption. However, the structure of incremental electricity consumption has experienced significant changes. Specifically, the demand for electricity in traditional industries has slowed down, while the contribution of strategic emerging industries to the growth of electricity demand has increased.

Under the requirements of green and low-carbon development, as the energy supply-side reform is pushed deeper and deeper, the renewable energy structure is evolving to a higher proportion, which requires that the impact of changes in demand-side energy use patterns and energy structure must be considered, concerning the speed of energy substitution and the path of energy transition. This involves enhancing the adaptability of energy supply to energy demand. With the continuously upgrading energy use patterns and demand structures, there will be an increased demand for high-quality energy products and services. Therefore, the supply of high-quality energy products and services is crucial. However, it is important to keep in mind that the optimal allocation and governance of green and low-carbon energy supply is not necessarily the optimal configuration that meets the requirements of coordinated low-carbon development for both energy supply and demand. Taking clean energy supply as an example, relying solely on economies of scale while ignoring the characteristics of reverse spatial distribution between energy supply bases and load centers is insufficient to support the long-term green development of the energy system. In contrast, the development mode of distributed energy based on local solutions to energy demand is more effective in driving the green and low-carbon development of the regional economy, effectively blocking the path of large-scale expansion dependent on fossil energy. In addition, energy supply-side reform needs to fully consider the potential dynamic changes in energy consumption patterns or investment. This helps to avoid a series of contradictions in the path of zero-carbon transition of energy, such as the accelerated decline in traditional energy production capacity and the slow development of low-carbon energy consumption, the rapid development of smart energy supply, and the low level of digitization of the demand side. To this end, it is important to focus on demand-side adaptation and to promote coordinated green development on both supply and demand sides of energy.

6.5.2.2 Energy Demand-Side Management: Demand Drives Supply

From the perspective of driving supply through demand, insufficient effective demand on the energy demand side significantly hinders the low-carbon transformation speed of the energy system. This shortage of effective demand is mainly manifested in the high proportion of high-carbon energy demand, low marketization level of energy prices, and imbalances in energy demand structures between urban and rural areas and industries. Under the strategic goal of carbon neutrality, based on the energy demand side, energy conservation, emission reduction, efficiency improvement, and other measures are key to promoting the low-carbon transformation of the energy system. Taking electricity load regulation as an example, meeting peak consumption on the demand side by simply adjusting the peak capacity on the supply side or expanding the transmission and distribution capacity of the power grid not only poses challenges to the operation of the power grid but also incurs high economic costs. In contrast, effective demand-side management, such as electricity conservation, peak shaving, and real-time demand response, not only helps ensure the security and reliability of the energy system but also contributes to reducing the additional costs of the coordinated development of energy supply and demand.

At the same time, the encouragement and advocacy of clean energy consumption and a green lifestyle under low-carbon development provide an important opportunity to promote low-carbon energy supply from the demand side and optimize the allocation of power resources. Electrification of energy consumption is crucial to improving overall energy efficiency and promoting green energy use. Expanding the space for electricity substitution on the demand side, and continuously increasing the electrification level of social energy consumption, contributes to positive incentives for large-scale clean energy generation on the supply side. Coupled with the low-cost and flexibility characteristics of demand-side regulation resources, the above approach helps mitigate the randomness, intermittency, and volatility of renewable energy, maintaining power balance in the electricity system. Therefore, effective demand management to drive green and low-carbon energy supply facilitates the coordinated and green development of energy supply and demand.

6.6 Path for Coordinated Development of Energy Supply and Demand Under the Context of Carbon Neutrality

Given the current constraints on the coordinated development of energy supply and demand under low-carbon conditions, and considering the evolving goals and driving forces of the future energy system's balanced development, this paper argues that the development of energy supply and demand in the context of carbon neutrality should adhere to a systemic perspective. It should be grounded in the operational characteristics and development issues of various energy subsystems, exploring feasible, realistic paths from a multidimensional and integrated perspective.

6.6.1 Promoting Deep Coupling of the Green and Low-Carbon Energy Industry Value Chain

From the perspective of industrial integration, promoting the nested coupling mechanism upstream and downstream of the industrial chain is necessary to break through the constraints of energy supply and demand and achieve coordinated development within and between industries.

6.6.1.1 Strengthening Industrial Coupling from the Circular Economy Perspective

The development of a circular economy requires enterprises to mitigate ecological impacts during the production process, recycling, and utilization of by-products and waste. Circular economy encourages enterprises to either extend their industrial chains, enhance their comprehensive utilization and processing capabilities for waste, or break industry boundaries horizontally to seek collaborative development and utilization opportunities for waste. This helps to form a coupled mode of multiple industries, promoting the coordinated reduction of carbon emissions in the energy supply and demand system.

6.6.1.2 Breaking Industry Monopoly Barriers and Regional Protection

Coordinated and green low-carbon development of energy supply and demand requires achieving horizontal industrial linkage and vertical industrial collaboration. This involves deepening vertically within industries to achieve the comprehensive cascade utilization of various energy sources, and horizontal collaboration between industries to ensure the complementary operation of multiple industries. Therefore, breaking the monopoly barriers in the energy industry is essential, allowing the efficiency of energy utilization to be improved across the entire energy supply and demand system.

6.6.1.3 Leveraging Digitalization to Facilitate the Transformation of the Energy Industry and Promote Coordinated Interaction Between Supply and Demand

Harnessing the power of digitalization is crucial for driving the transformation of the energy industry and facilitating seamless collaboration between the supply and demand sides. The efficiency and cost advantages of digital technologies position them as fundamental forces propelling the low-carbon transformation of the energy system. On the one hand, the integration of digitalization with cutting-edge low-carbon technologies provides new momentum for enterprises to achieve energy savings and emissions reduction. On the other hand, the construction of a digital internet centered around technologies such as 5G, artificial intelligence, and big data serves as a hub for the integration of the entire energy industry chain and provides the foundational support for information exchange. By consolidating information related to energy flow, data flow, and value flow, this digital infrastructure fosters industry integration that promotes both digitalization and greening across the energy supply and demand sides (Lin, 2020).

6.6.2 Promoting Coordinated Development of Energy Supply and Demand Networks and Spatial Layout

To foster green, low-carbon development on both the energy supply and demand fronts via spatial planning, there needs to be a paradigm shift in the developmental mindset. This involves capitalizing on the synergies and complementarities among regions to guide efforts, striving for a transition to spatially balanced growth. It is essential to consider the regional constraints on energy load due to varying natural resource endowments, industrialization levels, and infrastructure. This involves adapting the low-carbon transformation of the energy supply side according to the characteristics of population movement, industrial distribution, and urban layout in different regions, and strategically planning the allocation of supply and demand across different regions.

6.6.2.1 Inter-City Collaboration and Complementarity

Urban energy utilization and spatial layout structures evolve progressively, with the rapid expansion of transportation networks and infrastructure extending city boundaries. This has led to both a reduction in the utilization efficiency of energy infrastructure in city centers and increased resource wastage and traffic congestion. Achieving optimal urban layouts for coordinated green and low-carbon development in energy supply and demand requires a transition towards compact city layouts. This involves creating integrated functional zones for work, residence, and commerce to fundamentally reduce long-distance energy transport, forming a regionally balanced, self-sufficient energy supply system.

6.6.2.2 Inter-Urban and Rural Collaboration and Complementarity

The uneven construction of infrastructure and public services between urban and rural areas has resulted in lower penetration of liquefied gas, natural gas, and other clean energy sources in rural areas. The low-level development and utilization of clean energy, coupled with a predominant use of solid fuels such as coal, have led to increased waste in energy utilization and more severe environmental pollution in rural areas. In the low-carbon transformation of the energy supply side, urban–rural coordination and collaboration should consider the characteristics of rural areas, which have a dispersed population distribution and high space utilization. It is crucial to encourage early planning and rapid advancement of new energy industry deployment, providing financial support and policy incentives for clean energy projects. Particularly, accelerating the development of distributed clean energy and making increased efforts to develop wind, solar, and hydro energy resources according to local conditions is essential.

6.6.3 Establishing a Coupled Mechanism for Energy Technology Innovation and a Collaborative System

Technological innovation plays a pivotal role in driving the transformation of the energy supply and demand system, primarily in achieving three key aspects: firstly, realizing the vertical collaborative development of "source-grid-load-storage integration" from a coordinated perspective, addressing the randomness and volatility issues of the energy supply and demand sides. Secondly, achieving the horizontal collaborative scheduling of "multiple energy complementarity" from a linked perspective, effectively enhancing energy configuration and utilization efficiency. Thirdly, achieving the deep coupling of the energy supply and demand system through globally optimized technological breakthroughs to improve the coordinated development of various energy subsystems. The synergy of energy technology innovation is mainly reflected in the following aspects.

6.6.3.1 Collaboration Between Technologies

Collaboration between technologies involves promoting the deep integration and collaborative evolution of traditional low-carbon technologies and digital technologies. On the one hand, the gradual maturity of distributed energy and energy storage technologies will alter the real-time frequency characteristics of power generation, transmission, distribution, and utilization, making significant contributions to peak shaving, frequency regulation, and the integration of new energy. On the other hand, the technical characteristics of digital technology, such as "connection, aggregation, and empowerment", can facilitate the flow of data across the stages of energy production, transmission, consumption, and trading, promoting the formation of a new energy structure that is clean, low-carbon, safe, and efficient. Therefore, it is imperative to integrate digital technology into the transformation of traditional energy technologies, expand the boundaries of the energy system through technological collaboration, drive the digital transformation of relevant industries, and form a more advantageous technological trajectory within the energy system.

6.6.3.2 Collaboration Between Technology and Environment

The collaboration between technology and the environment involves the collaborative evolution of energy technology innovation with knowledge innovation, institutional innovation, service innovation, and other domains. The green and low-carbon development of the energy system towards carbon neutrality is a dynamic and continuously evolving process that relies on energy technology innovation. Given the significant uncertainty and risks associated with breakthrough developments in energy technology, it is necessary to leverage collaborative developments in various fields, such as knowledge creation, institutional coordination, market services, etc., to effectively identify and manage risks associated with energy technology projects and eliminate institutional obstacles to the iteration of energy technology. For instance, policy measures such as price subsidies, tax incentives, fund allocation, and service platform construction can be used to guide research and development efforts, technological supply, and the transformation of achievements in key areas such as smart grids and energy interconnection, providing strong support for the collaborative and green low-carbon transformation of the energy supply and demand sides.

6.6.4 Establishing a Robust Market Operation System for "Electricity-Carbon" Linkage

Electricity trading markets and carbon emissions trading markets are integral components of the comprehensive energy market. A well-functioning electricity market mechanism can drive supply and demand entities to obtain the autonomy of choice through data exchange and information sharing in the trading process. This not only provides more economical and high-quality electricity assurance for the demand side but also enhances the energy configuration efficiency on the supply side. The carbon market allocates carbon emission rights resources by market rules so that the main bodies of electricity supply and demand can complete the mandatory emission reduction tasks by quotas trade, thus realizing the overall flexibility of the balance between supply and demand of resources in the integrated energy system. The following methods can be considered to find a market-driven path for green synergistic development of energy supply and demand through the electricity and carbon trading markets.

6.6.4.1 Deepening Market-Oriented Reforms in the Electricity Market

The focus of electricity market reforms lies in streamlining price relationships to establish a market-oriented electricity pricing mechanism. This requires accelerating power system reforms in eligible areas, reasonably guiding electricity generation costs according to pricing policies, and restoring the commodity attributes of electricity prices to a moderate extent. Under the requirements of carbon neutrality, the low-carbon and clean development of the energy supply and demand structure necessitates further advancement of green electricity pilot trading initiatives, encouraging key power generation regions to actively engage in mid-to-long-term green electricity trading and promoting the optimization of power consumption structure.

6.6.4.2 Advancing the Comprehensive Construction of the Carbon Trading Market

The effectiveness of the carbon market in promoting the low-carbon transformation of the energy system depends on whether carbon prices adequately reflect information costs from all supply and demand parties and emission reduction. The carbon market must have the broadest possible coverage and market participants to form a fully effective competitive market. Additionally, the allocation of carbon emission quotas needs to reflect the emission reduction and compliance costs of participating entities. The future development of the carbon market requires comprehensive construction, including expanding the variety of carbon trading products, broadening the scope of carbon market trading, improving quota allocation methods, and strictly adhering to market trading rules.

6.6.4.3 Promoting the Coordinated Development of the Electricity-Carbon Market

The interplay between the electricity market and the carbon market can more effectively leverage market mechanisms in the optimization of resource allocation and green low-carbon transformation on both the supply and demand sides. While advancing the construction of both markets, it is necessary to further strengthen policy coordination and mechanism complementarity. In the short and medium term, the construction of the carbon market should drive the low-carbon transformation and green development of the entire electricity industrial chain. In the long term, efforts should be made to guide the coupling and coordinated development of the "electricity-carbon" market, allowing energy prices to reflect both the actual cost of electricity and the corresponding carbon emission costs of electricity production.

6.6.5 Improving the Policy Guarantee System for Low-Carbon Development of the Energy System

The collaborative green and low-carbon development of the energy supply and demand sides requires not only defining future development paths in industries, regions, technologies, and markets but also relying on the foundational support and adequate guarantees of top-level design and policy systems. This is a complex task to establish a comprehensive policy system for the green and low-carbon development of the energy supply and demand system, which requires the consideration of institutional reform, financial and tax support, legal system construction, public participation, and other aspects of the construction path.

6.6.5.1 Deepening Energy System Reform

China has entered a deep-water area in energy system reform. Deep-seated contradictions such as energy market access barriers, administrative and regional monopolies, and dispersed energy regulatory functions are evident. Stripping away institutional factors that affect energy market access and competition fairness, including administrative control intensity, market standardization, and legislative protection levels, is conducive to reducing the efficiency loss of energy resource allocation and creating favorable conditions for the low-carbon transformation of the energy system.

6.6.5.2 Harnessing the Guiding Roles of Green Finance and Green Taxation

Green finance can guide funds more precisely into green and low-carbon development projects such as clean energy, providing a source of funding for the low-carbon transformation of the energy system. Strengthening financial product innovation and actively developing market-oriented emission reduction tools, such as green finance and carbon finance, is beneficial for accelerating the extraction of funds from high-carbon industries and effectively supporting the low-carbon development needs of the energy supply and demand sides.

6.6.5.3 Establishing a Sound Legal Support System for Green Energy Development

Starting from the legal requirements for promoting the green and low-carbon transformation of the energy supply and demand sides, the construction of the legal system in the energy field needs to strengthen the top-level design of integrated development and coordinated management in the energy field. This includes regulations and legal norms related to energy market transactions, as well as the establishment of an efficient energy regulatory system and legal means, especially target responsibility systems and assessment mechanisms related to energy conservation and emission reduction.

6.6.5.4 Building a Comprehensive Public Participation and Feedback Mechanism

The collaborative green and low-carbon development on both sides of energy supply and demand cannot be achieved without public participation. Individual residents' green and low-carbon practices are of great significance to the low-carbon transformation. Building a comprehensive action guarantee and institutional system for the participation of the entire society and incentivizing the involvement of the entire population in the low-carbon transformation process are feasible and effective ways to assist in the green development of the energy system, improve energy utilization efficiency, and promote the use of clean energy.

References

Ai Q., & Hao, R. (2018). Key technologies and challenges for multi-energy complementarity and optimization of integrated energy system. *Power System Automation, 42*, 2–10+46.

Aldieri, L., Gatto, A., & Vinci, C. P. (2021). Evaluation of energy resilience and adaptation policies: An energy efficiency analysis. *Energy Policy, 157*, 112505.

Bi, Q. H., Fan, Y., Cai, S. H., & Xia, Y. (2013). Analysis of China's primary energy demand scenarios based on the CDECGE model. *China Population, Resources and Environment, 23*, 41–48.

Duan, H. B., & Wang, S. Y. (2019). From 2°C to 1.5°C: China's challenges to attain the global warming-limit targets. *Management World, 35*, 50–63.

Fan, Y., & Yi, B. W. (2021). Evolution, driving mechanism, and pathway of China's energy transition. *Management World, 37*, 95–105.

Han, J. G. (2016). Analysis on the ways to achieve soft landing of energy structure adjustment. *Management World* 3–7.

He, J. K. (2014). Energy revolution is an inevitable choice for my country's ecological civilization construction and energy transformation. *Economic Research Reference*, 71–73.

Li, B. J., & Zhang, Q. Q. (2017). Analysis of China's regional energy supply and demand structure balance and economic impact. *Exploration of Economic Issues*, 39–46.

Li, J. L., & Yang, X. W. (2021). Drivers of China's energy consumption: insights from the "new normal era". *Journal of Xiamen University Philosophy and Social Sciences Edition*, 43–56.

Liang, W., & Liu, M. F. (2017). A study on the coupling and coordinated development and tempo-spatial variation of China's strategic emerging industries and traditional industries. *Economic Geography, 37*, 117–126.

Lin, B. Q., & Li, J. L. (2015). Transformation of China's energy structure under environmental governance constraints: a peak value analysis of coal and carbon dioxide. *Chinese Social Sciences*, 84–107+205.

Lin, B. Q. (2018). The period of carrying out energy revolution to promote low carbon clean development in China. *China Industrial Economics*, 15–23.

Lin, B. Q. (2021). The key to the development of renewable energy lies in the construction of power marketization. *China Securities Journal*, A03.

Lin, B. Q. (2020). Energy Internet helps China's energy green and low-carbon transformation. *Coal Economic Research Journal, 40*, 1.

Liu, Y. W., & Hu, Z. Y. (2014). The impact of energy technology changes on China's economy and energy environment—An analysis based on a dynamic computable general equilibrium model. *China Soft Science*, 43–57.

Lu, Z. X., Huang, H., Shan, B. G., Wang, Y. H., Du, S. H., & Li, J. H. (2017). Morphological evolution model and power forecasting prospect of future electric power systems with high proportion of renewable energy. *Automation of Electric Power Systems, 41*, 12–18.

Ouyang, X., & Sun, C. (2015). Energy savings potential in China's industrial sector: From the perspectives of factor price distortion and allocative inefficiency. *Energy Economics, 48*, 117–126.

Tu, Q., Mo, J. L., & Fan, Y. (2020). The evolution and evaluation of China's renewable energy policies and their implications for the future. *China Population, Resources .and Environment, 30*, 29–36.

Wang, H., Qi, J. G., & Liu, J. C. (2013). A theoretical analysis of synergetic effectsof circular economy. *Quantitative Economics Technological Economics Research, 30*, 138–149.

Wu, L., Zhao, X. F., & Qi, Y. (2014). Demand, supply and governance of energy in reform-era China. *China Population, Resources and Environment, 24*, 147–152.

Yang, J. F., Yu, Y., Ma, T., Zhang, C. G., & Wang, Q. (2020). Evolution of energy and metal demand driven by industrial revolutions and its trend analysis. *China Population, Resources and Environment, 30*, 45–54.

Yao, X., & Kong, Q. B. (2010). China's integrated energy transportation system and its macro impact. *Journal of Financial Research*, 29–39.

Yao, X., Pan, S. Y., & Sun, C. W. (2017). City scale, spatial agglomeration and electricity intensity in China. *Economic Research Journal, 52*, 165–177.

Zhang, S. L. (2021). Research on the coordinated development of the electricity market and carbon market based on the "dual carbon" goal. *China Electric Power Enterprise Management*, 50–54.

Zhang, H., Cheng, J. H., & Wang, L. F. (2011). China's industrialization process and balance of supply and demand of energy minerals. *China Population, Resources and Environment, 21*, 165–170.

Zheng, X. Y. (2017). Promoting the full-scale liberation of energy price. *Price Theory and Practice*, 17–22.

Part IV
Pathways for Dual-Carbon Governance in China

Chapter 7
Does China's National Carbon Market Function Well? A Perspective on Effective Market Design

Yu Zheng and Bing Zhang

Abstract The emissions trading scheme (ETS) has piqued substantial interest among economists and policymakers. China officially launched the electricity sector's national carbon emissions trading market in 2021, making it the world's largest compliance carbon market. In contrast to the cap-and-trade (C&T) system prevalent in other economies, China's national carbon market employs a rate-based mechanism that implicitly subsidizes the output of regulated entities; however, is it effective? This study uses a market-design theoretical framework to explore whether China's national carbon market functions effectively and, more critically, what leads to its (slight) underperformance. We discover that policy design, policy conflicts, policy uncertainty, inexperienced market regulation, and excessive or inappropriate government intervention are the primary constraints on this emerging market, resulting in shrinking market thickness, congested market transactions, and lack of safety. For China to establish a better national carbon market, stronger market-oriented rules, appropriate market regulation, improved policy coordination, and greater electricity market reforms are required.

Keywords Emissions trading scheme (ETS) · Carbon market · Market design · China · Electricity sector

7.1 Introduction

Global climate change mitigation is being sought via market-based instruments such as carbon emissions trading (Stavins, 1997). Permitting allowance trading for plants involved within the emissions market would result in equal marginal abatement costs for each plant, ensuring that carbon abatement is cost-effective and minimizing overall social costs (Stranlund, 2002). Utilizing such market-based environmental

Y. Zheng (✉) · B. Zhang
State Key Laboratory of Pollution Control and Resource Reuse, School of Environment, Nanjing University, Nanjing, China
e-mail: yuzheng@stu.edu.cn

B. Gong et al. (eds.), *Chinese Governance and Transformation Towards Carbon Neutrality*, Resources, Environment and Agricultural Development,
https://doi.org/10.1007/978-981-97-9996-1_7

regulations effectively has become a global challenge. As the world's second-biggest economy and the largest carbon emitter (Guan et al., 2009; Zhu, 2012), China's stance and efforts on climate change have garnered international attention. After nearly a decade of exploration, China officially inaugurated its national carbon trading market (for the electricity sector) in July 2021, making it the world's largest carbon market to date and the first nation-level carbon market in a developing economy.[1] To achieve the 2060 carbon neutrality target,[2] the national carbon market is anticipated to play a significant role. However, compared to other big economies, China faces greater challenges in its quest for carbon neutrality.

Although China has transitioned from a regional to a national carbon market,[3] its approach may not simply result in carbon reductions. Given China's distinct political-economic context and institutional structure, issues concerning the efficiency of market-based policy instruments have been raised (Lo, 2013, 2016). Numerous studies show that China's carbon pilot programs lower emissions (Cao et al., 2021; Cui et al., 2021) although their cost-effectiveness may be constrained. Several discussions have taken place in China about potential hurdles to the performance of emissions trading, such as insufficient supply and demand, excessive administrative interventions, and inadequate regulatory infrastructure (Lo, 2016; Munnings et al., 2016; Zhang et al., 2016). However, little is known about the constraints affecting carbon market performance when market design and electricity sector–specific procedures are considered. The only sector to date to be included in China's national carbon market is the electricity sector, and its success will undoubtedly influence the inclusion of other emission-intensive industries (e.g. steel, cement, and electrolytic aluminum). Thus, regulators and regulated entities must swiftly understand the potential performance constraints of China's national carbon market.

We examine the performance of China's national carbon market using Roth's theoretical framework (Roth, 2007, 2008), which asserts that successful markets should not be 'thin, congested, or unsafe.' Basically, our systematic analysis reveals that this emerging market is somewhat thin, congested, and unsafe. First, using detailed firm-level data, we discover that the energy intensities among market participants are highly convergent, posing a barrier to market thickness. Furthermore, regional carbon controls tend to cause market segmentation, resulting in market thinning. Second, trading activity, which is concentrated near the compliance deadline of the carbon trading market, particularly bulk trading agreement, can impede participants from achieving satisfactory trading outcomes, leading to market congestion. Moreover, market congestion can result from excessive or inadequate government intervention caused by a lack of information. Third, data forgery, regulatory uncertainty, and potential strategic bargaining may degrade market safety and discourage potential

[1] See http://www.xinhuanet.com/english/2021-07/16/c_1310064614.htm.

[2] At the United Nations General Assembly (UNGA) on September 22, 2020, Chinese President Xi Jinping pledged to the world that China will peak CO_2 emissions by 2030 and achieve carbon neutrality by 2060. http://www.xinhuanet.com/politics/leaders/2020-09/22/c_1126527652.htm.

[3] Carbon markets are divided into two categories: primary and secondary. This paper focuses on the secondary market, where carbon allowances are traded between market participants (currently primarily emission-controlling enterprises), which is of greater public interest.

traders from entering the market. Furthermore, emissions trading programs are not implemented in a policy vacuum (Tietenberg, 2006). They have to interact directly or indirectly with various preexisting policies, which may result in inter-policy disputes and decline in the efficacy of the schemes (Dudek et al., 2004; Shin, 2013; Zhang et al., 2013a). Therefore, we systematically examine the indirect effects of the government-regulated electricity system, including generation rights and electricity prices, on the emission reduction effect of China's national carbon market and determine its effect both inside and outside the carbon market. Finally, we focus on these critical aspects and provide four major recommendations for a more efficient national unified carbon market.

The remainder of this paper will proceed as follows. The development and evolution of emissions trading in China are systematically reviewed, focusing on policy design and market trading performance. The following sections discuss and apply the theoretical framework for market design to evaluate China's national carbon market performance in three dimensions: market thickness, congestion, and safety. The final section presents recommendations for a more efficient carbon market.

7.2 Evolution and Practical Exploration of Emissions Trading in China

The emissions trading scheme (ETS) has been extensively studied by economists and policymakers throughout the years, demonstrating that it is an incredibly effective market-based instrument (Bosquet, 2000)[4] for minimizing pollution[5] externalities. Because of its cost-effectiveness (Montgomery, 1972), emissions trading has gained popularity worldwide, as demonstrated by the United States Acid Rain Program (US ARP) and the European Union Emissions Trading System (EU ETS), which has resulted in a massive collection of significant empirical research (Stavins, 1998; Martin et al., 2016). After more than two decades of learning by doing, China has amassed extensive expertise in the policy practice of carbon trading.

7.2.1 *SO_2 Emissions Trading Pilots*

In the field of emissions trading, the United States is a pioneer (Crocker, 1966; Dales, 1968). The significant success of the US ARP in the 1990s has strongly encouraged China to apply this market-based tool to reduce sulfur dioxide emissions. Although China began researching and testing the ETS in the 1980s, these

[4] In addition to the ETS, another important market-based environmental policy tool, usually compared with the ETS, is the environmental tax.

[5] It is worth noting that in addition to conventional pollutants (such as sulfur dioxide), greenhouse gases (such as carbon dioxide) are also included, especially after the Kyoto Protocol.

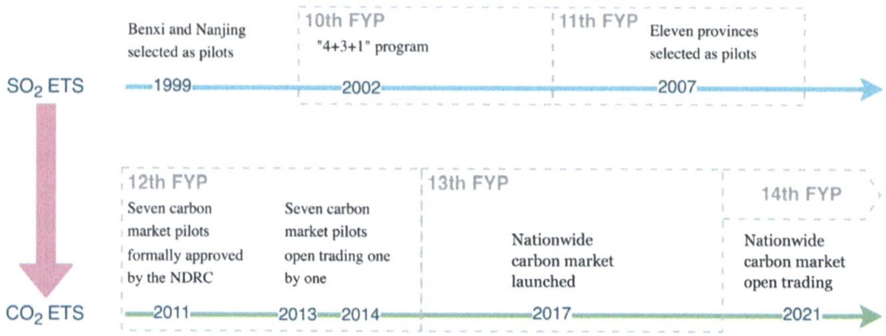

Fig. 7.1 Timeline of the introduction of China's carbon market. *Note* The authors compiled data from publicly available sources. For nearly a decade, China has been working to establish a full domestic carbon market since the 12th FYP. Furthermore, on 16 July 2021, China's nationwide CET launched online trading, involving 2162 key emission units in the electricity sector and encompassing over 4 billion tons of carbon emissions, making it the world's largest carbon market

experiments have mostly remained conceptual due to a lack of experience and implementation challenges. During the Ninth Five-Year Plan (FYP) period (1996–2000), however, substantial progress was made through the nationwide promotion of total emissions control (TEC) because national and regional experts acknowledged that this market-based strategy could reduce the cost of meeting TEC targets (Yang & Schreifels, 2003).

The US EPA introduced China's well-formed emissions trading (Dudek et al., 2004) when the State Environmental Protection Administration (SEPA) collaborated with the US EPA to evaluate the feasibility of introducing an SO_2 cap-and-trade program in 1999. Both organizations investigated the theories, conditions, foundations, and methods for implementing SO_2 emissions trading in China's electricity sector before selecting Benxi and Nanjing as the first two pilot sites. In March 2002, the two institutions started trading SO_2 emissions in four provinces (Shandong, Jiangsu, Shanxi, and Henan), three cities (Shanghai, Tianjin, and Liuzhou), and one enterprise (China Huaneng Group Co., Ltd.).[6] Since 2007, the Ministries of Environmental Protection (MEP), Finance (MOF), and the National Development and Reform Commission (NDRC) have selected eleven provinces (or direct-controlled municipalities)[7] to pilot emissions trading programs, all focusing on SO_2 pollution (Ministry of Environmental Protection (MEP), 2008). Figure 7.1 depicts the timeline of China's emissions trading implementation.

In general, China's SO_2 ETS has not been institutionalized, resulting in fewer transactions and lower cost savings than expected (Shin, 2013; Zhang et al., 2013a).

---

[6] This is also known as the "4 + 3 + 1" program. See "Notice on Beginning the Pilots of Promote the Research Program on China's Sulfur Dioxide Control and Emissions Trading Policy," State Environmental Protection Bureau (SEPA). SEPA (2002) This program was launched when the TEC was formalized during the 10th FYP period (2001–2005).

[7] In particular, Jiangsu, Zhejiang, Tianjin, Hubei, Hunan, Inner Mongolia, Shanxi, Chongqing, Shaanxi, Hebei and Henan are included.

This strategy has been the subject of numerous investigations, primarily from internal and external viewpoints. On the one hand, policy elements such as allocation of allowances, emissions measurements, and monitoring and verification are crucial to policy performance (Hart & Zhong, 2014). On the other hand, ETS must inevitably interact with other pre-existing regulations, both directly and indirectly, which frequently results in disagreements that reduce the program's efficacy (Chang & Wang, 2010; Sorrell & Sijm, 2003) Furthermore, the government's extensive intervention has weakened price signals, which may be a significant factor for China's failure to achieve the expected effectiveness of SO_2 emissions trading (Tao & Mah, 2009; Zhang et al., 2016). To summarize, while these pilot programs were never institutionalized or nationalized, China's previous SO_2 trading schemes provide valuable lessons and experiences for future carbon trading schemes. Despite the differences in pollution targets, the two ETS designs share certain characteristics. Exploration of ETS in policy design elements such as allowance allocation, emission measurement, monitoring, and verification is useful for subsequent carbon markets (regional and national). It should also be noted that the extensive government intervention in subsequent carbon markets has been somewhat weakened; however, this has not yet translated into a sufficiently appropriate and proportionate level of market intervention.

7.2.2 Regional Carbon Market Pilots

Recently, China has committed to decarbonizing to fulfill its responsibilities as the world's second-largest economy with the highest carbon emissions. Since the early 2000s, China has been actively involved in developing and trading in the international carbon market through the clean development mechanism (CDM) (Dechezleprêtre et al., 2009; Du & Takeuchi, 2019).[8] In the 12th FYP, the Chinese government began to focus on reducing carbon emissions, proposing a 17% reduction in carbon dioxide emissions per unit of GDP by 2015 compared to 2010 (State Council of the People's Republic of China, 2011). Several key policy instruments, such as the ten-thousand-enterprises program (The National Development and Reform Commission (NDRC), 2011a), were implemented during this period. The NDRC issued the Notice on Carrying Out the Pilot Project on Carbon Emissions Trading on 29 October 2011, approving seven carbon market pilots in Beijing, Tianjin, Shanghai, Chongqing, Hubei, Guangdong, and Shenzhen (The National Development and Reform Commission (NDRC), 2011b) to further reduce emission reduction costs and meet the emission reduction goal.

[8] The Clean Development Mechanism (CDM), defined in Article 12 of the Protocol, allows a country with an emission-reduction or emission-limitation commitment under the Kyoto Protocol (Annex B Party) to implement an emission-reduction project in developing countries. (UNFCC: https://unfccc.int/process-and-meetings/the-kyoto-protocol/mechanisms-under-the-kyoto-protocol/the-clean-development-mechanism) Studies have examined the impact of CDM on China, such as technology transfer and poverty.

We strive to present an overview of China's pilot carbon emissions trading markets by combining various sources of information and data, which differ considerably in terms of sectoral coverage, entry thresholds for qualifying installations, punitive measures for noncompliance, and other design features reflecting diverse settings and priorities (Chen & Xu, 2018; Zhang et al., 2017). Table 7.1 contains the detailed policy design of these seven pilot programs.

Generally, local governments in each pilot establish and determine their carbon markets differently based on their economic development state, industrial structure, and political goals, resulting in significant differences between the seven carbon markets described above. Furthermore, this is the situation preferred by the central government because it is the only way to gain as many valuable experiences in as many dimensions as possible while continuing to strive.[9]

Several distinguishing characteristics of carbon market pilots are discussed in greater detail below. First, all seven pilots include the electricity sector although they include various industries, some of which are nonindustrial (e.g. carbon markets in Beijing, Shanghai, and Shenzhen). The main factor might be that carbon emissions from the electricity sector are substantial and comparatively simple to account for. Second, interregional transactions are prohibited because each of the seven pilot markets is independent (i.e. 'segmented'). Third, carbon market pilots are constrained by the administrative region's emission reduction target (as shown in the third column of Table 7.1) and overlap with other energy-saving and emission-reduction policies during the same period (e.g. the ten-thousand-enterprises program).

Finally, characteristics of market performance should be given special consideration. (i) Overall price volatility is relatively high, as shown in Fig. 7.2a; although this is considered normal in most carbon pilots, caution is still advised because excessive volatility may impair price signal transmission. (ii) As illustrated in Fig. 7.2b, the average trading price of the seven pilots fluctuated significantly throughout the review period (June 2013–May 2022). Beijing's trading price (60.25 yuan/ton) is 3.38 times higher than Chongqing (17.84 yuan/ton).[10] (iii) The market thickness varies considerably across the seven pilots. Guangdong and Hubei account for 62.77% of the total trade volume (60.16% of total turnover).[11]

Numerous studies on the regional carbon emissions trading market have yielded significant, direct insights for China's nationwide application, particularly in terms of carbon emission reduction effectiveness, technological innovation, energy mix optimization, synergy effects, and carbon leakage issues (Almond & Zhang, 2021; Cao et al., 2021; Liu et al., 2021; Yu et al., 2021; Zhu et al., 2019).

---

[9] Geographically, at least one pilot market is located in each of China's eastern, central, and western regions, reflecting the Chinese government's strategic approach to exploring experience in a differentiated manner.

[10] The overall average price in the review period was 32.11 yuan/ton.

[11] The overall cumulative trading volume in the review period was 290.81 million tons (cumulative turnover is 7.77 billion yuan).

Table 7.1 Overview of the key features of China's seven pilot carbon emissions trading schemes

Pilots	Date of market initiation	Regional CO_2 intensity target for 2015 compared to 2010 (%)[A]	Emission threshold for coverage (1000 tons CO_2/year)	Historical emissions period	Number of covered industrial sectors[C]	Number of covered firms	Shares of total emissions (%)	Annual total allowance allocation (million tons CO_2)	Means of transaction	Object of transaction[D]	Allocation With auction[E]	Penalty
Shenzhen	06/18/2013	21	> 3	2009–2011	26	635	40	33	On-exchange	SZA, CCER	Yes	Fine
Shanghai	11/26/2013	19	> 20	2010–2011	10	197	57	150	On-exchange	SHEA, CCER	No	Fine
Beijing	11/28/2013	18	> 10	2009–2012	10	415	40	55	On-exchange: over the counter	BEA, CCER, carbon sink, and energy savings	No	Fine
Guangdong	12/19/2013	19.5	> 20	2009–2012	4	242	58	350	On-exchange	GDEA, CCER	Yes	Fine and allowance reduction
Tianjin	12/26/2013	19	> 20	2011–2012	5	114	55	160	On-exchange	TJEA, CCER	No	Policy

(continued)

Table 7.1 (continued)

Pilots	Date of market initiation	Regional CO_2 intensity target for 2015 compared to 2010 (%)[A]	Emission threshold for coverage (1000 tons CO_2/year)	Historical emissions period	Number of covered industrial sectors[C]	Number of covered firms	Shares of total emissions (%)	Annual total allowance allocation (million tons CO_2)	Means of transaction	Object of transaction[D]	Allocation With auction[E]	Penalty
Hubei	04/02/2014	17	> 150[B]	2010–2011	12	138	44	324	On-exchange	HBEA, CCER	No	Fine and allowance
Chongqing	06/19/2014	17	> 20	2008–2012	6	242	40	131	On-exchange	CQEA, CCER	No	Fine

Note Compiled by authors from publicly available figures, see, e.g. Liu et al., 'Has Carbon Emissions Trading Reduced $PM_{2.5}$ in China'; Zhang et al. (2014) 'Emissions trading in China'; and Zhu et al., 'Low-carbon Innovation Induced by Emissions Trading in China.' Statistics in this table refer only to the initial year of the carbon market pilots. (A) It should be noted that the emission reduction target here refers to the corresponding regional emission reduction target in the 12th FYP (2011–2015) period rather than for the carbon market. Meanwhile, the overall national emission reduction target for this period is 17%. (B) Hubei's emissions threshold is set at 60 thousand tons of coal equivalent, which is transferred into 150 thousand tons of CO_2 emissions to be comparable with other pilot projects. (C) The nonindustrial sector is not counted here; all pilots cover the electricity sector. (D) All carbon markets permit the trade of CCERs in addition to their respective emission permits (i.e. China Certified Emission Reductions). (E) Only Guangdong and Shenzhen designed auction mechanisms with relatively low auction percentages (3%)

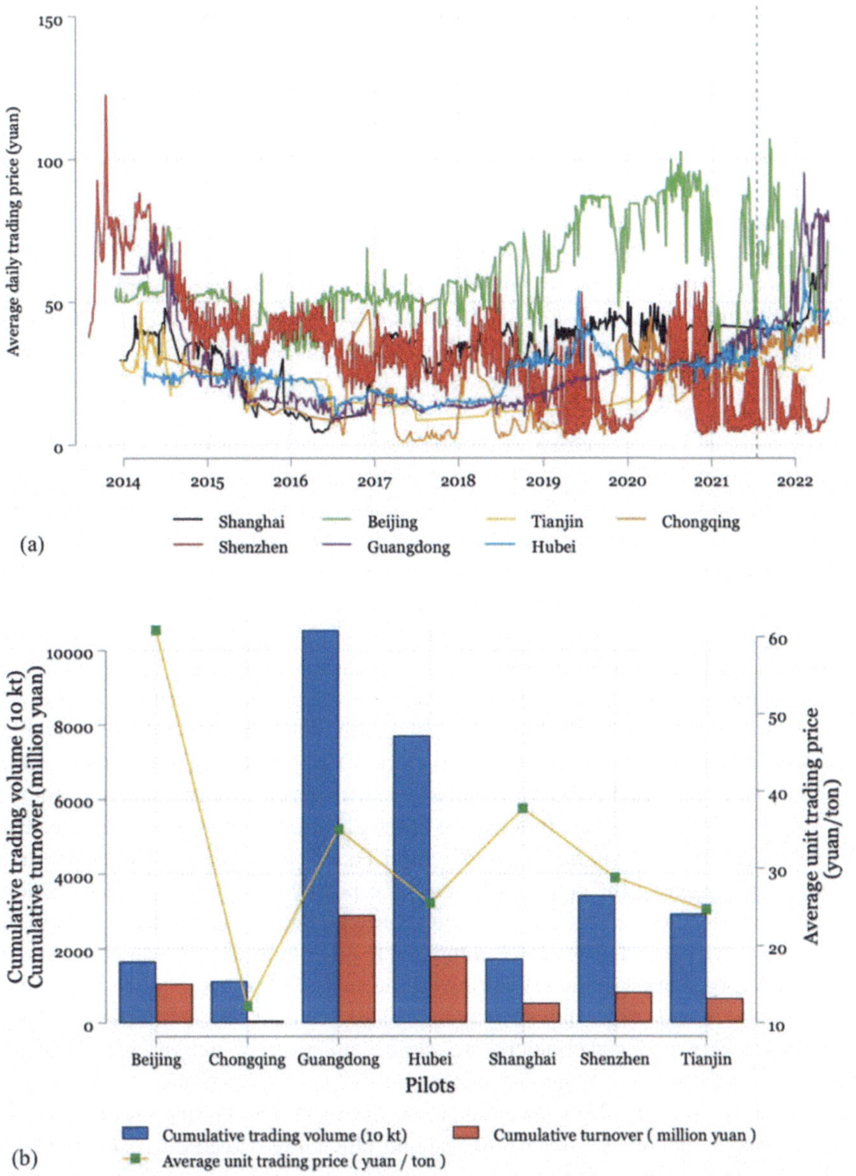

Fig. 7.2 Profile of China's regional carbon market pilots. **a** Average daily trading price trend. **b** Cumulative trading volume, cumulative turnover, and average unit trading price. *Note* The figure depicts the profile of China's seven regional carbon market pilots, including the trend of average daily trading price (**a**) and cumulative trading volume, cumulative turnover, and average unit trading price (**b**). The time interval for the statistics is from the launch of the pilot carbon market to May 27, 2022. The average unit trading price, total cumulative trading volume, and total cumulative turnover of the seven carbon markets are 32.11 yuan/ton, 290.81 million tons, and 7.77 billion yuan, respectively. In (**a**), the black vertical dashed line represents the start date for the national carbon market, which is July 16, 2021. Data source: China Stock Market & Accounting Research (CSMAR) Database

7.2.3 National Carbon Market for the Electricity Sector

The goal of the carbon market pilot is to generate valuable experiences that can be used to build a unified national market to further reduce the social cost of emission reductions. After 5 years of operation, China's national carbon market was officially launched on 18 December 2017 (The National Development and Reform Commission (NDRC), 2017). Prior to the market's official trading, ~ 2 years (2018–2019) were expected to be spent on market infrastructure construction (including data reporting, registration, trading, and market management systems) and simulation operation. However, due to the unexpected impact of COVID-19, China's national carbon market was slightly delayed and finally started trading in July 2021. Shanghai is in charge of the trading system, while Wuhan oversees the registration and settlement systems.

The national carbon market differs from pilot markets in the following ways. First, the national carbon market has been unified as opposed to the pilot program's segmented markets. Second, the regulatory authority has been transferred from the NDRC to the newly established Ministry of Ecology and Environment (MEE),[12] reflecting China's intention to integrate carbon trading with other environmental policies for better coordination. Finally, the electricity sector is the first and only sector chosen to fully participate in China's national carbon market, with 2,162 key compliance entities covering ~ 4 billion tons of carbon emissions.[13]

There are three primary reasons for limiting coverage to the electricity sector. (i) The electricity sector is typically energy- and emission-intensive with considerable decarbonization potential (Liu et al., 2013). In 2020, China's energy consumption accounted for ~88% of the total CO_2 emissions, with the electricity sector accounting for ~ 42.5%.[14] Thus, the decarbonization of the electricity sector is critical to China achieving its carbon-peak and carbon-neutral goals. (ii) In terms of inter-sectoral interactions, greening the electricity sector is especially important as a foundation for decarbonizing other sectors. (iii) The electricity sector ranks relatively high in terms of data richness and accuracy compared to other industries. Meanwhile, as the national carbon market gradually improves, the central government plans to expand the market to include other industries (such as steel, cement, and nonferrous metals).

Policymakers and stakeholders are closely monitoring market performance. Figure 7.3 depicts the volume and price trends of China's national carbon market from 19 July 2021, to 27 May 2022. First, the market is highly volatile, which raises concerns about its capacity to respond efficiently to carbon costs (Balietti, 2016). Second, except near the end of the compliance cycle, the trading volume is low. Compliance-driven markets would have few participants and few transactions.[15] Finally, the national carbon market's average trading price is only 50.23 yuan/ton,

---

[12] http://www.gov.cn/zhengce/2018-03/21/content_5276191.htm#1 (accessed 24 December 2021).

[13] Data source: Shanghai Environment and Energy Exchange (https://www.cneeex.com/).

[14] http://www.nea.gov.cn/2021-06/05/c_139993076.htm (accessed 24 December 2021).

[15] Approximately three-quarters of the transactions took place in December.

significantly lower than the EU ETS.[16] Furthermore, Xiao et al. (2021) demonstrated that carbon pricing could accelerate China's carbon peaking process and reduce peak height. The optimal carbon price is 21 USD/ton, more than twice as high as the current national carbon market average price for the electricity sector.

7.3 Theoretical Framework

Emissions trading markets are distinct from traditional markets in that policymakers developed and regulated them. Although markets vary in reality, we use a set of generic guidelines for constructing efficient markets, as summarized by Roth (2007), to assess the market efficiency of China's national carbon market from the market design perspective. Drawing upon research conducted in various markets such as labor, school choice programs, and kidney trading markets, Roth concludes that an effective market should satisfy three criteria (i.e. 'thick, uncongested, and safe') (Abdulkadiroğlu et al., 2005; Roth, 1991; Roth et al., 2005).

(1) The market must be thick to attract sufficient potential market participants (sellers and buyers) and allow them to engage in effective transactions (matching); (2) the marketplace must be secure and reliable. All potential market participants should be willing to trade in this market and reveal preferences truthfully and freely; and (3) this market should not be congested so that all participants have sufficient time to trade.

Such a framework for assessing market design has been shown to be broadly applicable in several theoretical and empirical studies (Gans & Stern, 2010; Zhang et al., 2016). In addition to the markets indicated above, this broad framework of Roth's three criteria for effective market design has been utilized in several subsequent studies to assess the functional performance of various types of markets, such as technology, idea creation, and pollution trading markets (Gans & Stern, 2010; Xu, 2011; Zhang et al., 2016). This general framework, we believe, is also applicable and instructive for carbon markets. The Roth criteria were established to build new markets (where they are lacking) or repair damaged ones, which, according to Xu (2011), could be especially useful for environmental protection because market failure is frequently the cause. To the best of our knowledge, no study has assessed the functioning market for carbon emissions trading using Roth's three effective market design criteria. Additionally, the state-regulated electricity system could have unforeseen consequences on the national carbon market, which is now limited to the electricity sector. Considering these factors, we use this framework to evaluate the market performance of China's national carbon market in the following sections. Figure 7.4 illustrates this framework.

[16] The average EU carbon price of 2021 exceeds 50 euros per ton and even hits a record above 90 euros per ton in February 2022. Data source: Trading Economics (https://tradingeconomics.com/).

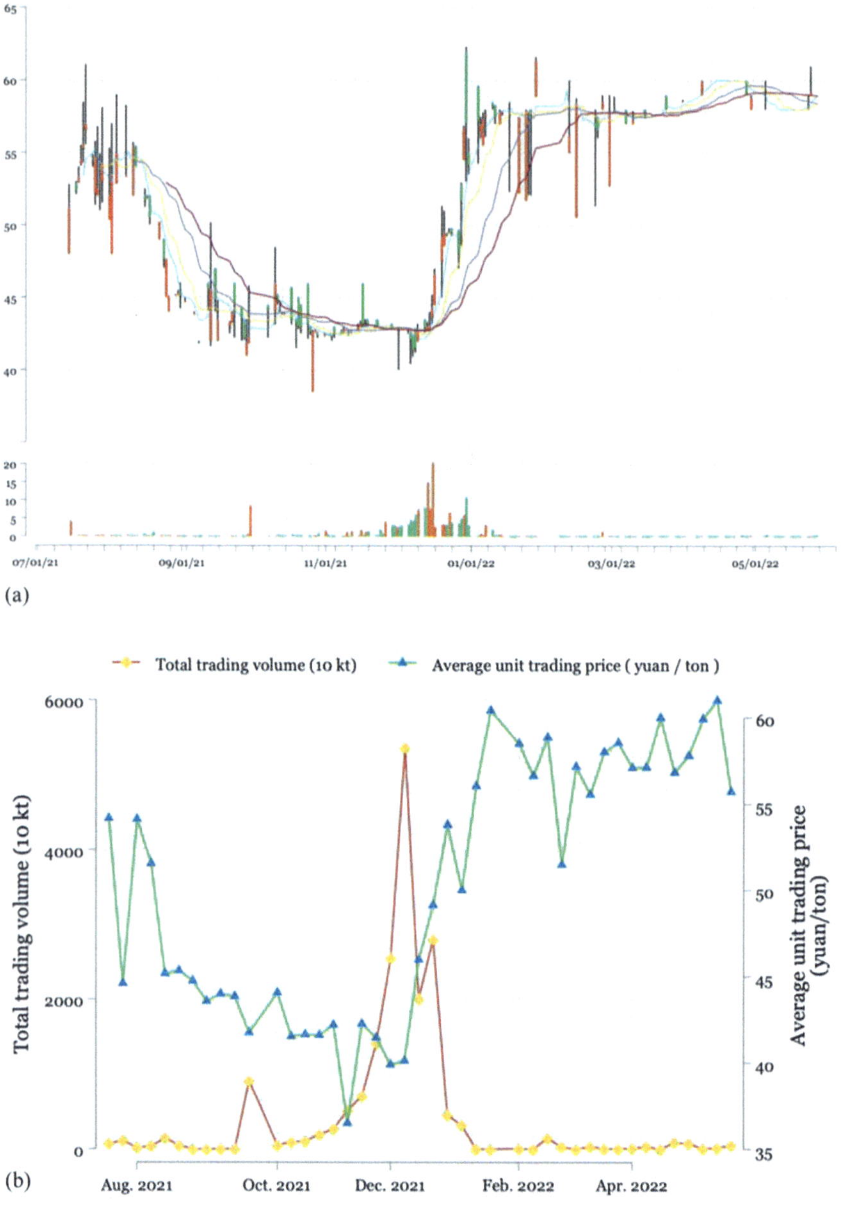

Fig. 7.3 Price and volume trends in China's national carbon market (07/16/2021–05/27/2022). **a** Daily candlestick chart. **b** Trends of (weekly) trading volume and average unit trading prices. *Note* The graph depicts China's national carbon market price and volume trends, including a daily candlestick chart (**a**). and total trading volume and average unit trading price trends (weekly) (**b**). The average unit trading price, total cumulative trading volume, and total cumulative turnover during the review period were 50.23 yuan/ton, 188.03 million tons, and 8.18 billion yuan, respectively. *Data source* CSMAR Database

Fig. 7.4 Research framework

7.4 Market Thickness

Several studies on various markets have determined providing thickness to be an important principle of a successful market. The market should generate sufficient potential market activity to produce reliable price signals. Thus, there should be a sufficient number of qualified market participants to act as buyers or sellers (Roth, 2007), and these participants should have incentives to trade.

7.4.1 Shrinking of Qualified Market Participants

Inadequately designed policies can reduce the number of qualified market participants. Potential sellers are becoming cautious and hesitant to join the carbon market owing to policy discontinuity and ambiguity, which has led to a decrease in market thickness. Due to their concerns that future climate policy restrictions and uncertainty regarding crucial carbon market information (such as benchmarks) may affect their allowance holdings, participants are hesitant to sell their allowances. In addition to reducing the number of potential transaction sellers, the weak penalty design of policies can reduce potential buyers. According to the current administrative rules (Montagnoli & de Vries, 2010), regulated enterprises that conceal their carbon emissions pay a fine of only CNY 10,000 to CNY 30,000. Such a low cost for noncompliance is enough to leverage millions of dollars in 'benefits' for regulated enterprises with a shortage of allowances. Stricter fines are required to minimize the number of regulatory violations by enterprises, as well as the intentional replacement of fines for allowance payments.

7.4.2 High Homogeneity of Energy Intensity Among Participants

In contrast to the other investigated markets,[17] China's national carbon market has > 2000 power enterprises,[18] and this remarkable figure ensures a high number of eligible participants. However, to increase the likelihood of effective matching (Gans & Stern, 2010), even a high number of participants is insufficient when participant diversity is low. Potential carbon trading market participants can act as carbon allowance buyers or sellers based on their marginal abatement costs or profits (Dickhaut et al., 2012). Therefore, the marginal abatement costs of power enterprises participating in the national carbon market considerably impact market thickness. When the marginal abatement costs of participating firms are remarkably convergent, the market thickness decreases.

To allocate allowances to covered facilities, China's national carbon market for the electricity sector relies on benchmarking, which bases the number of allowances granted to a facility on the technology- or fuel-specific emissions–output ratio.[19] More specifically, given a specific benchmark by the regulator, allowances would be granted to a given facility for the compliance cycle equal to its output during that period (Goulder & Morgenstern, 2018)[20] multiplied by the benchmark ratio and correction factor.[21] As the regulatory authorities set the benchmark ratio and adjustment factor, the difference between one facility's emissions–output ratio (i.e. carbon intensity) and the benchmark ratio determines whether the firm to which the facility belongs will be a buyer or a seller of allowances.[22] In cases where only two firms are in the market with only one facility each, no trading of allowances will occur if both facilities have the same emissions–output ratio. Thus, the diversity of the emissions–output ratios of market facilities plays a significant role in market thickness.

[17] For example, the number of participants in the study by Roth et al. (2005) does not exceed 100.

[18] Enterprises in the electricity sector (including autonomous power plants in other industries) that emit ≥ 26,000 tons of carbon dioxide equivalent (with a total energy consumption of ~ 10,000 tonnes of standard coal) in any one year from 2013 to 2019 were selected to participate in the first compliance cycle of the national carbon market.

[19] In the first phase of the market, benchmark ratios are divided into four categories based on the various fuel and technology of the facilities, with gas-fired facilities being the lowest.

[20] Although the allowance granted to a given coal-fired facility for a given compliance cycle is pre-established based on its output from the previous compliance cycle with an "initial allocation factor" (0.7 set in China's nationwide carbon market in the electricity industry), the ultimate allowance will be updated upon its output during the given compliance cycle. Thereby, the allowance allocation is a rate-based, not a mass-based system. (See the Implementation Plan for Setting and Allocating the Total Amount of Carbon Emission Trading Quotas in 2019–2020 (Power Generation Sector), and Goulder and Morgenstern (2018)).

[21] Indeed, the actual correction factor considers the cooling method, heat supply, and load factor.

[22] Here, assume that this firm has only one facility.

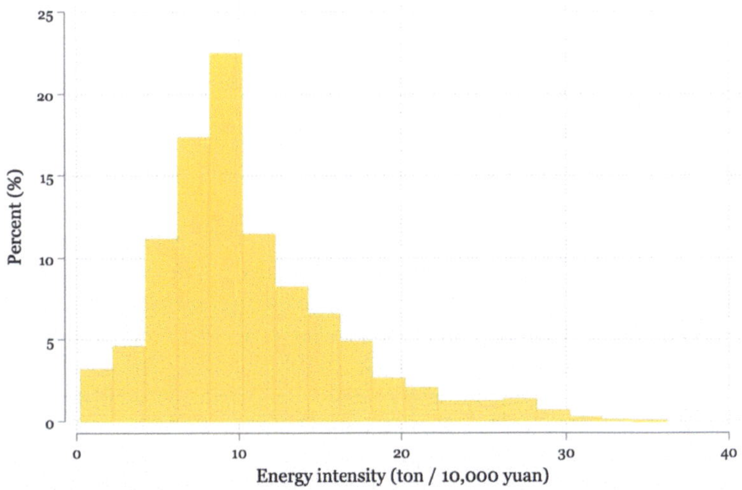

Fig. 7.5 Proportional distribution of energy intensity of the enterprises included in China's national carbon market. *Note* The figure depicts the proportional distribution of energy intensity of the firms included in China's national carbon market based on the CESD dataset. The energy intensity of firms is used as a proxy for their emission–output ratios, which refers to the total energy consumed per unit of output value. Autonomous power plants are not included. The bins are set at 2 tons/10,000 yuan. Four outliers are excluded. *Data source* CESD database and the NDRC

We examine the distribution of emissions–output ratios for covered firms using data from the China Environmental Statistics Database (CESD).[23] Firms' energy intensity is used as a proxy for their emissions–output ratios, which refer to the total amount of energy consumed per unit of output. Figure 7.5 depicts the energy intensity distribution of 719 covered firms matched with the CESD.[24]

The energy intensities of ~ 70% of the firms are concentrated in the range of 4–14 tons/yuan, significantly reducing the potential for trading in China's national carbon market system. Although former emissions trading markets such as the US SO_2 ETS, Chicago Climate Exchange, EU ETS, and China's regional carbon market (Montagnoli & de Vries, 2010; Sabbaghi & Sabbaghi, 2011; Wang & Wu, 2018) have low

[23] The CESD is the most comprehensive and extensive nationwide environmental database at the firm level in China. Since approximately 1998, the Ministry of Environmental Protection (MEP) has begun to establish a bottom-to-up system to collect environmental information covering all the major industrial emission sources all over China. All the data are self-reported by the point sources and then compiled by the MEP. Due to strict data collection procedures, the CESD is China's most reliable environmental microdata set. It is updated annually and contains > 400 data fields, including (1) basic plant information; (2) basic production information; (3) pollution emissions; (4) pollution abatement equipment; and (5) other environmental-relevant information, including total operating costs for pollution treatment. In this study, we mainly use the information on consumption of five types of energy (i.e. coal, fuel oil, natural gas, coke, and electricity) and the output value from this dataset to calculate the energy intensity.

[24] The list of enterprises included in the national carbon market was obtained from the NDRC. And autonomous power plants are not included.

thickness, the situation in China's national carbon market may be different because only the electricity sector is included. In other words, unlike in other markets, the high homogeneity of emission intensity or trading demand among different participants is extremely difficult to change.

Coal-fired power plants have continuously undergone upgrades and retrofits throughout the 11th (2006–2010), 12th (2011–2015), and 13th (2016–2020) FYP periods, and the coal consumption of power supply has continued to decline (Xu et al., 2013). In 2020, the national average coal consumption for thermal power plants ($\geq$ 6000 kW) was 305.5 g of standard coal per kWh, a ~ 20% decrease from 2005. Furthermore, by the end of the 14th FYP, the national average coal consumption for thermal power supply must be < 300 g of standard coal per kWh,[25] limiting energy consumption or carbon emissions per output. That is, upgrading and retrofitting coal-fired power plants will narrow the gap in emission–output ratios between covered plants, further thinning the market. However, the inclusion of other sectors is expected to thicken China's national carbon market.

7.4.3 Regional Total Carbon Emission Control

During the ninth FYP period (1996–2000), China began to promote a nationwide TEC system and made considerable progress in counteracting the increasing trend of environmental pollution and ecological damage.[26] In the 2010s, China's efforts to reduce pollution were bolstered by the TEC system. Under this system, China's central government sets a total control target every five years (i.e. the FYP), and the national total control is cascaded to provinces, cities, and counties. In other words, China's environmental governance system has relied heavily on a top-down target responsibility system. We have summarized China's national TEC targets since the 11th FYP (see Table 7.2), distributed down from the central government to local jurisdictions. China has preferred intensity control (Lo, 2013, 2016) to reduce emissions while maintaining economic development. This effort has unquestionably made remarkable contributions to China's environmental improvement.

However, China's total regional control is a boundary or administrative constraint. The vertical control target allocation from central to local levels has limited the emissions trading market, resulting in market segmentation. Studies have found that the electricity sector's SO_2 emissions trading program and carbon trading pilots are regionally segmented markets constrained by total regional control, making it difficult to develop real market power (Xu et al., 2011). Although China's national carbon market has been established, it is still limited by the regional emissions control system. Thus, China has begun implementing total controls in addition to previous intensity controls. Since the 14th FYP, China has implemented a system of dual management of carbon emission intensity and total emissions to address the

[25] http://www.gov.cn/zhengce/zhengceku/2021-11/03/content_5648562.htm.

[26] http://www.reformdata.org/1996/0903/16954.shtml.

Table 7.2 China's total emissions control targets

	11th FYP (2006–2010) (%)	12th FYP (2011–2015) (%)	13th FYP (2016–2020) (%)	14th FYP (2021–2025) (%)
Energy intensity reduction	~ 20	16	15	13.5
Carbon intensity reduction	–	17	18	18
Nonfossil share in primary energy mix	–	11.4	15	–
Total emissions of major pollutant reduction	10	8–10	10–15	–

Note The reduction targets are compared with the year before the first year of a given FYP, e.g. the energy intensity reduction in the 14th FYP is 13.5% lower than that in 2020. The attributes of all these targets are binding as distinct from the anticipatory goals (e.g. GDP growth rate) in the FYPs. The major pollutants include chemical oxygen demand, ammonia nitrogen, sulfur dioxide, and nitrogen oxides

challenge of climate change specifically.[27] This control system and the carbon market are two essential tools in China's policy toolbox for combating climate change. Limited evidence on the adverse effects of total regional control has been assessed. For example, Yu et al. (2018) found that the provincial abatement target would affect trading behaviors in the carbon trading market. Moreover, Zhang et al. (2013b) concluded that provincial targets are more expensive than a single national target under a given reduction in carbon intensity.

Notably, from the perspective of local governments, total regional control takes precedence over carbon markets; in fact, carbon markets are only binding on covered firms within their jurisdictions, not on local governments. Thus, Chinese environmental governance has an 'authoritarian environmentalism' overtone (Gilley, 2012). On the one hand, if local governments are under pressure to reach regional carbon or energy targets (especially near the end of the FYP), shutting down large swathes of industrial capacity may be a last-ditch measure. Once firms covered in the national carbon market are involved, the thickness will also be weakened, and in this case, sellers will be reduced. On the other hand, covered firms under local jurisdictions may stockpile excess allowances in anticipation of future pressure from local carbon regulations. Such unclear or inappropriate boundaries between the government and market may jeopardize the national carbon emissions trading market's performance (Roth, 2007). At the same time, during the transition phase from the pilot market to

[27] http://www.gov.cn/xinwen/2021-03/13/content_5592681.htm.

the national market, different local economic structures, trading rules, and emission calculation methods limit cross-regional trading, i.e. compatibility concerns (Zhang et al., 2013b).

7.5 Market Congestion

The second Roth criterion for efficient market design is to avoid congestion. A well-functioning market should give market participants ample time (or faster enough means to conduct transactions) to fully consider potential alternative options and close satisfactory deals. Thick markets attract a large number of market participants allowing them to bargain. However, they also risk 'congestion,' which is analogous to a traffic jam or a market panic in which everyone wants to get out but is unable to. Optimal market allocation can be challenging owing to market congestion, which can cause pricing distortions. While market thickness is necessary for the absence of congestion, the timing and specific rules of the market mechanism also influence the congestion level (Gans & Stern, 2010).

7.5.1 Congested Trading Near the End of the Compliance Cycle

China's national carbon market has failed to meet the second Roth criterion, indicating a risk of market congestion. Due to participants' limited time to comply, the market design results in congestion. As illustrated in Fig. 7.3, many transactions are in the run-up to the compliance deadline. The Chinese MEE issued a notice on 26 October 2021, requiring regulated enterprises to clear their allowances by 31 December 2021. In November and December 2021, enterprise transactions sharply surged, accounting for 90% of all transactions in the first compliance cycle. Li et al. (2022) Participants who need more allowances are under pressure to comply and must seek and complete transactions as soon as possible. However, due to time constraints, enterprises cannot fully consider alternative options and must rush to complete transactions instead. This limits the market's ability to achieve high-quality matches and prevents it from reaching optimal allocation. Because of the congestion, some participants have panicked and have had to pay an additional 2% commission to intermediaries to find a match (although there is currently no commission for trading in the national carbon market).

However, the deeper underlying cause is the participant sentiment of passive trading. This is demonstrated by the Guangdong pilot carbon market, with the electricity sector being the only one with a net inflow of allowances compared with other covered sectors (steel, cement, paper, civil aviation, and petrochemical).[28] That is, on the whole market level, only the electricity sector serves as a buyer. This passive trading behavior at the power plant level will be discussed further below.

Herein, we examine the decision-making process of market participants. According to Goulder and Morgenstern,[29] the profit of one covered plant is equal to its generation output revenues minus input costs[30] and emissions allowance expenses. When applied to a facility, the difference between its emission–output ratio and the benchmark equals the difference between its carbon emissions and its allowance (free) allocation. Although allowances are allocated at the facility level, decisions are made by enterprises that own various facilities. Figure 7.6 depicts a simplified decision-making process for participants in China's national carbon market. These decisions are critical to the effective functioning of the carbon market.

Generally, enterprises make three types of decisions: optimizing operations between various facilities, passing through additional costs, and increasing technical or fuel inputs. The state-regulated electricity market, however, significantly restricts businesses' strategic alternatives and forces them to adopt a passive role in the carbon market.

First, state-dispatched electricity generation rights restrict optimal inter-facility operation. Despite several rounds of power system reform, the state currently dominates China's electricity market, and electricity generation rights are distributed uniformly (Ngan, 2010). China's power dispatching system is based on the principle of open, equitable, and just dispatching (i.e. 'San Gong' dispatching)[31] and treats all market players equally under the premise of maintaining a safe, stable, and economic power system. More specifically, the mechanism of administrative allocation of annual generation quotas can be described as follows: at the end of each calendar year, the provincial government forecasts the overall electricity demand for the following year based on province-wide socioeconomic development and then allocates this demand to facilities within the province (as well as to those purchased outside the province). This process adheres to a facility-level 'fair dispatch' principle, in which facilities in each class (e.g. 300 GW) are allotted the same annual utilization hours (Mun et al., 2017; Ngan, 2010). Because of the administrative regulation of generation and benchmarking, it is difficult for a single plant to optimize resource allocation by adjusting the output of its various facilities in an integrated manner.

Furthermore, state-regulated electricity generation rights may, to some extent, discourage the closure of small-capacity or inefficient facilities. On the one hand, closing these inefficient facilities would reduce affiliated plant output because the reduced generation quota would not be transferred to other facilities under the current

[28] See, Guangdong Carbon Market's Transaction Data Report for the 2019 Compliance Year.GCEE (2021)

[29] See note 20 above.

[30] Different from Goulder and Morgenstern (2018), we consider three categories' input (i.e., fuel, technology, and other inputs) here instead of one single input, taking into account the means of potential emission reductions in power plants.

[31] http://www.gov.cn/ztzl/2006-07/01/content_324604.htm.

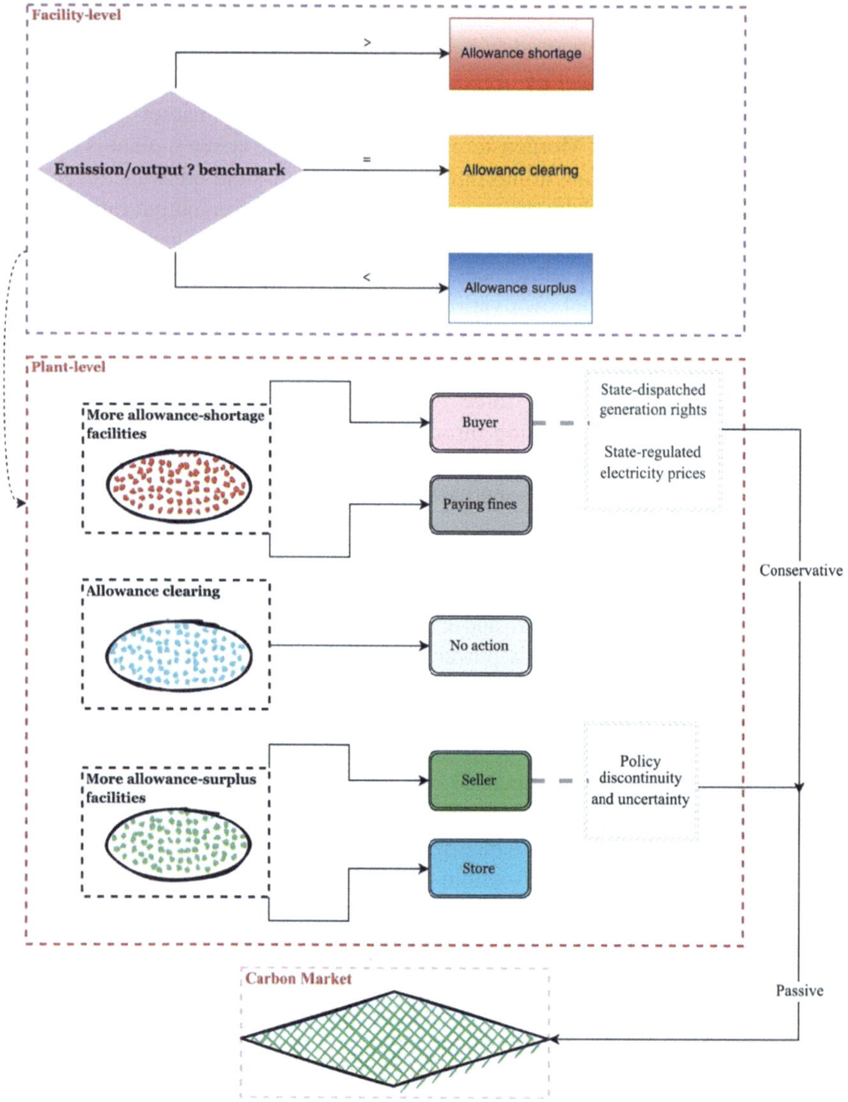

Fig. 7.6 Streamlined decision-making process for participants in China's national carbon market

facility-based generation quota allocation principle. On the other hand, allowances from closed facilities would be withdrawn in the national carbon market under the regulator's allowance allocation method,[32] reducing the affiliated plants' total carbon emissions allowances.

[32] See note 20 above.

Second, the cost pass-through strategy is constrained by state-regulated electricity prices. Because electricity prices are set by the government rather than by generating plants, cost pressures cannot be easily passed through to consumers (both industrial and residential). The government also sets transmission and distribution fees and retail electricity prices (Mun et al., 2017). Generators generate electricity with allocated quotas and connect to the corresponding grid at a regulated feed-in tariff, whereas consumers purchase it at a regulated retail price. Furthermore, power plants are under severe strain and have been severely impacted by declining electricity prices and rising coal prices in recent years. These pressures exacerbate power plants' overload and force them to participate passively in the carbon market. The carbon cost pass-through issue has received considerable attention (Kim et al., 2010), and it is critical to the survival of existing power plants. Several studies on carbon cost pass-through in electricity markets, both in the EU and US, have found pass-through rates of $\geq 50\%$ (Burtraw, 2008; Chen et al., 2011; Neuhoff et al., 2006; Sijm et al., 2006).

With a low carbon price, the strategy of increasing technology or fuel inputs often becomes the second-best alternative. When buying allowances is an alternative, increasing inputs to minimize carbon emissions can result in a lower emission–output ratio, thus getting closer to the regulator's benchmark. To maximize their profits, covered plants compare the cost of increasing their (fuel or technology) inputs to the cost of buying insufficient allowances. The overall abatement effects are undermined as covered plants prefer to buy allowances for compliance rather than increase inputs due to the abovementioned existing lower allowance prices.

Overall, the weakened response strategy has limited the active participation of power plants in the carbon market. Due to this passive participation, trading has been concentrated in the run-up to the compliance deadline, resulting in market congestion. Even if the policy is amended to give participants more time to comply in the future, congestion is unlikely to improve. The main impediment is the government's regulation of the electricity market, which includes electricity prices and generation rights. Regulated power plants must comply with both electricity generation rights and carbon allowance. Furthermore, they typically receive generation quotas before carbon allowances. Without market-driven incentives, the government allocates regulated plants' generation quotas so that they passively purchase any insufficient carbon allowances under a given generation capacity. Therefore, the carbon market is less effective at reducing emissions, and the carbon price discovery function is jeopardized.[33] The state dispatch of electricity generation rights acts as a shackle, reducing market-driven incentives and preventing regulated plants from adjusting response strategies. However, in the case of a deregulated electricity market, the strategy mix of regulated plants will be more adaptable. Tightly wound responses compel covered firms to conduct transactions passively. Although research on the association of the two markets is being conducted (Liu et al., 2017; Song et al., 2020), how China's carbon market can be developed concurrently with its electricity market reform remains unclear.

[33] Therefore, the carbon price is insufficient to guide firms' production decisions.

7.5.2 Massive Bulk Trading and Excessive Government Intervention

The prevalence of trading means based on bulk agreements may cause market congestion. Whether or not the compliance deadline is approaching, market participants prefer to trade in bulk agreements rather than listing agreements (see Fig. 7.7). During the first compliance cycle, the percentage of bulk agreements exceeded 80%. The pricing for bulk agreement transactions (> 0.1 Mt of carbon allowances) is negotiated between the parties over the counter. Unlike listing agreement trading, bulk agreement trading is conducted through a broker–dealer network rather than a centralized exchange. Participants bargain privately before agreeing on the trade. On the one hand, compared to open pooled bidding, this method provides insufficient information to the participants, thus deviating from market equilibrium; on the other hand, there is counter-party risk, which means that one party may default before the transaction or contract is completed.

Finally, government intervention can cause market congestion due to a lack of information (Zhang et al., 2016). Some local governments have intervened to find allowance sellers so that district enterprises can comply on time. The Shandong provincial government, for example, actively coordinated resources both within and outside the province through supply and demand trading negotiations, assisting eight enterprises in completing ~ 0.69 million tons of CCERs trading and six enterprises in completing ~ 1.39 million tons of Chinese emission allowances (CEAs) trading.

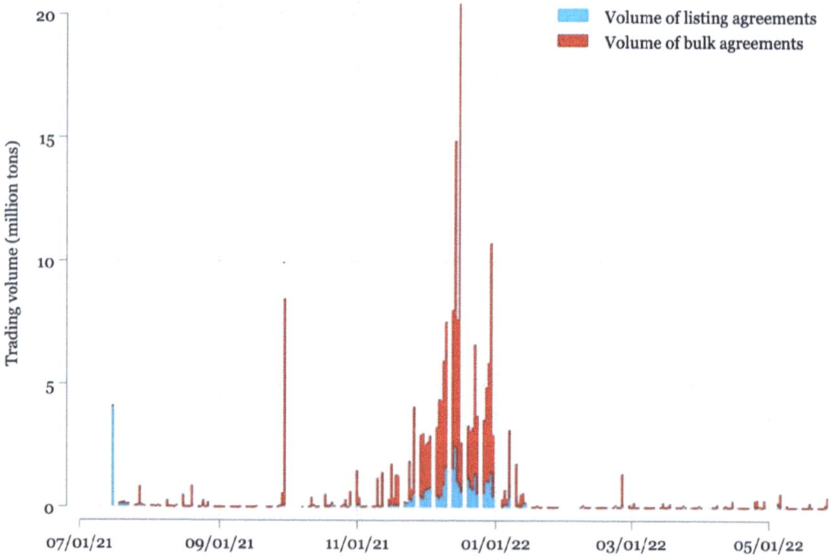

Fig. 7.7 Volume trends in China's national carbon market (bulk vs. listing agreement). *Data source* CESD database and the NDRC

7.6 Market Safety

The third Roth criterion for a well-functioning market is safety. It is critical to avoid strategic behavior, monopolies, or other undesirable factors that disrupt normal supply and demand and cause the market to become inefficient. Coase's Theorem states that the basis of emissions trading is the exchange of property rights produced by the internalization of commons (e.g. carbon emissions). Thus, genuine information regarding the quality of carbon allowances can be freely expressed in the market, and mutual satisfaction is essential.

7.6.1 Veracity of Carbon Emission Data

A critical requirement for the carbon market to function effectively is high-quality carbon emission data that approximates the actual carbon emissions of regulated entities. The monitoring, reporting, and verification (MRV) systems are widely used for ensuring the accuracy of carbon emission data. Effective MRV systems have significantly contributed to the success of the US ARP, and Heyes (2000) demonstrated that a 10% increase in EPA monitoring activities reduces emissions by ~ 0.6–4.2%. However, empirical studies conducted in developing countries indicate that misreporting of environmental data may be more prevalent (Duflo et al., 2013). Although Zhang et al. (2019) found no evidence of enterprises intentionally underreporting emissions data in Beijing and Hubei pilot carbon markets, it is too early to draw conclusions.

A recent MEE inspection report[34] reveals the existence of carbon emission data forgery in the national carbon market. This three-month special inspection focuses on four key aspects of coal sample collection, coal quality testing, verification, and reporting, and uncovers four technical service agencies that falsified test reports, manufactured false coal samples, or distorted report conclusions. It is also possible to uncover a conspiracy between key technical service agencies and the related emission-control businesses. The amount of carbon allowances allocated to enterprises is determined by the number of carbon emissions reported. The falsification of data creates significant uncertainty in carbon allowances, undermining the safety of the carbon market.

7.6.2 Regulatory Uncertainty

Regulatory uncertainty in China's carbon market also undermines the confidence of businesses to participate. Due to the delayed (near the end of the compliance cycle) issuance of allowances and the ambiguity around essential allowance information

[34] https://www.mee.gov.cn/ywgz/ydqhbh/wsqtkz/202203/t20220314_971398.shtml.

(such as banking), participants were reluctant to take part in the market. Some large power groups have a large surplus of allowances but are hesitant to sell them (thus limiting the supply of allowances), forcing some shortfall enterprises to seek sellers through intermediaries. The usage of CCERs in compliance[35] has increased due to the conservative approach toward allowances. In addition, a lack of policy certainty and continuity can make businesses feel insecure, discouraging them from participating in the carbon market or reducing emissions. Policy uncertainties such as tightening the total supply of carbon allowances, the implementation of allowance auctions, and the shift from intensity control to total control have resulted in more conservative decisions of businesses and thus lower market activity. Zhang et al. (2015) concluded that firms' willingness to reduce pollution is adversely affected by the perception of regulatory uncertainty in terms of social pressure and attitudes toward pollution control. Furthermore, excessive allowance concentration among the top players (such as the Big Five[36]) can lead to market near-monopolies or strategic bargaining, undermining potential market participants' confidence.

7.7 Concluding Remarks and Policy Implication

China's national carbon market, which currently includes the electricity sector only, has been operational for more than a year. The performance of the national carbon market for the electricity sector is critical for the inclusion of other carbon-intensive industries (such as the cement and steel industries) and the achievement of China's mid-century carbon neutrality goal (Wang et al., 2023; Zhao et al., 2023)[37]; thus, policymakers and stakeholders must act quickly to identify and address potential barriers affecting carbon market performance. The preceding systematic review investigates the evolution and practical application of the ETS in China, including SO_2 emissions trading pilots, regional carbon market pilots, and the electricity sector's national carbon market, focusing on scheme design and market performance. Certain obstacles to China's national carbon market for the electricity sector's subpar market performance can be overcome by considering a market-based theoretical framework (the Roth criteria of effective market design), policy interaction, and electricity sector–specific mechanisms. First, the low heterogeneity of participants' energy intensities and regional carbon controls result in limited trading opportunities and market segmentation, which thins the market. Second, falsified carbon emissions data and regulatory uncertainty jeopardize market safety. Third, market congestion

[35] Approximately 34 million tons of CCERs were used for offsets in the first compliance cycle of the national carbon market.

[36] The Big Five power generation companies in China, namely State Power Investment Corporation (SPIC), China Guodian Corporation (Guodian, GD), China Huaneng Group (Huaneng, HN), China Huadian Corporation (Huadian, HD), and China Datang Corporation (Datang, DT), together account for almost half of the total generation assets in the country.

[37] Aside from the electrical and industrial sectors, green transformation in other sectors (such as agriculture) is critical to China's carbon neutrality aspirations.

has been caused by the concentration of transactions, primarily in bulk, close to the compliance deadline and excessive government intervention. Finally, the government's regulation of the electricity system limits the ability of the carbon market to reduce emissions.

This paper contributes to a better understanding of China's national carbon market—the largest beyond the EU ETS—from a market design perspective. Using the Roth criterion and considering China's state-regulated electricity market, this study contributes to the body of knowledge on market–government relations in China. It is argued that for effective emission reduction, China's national carbon market, which is policy-driven and monitored by the central government, must rely on a thriving market function. A closer look into the Chinese carbon market can thus provide insights into the dynamic interaction between market forces and governmental regulation. Our research provides guiding policy insights for the development of China's carbon market and also outlines the significant implications for other countries (particularly developing economies that are about to apply this carbon pricing tool) in terms of establishing a thick, liquid, and safe carbon market.

We focus on these critical elements and conclude with four significant recommendations for a more efficient carbon market. First, a national unified carbon market must be established to ensure market thickness. The Chinese central government's *Opinions on Accelerating the Construction of the National Unified Market*,[38] published in April 2022, proposes fostering a nationwide unified ecological and environmental market (including the carbon market), hastening the establishment of nationwide unified market rules, and dismantling local protection and market segmentation. To remove the restrictions on cross-regional trade, regional total carbon regulations should be included in the design of the national carbon market, and more sectors should be included as soon as possible to thicken the market (Chen et al., 2023; Zhou et al., 2021).[39] The current national carbon market only includes the electricity sector, which limits the market's size, cost-efficiency, and ability to contribute to carbon neutrality. Indeed, firms in high-emission industries such as steel, nonferrous metals, and papermaking have been organized to report their carbon emission data,[40] paving the way for their inclusion in the national carbon market. We believe that once a unified national carbon market with more high-emitting companies is established, this market-based policy tool, led by China's central government and the most important policy tool in the policy toolkit for achieving the 2060 carbon neutrality target, will considerably weaken the original tier-based allocation of emission reduction mandates. It is also suggested that the China Certified Emission Reduction (CCER) mechanism be restarted to facilitate the carbon market's liquidity.

[38] http://www.gov.cn/zhengce/2022-04/10/content_5684385.htm.

[39] The achievement of carbon neutrality targets requires good coordination between different sectors and provinces in terms of emission reduction targets.

[40] See, the Notification on Key Points for Management of Enterprises' Greenhouse Gas Emissions Reporting in 2022.

Second, improving the management of enterprise carbon emissions disclosure is essential. For a functioning carbon market, accurate and dependable data are paramount. With the MEE having identified common issues such as the fabrication of carbon emission reporting data, further compliance will shift its emphasis toward the reinforcement of greenhouse gas (GHG) emission data management. The national carbon market is still nascent, so there must be further development in data management. To improve data accuracy, it is necessary to optimize information collection technology, such as via the use of Internet of Things and remote sensing technologies. Furthermore, improving and standardizing accounting standards for corporate carbon emissions and encouraging a continuous carbon emission monitoring system are critical. More importantly, from an institutional standpoint, stronger penalties for violations compromising data accuracy are needed to provide a safer market environment for participating entities. In short, a carbon market governed by more accurate big data is required.

Third, the central state must urgently find the right balance of oversight to regulate the carbon market properly and rationally. Ambiguous or inappropriate boundaries between the state and the market should be eliminated. During the initial compliance cycle, examples of state interference (particularly from local authorities) were observed. Therefore, to improve China's carbon market necessitate appropriate state oversight. In particular, the government should strive to develop good market rules, such as allowance allocation, allowance storage, and penalties for noncompliance, and provide a clear policy roadmap while minimizing inappropriate intervention in specific trading practices. The state must also improve its systems for preventing, spotting, and responding to potential speculations, monopolies, and other detrimental factors that threaten market stability. Furthermore, as most power companies in the carbon market are large state-owned enterprises, it is unknown whether these colossal companies with monopoly power will create market power and undermine carbon market safety as more carbon-intensive industries are included in the future. Therefore, additional optimization of carbon market management may be necessary to mitigate the threat that such potential market power poses to the healthy development of the carbon market.

Fourth, better coordination between the carbon market and other related policies is essential. Other policies must be coordinated and must complement carbon pricing to reduce emissions in a cost-effective manner. However, these policies may be developed by different institutions or at different stages, and they may have complex interactions that were not anticipated when they were created. Thus, the national carbon market must effectively coordinate with other policy mechanisms such as energy-use rights and green electricity trading to promote carbon neutrality. Concurrently, the MEE oversees the carbon market and will need to collaborate with other agencies, such as the NDRC.

Finally, it is critical to advance the reform of the electricity market (Wu et al., 2021). Several rounds of reform have yielded insufficient results. Strengthening administrative control over the electricity market while maintaining performance in the carbon market is a balancing act. If we are to play a decisive role in market resource allocation, we must shift government functions away from administrative control and toward management and services. The centralized distribution of electricity generation rights reduces businesses' willingness to trade freely and aggressively. Additionally, power firms find it challenging to successfully pass through the consequence of decreasing emissions to consumers due to government regulation of electricity prices. To rationalize electricity price regulation, it is crucial to support an orderly change in pricing; thus, China should develop its carbon market while also reforming its electricity market.

References

Abdulkadiroğlu, A., Pathak, P. A., & Roth, A. E. (2005). The New York City high school match. *American Economic Review, 95*(2), 364–367.

Almond, D., & Zhang, S. (2021). Carbon-trading pilot programs in China and local air quality. *AEA Papers and Proceedings, 111*, 391–395.

Balietti, A. C. (2016). Trader types and volatility of emission allowance prices. Evidence from EU ETS Phase I. *Energy Policy, 98*, 607–620.

Bosquet, B. (2000). Environmental tax reform: Does it work? A survey of the empirical evidence. *Ecological Economics, 34*(1), 19–32.

Burtraw, D. (2008). Regulating CO_2 in electricity markets: Sources or consumers? *Climate Policy, 8*(6), 588–606.

Cao, J., Ho, M. S., Ma, R., & Teng, F. (2021). When carbon emission trading meets a regulated industry: Evidence from the electricity sector of China. *Journal of Public Economics, 200*, 104470.

Chang, Y.-C., & Wang, N. (2010). Environmental regulations and emissions trading in China. *Energy Policy, 38*(7), 3356–3364.

Chen, Y., Liu, A. L., & Hobbs, B. F. (2011). Economic and emissions implications of load-based, source-based, and first-seller emissions trading programs under California AB32. *Operations Research, 59*(3), 696–712.

Chen, X., & Xu, J. (2018). Carbon trading scheme in the People's Republic of China: evaluating the performance of seven pilot projects. *Asian Development Review, 35*(2), 131–152.

Chen, M., Yu, D., Shi, X., & Wang, K. (2023). Emission reduction tournament would postpone carbon peaking in China. *Chinese Political Science Review, 8*(2), 273–303.

Crocker, T. D. (1966). The structuring of atmospheric pollution control systems. *The Economics of Air Pollution, 61*, 81–84.

Cui, J., Wang, C., Zhang, J., & Zheng, Y. (2021). The effectiveness of China's regional carbon market pilots in reducing firm emissions. *Proceedings of the National Academy of Sciences, 118*(52), e2109912118.

Dales, J. H. (1968). Land, water, and ownership. *The Canadian Journal of Economics, 1*(4), 791–804.

Dechezleprêtre, A., Glachant, M., & Ménière, Y. (2009). Technology transfer by CDM projects: a comparison of Brazil, China, Idia and Mexico. *Energy Policy, 37*(2), 703–711.

Dickhaut, J., Lin, S., Porter, D., & Smith, V. (2012). Commodity durability, trader specialization, and market performance. *Proceedings of the National Academy of Sciences of the United States of America, 109*(5), 1425–1430.

Du, Y., & Takeuchi, K. (2019). Can climate mitigation help the poor? Measuring impacts of the CDM in rural China. *Journal of Environmental Economics and Management, 95*, 178–197.

Dudek, D., Qing, H., & Zhang, J. (2004). *Environmental regulation capacity analysis: Report of* SO_2 *control and emissions trading cases in China*. Environmental Defense Fund.

Duflo, E., Greenstone, M., Pande, R., & Ryan, N. (2013). Truth-telling by third-party auditors and the response of polluting firms: Experimental evidence from India. *The Quarterly Journal of Economics, 128*(4), 1499–1545.

Gans, J. S., & Stern, S. (2010). Is there a market for ideas? *Industrial and Corporate Change, 19*(3), 805–837.

Gilley, B. (2012). Authoritarian environmentalism and China's response to climate change. *Environmental Politics, 21*(2), 287–307.

Goulder, L. H., & Morgenstern, R. D. (2018). China's rate-based approach to reducing CO_2 emissions: attractions, limitations, and alternatives. *AEA Papers and Proceedings, 108*, 458–462.

Guan, D., Peters, G. P., Weber, C. L., & Hubacek, K. (2009). Journey to world top emitter: An analysis of the driving forces of China's recent CO_2 emissions surge. *Geophysical Research Letters, 36*(4).

Guangzhou Carbon Emissions Exchange. (2021). Guangdong carbon market's transaction data report for the 2019 compliance year.

Hart, C., & Zhong, M. (2014). China's regional carbon trading experiments and the development of a national market: Lessons from China's SO_2 trading programme. *Energy and Environment, 25*(3–4), 577–592.

Heyes, A. (2000). Implementing environmental regulation: Enforcement and compliance. *Journal of Regulatory Economics, 17*(2), 107–129.

Kim, W., Chattopadhyay, D., & Park, J. (2010). Impact of carbon cost on wholesale electricity price: A note on price pass-through issues. *Energy, 35*(8):3441–3448

Li, J., Yao, Y., & Wang, X. (2022). The first compliance cycle of China's national emissions trading scheme: Insights and implications. *Carbon Neutrality, 1*(1), 34.

Liu, Z., Guan, D., Crawford-Brown, D., Zhang, Q., He, K., & Liu, J. (2013). Energy policy: A low-carbon road map for China. *Nature, 500*(7461), 143–145.

Liu, J., Woodward, R. T., & Zhang, Y. (2021). Has carbon emissions trading reduced PM2.5 in China? *Environmental Science and Technology, 55*(10): 6631–6643.

Liu, Y., Zhang, N., Kang, C., Xia, Q., Wu, H., & Chen, Z. (2017). Impact of carbon market on China's electricity market: An equilibrium analysis. In *2017 IEEE Power Energy Society General Meeting,* Chicago, IL, USA, pp 1–5

Lo, A. Y. (2013). Carbon trading in a socialist market economy: Can China make a difference? *Ecological Economics, 87*, 72–74.

Lo, A. Y. (2016). Challenges to the development of carbon markets in China. *Climate Policy, 16*(1), 109–124.

Martin, R., Muuls, M., & Wagner, U. J. (2016). The impact of the European Union emissions trading scheme on regulated firms: What is the evidence after ten years? *Review of Environmental Economics and Policy, 10*(1), 129–148.

Ministry of Environmental Protection (MEP). (2008). *Suggestion on the improvement of emissions trading policy*. Ministry of Environmental Protection of the People's Republic of China.

Montagnoli, A., & de Vries, F. P. (2010). Carbon trading thickness and market efficiency. *Energy Economics, 32*(6), 1331–1336.

Montgomery, W. D. (1972). Markets in licenses and efficient pollution control programs. *Journal of Economic Theory, 5*(3), 395–418.

Mun, H., Zhongmin, W., & Zichao, Y. (2017). *China's Power Generation Dispatch. Resources for the Future (RFF).* https://www.rff.org/publications/reports/chinas-power-generation-dispatch/.

Munnings, C., Morgenstern, R. D., Wang, Z., & Liu, X. (2016). Assessing the design of three carbon trading pilot programs in China. *Energy Policy, 96*, 688–699.

Neuhoff, K., Martinez, K. K., & Sato, M. (2006). Allocation, incentives and distortions: The impact of EU ETS emissions allowance allocations to the electricity sector. *Climate Policy, 6*(1), 73–91.

Ngan, H. W. (2010). Electricity regulation and electricity market reforms in China. *Energy Policy, 38*(5), 2142–2148.

Roth, A. E. (1991). A natural experiment in the organization of entry-level labor markets: Regional markets for new physicians and surgeons in the United Kingdom. *The American Economic Review, 81*(3), 415–440.

Roth, A. E. (2007). The art of designing markets. *Harvard Business Review, 85*(10), 118–126.

Roth, A. E. (2008). What have we learned from market design? *The Economic Journal, 118*(527), 285–310.

Roth, A. E., Sönmez, T., & Ünver, M. U. (2005). A kidney exchange clearinghouse in New England. *American Economic Review, 95*(2), 376–380.

Sabbaghi, O., & Sabbaghi, N. (2011). Carbon financial instruments, thin trading, and volatility: Evidence from the Chicago Climate Exchange. *The Quarterly Review of Economics and Finance, 51*(4), 399–407.

Shin, S. (2013). China's failure of policy innovation: The case of sulphur dioxide emission trading. *Environmental Politics, 22*(6), 918–934.

Sijm, J., Neuhoff, K., & Chen, Y. (2006). CO_2 cost pass-through and windfall profits in the power sector. *Climate Policy, 6*(1), 49–72.

Song, Y., Liu, T., Ye, B., & Li, Y. (2020). Linking carbon market and electricity market for promoting the grid parity of photovoltaic electricity in China. *Energy, 211*, 118924.

Sorrell, S., & Sijm, J. (2003). Carbon trading in the policy mix. *Oxford Review of Economic Policy, 19*, 420–437.

State Council of the People's Republic of China. (2011). Notice of the State Council on Issuing the Work Plan for Controlling Greenhouse Gas Emissions during the Twelfth Five-Year Plan. Beijing: The State Council No. [2011]41.

State Environmental Protection Bureau (SEPA). (2002). Notice on Beginning the Pilots of Promote the Research Program on China's Sulfur Dioxide Control and Emissions Trading Policy. Beijing: State Environmental Protection Bureau No. [2002]51.

Stavins, R. N. (1997). Policy instruments for climate change: How can national governments address a global problem rethinking environmental protection for the 21st century. *University of Chicago Legal Forum, 1997*, 293–330.

Stavins, R. N. (1998). What can we learn from the grand policy experiment? Lessons from SO_2 allowance trading. *Journal of Economic Perspectives, 12*(3), 69–88.

Stranlund, J. K., Chavez, C. A., & Field, B. C. (2002). Enforcing emissions trading programs: Theory, practice, and performance. *Policy Studies Journal, 30*(3), 343–361.

Tao, J., & Mah, D. N. (2009). Between market and state: Dilemmas of environmental governance in China's sulphur dioxide emission trading system. *Environment and Planning C: Government and Policy, 27*(1), 175–188.

The National Development and Reform Commission (NDRC). (2011a). Notice on Carrying out the Pilot Project on Carbon Emissions Trading. The NDRC No. [2011]2601.

The National Development and Reform Commission (NDRC). (2011b). Notice on Issuing the Implementation Plan for Energy Conservation and Low-Carbon Action of Ten Thousand Enterprises. The NDRC No. [2011]2873.

The National Development and Reform Commission (NDRC). (2017). National Development and Reform Commission on the Issuance of the National Carbon Emissions Trading Market Construction Plan (Power Generation Sector). The NDRC No. [2017]2191.

Tietenberg, T. (2006). Emissions trading: principles and practice. 2nd ed. Routledge.

Wang, Q., & Wu, S. (2018). Carbon trading thickness and market efficiency in a socialist market economy. *Chinese Journal of Population Resources and Environment, 16*(2), 109–119.

Wang, S., Yuan, L., & Gong, B. (2023). China's agricultural green transition and high-quality development toward carbon neutrality. *Chinese Political Science Review, 8*(2), 240–272.

Wu, X., Marín Del Valle, T., Zheng, L., Shi, Y., Du, Y., & Luo, W. (2023). Temporal changes in sectoral carbon productivity and corresponding driving factors: Implications for carbon governance in Zhejiang Province. *Journal of Chinese Governance, 8*(3), 322–348.

Xiao, J., Li, G., Xie, L., Wang, S., & Yu, L. (2021). Decarbonizing China's power sector by 2030 with consideration of technological progress and cross-regional power transmission. *Energy Policy, 150*, 112150.

Xu, Y. (2011). China's functioning market for sulfur dioxide scrubbing technologies. *Environmental Science & Technology, 45*(21), 9161–9167.

Xu, Y., Yang, C.-J., & Xuan, X. (2013). Engineering and optimization approaches to enhance the thermal efficiency of coal electricity generation in China. *Energy Policy, 60*, 356–363.

Yang, J., & Schreifels, J. (2003). Implementing SO_2 Emissions in China. Paper to OECD Global Forum on Sustainable Development: Emissions Trading. France.

Yu, P., Cai, Z., & Sun, Y. (2021). Does the emissions trading system in developing countries accelerate carbon leakage through OFDI? Evidence from China. *Energy Economics, 101*, 105397.

Yu, Z., Geng, Y., Dai, H., Wu, R., Liu, Z., Tian, X., & Bleischwitz, R. (2018). A general equilibrium analysis on the impacts of regional and sectoral emission allowance allocation at carbon trading market. *Journal of Cleaner Production, 192*, 421–432.

Zhang, B., Fei, H., He, P., Xu, Y., Dong, Z., & Young, O. R. (2016). The indecisive role of the market in China's SO_2 and COD emissions trading. *Environmental Politics, 25*(5), 875–898.

Zhang, B., Fei, H., Zhang, Y., & Liu, B. (2015). Regulatory uncertainty and corporate pollution control strategies: An empirical study of the 'pay for permit' policy in the Tai Lake Basin. *Environment and Planning C: Government and Policy, 33*(1), 118–135.

Zhang, B., Zhang, H., Liu, B., & Bi, J. (2013a). Policy interactions and underperforming emission trading markets in China. *Environmental Science and Technology, 47*(13), 7077–7084.

Zhang, D., Karplus, V. J., Cassisa, C., & Zhang, X. (2014). Emissions trading in China: Progress and prospects. *Energy Policy, 75*, 9–16.

Zhang, D., Rausch, S., Karplus, V. J., & Zhang, X. (2013b). Quantifying regional economic impacts of CO_2 intensity targets in China. *Energy Economics, 40*, 687–701.

Zhang, J., Wang, Z., & Du, X. (2017). Lessons learned from China's regional carbon market pilots. *Economics of Energy and Environmental Policy, 6*(2), 19–38.

Zhang, D., Zhang, Q., Qi, S., Huang, J., Karplus, V. J., & Zhang, X. (2019). Integrity of firms' emissions reporting in China's early carbon markets. *Nature Climate Change, 9*(2), 164–169.

Zhao, M., Shi, R., Du, R., & Yao, L. (2023). The pathway to China's carbon-neutral agriculture: Measures, potential and future strategies. *Chinese Political Science Review, 8*(2), 304–324.

Zhou, B., Zhou, F., Zhou, D., Qiao, J., & Xue, B. (2021). Improvement of environmental performance and optimization of industrial structure of the Yangtze River Economic Belt in China: Going forward together or restraining each other? *Journal of Chinese Governance, 6*(3), 435–455.

Zhu, X. (2012). Understanding China's growth: Past, present, and future. *Journal of Economic Perspectives, 26*(4), 103–124.

Zhu, J., Fan, Y., Deng, X., & Xue, L. (2019). Low-carbon innovation induced by emissions trading in China. *Nature Communications, 10*(1), 4088.

Chapter 8
Efficiency Versus Equity as China's National Carbon Market Meets Provincial Electricity Markets

Jian Cui, Feng Song, and Zhigao Jiang

Abstract Emissions reduction in the electricity sector is critical in achieving China's carbon neutrality target. While a national carbon trading market that covers the electricity sector has been established, its effectiveness depends on how this sector evolves into being a more integrated market. This study evaluated the impact of China's electricity market integration on the cost-effectiveness of carbon pricing. An integrated (regional electricity market) and a segmented (provincial electricity market) market scenario were used to identify possible reform paths going forward. Using high-frequency datasets of the five southern provinces in 2018, we assessed the impact of electricity market integration on the abatement potential and cost-effectiveness of carbon pricing. We found that carbon prices need to be as high as 200 yuan/ton to begin achieving overall carbon reduction. In this context, the regional market is more cost-effective in reducing emissions than the provincial one, as the abatement costs are saved by around 60% compared to the latter under the same emission reduction targets. However, the regional market may also raise potential equity issues. The provincial-level distribution of carbon emission reductions, as well as the withdrawal of coal power, are more concentrated in the regional market than in the provincial one, which indicates an inequitable social-economic-environmental impacts of market integration. Our research findings would help to improve policymakers' understanding of the interaction between carbon pricing and electricity market reforms. This would then assist them in coordinating an effective design of both the carbon and electricity markets, in addition to supporting China's carbon neutrality target.

Keywords Electricity market reform · Carbon market · Market integration · Carbon emissions · Equity and efficiency

J. Cui (✉) · F. Song
School of Applied Economics, Renmin University of China, Beijing, China
e-mail: jiancui@cup.edu.cn

Z. Jiang
Zhineng Consultant Company, Beijing, China

B. Gong et al. (eds.), *Chinese Governance and Transformation Towards Carbon Neutrality*, Resources, Environment and Agricultural Development,
https://doi.org/10.1007/978-981-97-9996-1_8

8.1 Introduction

As the world's current largest carbon emitter, China has announced its goal of achieving a carbon emission peak before 2030 and then carbon neutrality by 2060. To help in these endeavors, a national carbon trading market was launched in 2021. This market covers > 2000 thermal generators that are responsible for about half of China's carbon emissions, as well as about 10–14% of the world's total.

Carbon pricing is expected to encourage fuel switching within the electricity sector and, thus, reduce overall carbon emission; however, its effectiveness depends crucially on the existence of a well-functioning electricity market in order to pass through the carbon costs and to achieve equalized marginal abatement costs across both generators and regions. However, China's electricity sector had long been structured as a planning system, in which both the price and production were organized by the government and not determined by the merit order of generation costs. Even though China's electricity sector has experienced several rounds of restructurings and reforms since 1985 (Pollitt et al., 2017; Wang & Chen, 2012), a market-based resource allocation system is still in progress. Up to the end of 2020, the share of market-based electricity generation only accounted for 42% of the total generation.

The progress and characteristics of these electricity sector reforms will interact with and impact the effectiveness of the carbon market. One notable feature of China's electricity market reform is its provincial segmentation. Until now > 80% of electricity trade was transacted within the provincial markets, and cross-provincial electricity trading were limited and administratively implemented.

This market segmentation not only affects the efficiency of the electricity sector, but also weakens that of carbon pricing by restricting generation substitution across various provinces. While integrating electricity markets would help to improve the effectiveness of carbon pricing, it could also have certain distributional impacts across provinces, thereby raising equity concerns. As such, these impacts need to be quantitatively evaluated to improve both academic and policy understanding of the interaction between the electricity and carbon markets.

In this study, we adopted scenario simulations and the partial equilibrium model to evaluate and compare the effectiveness of carbon pricing on emission reduction efforts, as well as the distributional impacts between a regional versus a provincial electricity market scenario. Through using the unique high-frequency datasets of the five provinces in China Southern Electricity Grid in 2018, we simulated the emission reductions and abatement costs caused by the carbon pricing of the electricity sector under different scenarios, and then discuss the potential equity issues that may then arise.

This study's results can be summarized as follows. First, the carbon market cannot achieve any carbon emission until the carbon price increases to 200 yuan/ton in the regional electricity market scenario and 400 yuan/ton in the provincial market scenario, respectively, which is far higher than the current price. Second, the regional market is much more cost-effective in reducing carbon emissions compared with the provincial market. Given the same emission reduction targets, the abatement costs are reduced by around 60% more in the regional market than in the provincial market. This is because market integration amplifies the substitution effect of carbon pricing by allowing for the cross-provincial replacement of high-emission-efficiency units for low-emission-efficiency ones. Finally, the regional market also raises potential equity issues as electricity production and carbon emissions are then redistributed across various provinces. Compared with the provincial market scenario, emission reductions are more concentrated in Yunnan and Guizhou provinces within a regional market model. It is accompanied with the massive withdrawal of coal power in these provinces, which then indicates the occurrence of an inequitable impact of market integration on the electricity industry and economic development in each province.

Our study aimed to make two contributions to the existing literature and policy debates. First, we perform a detailed ex ante assessment of the potential impacts of China's newly launched carbon market on both its carbon reduction and electricity sectors, including its electricity generation structure, inter-provincial trading, and the resulting distributional impacts across provinces. Because the carbon market only covers the electricity sector, we analyzed how electricity market reforms and carbon market pricing interact with one another. Our results then illustrate how the electricity market's design affects the abatement potential and cost-effectiveness of carbon pricing.

Although there are many studies that have investigated the design and impact of carbon pricing in Europe and the US, there have been relatively few that have focused on China's carbon market specifically. In the Chinese context specifically, the studies by Cui et al. (2018) and Cao et al., (2021a, 2021b) both conducted an ex post evaluation of the effectiveness of China's pilot carbon trading programs across seven provinces. Among the few studies that have conducted an ex ante impact analysis of the national carbon market's potential effects, most have adopted the Computable General Equilibrium model, which assumes all industries are involved in the carbon market, with them then examining the relative impacts from the perspectives of different sectors, regions, and households (Cao et al., 2021a, 2021b; Fan et al., 2016; Huang et al., 2019).

In contrast with these prior studies, we adopted the partial equilibrium model as it provides a detailed depiction of the electricity sector characteristics as well as the unique features of China's carbon market using the high-frequency electricity load, production, and trade data. The use of this model would then help to improve the accuracy of assessments on the potential effects of carbon reduction and their overall cost-effectiveness. In addition, the scenario simulation considers electricity sector reform progress, as well as possible future directions. The results would then help improve policy makers' understanding of the interactions between the electricity and carbon markets, which would then allow them to coordinate the design of these two markets to help achieve China's carbon neutrality target.

Second, by simulating the heterogeneous impacts of carbon pricing on emissions across different provinces, we also addressed the CO_2 emission efficiency-equity trade-off between different electricity market reform designs. China is characterized by its diversity of resource endowments, electricity generation sources (and their associated carbon emission), and economic development by virtue of its large territory. Hence, a national carbon market can only achieve cost-effectiveness if it is able to equalize the resulting marginal abatement costs across regions, which would then require an integrated electricity market that encourages fuel-switching within a larger market through cross-province electricity trading and decreased carbon leakage across provinces. However, an equity-efficiency trade-off arises when provincial markets are integrated. Some provinces may be concerned with the negative economic and environmental impacts of these reforms. In this context, a quantitative assessment of these distributional impacts is a prerequisite in the formation of policy measures that are aimed at easing these concerns.

The rest of this paper is structured as follows. Section 8.2 analyzes the links between the carbon and electricity markets. Section 8.3 then introduces the scenarios and simulation methods used in this study and summarizes its datasets. Section 8.4 presents the simulation results of the carbon emission conditions at different carbon prices in different scenarios, as well as discussing the efficiency and equity of emission reduction. Section 8.5 then concludes this paper.

8.2 The Interactions Between the Electricity and Carbon Markets

In theory, the effect of carbon pricing in the electricity sector occurs through the merit order effect as this then encourages stakeholders to engage in fuel switching from high to low emission intensity, which then reduces the overall carbon emission rate. By equalizing the marginal abatement costs among generators across various regions, the cost-effectiveness could be achieved. However, the actual effectiveness depends on the interactions between the carbon market and the electricity market. Specifically, the carbon market's features, the electricity marketization reform, and the electricity supply profile would affect the potential effectiveness of carbon pricing strategies. Below, we analytically outline when and how carbon pricing works in the electricity sector, and then analyze the impact of electricity market integration on the effectiveness of carbon pricing.

8.2.1 Background on China's Carbon Market and Electricity Sector

China's carbon market has several important features that can affect its effectiveness. First, it is a national market as it allows trading of emissions allowances across regions. Second, it has adopted a tradable performance standard for its allowance allocation, which is different from the EU and US carbon markets. It is a rate-based instrument and does not have a predetermined absolute cap on the total number of emissions allowances. The number of emissions allowances granted to a given electricity plant is the product of the benchmark emission intensity assigned to the plant and the plant's level of output in that period. Third, four benchmarks are then applied to different technology categories, namely coal-fired units with a capacity of 300 MW and below, coal-fired units with a capacity of > 300 MW, gas-fired units, and other unconventional coal-fired units. Within each category, units with a carbon intensity below their benchmark will benefit from the sale of excess allowances, and tend to be allocated more output as carbon prices increase. As Fischer (2001), Fischer and Newell (2008) and Goulder et al. (2019) pointed out, a rate-based carbon market is less effective than a cap-based market given the same reduction target since it implicitly subsidizes the output. But it can have less impact on electricity output and price increase, thus has an attraction of fairness and political feasibility.

The progress of electricity sector reform and the interaction between electricity market and carbon market also affects the effectiveness of carbon pricing. A necessary condition for carbon pricing to be able to reduce generators' overall carbon emissions is that electricity plants need to sufficiently respond to changes in it. Before adopting the electricity marketization reform, China implemented a benchmark on-grid tariff in the electricity sector; that is, the same electricity generation technology would receive the same on-grid tariff as set by the government, resulting in no responses from these plants to changes in carbon prices. Therefore, in the absence of a market system that then reflects carbon costs, it is then difficult for carbon pricing to affect the generation structure, as well as to reduce the carbon emissions, of the electricity sector.

In 2015, China inaugurated a new reform with the goal of increasing the market-based allocation mechanism's role in both the electricity generation and retail segments, as well as to improve the regulation of distribution and transmission. This reform has, so far, helped the nation progress towards its marketization goal. The share of market-based electricity transactions within the total electricity consumption rate has increased from 13% in 2015 to 42% in 2020 (Fig. 8.1). However, this process is still far from being able to establish an efficient market due to both the common reform obstacles faced within international settings and the unique obstacles faced within China's institutional context. Based on this, several papers have provided a comprehensive review on this process and its potential pitfalls (Davidson & Pérez-Arriaga, 2020; Lin et al., 2019; Lin et al., 2019).

8.2.2 *Merit Order Effect of Carbon Pricing in the Electricity Market and the Related Abatement Costs*

8.2.2.1 Carbon Pricing and Carbon Reduction

In a perfectly competitive electricity market—which is the goal of China's electricity sector reform—wholesale markets determine the electricity price according

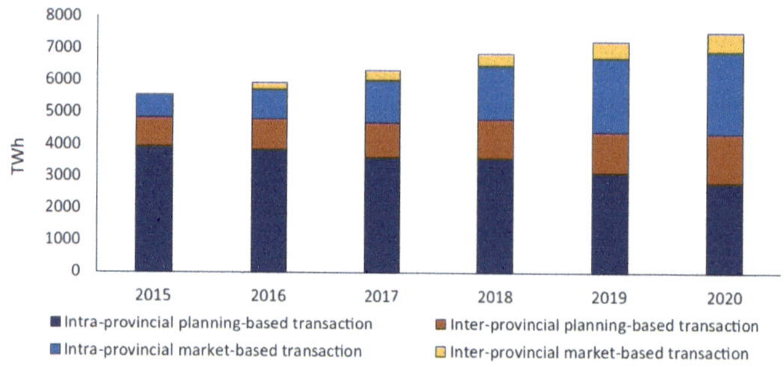

Fig. 8.1 China's electricity transaction from 2015 to 2020. *Note* Data are collected from the "Power Exchange Annual Report" published by the State Grid Corporation of China

to demand and supply bids (i.e., the "merit order curve"), wherein the latter is determined by the marginal costs of available electricity plants. Carbon pricing then affects the merit order of this supply curve by increasing the marginal costs of fossil-fuel electricity plants, inducing substitution among different emission-intensity generation, as well as promoting carbon reduction.

Consequently, the magnitude of this substitution effect depends on the current supply profile in the market. Intuitively speaking, if carbon pricing only induces the switch among the coal-electricity plants, it would then only induce a small degree of emissions reductions overall. As shown in Fig. 8.2, for Yunnan, because its installed capacity is only composed of coal power and hydropower, introducing carbon pricing might have minor effects on its adoption of the merit order if the substitution is constrained within in the province. For Guangdong, wherein the supply curve is composed of gas and coal power, a moderate carbon price would then encourage certain gas plants to shift their positions within their coal plants to be based more on the merit order, thereby reducing their overall carbon emissions. At higher carbon prices, carbon emissions will decrease significantly as a larger amount of coal is then substituted by gas.

8.2.2.2 Carbon Abatement Costs

Carbon pricing can influence the merit order so that it then switches plants' output from coal power to the more expensive gas power, production costs (e.g., generation and transmission costs) then increase as carbon prices increase. In addition, carbon pricing imposes additional allowance costs on electricity plants that are then passed onto consumers through biddings within the electricity market. Therefore, these abatement costs are measurable as increases in the production and allowance costs following the transition from a no-carbon pricing system to one that requires a carbon price for a given reduction target.

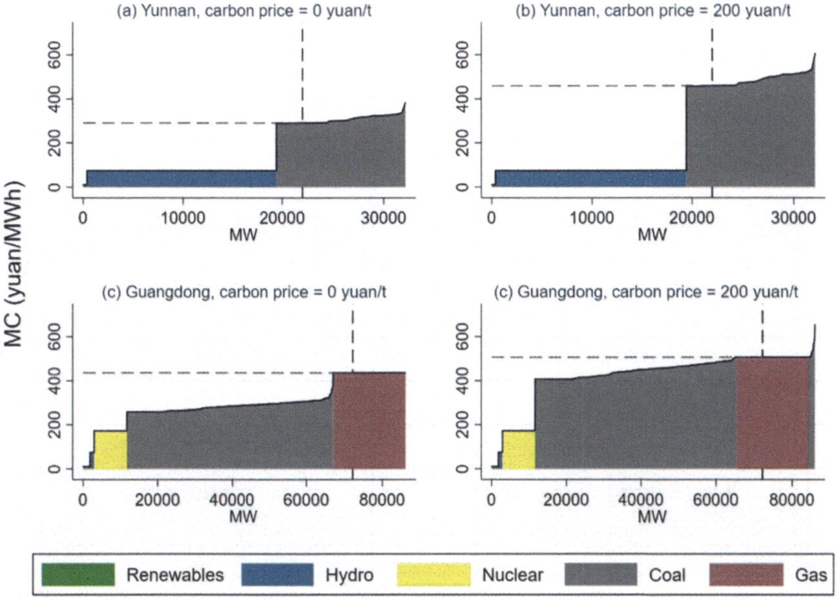

Fig. 8.2 An illustrative example of the merit order effects of different carbon prices: Yunnan and Guangdong. *Note* The vertical and horizontal dashed lines represent the demand curve and market clearing prices, respectively

8.2.3 Electricity Market Integration and Its Impact on Carbon Pricing Effectiveness

Regulatory fragmentation across provinces has been another longstanding feature of China's electricity system (Qi et al., 2019). Due to the nation's extensive history of electricity shortages, China's electricity supply and demand system was first balanced within each province. Provinces have traditionally been reluctant to increase their imports from other regions unless they are facing a specific shortage in order to protect their local generators. This is also related to the longstanding occurrence of interprovincial barriers arising from local protectionism in China's provincial market (Naughton, 2003; Poncet, 2003; Wei & Zheng, 2017; Young, 2000; Zhou, 2004).

A key step for China's electricity market reform is to achieve market integration among different provinces. Drawing lessons from the failure of the 2002 reform, a strategy of this round of reform is to start its implementation from provincial markets to incentivize local governments so that the reform can gain momentum. Provincial governments are responsible for market reform, while the central government only serves to provide general guidelines (Pollitt et al., 2017; Zhang et al., 2018). This can then lead to a significant amount of diversity in the nation's market designs, as

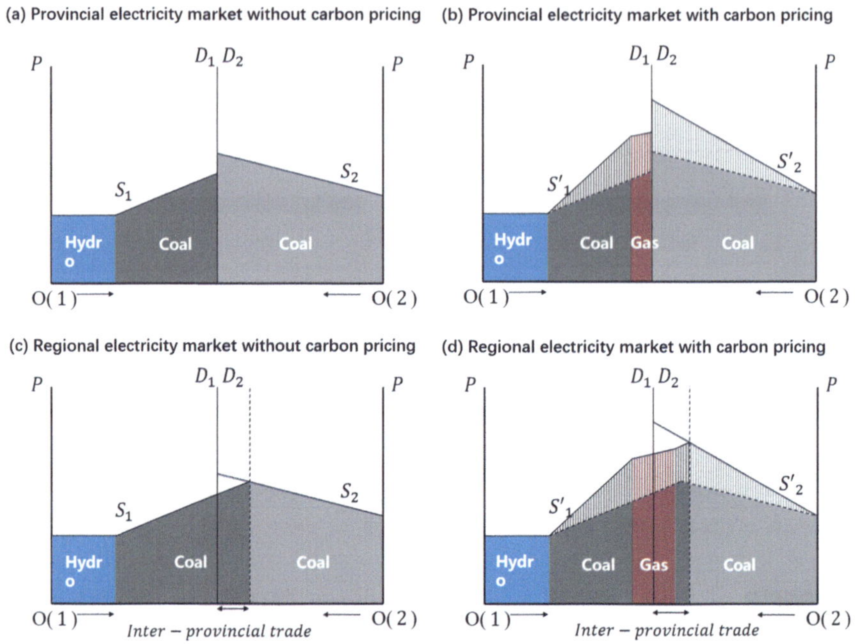

Fig. 8.3 The impact of market integration on abatement costs. *Note* The supply curve S1 for Province 1 is composed of high-emission-efficiency coal and gas power and the supply curve S2 for Province 2 is composed of low-emission-efficiency coal power. Without carbon pricing, the high marginal cost of gas-fired units results in no generation from market competition. Carbon pricing will shorten the cost gap between gas-fired units and coal-fired units, and promote the substitution of gas-fired units for coal-fired units. The vertical shaded areas in this figure (**b**) and (**d**) represent the abatement costs compared to (**a**) and (**c**)

well as increased difficulties in market integration (Chen et al., 2022; Davidson & Pérez-Arriaga, 2020).

Electricity market integration would serve to rearrange the merit order of plants by eliminating inter-provincial trade barriers, thereby improving the effectiveness of carbon pricing (Fig. 8.3).

8.2.3.1 Impact on Carbon Emission and the Associated Cost

Market integration facilitates the substitution of high-emission-efficiency plants for low-emission-efficiency ones through the introduction of inter-provincial electricity trade; in sum, it amplifies the substitution effect of carbon pricing and reduces the overall abatement costs. Given the assumption of a perfectly competitive market, the allowance cost is internalized into the electricity market by the carbon price, then the market is cleared by minimizing the social costs. And market integration will always reduce social costs by allowing inter-provincial substitution of power plants, thereby reducing the overall abatement costs.

Figure 8.3 visually depicts the impact of market integration on abatement costs. Figure 8.3a and c show production costs for provincial and regional market without carbon pricing, respectively. With the introduction of carbon pricing, the cost of allowances will be passed on to the electricity market and increase the competitiveness of gas-fired units to replace coal-fired units. Figure 8.3b and d show the total costs (production costs plus allowance costs) for provincial and regional market with carbon pricing, respectively. Comparing Fig. 8.3a, b, c and d, the vertical shaded areas in Fig. 8.3b and d are the abatement costs under the two market scenarios. And the difference between the vertical shaded areas of Fig. 8.3b and d represents the savings in abatement costs due to market integration. What's more, the abatement cost savings depend on how much the market integration can amplify the inter-provincial substitution effect of carbon pricing, which, itself, depends on the electricity supply profile of the study area.

8.2.3.2 Equity Concern

When market integration reallocates electricity production across provinces, carbon emissions are also redistributed across them. When electricity flows from provinces with high to those with low emission efficiency, carbon emissions then begin to flow in the opposite direction. As a result, greater amounts of carbon emissions are reallocated to provinces that possess a higher carbon emission efficiency. However, this increasingly concentrated distribution of carbon emission reductions in the regional market could then also increase regional equity concerns. Therefore, to assess the impact of electricity market integration on the abatement potential and cost-effectiveness of carbon pricing, we simulated and compared the emission reductions and abatement costs between the two market scenarios, following which we discussed the potential equity issues.

8.3 Data Description and Impact Simulation Model

In this section, we first introduced the study area and data. Then we described a partial market equilibrium model used to simulate the responses of electricity sector (including the generation, inter-provincial trade and associated carbon emission and costs) to the changing carbon price determined by the national market. Further, we discuss the differences in model settings between the segmented electricity market and the integrated electricity market.

8.3.1 Study Area and Data Description

Our study area included the five provinces in the China Southern Electricity Grid territory in 2018; namely, Guangdong, Guangxi, Yunnan, Guizhou, and Hainan. Our detailed high-frequency datasets on the electricity sector in these five provinces are comprised of:

(1) hourly electricity consumption, renewable energy generation, capacity utilization rates, and inter-provincial contracts in 2018 collected from the South China Energy Regulatory Office of the National Energy Administration; (2) installed capacity, energy consumption, and carbon emission intensity of coal-fired generators at the unit level, as well as of gas-fired generators at the provincial level, in addition to inter-provincial transmission capacities and technical loss rates as collected from Southern Electricity Grid's 2018 Dispatch Annual Report; (3) benchmark on-grid electricity tariffs and coal and gas prices in the electricity sector collected from the National Development and Reform Commission; and (4) the marginal costs of generation calculated using the price of fuel. Prices, costs, and other technical parameters are reported in this paper's appendix.

Figure 8.4 shows the actual supply profile for each province, as well as the inter-provincial trade in 2018. There exist sizable cross-province differences, because the technology mix of production capacities and ensuing fuel and generation mixes vary across provinces. Specifically, as the largest electricity consumer and carbon emitter in the Southern Power Grid, Guangdong's local power generation structure is mainly composed of thermal power. Among them, gas-fired power generation with the highest carbon emission efficiency accounts for 10.5%. Within coal-fired power generation, units with an installed capacity of 1000 and 600 MW account for 17.0% and 24.9% respectively, and units with an installed capacity 300 MW and below account for 22.9%. On the contrary, in Yunnan, which has the second largest power generation, the main power source is the non-emitting hydropower, accounting for as high as 74.7%. The power generation structures in Guangxi and Guizhou are relatively similar. The dominant power source in these two provinces is hydropower, followed by coal-fired power with an installed capacity of 600 MW. Hainan has the least power generation, mainly contributed by coal-fired units with an installed capacity of 300 MW. The large differences in supply profiles across provinces mean that the effects of carbon pricing on them will also vary widely. Supported by unit-level data, we can characterize the inter-provincial differences and evaluate the province-level distribution of carbon pricing impacts.

Figure 8.5 depicts the hourly electricity consumption, the hydroelectricity, and other renewable electricity generation at the regional/aggregate level. The electricity demand exhibits obvious seasonality and strong short-term fluctuations, while hydroelectricity and other renewable energy sources are significantly periodic and intermittent. It reflects the advantages of the high-frequency data used in this paper; that is, it allowed us to control for the short-term fluctuations in the simulation analysis to improve the accuracy of our results.

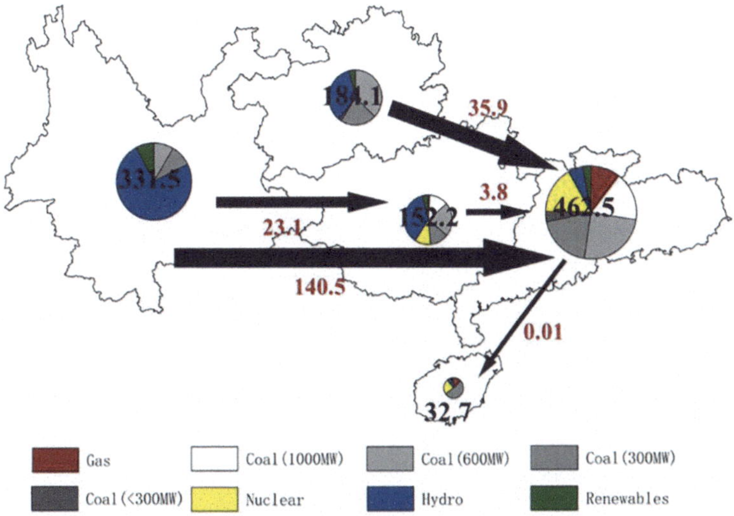

Fig. 8.4 Actual power generation and trade in 2018. *Notes* All numbers are in TWh

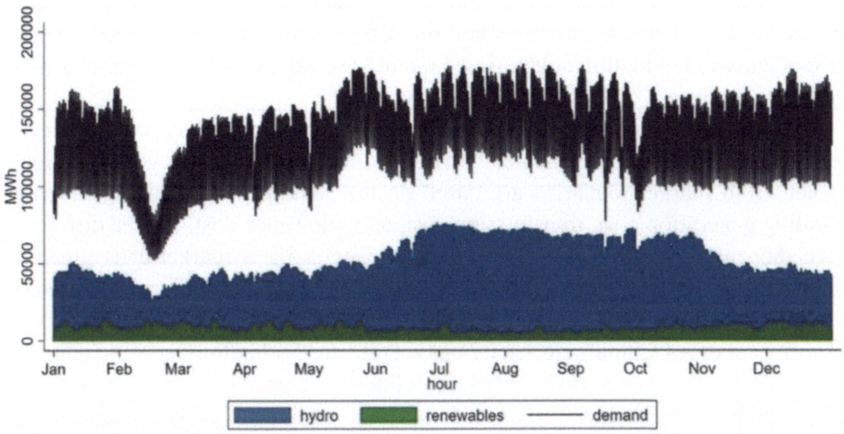

Fig. 8.5 Hourly electricity demand and the generation of hydroelectricity and other renewable energy sources at the regional level

8.3.2 Simulation Method

This subsection lays out the partial market equilibrium model used to simulate the electricity market equilibrium and assess the impact of carbon pricing. The research framework is shown in Fig. 8.6. Assuming perfectly competitive condition prevails in both electricity market and national carbon market, the generators are price-takers.[1] In the competitive electricity market, the market equilibrium can be obtained through

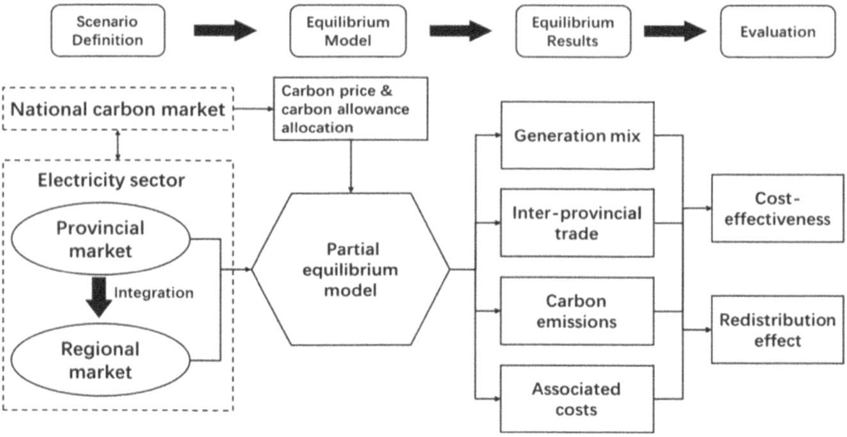

Fig. 8.6 Research framework

solving a cost minimization problem, of which the total costs consist of generation costs, transmission costs and allowance costs.[2] Given the demand, supply profile, and physical constraints, we can simulate the generation mix structure, the inter-provincial trade, carbon emissions and the associated costs for any given carbon price or emission reduction target. Based on these results, we can perform efficiency and equity analyses.

Based on the reform status and future direction of China's electricity sector, we define two scenarios, a segmented provincial market and an integrated regional market. Both market scenarios are based on the same cost-minimizing function, including generation cost, transmission cost, and allowance cost, but the difference is whether inter-provincial electricity trade is exogenous or market-determined. In the provincial market scenario, inter-provincial trade is predetermined by governmental contracts and is exogenous to the provincial market. This scenario is closer to the current stage of China's electricity market reform. Technology-specific marginal costs and installed generation capacities define the supply curve for domestically produced electricity in each province. Since inter- provincial trade is exogenous to the market, the inter-provincial transmission cost is also fixed and not affected by electricity market and carbon pricing. In contrast, in the regional market scenario, inter-provincial trade is determined by the market, and the generation capacity and demand are pooled together to form the aggregate supply curve and demand curve at the regional level. Since inter-provincial trade is market determined, the transmission cost is also affected by electricity market and varies with carbon prices.

The specific cost minimization model and related physical constraints are as follows, and the definitions of the parameters and variables in the model are shown in Table 8.1:

$$\min Cost = \underbrace{\sum_{t=1}^{8760}\sum_{i}\sum_{g} GEN_{t,i,g}MC_{i,g}}_{Generationcost} + \underbrace{\sum_{t=1}^{8760}\sum_{i}\sum_{j} TRA_{t,i,j}TC_{i,j}}_{Transmitioncost} + CP\underbrace{\sum_{t=1}^{8760}\sum_{i}\sum_{g} GEN_{t,i,g}\left(EI_{i,g} - \overline{EI_g}\right)}_{Allowancecost} \quad (8.1)$$

$$s.t. \sum_{g} GEN_{t,i,g} + \sum_{j}\left[TRA_{t,j,i}\left(1 - line_{j,i}\right) - TRA_{t,i,j}\right] = D_{t,i} \quad (8.2)$$

$$0 \le GEN_{t,i,g} \le \left(1 - loss_{i,g}\right)CAP_{i,g} g \in \{coal, gas, nuclear\} \quad (8.3)$$

$$0 \le GEN_{t,i,g} \le CAP_{i,g}CF_{t,i,g} g \in \{hydro, wind, solar\} \quad (8.4)$$

$$0 \le TRA_{t,i,j} \le TL_{i,j} \quad (8.5)$$

The objective function is the cost Eq. (8.1) which consists of electricity generation costs, transmission costs, and carbon allowance costs. The carbon market affects the equilibrium in the electricity market through the carbon price (*CP*) and the intensity benchmarks for allocating allowances (EI_g).

Equations (8.2–8.5) represent the specific constraints in the electricity sector:

Real-time supply and demand balance (8.2). In each province, the hourly total electricity generation plus the hourly net imports, after deducting line losses, should meet the hourly demand.

Electricity generation capacity constraints (8.3) and (8.4). Equation (8.3) represents the electricity generation capacity constraint of the stable electricity supply, wherein the generation capacity should not exceed the installed capacity after deducting for technical losses.

Equation (8.4) represents the electricity generation capacity constraints of variable electricity generation, including that within hydroelectricity, wind, and solar systems. Further, $CF_{t,i,g}$ is the capacity factor that represents the time-varying capacity utilization rate and is used to measure the intermittent and periodicity of variable electricity generation.

Inter-provincial flow constraints (8.5). The hourly trade flow between two provinces should not exceed their transmission capacity.

Table 8.1 The definitions of parameters and variables

Indices and parameters	Definitions
Subscripts:	
t	Hour in 2018, t ∈ 1, 8760]
i	Province, i ∈ {Guangdong, Guangxi, Yunnan, Guizhou, Hainan}
g	Unit index, including coal-fired, gas-fired, nuclear, hydro, wind, and solar power, where coal-fired power will be subdivided into each unit
Decision variables	
$GEN_{t,i,g}$	Power generation of unit g at time t
$TRA_{t,i,j}$	Power transmission from province i to j at time t Parameters:
Parameters	
$MC_{i,g}$	Marginal generation cost of unit g in province i
$TC_{i,j}$	Unit transmission cost from province i to j
CP	Carbon price in the national carbon market
$EI_{i,g}$	Carbon emission intensity of unit g in province i
EI_g	Benchmark emission intensity used for the allocation of carbon allowances to thermal unit g in the national carbon market
$D_{t,i}$	Power demand of province i at time t
$line_{j,i}$	Transmission line loss rate from province i to j
$CAP_{i,g}$	Generation capacity of unit g in province i
$loss_{i,g}$	Generation loss rate for coal-fired, gas-fired and nuclear power, including maintenance rate and self-consumption rate
$CF_{t,i,g}$	The capacity factor for hydro, wind, and solar power
$TL_{i,j}$	Transmission capacity limit from province i to j

Note In China's national carbon market, regulators set four benchmarks in the electricity sector for allocating allowances. These benchmarks are then applied to four technology categories, namely coal-fired units with a capacity of 300 MW and below, coal-fired units with a capacity of > 300 MW, gas-fired units, and other unconventional coal-fired units. In the provincial market scenario, inter-provincial trade is predetermined by governmental contracts, and $TRA_{t,i,j}$ is exogenous to the cost minimization model. In the regional market scenario, inter-provincial trade is determined by the market, and $TRA_{t,i,j}$ is the decision variable in the model

8.4 Results and Discussion

We first examined the effects of carbon pricing on carbon emissions reduction, as well as the induced costs increase between the two scenarios, at the regional level during which the cost-effectiveness of the two scenarios is compared. Then, we analyzed the distributional impact at the provincial level to examine why the equity issue is a matter of concern.

8.4.1 Comparing the Differential Effects on CO_2 Emissions Reduction of the Two Market Scenarios

Figure 8.7 depicts the regional-level emission reductions in the electricity sector as achieved by the two market reform scenarios at differing carbon prices. The first notable result is that changes in the carbon emission abatement are nonlinear when compared to the carbon price in both market scenarios (e.g., it is almost completely non-responsive at the low-price range and is only responsive at a higher price range).

Specifically, within the provincial market, the level of emissions does not change when the carbon price is below 100 yuan/ton, with it only slightly increasing when the price falls between 100 and 400 yuan/ton. Furthermore, carbon emission abatement is only effective when the price of carbon is above 400 yuan/ton. These novel findings are a result of the unique feature of China's carbon market in terms of its rate-based allocation of allowances, under which lower carbon prices within the provincial market only result in an output switch among similar coal power technologies within the same province. Although the low-emission-efficiency units are more polluting, they can benefit from rate-based carbon allowances and get more production due to the weak carbon intensity benchmark used for them, which is greater than their carbon emission intensity, thereby reducing the total costs but increasing their emissions. And across technology categories, high-capacity, high-emission-efficiency units face a stricter benchmark than low-capacity, low-mission-efficiency units, Carbon emissions may increase at low carbon price levels due to increased production of low-mission-efficiency units.

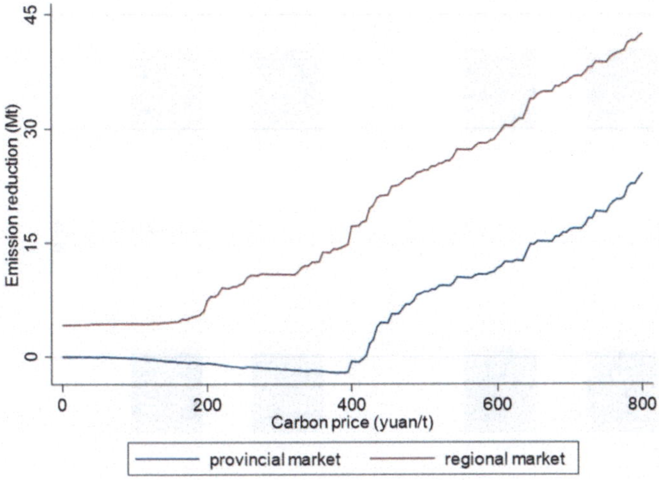

Fig. 8.7 Carbon emission reduction levels across the two market scenarios. *Note* The carbon emission reductions in this Figure were calculated by comparing emission levels within the provincial market without carbon pricing

Figure 8.8 reports the power generation structure at different carbon price levels, revealing the reason for the changes in carbon emissions. In the provincial market, when the carbon price rises from 0 yuan/ton to 100 yuan/ton, the power generation structure does not change much, resulting in almost no emission reduction. However, when the carbon price increases from 100 yuan/ton to 400 yuan/ton, the share of gas power generation then increased from 1.14% to 1.63%, while that of coal power generation with an installed capacity of less than or equal to 300 MW (which is relatively more carbon intensive) increased from 12.52 to 18.33%, with the share of coal power generation with an installed capacity of > 300 MW then dropping from 38.26 to 31.97%, resulting the increase in carbon emissions.

This observable output mismatch among coal plants is due to the different intensity standards in the allocation of emission allowances to coal plants of different capacities. In our sample, for 94% of the total capacity of coal-fired power generators, the carbon emission intensity is lower than the carbon intensity benchmark for carbon allocation (i.e. $EI_{i,g} < \overline{EI_g}$), among them, the low-emission- efficiency units with installed capacity less than or equal to 300 MW account for a 39.0% share. This suggests that as the carbon price increases from 100 yuan/ton to 400 yuan/ton, these low-emission-efficiency units will benefit from carbon allowances and produce more, reducing the total cost of the power sector but increasing emissions.

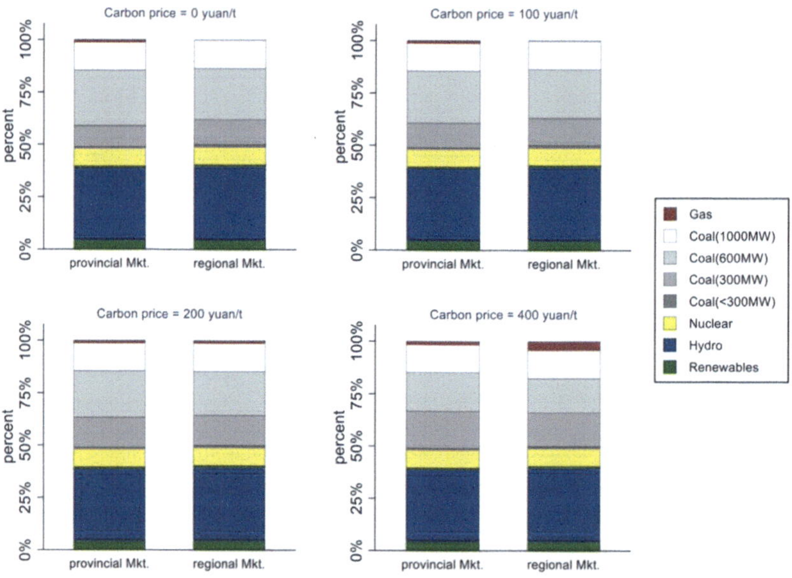

Fig. 8.8 Regional supply structure across the different market scenarios. *Note* Coal power units are divided into four groups based on their installed capacity

However, when the carbon price increases from 400 yuan/ton to 800 yuan/ton, the shares of gas power generation then rapidly increase from 1.63 to 9.59%, indicating that only the occurrence of a high carbon price level within the provincial market has a substitution effect and then promotes the output switching between gas and coal plants within the province.

In the regional market, we found that there is a more sensitive nonlinear response of emission reductions to carbon prices. At low carbon prices (i.e., those < 200 yuan/ton), carbon emissions respond relatively weakly to changes in carbon prices at around 0.84–1.49% less than emissions within the provincial market. This emission reduction is primarily due to increases in the shares of hydroelectricity generation. As shown in Fig. 8.8, when moving from the provincial to the regional market, there are relatively few changes in the thermal electricity generation structure; however, the shares of hydroelectricity generation would then increase from 34.82 to 35.53% due to them being dispatched across a larger region, with them then replacing 1.52% of thermal electricity generation.

Additionally, when the carbon price increases to above 200 yuan/ton, the total carbon emission reductions within the regional market respond significantly to the overall carbon price. Because the integration of the electricity market allows for the replacement of coal power with gas power across provinces, the shares in gas power generation within the regional market then respond more quickly to increases in carbon prices than they do in the provincial market, resulting in a more sensitive response curve. Furthermore, at a carbon price of 400 yuan/ton, the share of gas power generation then increases to 4.12% in the regional market, which is higher than the 1.63% observed within the provincial market, with the carbon emissions then being reduced by a further 12.97 million tons (2.61%), which confirms that electricity market integration amplifies the substitution effect of carbon pricing strategies.

8.4.2 The Cost-Effectiveness of Carbon Pricing Between the Two Market Scenarios

We have thus far analyzed the abatement effects of carbon pricing across two different electricity markets. Next, we assessed how much it would cost in total to reduce carbon emissions and to identify which market design is more efficient in reducing the overall emissions. As carbon pricing changes the overall merit order and imposes additional allowance costs that would be passed on to consumers through the electricity plant's bidding, we measured the abatement costs using increases in production and allowance costs. Given the same carbon reduction target, the required carbon price and the abatement costs for each market design are provided in Fig. 8.9.

As shown in Fig. 8.9, under the same emission reduction target, both the required carbon price and abatement costs are lower in the regional market than in the provincial, which indicates that the former is more cost-effective in reducing emissions. For example, when taking into consideration the total carbon reduction target of

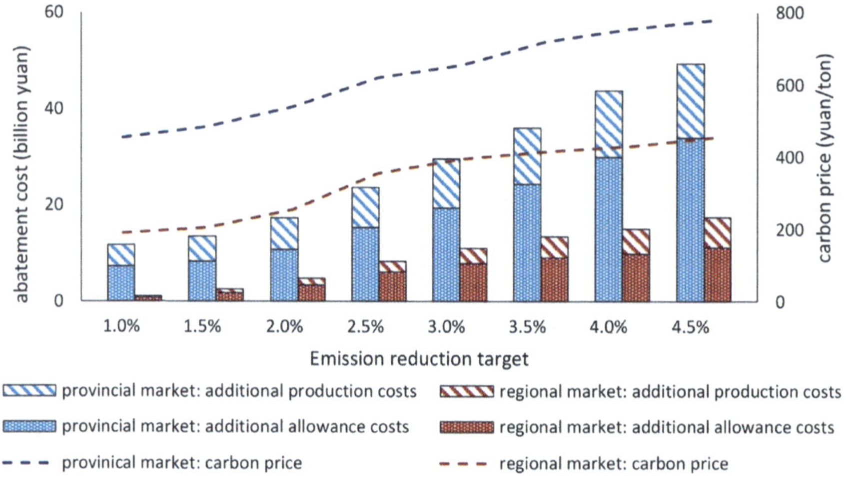

Fig. 8.9 The abatement costs of the different market scenarios. *Note* The abatement costs are calculated via increases in the production and allowance costs

1.0% (which is close to the annual total carbon emission reduction target required by China's 14th Five-Year Plan[3]), the carbon price needs to be as high as 455 yuan/ton and 190 yuan/ton in the provincial and regional markets, respectively. Additionally, the abatement costs in these two scenarios would need to be 11.76 billion yuan and 1.32 billion yuan, respectively. Among these two scenarios, the allowance costs would account for 62.6 and 70.2% of the total, with the remainder of expenses being generation and transmission costs. On average, across all the emission reduction targets, electricity market integration would save around 60% of abatement costs, meaning that market integration would significantly improve the cost-effectiveness of carbon pricing.

8.4.3 *Distributional Impacts and Equity Concerns*

The above results highlight the aggregate effects of the carbon market on the carbon emission abatement and its associated costs at the regional level. Another important evaluation criterion herein is the distributional impacts of the two market scenarios. To this end, Table 8.2 reports the carbon emissions of each province in the two market scenarios within the same 1.0% emission reduction target. It reveals that the abatement distribution across the studied provinces differ dramatically across the two market scenarios.

As reported in Table 8.2, abatement distribution at the provincial level is more concentrated within the regional market context compared to that within the provincial market. Comparing Figs. 8.4 and 8.10a, in the provincial market, Guangdong, Guangxi, and Hainan all experience a decline in their carbon emissions due to the

Table 8.2 The carbon emissions of each province in the two market scenarios under the same 1.0% emission reduction target

	Guangdong	Guangxi	Yunnan	Guizhou	Hainan
Provincial market					
Carbon price (yuan/ton)	455				
CO_2 emissions (million ton)	283.75	54.29	41.81	96.12	15.65
Shares (%)	57.72	11.04	8.50	19.55	3.18
Changes (%)	0.04	8.96	0.57	1.79	11.63
Regional market					
Carbon price (yuan/ton)	190				
CO_2 emissions (million ton)	314.46	84.93	10.32	62.72	19.26
Shares (%)	63.95	17.27	2.10	12.76	3.92
Changes (%)	10.78	42.42	75.18	33.58	8.74

Note The above change rates were calculated in comparison with the provincial market without carbon pricing. The reported carbon price is that when the two scenarios each reached the target of 1.0% total carbon emission reduction

resulting substitution of gas power for coal power. Furthermore, both Yunnan and Guizhou then experience a slight increase in their emissions because the rate-based allocation of allowances would then distort the carbon price incentives for coal power generation within these regions. In contrast, in the regional market scenario, carbon emission reduction would be largely concentrated in Yunnan and Guizhou (Table 8.2). Comparing Figs. 8.4 and 8.10b, electricity market integration redistributes electricity generation across these provinces, which would then reduce their electricity generation. Because the emission efficiency of coal-fired units in Yunnan and Guizhou is lower than that in Guangdong, Guangxi and Hainan, and high-emission-efficiency gas-fired units are installed in these three provinces. Market integration will reduce the share of coal power generation in Yunnan and Guizhou from 17.5 and 60.9% to 0.1 and 49.4%, increase the share of coal and gas power generation in Guangdong, Guangxi, and Hainan from 75.3%, 48.4%, and 65.3% to 78.1%, 53.1%, and 68.7%, respectively. Although Yunnan's hydroelectricity generation will increase, the reallocation of coal power generation is the main driver for the reallocation of electricity generation across provinces.

Additionally, when combined with the substitution of hydroelectricity for coal-fired electricity, as well as when considering the decrease in low-emission-efficiency thermal electricity generation, carbon emissions are then drastically reduced by 75.18% in Yunnan and 33.58% in Guizhou (Table 8.2). Conversely, Guangdong, Guangxi, and Hainan would then experience higher carbon emissions as market integration allocates more electricity generation to these regions specifically. The more concentrated distribution of emissions reductions in the regional market suggests that it is less effective in addressing carbon equity issues.

In addition to the emission allocation equity concern, market integration also raises an equity issue in terms of the development of the electricity industry. Comparing

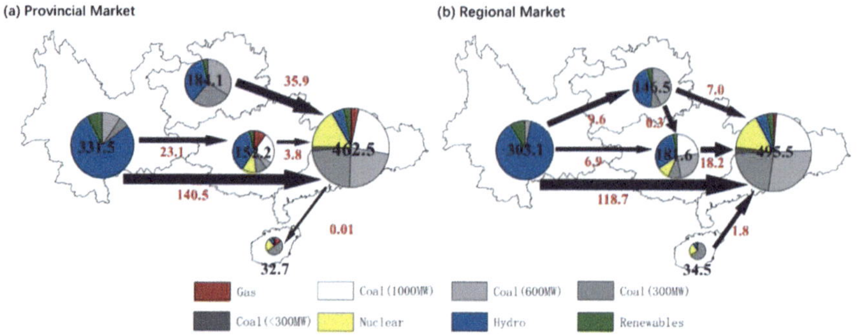

Fig. 8.10 Electricity generation and trade across the two market scenarios under the 1.0% emission reduction target. *Notes* All values are in TWh

Fig. 8.10a and b, in the regional market context, the optimization of inter-provincial trade leads to a decrease in exports from Yunnan and Guizhou, as well as a large withdrawal of coal power in these provinces. When compared with the provincial market, the coal-fired electricity generation in Yunnan and Guizhou would drop by 74.82% and 33.56% in the regional market scenario. This largescale withdrawal of coal power production would then make it difficult for coal power plants to recover their stranded costs from the regional wholesale market. Without other tools (e.g., ancillary service markets, capacity payment scheme etc.) to cover the investment costs of coal power plants, the development of the electricity sector in Yunnan and Guizhou would suffer within a market integration context. Moreover, these two provinces are rich in renewable resources (Fig. 8.4). Further, a lack of market incentives for the development of local coal power plants may then result in an insufficient adjustable capacity level in the long term that would be needed to meet the flexibility requirement for large-scale renewable energy integration (Chu et al., 2021). Therefore, although the regional market scenario does improve the efficiency of short-term emission reduction, it may also cause a potential inequity in the long-term development of the electricity industry between provinces.

8.5 Conclusions

In this study, we examined the impact of electricity market integration on the abatement potential and cost-effectiveness of carbon pricing. Through the designing of two potential electricity market scenarios (a provincial versus a regional market type), as well as through considering the rate-based allocation of allowances in China's national carbon market, we were able to quantify the responses of regional-level carbon emissions to changes in carbon prices in the context of the five southern provinces. Herein, we measured the abatement costs using increases in the production and allowance costs, with us then comparing the cost-effectiveness of abatement between the two market scenarios. We further assessed the equity issues arising from the redistribution of carbon emissions and electricity production at the provincial level in the regional market scenario.

Our study found that carbon pricing has a limited emission reduction effect in the context of a segmented electricity market. The carbon prices need to be as high as 400 yuan/ton to begin achieving overall carbon reduction. While within an integrated electricity market, carbon emission reductions are larger and more responsive to changes within carbon prices. To achieve the carbon emission intensity goal outlined in China's 14th Five-Year Plan, the carbon price needs to be as high as 455 yuan/ton and 190 yuan/ton in the provincial and regional markets, respectively, which are both much higher than the average carbon price of 42.85 yuan/ton in China's national carbon market as of 2021. Furthermore, given the same emission reduction targets, abatement costs are saved by around 60% in the regional market than in the provincial market, which indicates that the former is more cost-effective in reducing carbon emissions. This is because market integration amplifies the abatement effect of carbon pricing changes through allowing for the cross- provincial substitution of high-emission-efficiency units for low-emission-efficiency one.

However, the distribution effects of carbon emissions and electricity production at the provincial level suggests that the regional market scenario would then result in potential equity issues. This is because emission reductions at the provincial level are more concentrated in regional market, with the primary contributors being Yunnan and Guizhou herein. Because market integration would then reduce the number of exports from Yunnan and Guizhou by optimizing inter-provincial trade, it would then drastically reduce the output of their local coal plants. It would also result in an inequitable impact on the development of the electricity industry in each province. The coal power plants in Guangdong, Guangxi, and Hainan would then benefit from the increases in output caused by market integration. The withdrawal of coal power would mostly be concentrated in Yunnan and Guizhou, which would then lead to tax loss, employment loss and GDP loss in these provinces.

Our research reveals the role of electricity market design in the effectiveness of carbon pricing, with our results then helping to improve policymakers' understanding of the interaction between changes to carbon pricing and electricity market reform. To support China's carbon neutrality target, the integration of the provincial electricity market would be a cost-effective tool within the context of the current national carbon market within the electricity sector. Our results also show that electricity market integration would help to reduce the required carbon price and would then save on abatement costs. Furthermore, China is currently promoting the construction of integrated electricity markets, with it having set the target of establishing a national integrated electricity market system by 2030 (NDRC (National Development and Reform Commission), 2022). We would thus expect that, when the national carbon market is integrated with the national electricity market, it will effectively support the realization of China's carbon neutrality target.

However, there are certain equity issues to be resolved in promoting this integration of the electricity market. The first is the unfair distribution of carbon emissions and energy consumption. In addition to the national carbon market, an important policy in China aimed at reducing carbon emissions is the dual control on energy consumption. Under this policy, each province sets its own total energy consumption and intensity control targets. Because the regional electricity market will then redistribute the energy consumption and carbon emission between provinces, it may then cause conflicts with the dual control target in certain regions. To coordinate these policies, one feasible approach might be to set energy consumption and emission reduction targets at the regional level.

In addition, the inequitable impact on the electricity industry in each province is another issue that needs to be addressed during the process of market integration. Given that some provinces may suffer losses from the withdrawal of low-capacity, low-emission-efficiency coal plants caused by market integration, policy makers and other potential investors need to then recognize the potential risk of plant's becoming stranded and take this into account when making decisions. The massive withdrawal of coal power plants in the short term will the place enormous pressure on the local power sector. With the large-scale development of renewable energy in the future, how to maintain the stability and reliability of their own power supply will be a major challenge for these provinces. Therefore, regional ancillary service markets and capacity compensation mechanisms should be established to compensate for the stranded costs, meet the flexibility requirement, and to alleviate the equity issues.

Appendix

Marginal Cost

The marginal costs of the different technologies available are reported in Table 8.3. Because there are no official sources for the marginal cost of each unit type, these data were then estimated. For the coal- and gas-fired electricity units, we used fuel cost as a proxy variable for marginal cost. The coal and gas consumption at the unit level was collected from the Southern Electricity Grid 2018 Dispatch Annual Report. The coal and gas prices were 600 yuan/t and 2.7 yuan/m^3, respectively, which were the average fuel prices of coal and natural gas within the electricity sector in 2018 as published by the National Development and Reform Commission (NDRC). For the hydro and nuclear electricity units, we deducted the fixed costs from the levelized costs to estimate the overall marginal cost. The cost parameters are then derived from the Renewable Electricity Generation Costs in 2018, as published by the International Renewable Energy Agency (IRENA), as well as the Projected Costs of Generating Electricity that was published by the International Energy Agency (IEA) and the Nuclear Energy Agency (NEA).

Table 8.3 Marginal costs of the different electricity technologies

(yuan/kWh)	Solar	Wind	Hydro	Nuclear	Coal 1000 MW	Coal 600 MW	Coal 300 MW	Coal < 300 MW	Gas
Guangdong	0.000	0.000	0.074	0.172	0.265	0.288	0.297	0.338	0.436
Guangxi	0.000	0.000	0.074	0.172	0.273	0.287	0.305	–	0.615
Yunnan	0.000	0.000	0.074	–	–	0.292	0.322	–	–
Guizhou	0.000	0.000	0.074	–	–	0.291	0.310	0.349	–
Hainan	0.000	0.000	0.074	0.172	–	–	0.288	–	0.647

Table 8.4 Inter-provincial electricity transmission capacity in 2018

(GW)		To				
		Guangdong	Guangxi	Yunnan	Guizhou	Hainan
From	Guangdong	0	0	0	0	2 (0.057)
	Guangxi	6.8 (0.057)	0	0	0	0
	Yunnan	31.6 (0.080)	3.2 (0.057)	0	3 (0.057)	0
	Guizhou	12 (0.080)	3.4 (0.057)	0	0	0
	Hainan	2 (0.057)	0	0	0	0

Note The transmission costs are reported in parentheses and their unit is yuan/kWh

Inter-provincial Transmission Capacity

The inter-provincial transmission capacities between the five provinces in 2018 are shown in Table 8.4. The line loss rate herein is 5.51%, which is the average rate as calculated from the Southern Electricity Grid 2018 Dispatch Annual Report.

Notes

1. Since our study area is confined to the Southern grid provinces, referring to data from the IEA (https://www.iea.org/data-and-statistics/), in 2018, the power sector in this region emitted about 10.4% of the national electricity sector's CO_2. This relatively small share supports our assumption that the carbon price in the national carbon market is exogenous to the regional electricity market.
2. Since we focus on short-term partial equilibrium within the electricity sector, hourly demand curve can be assumed to be completely inelastic and met by the supply curve. Then according to the fundamental theorems of welfare economics (Lange, 1942), the welfare maximization problem of social planners can be reducible to the cost minimization problem of the electricity sector.
3. Based on the energy consumption and carbon emission intensity targets of GDP as established by China's 14th Five-Year Plan, assuming constant energy consumption, we estimated that total carbon emissions would need to be reduced by at least 1% per year. Given the constant short-term electricity demand assumed in this paper, the emission reduction target was initially set at 1% and then increased to 4.5 in 0.5% increments to account for tighter emission reduction targets.

References

Cao, J., Dai, H., Li, S., Guo, C., Ho, M., Cai, W., He, J., Hai, H., Li, J., Liu, Y., Wang, C., Wu, L., & Zhang, X. (2021a). The general equilibrium impacts of carbon tax policy in China: A multi-model comparison. *Energy Economics, 99*, 105284.

Cao, J., Ho, M. S., Ma, R., & Teng, F. (2021b). When carbon emission trading meets a regulated industry: Evidence from the electricity sector of China. *Journal of Public Economics, 200*, 104470.

Chen, H., Cui, J., Song, F., & Jiang, Z. (2022). Evaluating the impacts of reforming and integrating China's electricity sector. *Energy Economics, 108*, 105912.

Chu, Y., Gao, J., & Li, H. (2021). *Wind power, transmission congestion and regional allocative efficiency among fossil-fuel generators.* SSRN https://ssrn.com/abstract=3974592

Cui, J., Zhang, J., & Zheng, Y. (2018). Carbon pricing induces innovation: Evidence from China's regional carbon market pilots. *AEA Papers and Proceedings, 108*, 453–457.

Davidson, M. R., & Pérez-Arriaga, I. (2020). Avoiding pitfalls in China's electricity sector reforms. *The Energy Journal, 41*(3), 119–141.

Fan, Y., Wu, J., Xia, Y., & Liu, J. Y. (2016). How will a nationwide carbon market affect regional economies and efficiency of CO_2 emission reduction in China? *China Economic Review, 38*, 151–166.

Fischer, C. (2001). *Rebating environmental policy revenues: Output-based allocations and tradable performance standards* (RFF Discussion Paper: 01–22).

Fischer, C., & Newell, R. G. (2008). Environmental and technology policies for climate mitigation. *Journal of Environmental Economics and Management, 55*(2), 142–162.

Goulder, L. H., Long, X., Lu, J., & Morgenstern, R. D. 2019. *China's unconventional nationwide CO_2 emissions trading system: The wide-ranging impacts of an implicit output subsidy* (National Bureau of Economic Research No. w26537).

Huang, Y., Shen, L., & Liu, H. (2019). Grey relational analysis, principal component analysis and forecasting of carbon emissions based on long short-term memory in China. *Journal of Cleaner Production, 209*, 415–423.

Lange, O. (1942). The foundations of welfare economics. *Econometrica Journal of the Econometric Society, 10*(3/4), 215–228.

Lin, J., Kahrl, F., Yuan, J., Chen, Q., & Liu, X. (2019). Economic and carbon emission impacts of electricity market transition in China: A case study of Guangdong Province. *Applied Energy, 238*, 1093–1107.

Lin, J., Kahrl, F., Yuan, J., Liu, X., & Zhang, W. (2019). Challenges and strategies for electricity market transition in China. *Energy Policy, 133*, 110899.

Naughton, B. (2003). *How much can regional integration do to unify China's markets? How far across the river* (pp. 204–232).

NDRC (National Development and Reform Commission). (2022). *Guiding opinions on accelerating the construction of a national integrated electricity market.*

Pollitt, M. G., Yang, C. H., & Chen, H. (2017). *Reforming the Chinese electricity supply sector: Lessons from international experience* (In Cambridge Working Papers in Economics No. 1713).

Poncet, S. (2003). Measuring Chinese domestic and international integration. *China Economic Review, 14*(1), 1–21.

Qi, Y., Dong, W., Dong, C., & Huang, C. (2019). Understanding institutional barriers for wind curtailment in China. *Renewable and Sustainable Energy Reviews, 105*, 476–486.

Wang, Q., & Chen, X. (2012). China's electricity market-oriented reform: From an absolute to a relative monopoly. *Energy Policy, 51*, 143–148.

Wei, C., & Zheng, X. (2017). A new perspective on energy efficiency enhancement: A test based on market segmentation (in Chinese). *Social Sciences in China, 10*, 90–111.

Young, A. (2000). The razor's edge: Distortions and incremental reform in the People's Republic of China. *The Quarterly Journal of Economics, 115*(4), 1091–1135.

Zhang, S., Andrews-Speed, P., & Li, S. (2018). To what extent will China's ongoing electricity market reforms assist the integration of renewable energy? *Energy Policy, 114*, 165–172.

Zhou, L. A. (2004). The incentive and cooperation of government officials in the political tournaments: An interpretation of the prolonged local protectionism and duplicative Investments in China. *Economic Research Journal, 6*(1), 2–3.

Chapter 9
The Impact of Temperature Changes on Industrial Production in China and Its Mechanism Analysis

Lu Yang, Jingye Shi, and Xiaoguang Chen

Abstract This paper uses micro data of Chinese industrial enterprises from 1998 to 2007, combined with weather data from the same period, to examine the impact of temperature changes on industrial production and its mechanism. The study finds a nonlinear relationship between industrial output and temperature changes: rising summer temperatures significantly reduce industrial output, while rising winter temperatures increase industrial output; daily temperatures below or above [12 °C,15 °C) both negatively affect industrial output. In addition, seasonal temperature fluctuations also have adverse effects on industrial output. Further mechanism test results show that high temperatures indirectly affect output by reducing the total factor productivity, total fixed assets, investment, and innovation capability of industrial enterprises. From the estimation results of the sub-sample, the negative impact of rising summer temperatures on industrial output varies depending on the industry and ownership of the enterprise. Finally, the paper predicts that future global warming will lead to a decrease in China's industrial output by about 3.0–14.6% in the medium term and about 5.9–20.0% in the long term.

Keywords Temperature changes · Industrial production · Mechanism analysis

9.1 Introduction

Global warming is a widely concerned issue in human society. The convening of the 21st United Nations Climate Change Conference in November 2015 has pushed human society's attention to global warming to a new stage. According to the IPCC's

L. Yang
School of Accountancy, Nanjing University of Finance and Economics, Nanjing, China

J. Shi · X. Chen (✉)
School of Economics and Management, Southwest University of Finance and Economics, Chengdu, China
e-mail: cxg@swufe.edu.cn

B. Gong et al. (eds.), *Chinese Governance and Transformation Towards Carbon Neutrality*, Resources, Environment and Agricultural Development,
https://doi.org/10.1007/978-981-97-9996-1_9

fifth assessment report, from 1880 to 2012, the global surface average temperature rose by about 0.85 °C. The temperature rise in China over the past 60 years is particularly noticeable, rising about 0.23 °C every 10 years, almost twice the global temperature increase over the same period. Against the backdrop of increasingly severe global warming, the study of the relationship between climate change and economic development has become a hot topic of discussion among political scientists, sociologists, and governments, as global warming not only harms human health but also seriously affects industrial and agricultural production in human society (Dell et al., 2014).

This paper studies the impact of temperature changes on China's industrial production and explores possible impact channels. Currently, literature on the impact of climate change focuses on quantitatively analyzing the impact of high temperatures on the agricultural sector, as weather is one of the most important input factors affecting agricultural output. For example, Schlenker and Roberts (2009) used county-level panel data from the United States from 1950 to 2005 to study the impact of temperature changes on the yield of crops such as corn, soybeans, and cotton. The study found a nonlinear relationship between the yield of these crops and temperature. Based on county-level panel data from China from 2000 to 2009, Chen et al. (2016) also found a nonlinear relationship between the yield of corn and soybeans and temperature, and further pointed out that future climate change may lead to a decrease in the yield of corn and soybeans in China by 3–12% and 7–19% respectively by the end of this century.

Compared to agriculture, industry accounts for a larger proportion of GDP in many countries around the world. However, current research on the impact of climate change on industry is relatively scarce and focuses on the macro level, lacking empirical analysis at the micro level. For example, Hsiang (2010) used industry output data from 28 Caribbean countries from 1970 to 2006 to study the impact of temperature changes on agricultural and industrial sector output. The results showed that rising temperatures significantly reduced the output of the agricultural and industrial sectors in the region, but the impact on the industrial sector was greater. Specifically, for every 1 °C increase in summer temperatures, the output of the agricultural and industrial sectors in Caribbean countries will decrease by 0.1% and 2.4% respectively. Dell et al. (2012) used panel data from 125 countries worldwide from 1950 to 2003 for their research. They found that rising temperatures significantly reduced the level of industrial output in poor countries (−2%/+1 °C), but had no impact on the output of wealthy countries. In contrast, there are very few studies using micro data to study the impact of temperature changes on industrial output. Among the few studies, Chen and Yang (2019) and Zhang et al. (2018) used the Chinese industrial enterprise database from 1998 to 2007 to empirically test the impact of temperature changes on China's industrial output. Their research shows that there is an inverted U-shaped relationship between temperature and industrial output. Industrial output will increase with the rise in temperature until it reaches an optimal temperature range, after which industrial output will sharply decrease with further increases in temperature.

However, how does temperature change affect industrial output? Existing literature is relatively weak in this area. Using micro data from India's manufacturing industry, Somanathan et al. (2015) found that rising temperatures significantly reduced labor productivity, increased absenteeism, and led to a decrease in industrial output. Zivin and Neidell (2014) used micro data from the United States from 2003 to 2006 to examine the impact of temperature changes on workers' working hours. The study found that when the average daily temperature exceeds 29 °C, outdoor workers will reduce their working hours for the day. Zhang et al. (2018) found that rising temperatures mainly affect industrial output indirectly by reducing the total factor productivity (TFP) of industrial enterprises. The above literature discusses one or several channels through which temperature changes affect industrial output, but does not comprehensively examine all possible impact channels.

Based on the research of Chen and Yang (2019) and Zhang et al. (2018), this paper focuses on how temperature change affects industrial output, utilizing a database of Chinese industrial enterprises and daily meteorological data from the China Meteorological Administration (CMA) for the period 1998–2007. To answer this question, this paper first clarifies the mechanism of how temperature changes affect industrial output through a theoretical model, and then empirically tests the predictions of the theoretical model. Our research results show that rising summer temperatures will significantly reduce industrial output, and this negative impact has a lagging effect. Compared to the temperature range of [12 °C, 15 °C), daily average temperatures in higher or lower ranges will negatively affect the industrial added value of enterprises. We also found that, except for spring, the increase in temperature fluctuations in other seasons will also reduce the output of industrial enterprises.

Similar to the research results of Zhang et al. (2018), we found that temperature changes will indirectly affect industrial output by affecting the TFP of industrial enterprises. Unlike Zhang et al. (2018), our research results indicate that temperature changes can indirectly affect industrial output by influencing the total value of fixed assets, investment, and the ratio of new products. Moreover, from the estimation results of the sub-samples, the negative impact of rising summer temperatures on industrial output varies depending on the ownership attributes of the enterprises. Specifically, the increase in summer temperature does not significantly affect the output of state-owned and foreign-funded enterprises, but it significantly reduces the output of collective and private enterprises, with a greater impact on private enterprises. Finally, using temperature data for the mid-twenty-first century (2040–2069) and the long term (2070–2090), this paper predicts the potential impact of global warming on China's industrial output in the future. The results show that, all other factors being equal, global warming in the future may lead to a decrease in China's industrial output by about 3.0–14.6% in the medium term and about 5.9–20.0% in the long term.

The main contributions of this paper are reflected in the following aspects. Firstly, from a research perspective, this paper comprehensively examines the mechanism of temperature changes affecting industrial output. A few studies, such as Chen and Yang (2019), quantitatively analyze the impact of temperature changes on industrial output using micro-data, but do not investigate the channels of impact. Some literature, including Somanathan et al. (2015), Zivin and Neidell (2014), and Zhang et al. (2018), discuss the impact of temperature changes on industrial output around one or several channels, but do not comprehensively examine the channels of impact. Second, in terms of research methods, unlike most existing literature, this paper constructs temperature variables in two ways in empirical analysis (using average seasonal temperature and temperature range as temperature variables), which can not only test whether there are seasonal differences in the impact of temperature changes on industrial output, but also estimate the marginal impact of different temperature ranges on industrial output. Third, existing literature only considers the impact of changes in average temperature levels (level) when examining the impact of temperature changes on industrial output, ignoring the impact of changes in temperature variability. Unlike existing research, this paper not only considers changes in average temperature levels, but also the impact of changes in temperature variability on industrial output.

The rest of this paper is arranged as follows: the second part explains the theoretical model; the third part is the econometric model setting and variable explanation; the fourth part describes the data used; the fifth part reports the estimated results and analysis; the sixth part is the extension analysis; the seventh part predicts the impact of future global warming on China's industrial output; the last part is the conclusion and policy implications of this paper.

9.2 Theoretical Model

This part of the paper clarifies through a simple theoretical model the channels through which temperature changes affect the output of industrial enterprises. Consider a standard Cobb Douglas production function:

$$Y_t = A_t L_t^{\alpha} K_t^{\beta} \tag{9.1}$$

In this function, Y_t represents the output of the enterprise in the t-th period, L_t and K_t respectively represent the labor and capital input of the enterprise in the t-th period. A_t is the TFP of the enterprise, reflecting the comprehensive output efficiency of input factors such as capital and labor (Lu & Lian, 2012). α and β respectively represent the output elasticity of labor and capital. From Eq. (9.1), it can be seen that when any factor in the TFP, labor, and capital input of the enterprise changes, the output of the enterprise will also change accordingly.

When the temperature exceeds the most suitable temperature range for the human body, the continued rise (or fall) in temperature will cause workers to experience physical discomfort, fatigue, and even symptoms of illness, thereby negatively affecting the productivity of workers (Adhvaryu et al., 2014; González-Alonso et al., 1999; Somanathan et al., 2015; Zhang et al., 2015). At the same time, temperature changes will also directly affect the productivity of capital (Lilja, 2000; Mostafavi & Agnew,

1996). Therefore, when the temperature exceeds a certain level, both too high or too low temperatures will cause the productivity of labor and capital to decline, thereby negatively affecting TFP and causing the output of the enterprise to decline.[1]

Also, temperature changes may indirectly affect a company's output by affecting its labor and capital. First, people may alleviate the negative effects of high temperatures by reducing working hours (Somanathan et al., 2015; Zivin & Neidell, 2014). When labor input decreases, the output of the enterprise will decrease accordingly. Secondly, high temperatures will exacerbate the wear and tear of capital, leading to a decrease in the capital stock of the enterprise (Moore & Delavane, 2015). When the capital stock of the enterprise decreases, its output will also decrease accordingly.

It is obvious that temperature indirectly affects a company's output through three channels: TFP, labor, and capital. However, will temperature indirectly affect a company's output by affecting its investment? According to the accounting method of macro capital stock:

$$K_t = K_{t-1} + I_t - \delta K_{t-1} \tag{9.2}$$

where, K_t represents the capital stock of the enterprise at the end of period t, K_{t-1} represents the capital stock of the enterprise at the end of period t − 1, I_t represents the fixed capital investment of the enterprise in period t, δ represents the depreciation rate of capital. Existing literature shows that temperature changes can indirectly affect investor behavior by affecting investor sentiment (Cao & Wei, 2005). From Eq. (9.2), we can see that the fixed capital investment of the enterprise in period t (I_t) will affect the current capital stock of the enterprise (K_t), and changes in the enterprise's capital stock will in turn affect the enterprise's output. Therefore, temperature changes may also indirectly affect the capital stock of the enterprise by affecting the investment behavior of the enterprise, thereby affecting the output of the enterprise.

Finally, previous studies have shown that high temperatures can reduce people's cognitive abilities (Hancock et al., 2007; Zivin et al., 2018). At the same time, if companies adopt adaptive behaviors to cope with global warming, it will reduce their research and development funds, reduce their ability to develop new products and have a negative impact on their total output. Therefore, unlike Zhang et al. (2018), this paper not only considers TFP, labor, and capital input as channels through which temperature changes affect industrial output, but also examines whether temperature changes indirectly affect output by affecting investment and innovation of enterprises.

In addition, other policies or sudden factors can also affect the output of industrial enterprises, which cannot be reflected in the theoretical model. For example, during the high temperature heat wave period, continuous high temperature weather can cause abnormal operation of production equipment and physical and mental fatigue of operators, which can easily trigger various safety accidents. In order to protect the life and health of workers and prevent production safety accidents caused by extreme high temperature weather, the government will require enterprises to stop production and business activities when the temperature exceeds a certain level. In addition, during the continuous high temperature period in summer, in order to prevent electricity overload and ensure the principle of priority use of electricity in hospitals and schools, some areas will take measures such as peak shifting, peak avoidance and even power rationing. These measures and government actions will have a negative impact on enterprise output. However, due to the unavailability of relevant data, we will not analyze these measures and government actions as channels for temperature changes to affect enterprise output in the following empirical analysis.

9.3 Model Setting and Variable Description

In order to examine the impact and mechanism of temperature changes on industrial output, this article adopts the following econometric model settings:

$$\begin{aligned}\ln y_{i,t} &= \alpha_0 Temp_{i,t} + \alpha_1 Temp_{i,t-1} + \beta_0 W_{i,t} \\ &\quad + \beta_1 W_{i,t-1} + \gamma \Psi_t^j + \delta \Phi_t^r + c_i + \varepsilon_{i,t}\end{aligned} \tag{9.3}$$

where, the subscript i represents the enterprise, t represents the year, j represents the manufacturing industry, r represents the six major regions divided according to the geographical area of China. The explained variable $lny_{i,t}$ includes the natural logarithm value of industrial output (Ln(Output)), measured by the natural logarithm value of the added value of industrial enterprises, as well as various "channel variables" expounded by the theoretical model. These "channel variables" include: the natural logarithm value of the total factor productivity of the enterprise (Ln(TFP)), where we use the extended OP method to estimate the TFP of the enterprise; the natural logarithm value of the labor input of the enterprise (Ln(Labor)), measured by the natural logarithm value of the number of employees in the enterprise; the natural logarithm value of the capital input of the enterprise (Ln(Capital)), measured by the natural logarithm value of the total fixed assets of the enterprise; the natural logarithm value of the investment of the enterprise (Ln(Investment)), represented by the difference between the total fixed assets of the enterprise in the current year and the previous year plus the depreciation of the enterprise in the current year and taking the natural logarithm; the innovation ability of the enterprise, represented by the ratio of the output value of new products of the enterprise to the total industrial output value of the enterprise (New product ratio).

$\mathrm{Temp}_{\mathrm{i,t}}$ represents the temperature variable, borrowing the method of Hsiang (2010), here we use the seasonal average temperature ($\mathrm{Temp}^{\mathrm{spring}}$, $\mathrm{Temp}^{\mathrm{summer}}$, $\mathrm{Temp}^{\mathrm{fall}}$, and $\mathrm{Temp}^{\mathrm{winter}}$) to measure. In addition to the temperature variable, this paper also controls other weather variables related to temperature in the model, represented by $\mathrm{W}_{\mathrm{i,t}}$, including total seasonal precipitation, total sunshine hours, average atmospheric pressure, average relative humidity, and average wind speed. In addition, in order to test whether the impact of weather variables on various economic variables has a lag, we also added the lag terms of these weather variables which are denoted by $\mathrm{Temp}_{\mathrm{i,t-1}}$ and $\mathrm{W}_{\mathrm{i,t-1}}$.

This paper attributes other uncontrolled factors that may affect industrial output to the error term. These error terms mainly include four parts: ① c_i denotes unobservable firm heterogeneity that does not change over time, such as the geographical location of the firm; ② Ψ_t^j denotes industry and time fixed effects, such as technological progress in a specific industry, price shocks, and policy changes; ③ Φ_t^r denotes regional and time fixed effects, such as environmental changes and policy shocks in a specific region, here we divided China into six major regions according to geographical divisions: North China, Northeast, East China, Central South, Southwest, Northwest; and ④ε_{it} denotes other unobservable random disturbances. In addition, in the regression analysis, we also controlled for heteroscedasticity, autocorrelation, and spatial correlation of the residuals.

Unlike the empirical strategy of Zhang et al. (2018), we constructed temperature variables in two ways in the empirical analysis, using average seasonal temperature and temperature range as temperature variables.[2] Therefore, we can not only test whether the impact of temperature changes on industrial output has seasonal differences, but also estimate the marginal impact of different temperature ranges on industrial output.

9.4 Data Sources and Descriptive Statistics

The empirical analysis of this paper uses two sets of micro data. The first set of data comes from the Chinese Industrial Enterprise Database from 1998 to 2007, which covers all state-owned enterprises and "above-scale" (i.e., main business income exceeds 5 million yuan) enterprises among non-state-owned enterprises. The sample statistics increased year by year from about 160,000 in 1998 to about 330,000 in 2007. These enterprises contributed 85% of China's industrial output (Jefferson et al., 2003), so they can represent the overall level of national industrial enterprises well. The database includes more than eighty variables from corporate balance sheets, income statements, and cash flow statements, and provides detailed information about corporate identity, ownership, industrial added value, employment, total fixed assets, depreciation, and new product output value. Using this database, we calculated the TFP of the enterprises. In the process of data processing, we referred to Cai and Liu (2009), we removed observations that met any of the following conditions: ① Observations with missing key indicators (such as total assets, number of employees, total industrial output value, net value of fixed assets, and sales); ② Observations that do not meet the "above scale" standard, i.e., sales less than 10 million yuan, or observations with fewer than 8 employees; ③ Observations that clearly violate accounting principles, such as total assets less than current assets, total assets less than the net value of fixed assets, or accumulated depreciation less than current depreciation; ④ Extreme values (top and bottom 0.5%) of key indicators (including industrial added value, sales revenue, and total industrial output value) were excluded.

The second set of data comes from the Meteorological Data Sharing Service System of the China Meteorological Administration, which records daily average temperature, rainfall, sunshine duration, atmospheric pressure, relative humidity, and wind speed of 820 meteorological stations in China from 1998 to 2007. The database also contains detailed coordinate information for each meteorological station. Based on this, we matched the weather data with the boundaries of Chinese counties to obtain county-level weather data. Among the 2811 counties in the sample, for counties with multiple meteorological stations, we used the average of the data from each station to construct their weather data. For counties without a meteorological station, we used the weather information of the neighboring county to construct the weather data. According to the weather data provided by this database, we can calculate the weather variables for the four seasons of spring, summer, autumn, and winter in each county in China from 1998 to 2007.

After merging the above industrial enterprise data with the weather data, our final sample is an unbalanced panel of about 1.8 million observations. Table 9.1 provides descriptive statistics for the main variables.[3]

9.5 Estimation Results and Analysis

9.5.1 The Impact of Temperature Changes on Industrial Output

9.5.1.1 Baseline Results

This paper first examines the impact of temperature changes on industrial output, and the regression results are shown in Table 9.2. The results of column (1) only control for current weather variables, showing that the output of industrial enterprises has a significant negative correlation with summer temperature, with an estimated parameter value of − 0.0591. This indicates that, with other explanatory variables held constant, for every 1 °C increase in summer temperature, the industrial added value of the enterprise will decrease by 5.91%, and this negative impact is significant at the 1% level. Conversely, the output of industrial enterprises has a significant positive correlation with winter temperature, with an estimated parameter value of 0.0181. This indicates that, with other explanatory variables held constant, for every 1 °C increase in winter temperature, the output of industrial enterprises will increase by 1.81%, and this positive impact is also significant at the 1% level. The temperature changes in other seasons do not have a significant impact on the output of industrial enterprises.

To test whether the impact of temperature changes on industrial output has a lag, we further controlled for lagged weather variables in the model. As can be seen from column (2) of Table 9.2, adding lagged weather variables as explanatory variables, the negative correlation between summer temperatures and industrial output remains,

Table 9.1 Main variable statistical characteristics

Variable name	Variable meaning	Sample size	Mean value	Standard deviation	Minimum value	Maximum value
Ln(Output)	The natural logarithm of industrial added value	1,803,482	8.6233	1.3014	4.7449	12.4772
Ln(Labor)	The natural logarithm of the number of employees	1,803,482	4.8013	1.0820	2.0794	11.9823
Ln(Capital)	The natural logarithm of the total value of fixed assets	1,799,402	8.4543	1.6511	0.0000	16.4471
Ln(TFP)	The natural logarithmic value of TFP	1,801,322	3.1281	1.0276	− 3.7805	10.0428
Ln(Investment)	The natural logarithm of investment	983,330	6.9060	1.9093	− 7.1634	15.6322
New products ratio	New product ratio	1,567,431	0.0296	0.1377	0.0000	1.0000
$Temp^{spring}$	Spring average temperature (°C)	1,803,482	16.0323	3.7237	− 6.2435	27.8217
$Temp^{summer}$	Summer average temperature (°C)	1,803,482	26.3717	2.3915	4.8435	32.7565
$Temp^{fall}$	Autum average temperature (°C)	1,803,482	17.5138	4.5235	− 6.5077	27.6363
$Temp^{winter}$	Winter average temperature (°C)	1,803,482	4.9121	6.7872	− 28.7890	23.5678
$Tsdv^{spring}$	Spring temperature standard deviation (°C)	1,795,839	5.8782	1.1443	1.5949	13.2471

(continued)

Table 9.1 (continued)

Variable name	Variable meaning	Sample size	Mean value	Standard deviation	Minimum value	Maximum value
$Tsdv^{summer}$	Standard deviation of summer temperature (°C)	1,795,839	2.7420	0.6452	0.7558	6.6549
$Tsdv^{fall}$	Standard deviation of autumn temperature (°C)	1,795,839	5.6911	1.4867	1.3770	15.4902
$Tsdv^{winter}$	Standard deviation of winter temperature (°C)	1,795,839	3.8337	0.8613	1.2790	9.4573

as does the positive correlation between winter temperatures and industrial output, with estimated parameter values of − 0.0565 and 0.0140, respectively. In addition, an increase in summer temperature in the previous year will also significantly reduce the industrial output of the enterprise in the current year, but compared with the current impact, the impact of the lagged period is slightly smaller, with a coefficient of − 0.0358. Furthermore, we found that for every 1 °C increase in both current and lagged summer temperatures, the current industrial output of the enterprise will decrease by 9.23%.

9.5.1.2 Robustness Test

To examine the reliability of the above results, we conducted robustness tests from four aspects. Due to space limitations, the robustness test only reports the estimated coefficients of summer temperature variables.

Firstly, in baseline regression, we group the samples by "city year", allowing for mutual independence between groups, and adjust the covariance matrix of the residuals accordingly. Here, we re-group the samples by "county-year" and perform cluster analysis. The results are reported in column (1) of Table 9.3. Secondly, in the previous study, the regional division was based on geographical divisions, dividing China into six major regions. As the second robustness check, we use economic divisions, dividing China into Northeast, East, Central, and West four major regions, constructing a new region × year fixed effect, and re-estimating the model. The regression results are reported in column (2) of Table 9.3. Thirdly, in the third robustness check, we replace the region × year fixed effect in the benchmark model with city fixed effect × time trend in the model. The regression results are reported in column

Table 9.2 Impact of temperature changes on industrial output (baseline results)

	Ln(Output)	
	(1)	(2)
$Temp^{spring}$	− 0.0029	− 0.0056
	(0.0090)	(0.0087)
$Temp^{summer}$	− 0.0591***	− 0.0565***
	(0.0088)	(0.0090)
$Temp^{fall}$	− 0.0007	0.0132
	(0.0079)	(0.0087)
$Temp^{winter}$	0.0181***	0.0140**
	(0.0067)	(0.0068)
$L.Temp^{spring}$		0.0084
		(0.0083)
$L.Temp^{summer}$		− 0.0358***
		(0.0094)
$L.Temp^{fall}$		0.0187**
		(0.0081)
$L.Temp^{winter}$		− 0.0042
		(0.0075)
Sum of $Temp^{spring}$		0.0028
		(0.0134)
Sum of $Temp^{summer}$		− 0.0923***
		(0.0139)
Sum of $Temp^{fall}$		0.0319**
		(0.0135)
Sum of $Temp^{winter}$		0.0098
		(0.0109)
Other weather variables	YES	YES
industry × Year fixed effect	YES	YES
Geographical region × Year fixed effect	YES	YES
Observed value	1,803,482	1,801,581
R^2	0.7998	0.8001

Note The robust standard deviation is shown in parentheses. ***, **, * represent Significance at the 1%, 5%, and 10% levels respectively

(3) of Table 9.3. Finally, the previous study did not consider the impact of weekends and statutory holidays when examining the impact of temperature changes on industrial output. In China, most industrial production activities occur on weekdays. Therefore, in the last robustness check, we exclude the weather information of weekends and statutory holidays and reconstruct the weather variables, then re-estimate

Table 9.3 Impact of temperature changes on industrial output (robustness test)

	Cluster analysis at the county year level	Control economic regions × Year fixed effect	Controlling urban fixed effects × Time trend	Weather variables constructed using weather information from weekdays
	(1)	(2)	(3)	(4)
$Temp^{summer}$	− 0.0565***	− 0.0337***	− 0.0288***	− 0.0555***
	(0.0061)	(0.0095)	(0.0067)	(0.0088)
$L.Temp^{summer}$	− 0.0358***	− 0.0178*	− 0.0124	− 0.0293***
	(0.0064)	(0.0096)	(0.0077)	(0.0085)
Sum of $Temp^{summer}$	− 0.0923***	− 0.0515***	− 0.0411***	− 0.0848***
	(0.0095)	(0.0139)	(0.0106)	(0.0129)
Other weather variables	YES	YES	YES	YES
Industry × Year fixed effect	YES	YES	YES	YES
Geographical region × Year fixed effect	YES	NO	NO	YES
Economic region × Year fixed effect	NO	YES	NO	NO
Urban fixed effects × Time trend	NO	NO	YES	NO
Observed value	1,801,581	1,801,581	1,801,581	1,801,581
R^2	0.8001	0.7999	0.8032	0.8001

Note The robust standard deviation is shown in parentheses. ***, **, * represent Significance at the 1%, 5%, and 10% levels respectively

the model. The last column of Table 9.3 reports the regression results. From these results, it can be seen that the core conclusions of this paper have good robustness.

9.5.2 *Mechanism of Temperature Change Affecting Industrial Output*

To explore the channels through which temperature changes affect the output of industrial enterprises, in conjunction with the theoretical analysis in the second part of this paper, we choose total factor productivity, employment, total value of fixed assets, investment, and the ratio of new products as channel variables, and regress them as the dependent variables in Eq. (9.3). Since the rise in summer temperature has a significant negative impact on industrial output, we only report the estimated coefficients of the summer temperature variable here.

For simplicity, we only controlled the current weather variables in the model. Columns (1)–(5) of Table 9.4 report the estimated results of the above 5 channel variables as dependent variables. The results show that, except for the number of employees, summer temperature is significantly negatively correlated with the TFP, total fixed assets, investment, and new product ratio of industrial enterprises. Specifically, with other explanatory variables unchanged, for every 1 °C increase in summer temperature, the TFP, total fixed assets, investment, and new product ratio of industrial enterprises will decrease by 4.06%, 2.78%, 7.33%, and 0.21% respectively.

It should be emphasized that Zhang et al. (2018) found that the main channel through which temperature changes affect industrial output is enterprise TFP, while temperature changes have no significant impact on the total value of fixed assets of enterprises. Our analysis shows that temperature changes not only affect a firm's TFP but also indirectly affect industrial output by affecting the total value of a firm's fixed assets, investment, and the ratio of new products. The following factors may have led to the differences between the conclusions of Zhang et al. (2018) and our study. First, the construction of the temperature variable is different. Zhang et al. (2018) used temperature bins as the temperature variable, while the results we report here use the seasonal average temperature as the temperature variable.[4] Second, the sources of weather data are different. The weather data in Zhang et al. (2018) comes

Table 9.4 Channel analysis of the impact of temperature changes on industrial output

	Ln(TFP)	Ln(Labor)	Ln(Capital)	Ln(Investment)	New product ratio
	(1)	(2)	(3)	(4)	(5)
$Temp^{summer}$	− 0.0406***	− 0.0033	− 0.0278***	− 0.0733***	− 0.0021*
	(0.0081)	(0.0050)	(0.0068)	(0.0176)	(0.0012)
Other weather variables	YES	YES	YES	YES	YES
industry × Year fixed effect	YES	YES	YES	YES	YES
Geographical region × Year fixed effect	YES	YES	YES	YES	YES
Observed value	1,801,322	1,803,482	1,799,402	983,330	1,567,431
R^2	0.7039	0.8914	0.8889	0.6903	0.6236

Note The robust standard deviation is shown in parentheses. ***, **, * represent Significance at the 1%, 5%, and 10% levels respectively

from the National Oceanic and Atmospheric Administration of the United States, while our data comes from the Meteorological Data Sharing Service System of the China Meteorological Administration. Third, in the analysis of Zhang et al. (2018), other than TFP, labor, and capital input, no other potential impact channels were considered. In contrast, our empirical research conducted a more comprehensive channel analysis.

9.5.3 Temperature Changes and Industrial Output: Does the Type of Ownership of the Firm Matter?

Table 9.5 reports the regression results by ownership. The results show that the increase in summer temperature does not have a significant impact on the output of state-owned and foreign-funded enterprises. However, higher temperatures will lead to a decrease in the output of private and collective enterprises, and the impact on private enterprises is greater. Specifically, controlling for other explanatory variables, for every 1 °C increase in summer temperature, the output of private and collective enterprises will decrease by 10.81% and 9.62% respectively, and this negative impact is significant at the 1% level. We believe that the reason for the above phenomenon may be that in our country, compared with private and collective enterprises, state-owned and foreign-funded enterprises have a more complete labor system, stricter implementation of national regulations, and a more relaxed financing environment. State-owned and foreign-funded enterprises in our country can use their institutional and capital advantages to take a series of adaptive measures, such as setting up rest places in high-temperature working environments, equipping with air-conditioning and other heatstroke prevention and cooling equipment to alleviate the negative impact of high temperature on their output. Private and collective enterprises are smaller in scale, have lower technical levels, and face greater financing constraints, so their ability to cope with global warming is weaker.

9.5.4 Does the Negative Impact of High Temperatures on Industrial Output Vary Across Industries?

To analyze whether the impact of temperature changes on industrial output varies across industries, we regress the output of different industries according to the two-digit industry code, controlling for current and lagged weather variables in all sub-industry regression models. Figure 9.1 shows the estimated results by industry, where the point estimate coefficients are the total impact of current and lagged summer temperature changes on the output of each industry. As can be seen, out of 39 industrial sectors, 18 are negatively affected by high temperatures. These sectors include both labor-intensive and capital-intensive industries. Among them, the "furniture

Table 9.5 The impact of temperature changes on the output of enterprises with different ownership systems

	State-owned	Collective	Private	Foreign
	(1)	(2)	(3)	(4)
$Temp^{summer}$	− 0.0138	− 0.0689***	− 0.0653***	− 0.0173
	(0.0092)	(0.0134)	(0.0111)	(0.0149)
$L.Temp^{summer}$	0.0006	− 0.0273**	− 0.0428***	− 0.0077
	(0.0100)	(0.0120)	(0.0125)	(0.0149)
Sum of $Temp^{summer}$	− 0.0133	− 0.0962***	− 0.1081***	− 0.0249
	(0.0154)	(0.0196)	(0.0177)	(0.0229)
Other weather variables	YES	YES	YES	YES
industry × Year fixed effect	YES	YES	YES	YES
Geographical region × Year fixed effect	YES	YES	YES	YES
Observed value	233,368	252,815	807,494	339,807
R^2	0.8870	0.7949	0.7882	0.7727

Note The robust standard deviation is shown in parentheses. ***, **, * represent Significance at the 1%, 5%, and 10% levels respectively

manufacturing", "rubber products", and "electrical machinery and equipment manufacturing" industries are the most affected by high temperatures. For every 1 °C increase in summer temperature, the output of these three industries will decrease by 23.13%, 21.25%, and 18.88% respectively.

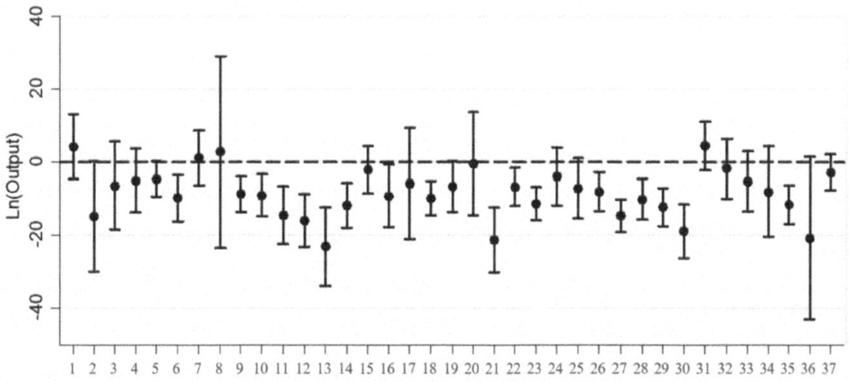

Fig. 9.1 Impact of summer temperature changes on output of different industries (%) (Serial numbers 1 to 37 correspond to different industries as follows)

1-Coal mining and washing industry\2-Ferrous metal ore mining\3-Non-ferrous metal mining\4-Non-metallic mining\5-Agri-food processing industry\6-food manufacturing\7-Beverage manufacturing\8-Tobacco products industry\9-Textile industry\10-Textile,clothing,shoes and hats manufacturing\11-Leather,fur, feather (down) and their products industry\12-Wood processing and wood, bamboo, rattan, palm and grass products industry\13-Furniture manufacturing\14-Paper and paper products industry\15-Printing and reproduction of recorded media\16-Manufacture of educational and sports goods\17-Petroleum processing, coking and nuclear fuel processing industries\18-Chemical raw materials and chemical products manufacturing\19-Medicine Manufacturing\20-Chemical fibre manufacturing\21-Rubber products industry\22-Plastic industry\23-Non-metallic mineral products industry\24-Ferrous metal smelting and rolling industry\25-Non-ferrous metal smelting and rolling processing industry\26-Metal products industry\27-General equipment manufacture\28-Specialized equipment manufacturing\29-Transportation equipment manufacturing\30-Electrical machinery and equipment manufacturing\31-Communications equipment, computers and other electronic equipment manufacturing\32-Instruments, meters and machinery for cultural and office use manufacturing\33-Crafts and other manufacturing\34-Waste resources and waste materials recycling and processing industry\35-Electricity, heat production and supply\36-Gas production and supply industry\37-Water production and supply industry.

9.6 Extension Analysis

9.6.1 Extension I: Does the Change in Temperature Fluctuation Affect Industrial Output?

The previous study only considered the impact of average temperature changes on industrial enterprises, ignoring the impact of temperature fluctuation amplitude changes. Will changes in temperature fluctuations affect the output of industrial enterprises? What is its internal mechanism? An in-depth study of this issue is of great practical significance, for example, it is conducive to evaluate the impact of temperature changes on the output of China's industrial enterprises in a more comprehensive and systematic way.

To test the impact of changes in temperature fluctuation on industrial output, we adopt the following econometric model setting:

$$\begin{aligned} \ln y_{i,t} &= \alpha_0 Temp_{i,t} + \rho_1 Tsdv_{i,t} + \beta_0 W_{i,t} \\ &+ \gamma \Psi_t^j + \delta \Phi_t^r + c_i + \varepsilon_{i,t} \end{aligned} \tag{9.4}$$

where, $Tsdv_{i,t}$ represents the fluctuation of temperature, measured by the standard deviation of temperatures in the four seasons of spring, summer, autumn, and winter. The calculation method of the standard deviation of temperature for each season is as follows: First, we calculate the average seasonal temperature for each county during the sample period; then, we subtract the average temperature of the corresponding season from the daily average temperature of each county in each year of a season, square the result, and sum up to get the sum of squared deviations; finally, we take the average of the sum of squared deviations and take the square root, to get the standard deviation of the seasonal temperature for each county in different years. The construction method for other weather variables and fixed effects in Model (9.4) is consistent with Eq. (9.3). For simplicity, we don't control lagged weather variables.

Table 9.6 reports the regression results. Due to space limitations, we only report the estimated coefficients of temperature standard deviation variables. Firstly, we regress industrial output as the dependent variable, and the regression results are shown in column (1) of Table 9.6. The results show that there is a significant negative correlation between the standard deviation of temperatures and the output of industrial enterprises in all seasons, except for spring. Specifically, for every increase in the fluctuation amplitude of summer temperature, autumn temperature, and winter temperature by one unit, the output of industrial enterprises will decrease by 2.31%, 2.63%, and 1.62%, respectively.

Next, we further analyze how the changes in temperature fluctuation amplitude affect the output of industrial enterprises through various channels. We again take the various channel variables mentioned above as the dependent variables for regression analysis, and the estimated results are shown in columns (2)–(6) of Table 9.6. The results show that for every unit increase in the amplitude of summer temperature fluctuations, the TFP of industrial enterprises will decrease by 4.01%. In contrast, there is a positive correlation between the standard deviation of summer temperature and the ratio of new products, which may be because, in order to reduce the negative impact of increased temperature fluctuation amplitude on output, enterprises may have increased R&D investment.

The standard deviation of autumn temperature has a significant negative correlation with the TFP, total fixed assets, and investment of industrial enterprises, with coefficients of – 0.0173, – 0.0164, and – 0.0379, respectively, and is significant at the 5% level. There is also a significant negative correlation between the standard deviation of winter temperature and the TFP and investment of industrial enterprises.

In summary, an increase in the amplitude of summer temperature fluctuations will indirectly affect industrial output through the channels of enterprise TFP and the ratio of new products. An increase in the amplitude of autumn temperature fluctuations will lead to a decrease in industrial output by reducing the TFP, total fixed assets, and investment of enterprises. An increase in the amplitude of winter temperature fluctuations will negatively affect industrial output by reducing the TFP and investment of enterprises.

Table 9.6 The impact of temperature fluctuation amplitude on industrial output and its influencing channels

	Ln(Output)	Ln(TFP)	Ln(Labor)	Ln(Capital)	Ln(Investment)	New product ratio
	(1)	(2)	(3)	(4)	(5)	(6)
$Tsdv^{spring}$	0.0015	0.0095	− 0.0020	− 0.0107	− 0.0158	− 0.0024**
	(0.0090)	(0.0083)	(0.0048)	(0.0073)	(0.0181)	(0.0010)
$Tsdv^{summer}$	− 0.0231**	− 0.0401***	0.0125	0.0109	0.0325*	0.0026**
	(0.0098)	(0.0090)	(0.0079)	(0.0080)	(0.0167)	(0.0012)
$Tsdv^{fall}$	− 0.0263***	− 0.0173**	0.0038	− 0.0164***	− 0.0379***	0.0006
	(0.0076)	(0.0067)	(0.0058)	(0.0055)	(0.0135)	(0.0008)
$Tsdv^{winter}$	− 0.0162**	− 0.0168**	0.0027	− 0.0042	− 0.0357**	0.0013
	(0.0077)	(0.0073)	(0.0068)	(0.0058)	(0.0161)	(0.0009)
Other weather variables	YES	YES	YES	YES	YES	YES
industry × Year fixed effect	YES	YES	YES	YES	YES	YES
Geographical region × Year fixed effect	YES	YES	YES	YES	YES	YES
Observed value	1,803,482	1,801,322	1,803,482	1,799,402	983,330	1,567,431
R^2	0.7999	0.7040	0.8914	0.8890	0.6904	0.6237

9.6.2 Extension II: Constructing Temperature Intervals as Temperature Variables

Here, we use temperature bins as temperature variables to test the robustness of the results. The specific model settings are as follows:

$$\ln y_{i,t} = \sum_{m} \alpha^{m} Tbin_{i,t}^{m} + \beta W_{i,t} + \gamma \Psi_{t}^{j} + \delta \Phi_{t}^{r} + c_{i} + \varepsilon_{i,t} \tag{9.5}$$

where, $Tbin_{i,t}^{m}$ represents the number of days in the t th year when the average daily temperature in the region where company i is located falls into the m th temperature interval. We divide the average daily temperature into 12 intervals, each with a span of 3 °C. Here we define $Tbin_{i,t}^{1}$ = the number of days in the t th year when the average daily temperature in the region where company i is located falls into the interval (−∞, 0 °C); $Tbin_{i,t}^{2}$ = the number of days in the t th year when the average daily temperature in the region where company i is located falls into the interval [0 °C, 3 °C). And so on, $Tbin_{i,t}^{12}$ = the number of days when the company i The number of days in the t th year when the average daily temperature in my region falls into the interval [30 °C, +∞). The construction methods of other weather variables and fixed effects are consistent with model (9.3). In addition, since the total number of days in all temperature intervals adds up to 365, to avoid multicollinearity, we removed the 6th temperature interval [12 °C, 15 °C) from the regression.[5] Therefore, the regression coefficient α^m measures the marginal impact on industrial output for each additional day that the average daily temperature falls into the interval m, relative to the temperature interval [12 °C, 15 °C). We chose [12 °C, 15 °C) as the reference interval because it is in the middle of all temperature intervals. Our regression results will not change due to the selection of other reference temperature intervals.

We use industrial output as the dependent variable for regression, and the regression results are shown in column (1) of Table 9.7. First, there is a nonlinear relationship between temperature and industrial output. Specifically, when the temperature is below [12 °C, 15 °C), the temperature has a slight negative impact on industrial output, and the estimated coefficients of most low-temperature intervals are not significant. When the temperature exceeds [12 °C, 15 °C), industrial output will decrease with the further increase in temperature, and the rate of decrease will gradually increase. For each additional day that the average daily temperature falls into the [27 °C, 30 °C) and [30 °C, +∞) intervals, the output of industrial enterprises will decrease by 0.30% and 0.43% respectively, and this negative impact is significant at the 1% level, which is similar to the conclusion of Zhang et al. (2018).

Next, in order to further analyze whether there is also a non-linear relationship between the various channel variables and temperature mentioned earlier, we will use the 5 channel variables above as the dependent variables for regression. The regression results are shown in columns (2)–(6) of Table 9.7. The results in column (2) of Table 9.7 show that there is also a similar non-linear relationship between temperature and industrial enterprise TFP. When the temperature is below [12 °C, 15 °C], the temperature has a slight negative impact on the TFP of industrial enterprises; when the temperature exceeds [12 °C, 15 °C], the negative impact of temperature on TFP gradually increases with the increase of temperature, which is similar to the research conclusion of Zhang et al. (2018).

Columns (3) and (4) of Table 9.7 report the estimated results of the impact of different temperature intervals on the number of employees and the total value of fixed assets of enterprises respectively. Column (3) of Table 9.7 shows that, relative to the temperature interval [12 °C, 15 °C), for each additional day that the average daily temperature falls into the [24 °C, 27 °C) and [27 °C, 30 °C) intervals, the number of employees in industrial enterprises will decrease by 0.1% and 0.13% respectively. Column (4) of Table 9.7 shows that when the temperature is low, the temperature has no significant impact on the total value of fixed assets of industrial enterprises; when

Table 9.7 Marginal impact and impact channels of different temperature ranges on industrial output

	Ln(Output)	Ln(TFP)	Ln(Labor)	Ln(Capital)	Ln(Investment)	New product ratio
	(1)	(2)	(3)	(4)	(5)	(6)
< 0 °C	– 0.0013	– 0.0010	0.0009*	– 0.0007	– 0.0059***	0.0001
	(0.0009)	(0.0008)	(0.0005)	(0.0007)	(0.0017)	(0.0001)
[0 °C, 3 °C)	– 0.0001	0.0001	0.0007*	– 0.0006	– 0.0055***	0.0000
	(0.0007)	(0.0007)	(0.0004)	(0.0005)	(0.0014)	(0.0001)
[3 °C, 6 °C)	– 0.0014**	– 0.0011**	0.0008**	– 0.0005	– 0.0034***	– 0.0000
	(0.0006)	(0.0006)	(0.0004)	(0.0005)	(0.0011)	(0.0001)
[6 °C, 9 °C)	0.0005	0.0004	0.0005	0.0001	– 0.0028**	– 0.0001
	(0.0006)	(0.0005)	(0.0003)	(0.0005)	(0.0011)	(0.0001)
[9 °C, 12 °C)	– 0.0005	– 0.0009*	0.0005	0.0001	– 0.0017*	0.0000
	(0.0005)	(0.0005)	(0.0003)	(0.0004)	(0.0010)	(0.0001)
[12 °C, 15 °C)	–	–	–	–	–	–
[15 °C, 18 °C)	– 0.0013**	– 0.0016***	0.0001	– 0.0003	0.0007	– 0.0001
	(0.0005)	(0.0005)	(0.0004)	(0.0004)	(0.0009)	(0.0001)
[18 °C, 21 °C)	– 0.0009	– 0.0006	– 0.0002	– 0.0012**	– 0.0012	– 0.0001*
	(0.0006)	(0.0005)	(0.0004)	(0.0005)	(0.0011)	(0.0001)
[21 °C, 24 °C)	– 0.0004	– 0.0002	– 0.0006	– 0.0012**	– 0.0002	– 0.0003**
	(0.0007)	(0.0007)	(0.0005)	(0.0005)	(0.0012)	(0.0001)
[24 °C, 27 °C)	– 0.0020**	– 0.0011	– 0.0010**	– 0.0015***	– 0.0031***	– 0.0003***
	(0.0008)	(0.0007)	(0.0004)	(0.0006)	(0.0012)	(0.0001)
[27 °C, 30 °C)	– 0.0030***	– 0.0018**	– 0.0013***	– 0.0021***	– 0.0046***	– 0.0003**
	(0.0009)	(0.0008)	(0.0005)	(0.0007)	(0.0015)	(0.0001)
≥ 30 °C	– 0.0043***	– 0.0033***	– 0.0005	– 0.0025***	– 0.0057***	– 0.0003**
	(0.0010)	(0.0009)	(0.0006)	(0.0008)	(0.0017)	(0.0001)
Other weather variables	YES	YES	YES	YES	YES	YES
industry × Year fixed effect	YES	YES	YES	YES	YES	YES

(continued)

Table 9.7 (continued)

	Ln(Output)	Ln(TFP)	Ln(Labor)	Ln(Capital)	Ln(Investment)	New product ratio
	(1)	(2)	(3)	(4)	(5)	(6)
Geographical region × Year fixed effect	YES	YES	YES	YES	YES	YES
Observed value	1,803,482	1,801,322	1,803,482	1,799,402	983,330	1,567,431
R^2	0.7998	0.7040	0.8914	0.8889	0.6904	0.6236

Note The robust standard deviation is shown in parentheses. ***, **, * represent Significance at the 1%, 5%, and 10% levels respectively

the average daily temperature exceeds 18 °C, the further increase in temperature will lead to a decrease in the total value of fixed assets of industrial enterprises, and the rate of decrease will gradually increase as the temperature rises. These findings are different from the research conclusions of Zhang et al. (2018), who found that changes in most temperature intervals have no significant impact on the labor and capital of industrial enterprises. The difference in the source of weather data is the main reason for the difference between the findings of Zhang et al. (2018) and our research.[6]

Column (5) of Table 9.7 reports the estimated results of different temperature ranges on corporate investment. The results show that too high or too low temperatures have a significant negative impact on industrial corporate investment. The last column of Table 9.7 reports the estimated results of different temperature ranges on the ratio of new products of enterprises. Similar to the estimated results with seasonal temperature as the temperature variable, the negative impact of temperature changes on the ratio of new products of industrial enterprises is relatively small.

9.6.3 Extension III: Expand Sample

In this section, we extend the sample from 1998–2007 to 1998–2013. However, as Wang et al. (2018) and Chen (2018) pointed out, the industrial enterprise data from 2008 to 2013 have serious missing indicators, including (1) no statistical industrial added value, and all industrial intermediate input indicators are missing, so it is impossible to calculate the industrial added value from 2008 to 2013 and estimate TFP; (2) the database has partial missing indicators such as depreciation and new product output value, making it impossible to calculate investment and innovation as channel variables. Therefore, due to the above problems with the 2008–2013 data, we choose in this section to use gross industrial output as a proxy for industrial value added and to test the effect of temperature change on the two channel variables, labor and capital.

First, we regress the total industrial output from 1998 to 2007, and the regression results are reported in column (1) of Table 9.8. The results show that when comparing the estimates of temperature change on industrial value added reported in Table 9.2 earlier, summer temperatures in the current and lagged periods are essentially unchanged significantly, both in terms of the magnitude of the coefficients and in terms of the level of significance. Specifically, for every 1 °C increase in current and lagged summer temperatures, the industrial added value and total industrial output of enterprises will decrease by 9.23% and 9.32% respectively, and this negative impact is significant at the 1% level. Therefore, the impact of temperature changes on total industrial output and industrial added value is quite close.

Secondly, column (2) of Table 9.8 reports the estimated results of the impact of rising summer temperatures on total industrial output using data from 1998 to 2013.[7] Compared with the estimated results of column (1) from 1998 to 2007, the coefficients of the current and lagged summer temperatures have significantly decreased, but their cumulative impact on total industrial output is still negative and has passed the 1% level of significance test. For every 1 °C increase in the current and lagged summer temperatures, the total industrial output of enterprises will decrease by 2.64%, and this negative impact is significant at the 1% level. This result suggests that when

Table 9.8 The impact and channel of temperature changes on industrial output (1998–2013)

	Ln(Total industrial output)		Ln(Labor)	Ln(Capital)
	1998–2007	1998–2013	1998–2013	1998–2013
	(1)	(2)	(3)	(4)
$Temp^{summer}$	– 0.0536***	– 0.0117**	0.0027	0.0391***
	(0.0073)	(0.0059)	(0.0045)	(0.0090)
$L.Temp^{summer}$	– 0.0396***	– 0.0147**		
	(0.0078)	(0.0057)		
Sum of $Temp^{summer}$	– 0.0932***	– 0.0264***		
	(0.0117)	(0.0087)		
Other weather variables	YES	YES	YES	YES
industry × Year fixed effect	YES	YES	YES	YES
Geographical region × Year fixed effect	YES	YES	YES	YES
Observed value	1,801,581	3,214,428	3,217,274	3,194,100
R^2	0.8661	0.8584	0.8462	0.8704

Note The robust standard deviation is shown in parentheses. ***, **, * represent Significance at the 1%, 5%, and 10% levels respectively

enterprises are in high temperatures for a long time, they may take a series of adaptive measures to alleviate the negative impact of high temperatures on their output.

Finally, columns (3) and (4) of Table 9.8 respectively report the estimated results of the impact of temperature changes on employment and capital using data from 1998 to 2013. For simplicity, in the regressions of columns (3) and (4), we only controlled for current weather variables. We found that, on the one hand, the rise in summer temperatures does not have a significant negative impact on the number of employees in enterprises, which is similar to the estimated results from 1998 to 2007. On the other hand, contrary to the estimated results from 1998 to 2007, the rise in summer temperatures has a significant positive impact on the fixed assets of enterprises, indicating that enterprises may alleviate the negative impact of high temperatures on their output by increasing their capital stock.

9.7 Future Impact of Global Climate Change

Using the estimated coefficients from the benchmark model (9.3) (average seasonal temperature as the temperature variable), we predict the potential impact of future climate change on China's industrial output. The future temperature data used in this paper comes from Climate Wizard. The website provides mid-term (2040–2069) and long-term (2070–2099) temperature data predicted based on different global climate change models, including monthly average temperature and seasonal average temperature. These temperature data predictions are based on A2, A1B, and B1, three possible socio-economic development scenarios, corresponding to high, medium, and low greenhouse gas emission scenarios.[8] Following Schlenker and Roberts (2009), we use the temperature data predicted by the UKMO-HadCM3 climate change model for the following analysis.

We first calculated the mid-term and long-term variation values of spring, summer, autumn, and winter temperatures in various districts and counties in China based on future temperature data and average temperatures from 1998 to 2007. Then, combining the estimation coefficients of the benchmark model (Table 9.2) and robustness test (Table 9.3) mentioned earlier, we predicted the mid-term and long-term effects of future temperature changes on China's industrial output. The results show that under the A2, A1B, and B1 scenarios, the UKMO-HadCM3 model predicts that China's industrial output will decrease by 3.04–14.64% in the medium term. Compared to the mid-term, long-term temperature changes have a greater negative impact on China's industrial output. Specifically, in the A2, A1B, and B1 scenarios, the UKMO-HadCM3 model predicts that China's industrial output will decrease by 5.87–19.99% in the long term.

9.8 Conclusion and Policy Implications

This paper uses the Chinese industrial enterprise database and daily weather data to explore the impact of temperature changes on industrial output and its internal impact mechanism. We found: First, there is a non-linear relationship between industrial output and temperature changes. Specifically, an increase in summer temperature significantly reduces industrial output, while an increase in winter temperature increases industrial output. Compared to the temperature range [12 °C, 15 °C), daily average temperatures in higher or lower ranges both negatively affect industrial output. Second, seasonal fluctuations in temperature also have adverse effects on industrial output. Third, high temperatures indirectly affect output by reducing the TFP, total fixed assets, investment, and innovation capabilities of industrial enterprises. Fourth, the negative impact of increased summer temperatures on industrial output varies by industry and ownership. Finally, this paper predicts that future temperature changes will cause China's industrial output to decrease by about 3.0–14.6% in the mid-term and about 5.9–20.0% in the long term.

The theoretical and practical significance of the conclusions of this study is clear. On the one hand, this paper is a useful supplement to existing climate change related research. Existing literature, both domestic and foreign, focuses more on the impacts of climate change on agricultural and industrial outputs, with relatively few studies on the mechanisms of their internal impacts. On the other hand, the conclusions of this study highlight the importance and urgency of addressing global warming. Although China's industrial enterprises have taken measures to adapt to climate change and reduce the adverse effects of global warming, given the adverse effects that global warming has had and will have on China's industrial sector, it is necessary for the government to formulate relevant policies to cope with and adapt to global warming, such as imposing carbon taxes, developing clean energy, and increasing research and development of climate change adaptive technologies. In addition, this paper points out that due to various imperfect regulations and financial disadvantages, private enterprises and collective enterprises have suffered significant economic losses in hot weather. Therefore, the Chinese government should further improve the various systems of private and collective enterprises, increase their financial input, improve their financing environment, and ensure their healthy and stable development.

Notes

1. Both high and low temperatures negatively affect the productivity of labor and capital. For the sake of illustration, in the following theoretical analysis, we will only describe the effects of high temperatures on output and the possible channels of influence.
2. In the part 9.6, the expansibility analysis discusses the results when temperature interval is used as temperature variable.
3. Due to space constraints, we do not report descriptive statistics for other weather variables.

4. In the part 9.6, we also take the temperature box as the temperature variable to analyze the channel of temperature change affecting industrial output, and the main research conclusions have not changed.
5. In order to ensure that the sum of all temperature ranges in different years during the sample period is 365, we exclude the weather information of February 29 from the sample.
6. Zhang et al. (2018) also differed from us in the construction of temperature zones. In order to test whether the difference in the structure of the temperature range is one of the reasons for the difference in the research conclusions, we reconstructed the temperature range according to the method of Zhang et al. (2018) and used the same model settings as Zhang et al. (2018), but the differences in the research conclusions still exist. Therefore, we believe that different sources of weather data are the main reason for the differences in research conclusions.
7. The 2010 data had major quality problems, the capital structure was abnormal, and all important variables such as total industrial output were missing, so we did not include the 2010 data for regression analysis.
8. The three scenarios differ mainly in the assumptions made about population growth, economic development, technological progress, and energy sources and efficiency.

References

Adhvaryu, A., Kala, N., & Nyshadham, A. (2014). *The light and the heat: Productivity co-benefits of energy-saving technology* (Working Paper).

Burke, M., Hsiang, S. M., & Miguel, E. (2015). Global non-linear effect of temperature on economic production. *Nature, 527*(7577), 235–239.

Cao, M., & Wei, J. (2005). Stock market returns: A note on temperature anomaly. *Journal of Banking and Finance, 29*(6), 1559–1573.

Cai, H., & Liu, Q. (2009). Competition and corporate tax avoidance: Evidence from Chinese industrial firms. *Economic Journal, 119*(537), 764–795.

Chen, L. (2018). Re-exploring the usage of China's industrial enterprise database. *Economic Review, 6*, 140–153.

Chen, S., Chen, X., & Xu, J. (2016). Impacts of climate change on agriculture: Evidence from China. *Journal of Environmental Economics and Management, 76*, 105–124.

Chen, X., & Yang, L. (2019). Temperature and industrial output: Firm-level evidence from China. *Journal of Environmental Economics and Management, 95*, 257–274.

Dell, M., Jones, B. F., & Olken, B. A. (2012). Temperature shocks and economic growth evidence from the last half century. *Journal of Economic Literature: Macroeconomics, 4*(3), 66–95.

Dell, M., Jones, B. F., & Olken, B. A. (2014). What do we learn from the weather? The new climate-economy literature. *Journal of Economic Literature, 52*(3), 740–798.

González-Alonso, J., Teller, C., Andersen, S. L., Jensen, F. B., Hyldig, T., & Nielsen, B. (1999). Influence of body temperature on the development of fatigue during prolonged exercise in the heat. *Journal of Applied Physiology, 86*(3), 1032–1039.

Hancock, P. A., Ross, J. M., & Szalma, J. L. (2007). A Meta-analysis of performance response under thermal stressors. *Human Factors, 49*(5), 851–877.

Hsiang, S. M. (2010). Temperatures and cyclones strongly associated with economic production in the Caribbean and Central America. *Proceedings of the National Academy of Sciences, 107*(35), 15367–15372.

Jefferson, G., Hu, A., Guan, X., & Yu, X. (2003). Ownership, performance, and innovation in China's industrial enterprise sector. *China Economic Review, 14*(1), 89–113.

Lilja, D. J. (2000). *Measuring computer performance: A practitioner's guide*. Cambridge University Press.

Lu, X. D., & Lian, Y. J. (2012). Estimation of total factor productivity of industrial enterprises in China: 1999–2007. *China Economic Quarterly, 2*, 542–558.

Mostafavi, M., & Agnew, B. (1996). The Impact of ambient temperature on lithium-bromide/water absorption machine performance. *Applied Thermal Engineering, 16*(6), 515–522.

Moore, F. C., & Delavane, B. D. (2015). Temperature impacts on economic growth warrant stringent mitigation policy. *Nature Climate Change, 5*(2), 127–131.

Olley, G. S., & Pakes, A. (1996). The dynamics of productivity in the telecommunications equipment industry. *Econometrica, 64*(6), 1263–1297.

Schlenker, E., & Roberts, M. J. (2009). Nonlinear temperature effects indicate severe damages to U.S. crop yields under climate change. *Proceedings of the National Academy of Sciences, 106*(37), 15594–15598.

Somanathan, E., Somanathan, R., Sudarshan, A., & Tewari, M. (2015). *The impact of temperature on productivity and labor supply: Evidence from Indian manufacturing* (Working Paper).

Wang, Y., Li, W., & Dai, Y. (2018). How do zombie firms affect innovation?—Evidence from China's industrial firms. *Economic Review, 11*, 99–114.

Zhang, J. G., Yang, S. H., & Suo, C. Y. (2015). Research on effects of high temperature and high humidity environment on miners' physiology and psychology. *China Safety Science Journal, 1*, 23–28.

Zhang, P., Deschenes, O., Meng, K., & Zhang, J. (2018). Temperature effects on productivity and factor reallocation: Evidence from a half million Chinese manufacturing plants. *Journal of Environmental Economics and Management, 88*, 1–17.

Zivin, J. G., Hsiang, S. M., & Neidell, M. (2018). Temperature and human capital in the short-and long-run. *Journal of the Association of Environmental and Resource Economists, 5*(1), 77–105.

Zivin, J. G., & Neidell, M. (2014). Temperature and the allocation of time: Implications for climate change. *Journal of Labor Economics, 32*(1), 1–26.

Chapter 10
The Pathway to China's Carbon–Neutral Agriculture: Measures, Potential and Future Strategies

Minjuan Zhao, Rui Shi, Ruirui Du, and Liuyang Yao

Abstract Achieving China's agriculture carbon neutrality by 2060 aligns with national and transnational policy efforts. This paper aims to set forth a possible way for China's carbon–neutral agriculture, which needs to produce more food with lower emissions, based on an overview of the agricultural greenhouse gas emissions from 1990 to 2060. Our results show that China has made impressive progress in food production in the past decades with relatively low per-unit output emissions. At the same time, agricultural emissions peaked in 2016 with 842.21 million tons of carbon dioxide equivalent. We predict that a reduced carbon budget will offset the emissions in 2060 with a 65% increase in food production by proper mitigation measures. In addition, we put forth several strategies, including carbon–neutral capacity building, GHG emission avoidance, carbon storage, and low-carbon agri-food system establishment, to push China's agriculture to carbon neutrality. This study provides a national perspective on achieving agricultural carbon neutrality and will interest policymakers in making low-carbon development plans.

Keywords Carbon neutrality · Agriculture · Greenhouse gas emissions · Mitigation potential

10.1 Introduction

Global emissions of carbon dioxide (CO_2) and other greenhouse gas (GHG) from human activities have brought multiple challenges to human society and economic activities (IPCC, 2007). In response to the threats posed by excessive GHG emissions, nearly 200 countries committed to the Paris Climate Agreement in December 2016 (Glemarec, 2019; Keohane, 2019) (a set of binding procedural commitments aiming to reduce GHG emissions and limit global warming to 1.5 °C or well below 2 °C). The

M. Zhao (✉) · R. Shi · R. Du · L. Yao
College of Economics and Management, Northwest A&F University, No. 3 Taicheng Road, Yangling, Xianyang 712100, Shaanxi, People's Republic of China
e-mail: minjuan.zhao@nwsuaf.edu.cn

B. Gong et al. (eds.), *Chinese Governance and Transformation Towards Carbon Neutrality*, Resources, Environment and Agricultural Development,
https://doi.org/10.1007/978-981-97-9996-1_10

agriculture sector is the second contributor to climate change, accounting for 12.23% of global GHG emissions (Climate Watch, 2021). Meanwhile, agriculture occupies almost half of the global vegetated land, which has a great potential for climate change mitigation by reducing GHG emissions and increasing soil carbon sequestration (Lal et al., 1998; Lehner & Rosenberg, 2017; Soil Management CRSP, 2002). As more people populate the earth and the affluent population continues to grow, the need for food will increase by 35 to 56% between 2010 and 2050 (van Dijk et al., 2021). This need means that, unless actively addressed, agricultural GHG emissions are likely to increase at least proportionally with the rising food demand and pose threats to achieving GHG emissions goals (Searchinger et al., 2019). Thus, the pathway to carbon–neutral agriculture faces the challenge of satisfying the growing food demand alongside GHG reduction goals.

Despite the great challenge of achieving carbon–neutral agriculture, some developed countries have proposed policy strategies but differ in their goals and pathways. Australia's leading agricultural organizations are committed to achieving carbon–neutral agriculture by 2050 (Kingwell, 2021). The British Farmers' Union (NFU) proposes three practical ways to achieve carbon neutrality in agriculture by 2040, including increasing agricultural productivity, enhancing carbon storage, and developing biomass energy and material (NFU, 2020). Demark, which believes that it can neither reduce agricultural production nor shift the production of high-carbon emission food to other countries, contributes to achieving carbon–neutral agriculture by 2050 (Searchinger et al., 2021).

Nevertheless, the way to carbon–neutral agriculture still needs to be discovered, especially in developing countries. China, the world's largest developing country, has announced its commitment to achieving a carbon peak before 2030 and carbon neutrality before 2060. In addition, its agriculture sector's role needs to be further understood, considering the rising food production pressures caused by the large population size and growing middle-income population, as well as the tightening environmental constraints from the degraded natural resources and policy stringency (Chen & Huang, 2021; Kuhn, 2018; Zhang, 2021). Meanwhile, China's pursuit of carbon–neutral agriculture also provides a vital opportunity for implementing its major sustainable development strategies, such as ecological civilization construction and rural vitalization (Altiparmak, 2022; Bondes, 2022; Liu et al., 2022; Shapiro et al., 2011). The carbon–neutral target, alongside the investment in technologies and practices in proactively addressing emissions, has the promise to improve the productivity and sustainability of agriculture development in China.

The literature has covered a set of critical issues related to carbon–neutral agriculture. The first set of research has modeled future scenarios relating to agricultural GHG emissions considering the potential GHG emissions reduction technologies and practices (Auvikki et al., 2021; Eastwood et al., 2019; Joseph, 2023; Klerkx & Rose, 2020; Pan et al., 2015; Stilgoe et al., 2013). These models include the global scale land-use models, MAgPIE and IMAGE (Popp et al., 2010; Stehfest et al., 2009), the scenario-based model at the European scale (Westhoek et al., 2015), the carbon opportunity cost and production emissions method (Searchinger et al., 2018), and the global balance model, GlobAgri-WRR (Ranganathan et al., 2016). The second set of research has analyzed the cost-effectiveness of different agriculture GHG emissions reduction measures. Recent reports by McKinsey and the World Resources Institute assess the mitigation potential and the related cost-effectiveness of different proven measures for mitigating agricultural GHG emissions (Ahmed et al., 2020; Searchinger et al., 2021). Researches also show that protective measures such as no-tillage agricultural practices, payments for agricultural soil carbon sequestration, and climate-resilient agriculture have significantly higher economic benefits (Antle & Stoorvogel, 2008; Jamil et al., 2021; Suresh et al., 2021). The third set of research has focused on the management practices to create incentives for adopting low-carbon agricultural practices, such as payment and financing schemes (Lewandrowski et al., 2004). However, there is still little scientific information about China's carbon–neutral agriculture in China. According to the current retrieval, only a few studies have reviewed the adoption and effectiveness of greenhouse gas emission reduction measures at the farm level, while there is no report on achieving agricultural carbon neutrality at the national level.

Accordingly, our study aims to analyze the carbon neutrality of China's agriculture while meeting the food production target by 2060. Our analysis shows that China's agricultural carbon intensity is lower than the leading exporter of agricultural products, which means that shifting China's domestic food demand in the future to other countries will increase GHG emissions elsewhere. As a major responsible country in addressing climate change, China has promised to maintain an overall 95% food self-sufficiency in the future and will share equally in the mitigation burden to increase yields. Thus, our baseline scenario of agricultural GHG emissions has been a proportionate global growth in food production. The mitigation scenarios to achieve carbon–neutral agriculture have been outlined considering the potential of different mitigation measures. Finally, concluding remarks are made regarding the various strategies to secure the achievement of China's carbon–neutral agriculture.

The paper fills the literature gap from two aspects. First, we set forth a possible pathway to China's carbon–neutral agriculture considering China's food production target. We predict a baseline scenario of China's agricultural GHG emissions in 2030 and 2060 considering the food demand growth, and plan a phased pathway to carbon neural agriculture, including the peak period (before 2016), prepare period (2016–2030), development and scaling up period (2030–2050), and refine period (2050–2060). Given that the pathway to China's carbon–neutral agriculture still needs to be discovered in existing literature, our findings are intended to provide government and agricultural stakeholders with information on the scale of potential mitigation opportunities and a pathway to China's carbon–neutral agriculture.

Second, the paper set forth phased strategies for achieving carbon–neutral agriculture according to the characteristics of carbon neutral pathway, providing a policy reference for China's carbon–neutral agriculture. The proposed strategies consist of four main areas: carbon–neutral capacity building, GHG emission avoidance, carbon storage, and low-carbon agrifood system establishment, providing a more scientific and comprehensive strategy for achieving carbon–neutral agriculture. Moreover, the strategies are synergistic with China's food security goal, which means we should improve agriculture productivity and save land and forests simultaneously, providing a strategic direction for the transformation of China's agriculture food system with carbon neutrality goals.

The following is the layout of the article. Section 10.2 reviews the historical GHG emission of China's agriculture and makes an international comparison of GHG emissions due to agriculture. Section 10.3 explores the potential GHG emissions from China's agriculture and the pathway to carbon–neutral agriculture. We set forth the strategies for achieving agricultural carbon neutrality in Sect. 10.4. The conclusions and policy implications are summarized in Sect. 10.5.

10.2 Overview of GHG Emissions from China's Agriculture

China's agriculture is characterized by smallholders with less than 0.82 mu cultivated land per capita, feeding a population of 1.46 billion with 1.19 billion mu cultivated land. In 2018, the agricultural output value from China accounted for 24.89% of the world. However, the input intensity of fertilizer and pesticides in China's agriculture is higher than the global average level, leading to soil quality degradation. Furthermore, the utilization efficiency of agricultural by-products (such as straw and manure) is relatively low, causing lots of GHG emissions. China's GHG emissions inventory shows that agriculture accounted for 6.85% of the country's total emissions in 2018, while non-CO_2 emissions were up to 33.7%. Agriculture activities from crops and livestock production release significant non-CO_2 emissions such as methane (CH_4) and nitrous oxide (N_2O), which have a more potent global warming potential than CO_2. Therefore, measuring and analyzing these carbon emission sources in agriculture are essential, which is the precondition of mitigation potential analysis.

10.2.1 The Historical Trend of GHG Emission from China's Agriculture

We provide a comprehensive description of the three most relevant GHG emissions, methane (CH_4), nitrous oxide (N_2O), and carbon dioxide (CO_2), from agriculture and total sectors in China over the period 1990–2018 in Table 10.1. Many databases can measure GHG emissions from agriculture. However, according to the IPCC guidelines, the FAO database is currently considered to be the only known database that can break down the sources of agricultural greenhouse gas emissions. It allows us to analyze agricultural GHG emissions in depth.

The GHG emissions from total sectors exhibited an upward trend during the 1990–2018 period and reached 11,705 million tons of carbon dioxide equivalent (denoted as Mt CO_2eq) in 2018. Moreover, the GHG emissions due to agriculture contributed 801.61 Mt CO_2eq in 2018, a roughly 14% growth since 1990, accounting for approximately 7% of the total GHG emissions. The methane and nitrous oxide

Table 10.1 Historical overview of China's agricultural GHG emissions

Resource institute							
	1990	1995	2000	2005	2010	2015	2018
Unit	Mt CO_2eq						
Carbon dioxide	1823.96	2735.48	2994.73	5486.88	8138.34	9120.27	9663.36
Methane	730.78	798.90	830.59	837.94	1064.20	1237.79	1238.95
Nitrous oxide	313.21	371.35	386.72	428.39	487.17	543.19	539.14
HFCs, PFCs and SF6	5.76	12.57	37.66	109.60	182.65	248.43	264.36
Total China GHG emissions	2873.71	3918.30	4249.70	6862.81	9872.37	11,149.68	11,705.81
Agricultural sector emissions	703.44	785.32	792.77	799.46	810.54	837.61	801.61
Carbon dioxide	87.35	89.88	91.59	92.49	98.64	121.53	114.86
On-farm energy use	85.77	88.28	89.96	90.84	96.98	119.86	113.19
Drained organic soils	1.58	1.60	1.63	1.65	1.66	1.66	1.66
Ratio	0.12	0.11	0.12	0.12	0.12	0.15	0.14
Methane	386.25	418.82	424.89	406.25	395.12	390.95	377.45
Enteric fermentation	186.55	225.68	235.52	221.68	201.76	191.55	185.47
Rice cultivation	164.92	153.04	149.07	143.23	148.15	152.67	149.84
Manure MANAGEMENT	25.85	31.36	32.45	33.05	35.49	35.09	31.33
On-farm energy use	4.74	4.61	3.83	4.13	4.88	6.00	5.44
Burning-crop residues	4.00	3.95	3.87	3.96	4.53	5.51	5.26
Savanna fires	0.19	0.19	0.15	0.20	0.30	0.13	0.11
Ratio	0.55	0.53	0.54	0.51	0.49	0.47	0.47
Nitrous oxide	229.84	276.61	276.29	300.72	316.78	325.14	309.30
Synthetic fertilizers	107.91	131.22	122.16	148.01	163.90	170.80	156.19
Manure left on pasture	45.12	55.46	60.09	59.69	56.48	54.27	54.65
Manure management	27.95	34.64	36.04	33.31	32.29	30.82	30.47
Manure applied to soils	23.89	24.51	24.22	24.98	28.11	33.26	33.10
Crop residues	20.04	25.49	27.51	28.60	29.87	28.77	27.85

(continued)

Table 10.1 (continued)

Resource institute							
On-farm energy use	3.30	3.68	4.70	4.49	4.26	5.25	5.15
Burning- crop residues	0.98	0.97	0.95	0.97	1.11	1.35	1.29
Drained organic soils	0.48	0.49	0.49	0.50	0.50	0.50	0.50
Savanna fires	0.16	0.16	0.13	0.17	0.26	0.12	0.10
Ratio	0.33	0.35	0.35	0.38	0.39	0.39	0.39

Data source The GHG emission due to agricultural sector origins from FAO database; the GHG emission due to all sectors origins from Climate Watch database, an open data platform managed by the World Resource Institute

emissions within the farm gate generated most of the GHG emissions in agriculture, reaching 686.75 Mt CO_2eq in 2018, while carbon dioxide reached nearly 114.86 Mt CO_2eq.

As for the proportion of different GHG emissions, methane contributed significantly, with a ratio of 47.09% in 2018. From 1990 to 2018, the methane emissions from the agricultural sector first experienced a continuous rise, peaked at 424.89 Mt CO_2eq in 2000, and then showed a fluctuant declining trend. The proportion of methane emissions showed a continuous decline from 1990 to 2018. In particular, enteric fermentation and rice cultivation are the two significant sources of methane emissions (88.84%), generating emissions of 335.31 Mt CO_2eq in 2018. It is clear that the methane due to enteric fermentation increased and peaked in 1995 and declined for the following 20 years. In addition, the methane emissions caused by rice cultivation fluctuated and showed a declining global trend from 1990 to 2018.

The second-largest GHG component of China's agriculture, nitrous oxide, first experienced a rising trend, peaked at 325.14 Mt CO_2eq in 2015, and then decreased significantly in 2018. Moreover, its proportion showed an upward trend from 1990 to 2018. Synthetic fertilizer was the most significant source of nitrous oxide emissions (50.50%) in 2018. The emissions from synthetic fertilizer increased from 107.91 Mt CO2eq to 156.19 Mt CO_2eq from 1995 to 2018, with a growth rate of 44.74%.

Moreover, for carbon dioxide, the emissions and the proportion increased overall from 1990 to 2018. On-farm energy use was the primary source of carbon dioxide (98.55%) in 2018, generating annual emissions of 113.19 Mt CO_2eq. In particular, the GHG emissions from on-farm energy use experienced a rising trend during the study period.

10.2.2 The International Comparison of GHG Emissions Due to Agriculture

China's per capita GHG emissions and GHG emissions intensity have been compared internationally in Figs. 10.1 and 10.2. The per capita GHG emissions from the agriculture sector and total sectors of the top ten countries are illustrated in Fig. 10.1, including China, the United States, India, Russia, Indonesia, Brazil, Japan, Iran, Germany, and Canada. In 2018, Canada had the highest per capita GHG emissions of total sectors, reaching 20.59 tons CO_2eq per capita, as large as 2.57 times than China. The United States and Russia were 17.71 and 13.67 tons CO_2eq per capita, respectively. China's per capita GHG emission was 8.02 tons CO_2eq, relatively lower than other countries. When ranking countries in terms of per capita GHG emissions of agriculture sector, Brazil, Canada, and Indonesia were the top three emitters, reaching 5.74, 5.24, and 3.44 tons CO_2eq, respectively. Nevertheless, the per capita GHG emission from agriculture sector in China was only 0.55 tons CO_2eq, significantly lower than most countries. It indicates that although China has the highest GHG emission globally, the per capita GHG emissions from the total and agriculture sectors are relatively low, especially compared with developed countries, such as the United States and Germany. The per capita GHG emissions can illustrate the equity of agricultural GHG emissions to a certain extent. To further analyze the relationship between agricultural output value and GHG emissions, we compared the GHG emissions intensity among the top 10 emitters.

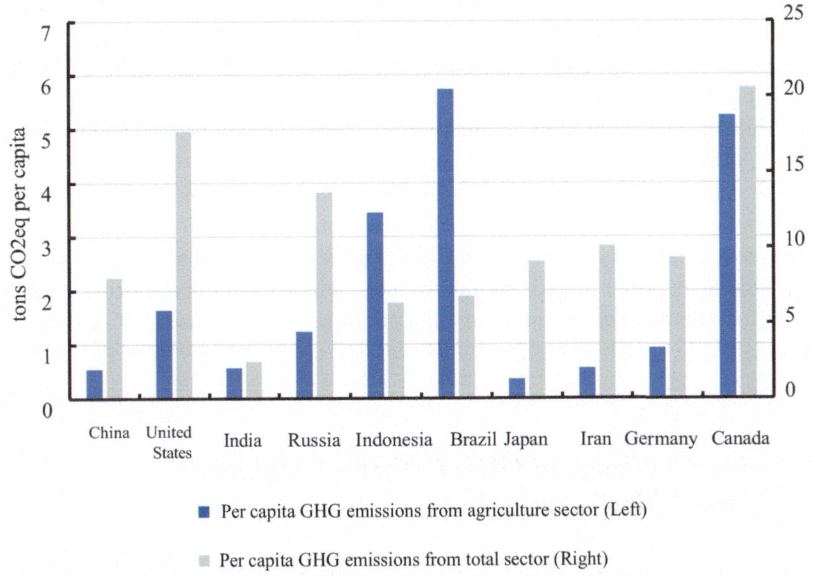

Fig. 10.1 Per capita GHG emissions of top ten carbon emission countries

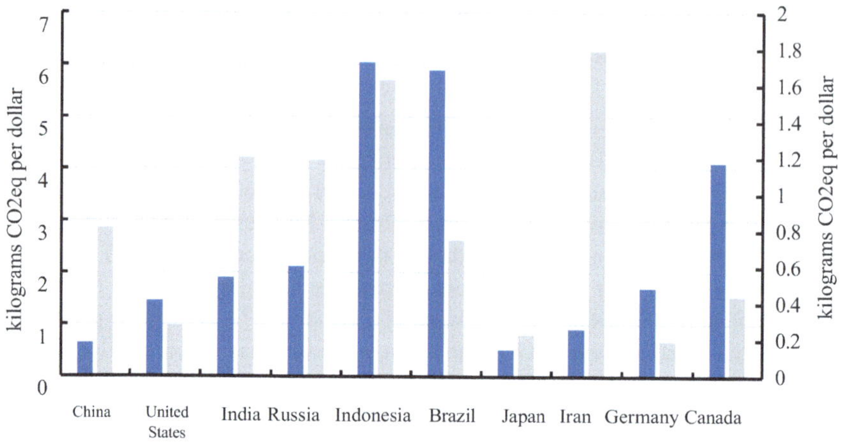

Fig. 10.2 GHG emissions intensity of top ten carbon emission countries. *Data resource* The GHG emissions due to agriculture, agricultural output value, country's population, and country's output value origin from FAO database; the carbon emissions due to total sectors origins from Climate Watch database

In Fig. 10.2, we analyzed the GHG emissions intensity from the entire sectors and agriculture sector of the top ten emitters. For GHG emissions intensity from total sectors, Iran had the highest emissions intensity among these countries, reaching 1.79 kg CO_2eq per dollar in 2018. Indonesia, India, and Russia followed with over 1 kg CO_2eq per dollar. In contrast, China had a relatively low GHG emissions intensity, half less than Iran. When ranking GHG emissions intensity from the agriculture sector, Indonesia, Brazil, and Canada were the top three emitters, reaching 6.05 kg CO_2eq per dollar, 5.91 kg CO_2eq per dollar, and 4.12 kg CO_2eq per dollar, respectively. While the GHG emissions intensity from China's agriculture is 0.65 kg CO_2eq per dollar, ranking ninth among these countries. It indicates that China is at a relatively low carbon emissions stage in agriculture according to the GHG emissions intensity indicator, although the total GHG emissions due to agriculture are significant. Moreover, our analysis shows that China's agricultural carbon intensity is lower than the leading exporter of agricultural products, which means that shifting China's domestic food demand in the future to other countries will increase GHG emissions elsewhere.

10.2.3 The Challenge of GHG Emissions Mitigation from China's Agriculture

The agriculture sector is the second contributor to GHG emissions in China, releasing significant amounts of non-CO_2 emissions such as methane and nitrous oxide, both potent greenhouse gas, totaling 686.75 Mt CO_2eq in 2018. Enteric fermentation, rice cultivation, and synthetic fertilizer contribute the most GHG emissions, accounting for 61.26% of total emissions due to agriculture. Furthermore, the growth in livestock and crop production, caused by population growth and changes in dietary preference, drives the increase in the GHG emissions from animal husbandry and crop production. Hence, reducing GHG emissions in China's agriculture would be a challenge in ensuring food security in the future.

Moreover, through international comparison of GHG emission intensity, we conclude that although China has the most significant GHG emissions from agriculture worldwide, the GHG emissions intensity is relatively low compared with other countries, especially the developed countries, such as the United States and Canada. Therefore, it would be a huge challenge for China's agriculture to reduce GHG emissions, pursuing production and output value growth with relatively low per capita GHG emissions and GHG emissions intensity compared with other countries. Low-carbon technology innovation in agriculture may be vital to tackling these problems.

10.3 GHG Emissions Mitigation Potential from China's Agriculture

Forecasting the GHG emissions mitigation potential is the basis of realizing carbon–neutral agriculture.[1] We forecasted the GHG emission mitigation potential from agriculture considering the mitigation measures of agriculture production and stakeholder engagement and collaboration. To define the mitigation measures of agriculture production, it is essential to identify the primary sources of emissions, mainly crop production, animal management, on-farm energy use, and land use and land-use change. Considering stakeholder engagement and collaboration, agriculture's GHG emissions mitigation potential is much more enormous. The collaboration mitigation measures mainly include crop straw energy utilization, the cultivated land converted to forest land, and food carbon footprint reduction. We illustrated the specific mitigation measures from agriculture production and stakeholder engagement and collaboration in Table 10.2.

10.3.1 GHG Emissions Mitigation Potential from Agriculture Production

We forecasted the GHG mitigation potential from agriculture production in 2030 and 2060 with mitigation measures that refer to removing carbon from the air from agriculture production.[2] Moreover, our mitigation measures identify various promising ways of reducing production emissions with mitigation potential summarized in Table 10.3. Considering the rising food demand and diet preference change, we

Table 10.2 Mitigation measures for carbon neutrality in agriculture

Scope	Source reduction	Mitigation measures
Agriculture production	Crop production	Prohibit straw burning Optimize flood irrigation and drainage in rice cultivation Employ organic farming and other more climate-friendly farming systems Improve management practices for synthetic fertilizers
	Animal management	Improve forage digestibility by forage processing Improve animal health to decrease the mortality rate Improve manure management Develop methane inhibitors and vaccines
	On-farm energy use	Rural solar panel promotion Rural biogas digester construction
	Land use and land-use change	Residue incorporation Reduce or eliminate tillage Add soil amendments
Stakeholder engagement and collaboration	Energy industry Land-use change Consuming sector	Energy utilization of crop straw to reduce primary energy use Cultivated land converted to forest land Food waste reduction

forecasted an 18% structural growth of GHG emissions in 2030 and 65% in 2060 without mitigation measures (Springmann et al., 2018). The GHG emissions due to agriculture are 765.30 Mt CO_2eq in 2030 and 341.36 Mt CO_2eq in 2060, with mitigation measures from agriculture production. Among the agricultural emissions sources, nitrous oxide and methane emissions have huge mitigation potential. Due to agriculture, the methane would come to 351.66 Mt CO_2eq in 2030 and 161.43 Mt CO_2eq in 2060. By taking mitigation measures such as improving forage digestibility, improving manure management, decreasing animal mortality rate, and optimizing flood irrigation and drainage in rice cultivation, we can reduce methane emissions by 18% in 2030 and 73% in 2060. Furthermore, the nitrous oxide emissions due to agriculture would come to 309.53 Mt CO_2eq in 2030 and 161.32 Mt CO_2eq in 2060. We can reduce nitrous oxide emissions by improving management practices for synthetic fertilizers, incorporating residue, reducing or eliminating tillage, and employing organic farming and other climate-friendly farming systems by 11% in 2030 and 71% in 2060. It indicates that the effect of these mitigation measures is better with the extension of time.

Table 10.3 Forecasting of agricultural carbon emissions and potential mitigation in China

	2030		2060	
	18% higher production baseline	After mitigation	65% higher production baseline	After mitigation
Unit	Mt CO_2eq			
Carbon dioxide	129.79	104.11	170.95	18.62
On-farm energy use	127.91	102.32	167.92	18.47
Drained organic soils	1.88	1.79	3.03	0.15
Methane	426.51	351.66	594.93	161.43
Enteric fermentation	209.58	167.66	329.69	105.50
Rice cultivation	169.32	152.39	190.01	34.20
Manure management	35.40	26.56	58.00	20.30
On-farm energy use	6.15	4.92	8.46	0.93
Burning-crop residues	5.94	0.00	8.28	0.00
Savanna fires	0.13	0.13	0.49	0.49
Nitrous oxide	349.51	309.53	556.08	161.32
Synthetic fertilizers	176.49	158.84	299.72	80.93
Manure left on pasture	61.76	56.04	92.30	25.84
Manure management	34.44	25.82	52.77	18.47
Manure applied to soils	35.24	31.71	45.94	12.40
Crop residues	31.47	29.88	54.61	22.39
On-farm energy use	5.82	4.65	7.37	0.81
Burning-crop residues	1.46	0.00	2.03	0.00
Drained organic soils	0.56	0.53	0.91	0.05
Savanna fires	0.11	0.11	0.43	0.43
Total	905.81	765.30	1321.96	341.36

10.3.2 GHG Mitigation Potential Considering Stakeholders' Engagement and Collaboration

We predicted the GHG mitigation potential considering stakeholders' engagement and collaboration, and Fig. 10.3 presents the pathway to carbon–neutral agriculture. Here, the mitigation measures refer to the removal of carbon from the air or emission reduction by another sector that we count compensating for actual physical emissions due to China's agriculture. The scope boundary of mitigation measures

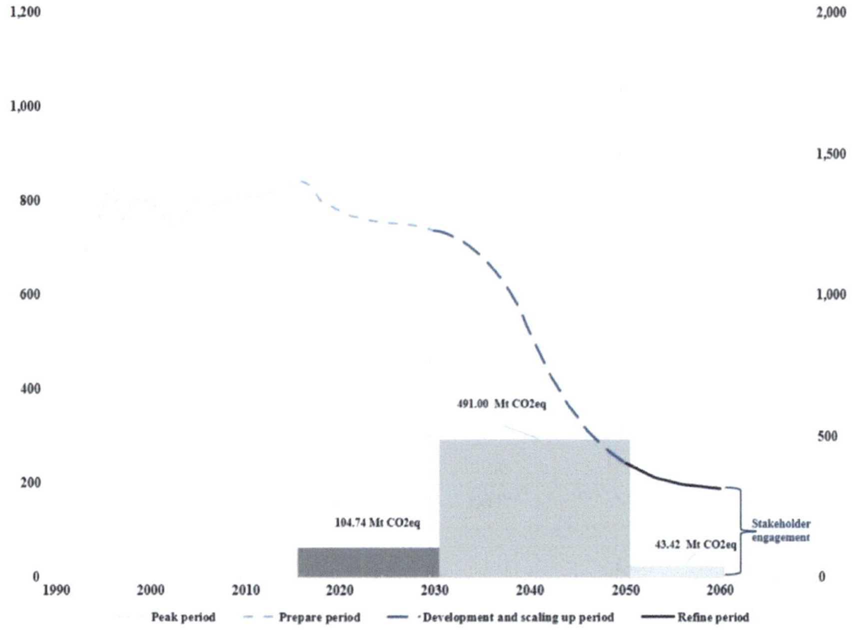

Fig. 10.3 The pathway to carbon–neutral agriculture

is broader than that in Table 10.3. Results in Fig. 10.3 consider the specific mitigation measures, including bioenergy (which reducing emissions from fossil fuel use), reforestation and soil carbon gains (which absorb carbon dioxide from the atmosphere), and food carbon footprint reduction (which reducing emissions from the food-making process).

Referring to Springmann et al. (2018), we predicted the baseline of China's agricultural GHG emissions in 2030 and 2060. Following Searchinger et al. (2021), we set the other mitigation factors for agricultural carbon emissions. The author of the original paper developed a model with a separate spreadsheet to estimate mitigation factors for different abatement measures. The results of this study are considered an important research reference by experts around the world. Particularly, straw burning is expected to be banned entirely in China by 2030. Thus, the GHG emissions from straw burning were set to zero in 2030 and 2060. Moreover, considering that savanna fires are unstable, we set their migration factor to zero in 2030 and 2060.

We assumed that the accumulative GHG emissions budget is 28,137.22 Mt CO_2eq (Shu et al., 2021). Furthermore, we divide the pathway to realizing carbon–neutral agriculture into four stages according to the development trend of agricultural carbon emissions and the time point of China's carbon peak and carbon neutrality policy. The first stage is called the peak period (before 2016). The agricultural GHG emissions showed a fluctuating upward trend and peaked in 2016. Due to the extreme pursuit of increased food production at this stage, there were severe ecological and environmental issues during this period.

The second stage is from 2016 to 2030, called prepare period. The objective at this stage is to build leadership capacity and competency among industry stakeholders. The agriculture industry will develop skills and knowledge to adopt low-carbon technologies by investing human capital. Mitigation measures in this period include developing capability-building initiatives for agriculture and developing science communication initiatives for all stakeholders. The GHG emissions due to agriculture peaked in 2016 and began to decrease. Moreover, from 2016 to 2030, the GHG emissions in agriculture decrease slowly with short-term mitigation measures, such as promoting residue incorporation, improving manure management, prohibiting crop-straw burning, and using clean energy.

The third stage is from 2030 to 2050, called the development and scaling up period (2030–2050). The objective of the stage is to minimize emissions due to agriculture. After 2030, the GHG emissions due to agriculture will decrease rapidly and step into a scaling-up period. The mitigation measures at this period include energy utilization of crop straw, developing methane inhibitors and vaccines, and adopting low-carbon technologies in agriculture production.

The fourth stage is from 2050 to 2060, called refine period. At this stage, the GHG emissions due to agriculture are relatively low. The stage aims to continuously improve agriculture's measures, methods, and products and sustain a stable low carbon emissions status. At this stage, the main mitigation measures include the increased forest land converted from cultivated land in agriculture and a stable high level of soil carbon sequestration. We can only maintain a sustainable low-carbon agriculture production pattern through these mitigation measures.

10.3.3 Discussion on China's Agriculture Carbon Neutrality

We calculated the mitigation potential in agriculture with the mitigation measures from agriculture production and stakeholder engagement and collaboration. By illustrating the pathway to realizing carbon–neutral agriculture, we arrived at the point that agricultural GHG emissions peaked in 2016. After 2016, the GHG emissions in agriculture decreased slowly from 2016 to 2030 and rapidly from 2030 to 2050. Finally, agriculture's GHG emissions will remain relatively low after 2050. Mitigation measures play a vital role in agriculture during the agricultural GHG emissions reduction and low-carbon production periods.

It is worth noting that the cost and benefits of the mitigation measures would change during different stages, considering the technology development, marginal benefits change, and upfront cost. Therefore, we should reduce the GHG emissions due to agriculture by mitigation measures with the maximum profit constraint. Besides, stakeholders' engagement and collaboration with other sectors can improve agriculture's GHG emission mitigation potential. Accordingly, the challenges in China's agricultural emission reduction pathway include choosing efficient mitigation measures with maximum profit constraints and maximizing the mitigation potential in agriculture through stakeholders' engagement and collaboration.

Most of the existing literature on agricultural carbon neutrality usually focuses on developed countries such as the United States and Denmark (Kingwell, 2021; Lehner & Rosenberg, 2017; Puupponen et al., 2022; Searchinger et al., 2021) while seldomly discusses on developing countries. Moreover, the research has conducted economic evaluations of carbon–neutral agriculture policy in terms of feasibility (Searchinger et al., 2021), input–output (Scuderi et al., 2021), and cost-effectiveness (Kingwell, 2021). In the study of carbon–neutral pathways in agriculture, our study holds the same viewpoint as most scholars: carbon–neutral agriculture is geared towards a sustainable food system, considering the challenges of human health, conservation of natural resources and biodiversity, and adaptation to climate change. We discussed the potential of mitigation measures for carbon–neutral agriculture and proposed a future carbon–neutral pathway roadmap for China's agriculture, and provided a more scientific and comprehensive strategy for achieving carbon–neutral agriculture. Furthermore, it can provide a valuable reference for achieving carbon–neutral agriculture for other developing countries.

Moreover, China still needs to issue policies or regulations to achieve carbon–neutral agriculture at this stage. However, China has covered several policies and regulations related to agricultural emissions reduction and storage in ecological civilization construction and green agriculture transition. For examples, in 2021, the Ministry of Agriculture and Rural Affairs released the top ten technology models for carbon reduction and storage in agriculture and rural areas. Furthermore, China's State Council issued the Fourteenth Five-Year Plan to promote agricultural and rural areas to reduce carbon emissions and improve carbon storage. Moreover, China's first agricultural carbon trading platform was launched in Fujian province, which further promotes agricultural carbon storage through the market. China initially formed a policy system for agricultural carbon reduction and storage, while the policy objectives remain to be clarified and refined, and technological innovation and resource utilization efficiency need to be further promoted.

10.4 Strategies for Achieving Agricultural Carbon Neutrality

Carbon–neutral agriculture is an ambitious target for China's agriculture industry to achieve net zero GHG in 2060. Regarding the food security goal, China's agricultural carbon neutrality means that we should reduce net GHG emissions from agriculture and satisfies food demand growth. Although many technological and practical options exist to reduce emissions from agriculture, there is still a need to develop strategies to make carbon–neutral agriculture a mutually beneficial way for society, environment, and farmers. According to the carbon–neutral agriculture pathway analysis, we proposed strategies in four areas: carbon–neutral capacity building, GHG emissions avoidance, carbon storage, and a low-carbon agrifood system establishment. Table 10.4 presents these strategies.

Table 10.4 Strategies for carbon neutrality in agriculture

Strategy type	Strategies
Carbon neutrality capacity building	Knowledge communication and building of carbon neutrality Develop related tool and measures Clear goal policy set
GHG emissions avoidance	Low-carbon crop production Low-carbon animal husbandry
Carbon storage	Soil management Peatland conservation Afforestation
Low-carbon agrifood system establishment	Increasing food productivity Low-carbon diet Reduce food loss and waste

10.4.1 Carbon Neutrality Capacity Building

During the prepare period for carbon–neutral agriculture (2016–2030), developing agricultural carbon neutrality capacity is essential, which is vital to enable the agricultural transition to a carbon–neutral position by 2060. First, we should pay attention to the development of carbon neutrality capability and the training of all stakeholders, such as providing active and visible recognition and support to industry leaders and developing science communication initiatives for all stakeholders to ensure a shared understanding of knowledge and technology. Second, it is vital to developing agricultural carbon reduction and storage tools. For instance, establishing a monitoring and assessment system for agricultural carbon reduction and storage potential will help analyze China's carbon–neutral agriculture progress. Third, setting a series of clear and stable policies and regulations related to carbon–neutral agriculture will help provide a clear understanding of carbon–neutral agriculture strategy for all stakeholders.

10.4.2 GHG Emissions Avoidance

During the prepare period (2016–2030) and development and scaling up period (2030–2050) of agricultural carbon neutrality, agricultural GHG emissions avoidance is an important work area. It includes low-carbon crop production and low-carbon animal husbandry. First, in crop production, the application of nitrogen fertilizers, rice cultivation, and energy use are the primary sources of GHG emissions. It is suggested to increase the nitrogen use efficiency for nitrogen fertilizer application. For example, the percentage of applied nitrogen absorbed by crops. It involves improving fertilizer management or fertilizer composition to increase the nitrogen uptake rate, thus reducing the amount of fertilizer needed. For rice cultivation, we can shorten the duration of field flooding and reduce the water levels to decrease the growth of methane-producing bacteria, which can reduce emissions by up to 90%, save water and increase rice yields on some farms. Moreover, some rice varieties also generate less methane. For agricultural energy use, actions include integrating low-carbon energy sources such as solar and wind, efficiency programs into agriculture, and using renewable energy in nitrogen fertilizer manufacturing.

Furthermore, in animal husbandry, enteric fermentation, manure management, and manure left on pasture are the three main sources of GHG emissions. For enteric fermentation, increasing ruminants' productivity can reduce methane emissions, mainly because more milk and meat are produced per kilogram of feed. In addition, new technologies can reduce enteric fermentation, such as 3-nitrooxypropan (3-NOP), a chemical additive that inhibits microbial methane tested in New Zealand and cut methane emissions by 30%. Improving manure management by better separating liquids from solids and capturing methane can significantly reduce emissions. For manure left on pasture, the emerging approach involves applying chemicals that prevent nitrogen from turning into nitrous oxide and growing grasses that prevent this process naturally. The government can consider increasing support for the research and development of such chemical and biological nitrification inhibitors and encouraging farmers to adopt them.

10.4.3 Carbon Storage

During the development and scaling up period and the refine period of carbon–neutral agriculture (2030–2060), the effort should focus on carbon storage which is a long process. Given that improving agricultural productivity can cause more land clearing locally in some cases, we must explicitly link it with efforts to protect natural ecosystems from conversion to agriculture. The strategy contains three main work areas: soil management, peatland conservation, and reforestation.

First, in terms of soil carbon, many soils have been degraded over time and thus it is an excellent opportunity to improve soil health and microbial diversity through better grazing management and planting deep-rooted perennial grasses or forage species. Essential strategies include avoiding further loss of carbon from soils by halting the conversion of forests and protecting or increasing soil carbon by boosting the productivity of grasslands and croplands.

Second, peatlands' agriculture conversion requires drainage, releasing large amounts of carbon into the atmosphere. Thus, restoring carbon to wetlands should be a high priority and would improve the GHG mitigation potential. Actions to take include providing funds for peatland restoration, improving peatland mapping, and establishing laws that prevent peatlands from being drained.

Moreover, agriculture has a history of sacrificing trees for increasing agricultural productivity; however, the perception is now changing. It is proven that trees provide a range of benefits, including lamb survival, shade, and shelter for livestock in heatwaves, biodiversity restoration, and wind erosion reduction. Afforestation is a crucial way to increase biomass and soil carbon. Evidence shows that the above-ground forest system ecosystems contain approximately the same amount as present in the earth's atmosphere in the form of CO_2 (Nilsson & Schopfhauser, 1995). China has proposed a strategic objective to increase the forest coverage rate to 24.1% in 2025 and 25% in 2030. The forest coverage rate can increase agriculture resilience to climate extremes through improved water retention and soil fertility. It includes the mitigation measures in agriculture that convert surplus cultivated land to forest land, which is a long-term process.

10.4.4 Low-Carbon Agrifood System Establishment

To achieve agricultural carbon neutrality and ensuring achievement, we should establish an efficient food system and transition to a sustainable low-carbon food diet during the process. First, given that demand for animal-based foods is projected to grow significantly and pastureland accounts for more than half of agricultural land use in China, boosting pasture productivity is an effective solution. Second, the rising demand for food puts enormous pressure on carbon–neutral farming. Therefore, there is a need to promote a low-carbon diet, which is not a ban on meat-eating habits but a focus on improving the efficiency of food provision, buying local and seasonal food, and reducing consumption of carbon footprint. Third, as food loss and waste occur all along the food chain, from the field to the fork, measuring food waste, setting reduction targets, and improving food preservation time are recommended.

10.5 Conclusions and Policy Implications

Agriculture plays a vital role in climate change, as it emits lots of GHG emissions and has a considerable carbon sequestration potential. The achievement of carbon–neutral agriculture is challenging but meaningful for meeting future climate targets. Our analysis reveals agriculture sectors' GHG emissions, offers a possible path to carbon–neutral agriculture in China, and sets forth many strategies for achieving the carbon–neutral target. We have arrived at several conclusions. First, enteric fermentation, rice cultivation, fertilizer use, on-farm energy use, and manure management are the primary sources of agricultural carbon emissions. Second, despite the most considerable amount of total agricultural GHG emissions, both per capita and per unit output GHG emissions from agriculture are relatively low compared with other countries, making mitigating GHG emissions from China's agriculture sector more challenging. Third, China's agricultural sector has great potential to produce more food and sharply reduce GHG emissions. Fourth, our data show that the GHG emissions in agriculture peaked in 2016 and then decreased slowly since 2016. We predict that agriculture emissions will steadily decrease to 2030, decrease rapidly from 2030 to 2050, and finally remain at a low level from 2050 to 2060. Fifth, considering the current status and prediction of mitigation potential in agriculture, this paper sets forth the strategies for carbon–neutral agriculture according to estimation results, including carbon–neutral capacity building, GHG emissions avoidance, carbon storage, and low-carbon agrifood systems establishment.

The further direction is that China could also seek to achieve carbon neutrality with the consideration of imported food carbon emissions through further GHG emissions reduction and international cooperation. It could be achieved by documenting the international emissions from imported agricultural products and reducing carbon on an explicit aspect of our procurement processes for imported food. China could also make positive moves to develop partnerships with countries from which we import the food and help to lower GHG emissions from agriculture production in the future. We make the following policy recommendations based on the finds of our study.

First, we should improve the top-level design of China's agricultural carbon neutrality policy. It is advised to make strategic deployment in an organized and systematic manner, scientifically determine the timeline and roadmap for realizing carbon–neutral agriculture, and formulate short-term, medium-term, and long-term goals and action plans. Considering other policy objectives in agriculture, coordinate the development of different regions to make agricultural GHG emissions reduction tasks that meet local conditions. Moreover, it is advised to publish an annual Environmental Sustainability Report detailing China's carbon impact and reduction journey, beneficial for understanding the progress of China's carbon–neutral agriculture.

Second, we should develop a monitoring, reporting, and verification (MRV) system for agricultural GHG emissions. We could organize experts to develop an agricultural GHG emissions monitoring, reporting, and verification system to guarantee accurate estimations of China's agricultural emissions, facilitating precise policy-making and local adaptation. To start with, referring to international calculation standards and models, combining with domestic farming levels, and developing agricultural emission standards consistent with national conditions. Furthermore, establishing a set of digital carbon reduction navigation templates and constructing a whole life cycle agricultural emission data index system. Last, strengthening the verification of agricultural data via the monitoring platform to enhance data accuracy.

Third, we should develop carbon-neural climate investment and financing for agriculture. It is advised that the Ministry of Finance of China should actively promote climate investment and financing related to carbon and promote the agricultural low-carbon transformation through diverse policy instruments and combinations. First, the Ministry of Finance should lead in government investment and build a phased, multi-level, multi-functional investment and financing support system for agricultural carbon–neutral technologies and products. Second, the government should design agricultural carbon trading market systems, improve policies to support social capital participation, and promote the investment vigor of market players in carbon–neutral agriculture. Last, the government should carry out a pilot project for agricultural GHG emissions reduction, technology investment, and financing reform, and encourage the participation of society, enterprises, and farmers in pilot projects.

Fourth, we should strengthen the publicity and guidance of carbon–neutral agriculture. Carbon–neutral agriculture is still a relatively new concept in China, and enterprises and farmers lack the motivation and knowledge reservation to participate in its construction. First, we should use new media to strengthen the knowledge and popularization of carbon–neutral agriculture and actively guide stakeholders to participate in its construction. Second, we should improve carbon–neutral agriculture's information release mechanism, actively respond to social and public concerns and creating an excellent social atmosphere. Third, we should encourage the practical transformation of advanced agricultural carbon–neutral research results and increase the subsidies for agricultural GHG emission reduction behaviors. It would be beneficial for improving farmers' awareness of emission reduction and guiding them toward transforming low-carbon production.

Fifth, we should strengthen international cooperation in carbon–neutral agriculture. We could use the BRICS, G20, UNFCCC, and other international multi-bilateral dialogue platforms, and actively participate in international agricultural emission reduction exchanges and cooperation. Moreover, it is advised to firmly grasp the Asian Infrastructure Investment Bank, World Bank, Asian Development Bank and other strategic opportunities to support green, low-carbon development and increase the introduction of progressive ideas, cutting-edge technologies, unique talents, and preferential funding. Last but not least, we should accelerate the cultivation of domestic carbon–neutral agriculture demonstration projects, promoting the Chinese experience of carbon reduction and storage from agriculture and gradually achieving the goal of leading carbon–neutral agriculture governance.

Notes

1. The carbon neutral agriculture in the paper refers that the GHG emissions with mitigation are less than the GHG emissions budget for the agriculture sector (Shu et al., 2021).
2. Referring to the future global food demand growth rate predicted by the Food-system model (Springmann et al., 2018), we forecasted the baseline of China's agricultural GHG emissions in 2030 and 2060. Particularly, we set the growth rate of carbon emissions from the planting industry to change in the same proportion as the grain demand growth rate and the growth rate of carbon emission from the livestock industry to change in the same proportion as the meat demand growth, considering the dietary structure shift. However, according to Liu et al. (2021) and Zhao et al. (2021), China's food demand will likely grow faster than the global average. Therefore, there is a risk that the prediction results in this paper will be underestimated.

References

Ahmed, J., Almeida, E., Aminetzah, D., Denis, N., Henderson, K., Katz, J., Kitchel, H., & Mannion, P. (2020). *Agriculture and climate change: Reducing emissions through improved farming practices*. McKinsey & Company.

Altiparmak, S. O. (2022). China and lithium geopolitics in a changing global market. *Chinese Political Science Review*. https://doi.org/10.1007/s41111-022-00227-3

Antle, J. M., & Stoorvogel, J. J. (2008). Agricultural carbon sequestration, poverty, and sustainability. *Environment and Development Economics, 13*(3), 327–352. https://doi.org/10.1017/S1355770X08004324

de Auvikki, B., Camilla, S., & David, C. R. (2021). Governing agricultural innovation: A comprehensive framework to underpin sustainable transitions. *Journal of Rural Studies, 89*, 407–422.

Bondes, M. (2022). Yanzhong Huang, toxic politics: China's environmental health crisis and its challenge to the Chinese State. *Journal of Chinese Political Science, 27*, 415–417. https://doi.org/10.1007/s11366-021-09782-z

Chen, J., & Huang, C. (2021). Policy reinvention and diffusion: Evidence from Chinese provincial governments. *Journal of Chinese Political Science, 26*, 723–741. https://doi.org/10.1007/s11366-021-09725-8

Climate Watch. (2021). https://www.climatewatchdata.org/sectors/agriculture#resources-for-action. Accessed 27 May 2022.

Eastwood, C., Klerkx, L., Ayre, M., & Dela Rue, B. (2019). Managing socio-ethical challenges in development of smart farming: From a fragmented to a comprehensive approach for responsible research and innovation. *Journal of Agricultural & Environmental Ethics, 32*, 741–768.

Glemarec, Y. (2019). Aligning national interests and global climate justice: The role of human rights in enhancing the ambition of nationally determined contributions to Combat climate change. *Fudan Journal of the Humanities and Social Sciences, 12*, 309–327. https://doi.org/10.1007/s40647-018-0249-4

IPCC. (2007). *Climate change 2007: The physical science basis*. Cambridge University Press.

Jamil, I., Jun, W., Mughal, B., Waheed, J., Hussain, H., & Waseem, M. (2021). Agricultural innovation: A comparative analysis of economic benefits gained by farmers under climate resilient and conventional agricultural practices. *Land Use Policy*. https://doi.org/10.1016/j.landusepol.2021.105581

Joseph, J. (2023). State, society and environmental security in international relations theory. *Fudan Journal of the Humanities and Social Sciences*. https://doi.org/10.1007/s40647-022-00363-9

Keohane, R. O. (2019). Institutions for a world of climate injustice. *Fudan Journal of the Humanities and Social Sciences, 12*, 293–307. https://doi.org/10.1007/s40647-018-0241-z

Kingwell, R. (2021). Agriculture's carbon neutral challenge: The case of Western Australia. *The Australian Journal of Agricultural and Resource Economics, 3*(65), 566–595. https://doi.org/10.1111/1467-8489.12440

Klerkx, L., & Rose, D. 2020. Dealing with the game-changing technologies of agriculture 4.0: How do we manage diversity and responsibility in food system transition pathways? *Global Food Security, 24*, 100347.

Kuhn, B. M. 2018. China's commitment to the sustainable development goals: An analysis of push and pull factors and implementation challenges. *Chinese Political Science Review, 3*, 359–388. https://doi.org/10.1007/s41111-018-0108-0

Lal, R., Kimble, J. M., Follett, R. F., & Cole, C. V. (1998). *The potential of US cropland to sequester carbon and mitigate the greenhouse effect* (p. 128). Ann Arbor Press.

Lehner, P., & Rosenberg, N. (2017). *Legal pathways to carbon-neutral agriculture*. Social Science Electronic Publishing.

Lewandrowski, J., Peters, M., Jones, C. A., House, R. M., Sperow, M., Eve, M., & Paustian, K. H. (2004). Economics of sequestering carbon in the US agricultural sector. *Technical Bulletin*. https://doi.org/10.22004/ag.econ.33569

Liu, H., Zhang, Z., Wang, Y., Zhang, C., & Wang, D. (2022). Testing the correlation between eco-environmental performance and provincial official promotion in China. *Journal of Chinese Political Science, 28*(3), 375–399. https://doi.org/10.1007/s11366-022-09834-y

Liu, X., Dou, Y., Guan, D., Hewings, G., & Wang, S. (2021). Forecasting China's food grain demand 2021–2050 with attention to balanced dietary and fertility policies. *SSRN Journal*. https://doi.org/10.21203/rs.3.rs-675464/v1

NFU. (2020, January 1). *Achieving net zero: Farming's 2040 goal*. https://www.nfuonline.com/updates-and-information/achieving-net-zero-meeting-the-climate-change-challenge/. Accessed 30 January 2022.

Nilsson, S., & Schopfhauser, W. (1995). The carbon-sequestration potential of a global afforestation program. *Climatic Change, 30*(3), 267–293.

Pan, S. Y., Lin, Y. J., Snyder, S. W., Ma, H. W., & Chiang, P. C. (2015). Development of low-carbon-driven bio-product technology using lignocellulosic substrates from agriculture: Challenges and perspectives. *Current Sustainable/renewable Energy Reports, 2*, 145–154. https://doi.org/10.1007/s40518-015-0040-y

Popp, A., Lotze-Campen, H., & Bodirsky, B. (2010). Food consumption, diet shifts and associated non CO_2 greenhouse gases from agricultural production. *Global Environmental Change, 20*(3), 451–462. https://doi.org/10.1016/j.gloenvcha.2010.02.001

Puupponen, A., Lonkila, A., Savikurki, A., Karttunen, K., Huttunen, S., & Ott, A. (2022). Finnish dairy farmers' perceptions of justice in the transition to carbon-neutral farming. *Journal of Rural Studies, 90*, 104–112. https://doi.org/10.1016/j.jrurstud.2022.01.014

Ranganathan, J., Vennard, D., Waite, R., Lipinski, B., Searchinger, T., Dumas, P., & Lipinski, B. (2016). Shifting diets: Toward a Sustainable food future. *Global Food Policy Report*. https://doi.org/10.2499/9780896295827_08

Scuderi, A., Cammarata, M., Branca, F., & Timpanaro, G. 2021. Agricultural production trends towards carbon neutrality in response to the EU 2030 green deal: Economic and environmental analysis in horticulture. *Agricultural Economics, 11*(67), 435–444. https://doi.org/10.17221/145/2021-AGRICECON

Searchinger, T. D., Wirsenius, S., Beringer, T., & Dumas, P. (2018). Assessing the efficiency of changes in land use for mitigating climate change. *Nature, 564*, 249–253. https://doi.org/10.1038/s41586-018-0757-z

Searchinger, T., Richard, W., Craig, H., Janet, R., Patrice, D., & Emily, M. 2019. *World resources report: Creating a sustainable food future—A menu of solutions to feed nearly 10 billion people by 2050*. World Resources Institute, World Bank, UN Development Programme, and UN Environment Programme.

Searchinger, T., Zionts, J., Wirsenius, S., Wirsenius, S., Beringer, T., & Dumas, P. (2021). *A pathway to carbon neutral agriculture carbon-neutral agriculture in Denmark*. World Resources Institute. https://doi.org/10.46830/wrirpt.20.00006

Shapiro, J., Esarey, A., Haddad, M. A., Lewis, J. I., & Harrell, S. (2011). Greening East Asia the rise of the eco-developmental state. *Journal of Chinese Political Science, 26*, 433–435. https://doi.org/10.1007/s11366-021-09724-9

Shu, Y., Zhang, L., Zhang, Y., Wang, Y., Lu, G., Yuan, B., & Xia, P. (2021). Carbon peak and carbon neutrality path for China's power industry. *Strategic Study of CAE, 23*(6), 1–14 (in Chinese).

Soil Management, C. R. S. P. (2002). *A soil carbon accounting and management system for emissions trading. Special publication SM CRSP 2002–04, soil management collaborative research support program*. University of Hawaii.

Springmann, M., Clark, M., Mason-D'croz, D., Wiebe, K., Bodirsky, B. L., Lassaletta, L., de Vries, W., Vermeulen, S. J., Herrero, M., Carlson, K. M., Jonell, M., Troell, M., DeClerck, F., Gordon, L. J., Zurayk, R., Scarborough, P., Rayner, M., Loken, B., Fanzo, J., … Willett, W. (2018). Options for keeping the food system within environmental limits. *Nature, 562*, 519–525.

Stehfest, E., Bouwman, L., van Vuuren, D. P., den Elzen, M. G. J., Eickhout, B., & Kabat, P. (2009). Climate benefits of changing diet. *Climatic Change, 95*, 83–102. https://doi.org/10.1007/s10584-008-9534-6

Stilgoe, J., Owen, R., & Macnaghten, P. (2013). Developing a framework for responsible innovation. *Research Policy, 42*(9), 1568–1580.

Suresh, K., Khanal, U., Wilson, C., Managi, S., Quayle, A., & Santhirakumar, S. (2021). An economic analysis of agricultural adaptation to climate change impacts in Sri Lanka: An endogenous switching regression analysis. *Land Use Policy, 109*(1), 105601.

van Dijk, M., Morley, T., Rau, M. L., & Saghai, Y. (2021). A meta-analysis of projected global food demand and population at risk of hunger for the period 2010–2050. *Nature Food, 2*, 494–501. https://doi.org/10.1038/s43016-021-00322-9

Westhoek, H., Lesschen, J. P., Leip, A., Rood, T., Wagner, S., & De Macro, A. (2015). *Nitrogen on the table: The influence of food choices on nitrogen emissions, greenhouse gas emissions and land use in Europe* (European Nitrogen Assessment Special Report on Nitrogen and Food).

Zhang, C. (2021). Yifei Li and Judith Shapiro, China Goes Green: Coercive environmentalism for A troubled planet. *Journal of Chinese Political Science, 26*, 769–770. https://doi.org/10.1007/s11366-021-09741-8

Zhao, H., Chang, J., Havlík, P., van Dijk, M., Valin, H., Janssens, C., Ma, L., Bai, Z., Herrero, M., Smith, P., & Obersteiner, M. (2021). China's future food demand and its implications for trade and environment. *Nature Sustainability, 4*(12), 1042–1051.

Chapter 11
China's Agricultural Green Transition and High-Quality Development Toward Carbon Neutrality

Shuo Wang, Lingran Yuan, and Binlei Gong

Abstract Chinese green governance aims to achieve green transition and high-quality development in agriculture. Economic growth theory uses total factor productivity (TFP), an index of input–output ratio, to measure development quality, which provides a classic framework to assess the process of green transition and high-quality development. On the way to carbon neutrality, the goal of green governance is to achieve a balancing act between "pollution reduction" and "greenhouse gas (GHG) reduction," in addition to food security. Besides green policies, the government and other market entities can use non-institutional measures, including green technologies and finance, as green governance tools to achieve this end. This study clarifies the goals and tools of green governance and establishes a new analytic framework to investigate how to use these tools to achieve the aforementioned goals efficiently and effectively. The theoretical foundation, econometric method, and design of the new framework are introduced based on a TFP analysis. This framework sheds light on how to evaluate the achievement of these goals and how to accelerate green transition and high-quality development in the future.

Keywords Carbon neutrality · Total factor productivity · Green governance and transition · High-quality development · China's agricultural sector

---

S. Wang · B. Gong (✉)
School of Public Affairs, Zhejiang University, Hangzhou, China
e-mail: gongbinlei@zju.edu.cn

B. Gong
Academy of Social Governance, Zhejiang University, Hangzhou, China

China Academy for Rural Development, Zhejiang University, Hangzhou, China

L. Yuan
School of Advanced Agricultural Sciences, Peking University, Beijing, China

B. Gong et al. (eds.), *Chinese Governance and Transformation Towards Carbon Neutrality*, Resources, Environment and Agricultural Development,
https://doi.org/10.1007/978-981-97-9996-1_11

11.1 Introduction

Climate change is one of the most urgent issues worldwide. Many countries have planned their national climate strategies and formulated emission reduction programs based on nationally determined contributions to achieve the goal adopted by the Paris Agreement. In September 2020, President Xi Jinping pledged at the 75th UN General Assembly General Debate that China will strive to reach peak CO_2 emissions by 2030 (i.e., "carbon peaking") and achieve "carbon neutrality" by 2060 (Ma et al., 2022). This initiative is also referred to as the "3060 Target" or the "carbon peaking and carbon neutrality goals." Subsequently, it was clarified that China's "carbon peaking" refers to the peak of CO_2, whereas "carbon neutrality" refers to the achievement of net zero emissions of CO_2, the balance of emissions, and CO_2 sinks.

However, special attention should be paid to non-CO_2 greenhouse gas (GHG) emissions as they are easily overlooked or ignored when "carbon peaking" and "carbon neutrality" are heavily hyped. According to the last publicly available national GHG inventory, the top three net GHG emissions in China in 2014 were CO_2 (8.93 billion tons of CO_2eq, 81.6%), methane (CH_4) (1.16 billion tons of CO_2eq, 10.4%), and nitrous oxide (N_2O) (0.61 billion tons of CO_2eq, 5.5%) (The People's Republic of China—Ministry of Ecology and Environment, 2018). Despite the small share of non-CO_2 GHG emissions, their warming and emission reduction effects cannot be ignored. An example is CH_4 whose 20-year global warming potential (GWP) after emissions is 84 times that of CO_2 and has a relatively short atmospheric lifetime (IPCC, 2013). This means that CH_4 emission reductions are faster than CO_2 emission reductions and significantly help slow the warming trend in the short term.

Recently, China has been actively exploring the green transition of agriculture to achieve high-quality agricultural development,[1] yet agricultural GHG emission reduction has not received sufficient attention. The policy focusing on the green transition and high-quality development of agriculture mainly concerns "pollution reduction" rather than "GHG reduction." However, in China, the agricultural sector accounts for a small share of CO_2 emissions (CO_2 emissions from agriculture have not even been included in the National Greenhouse Gas Inventory Program in 2014), but the highest share of non-CO_2 GHG emissions (approximately 40.3%, compared with approximately 30.7% in the energy sector), contributing over 40% of the country's CH_4 emissions and approximately 60% of N_2O emissions (Department of Climate Change, Ministry of Ecology and Environment, 2018).

To summarize, in China, existing climate policies primarily focus on CO_2 reduction, and agricultural policies mainly focus on pollution reduction, which makes GHG reduction in China's agriculture a blind spot as neither climate nor agricultural policies cover it well. However, it is noteworthy that our final goal is to prevent climate change. Therefore, urgent action is needed to reduce GHG emissions in agriculture, and the best way is to highlight its role and importance in China's agricultural green growth strategy. More specifically, it is necessary to clarify the difference between "pollution reduction" and "GHG reduction" in agricultural production and make these two targets equally crucial in China's agricultural green development.

In the literature, an important indicator to assess the green agricultural transition and high-quality development process is agricultural TFP, a measure of agricultural technological progress and efficiency improvement. Using TFP as a framework to analyze the achievement of high-quality growth in agriculture has been widely recognized in academia. With increasing environmental concerns, the traditional TFP measure was gradually replaced by green total factor productivity (GTFP), as the latter considers the non-desired output of agricultural production (e.g., water pollutant emissions). However, some issues exist in the current GTFP framework: (1) GTFP is an "all-in-one" index that cannot be further decomposed into economic and environmental efficiency. In other words, we cannot identify the economic and environmental performance. (2) Existing agricultural GTFP studies primarily consider pollution (e.g., air, water, and soil pollution) as undesired outputs without considering GHG emissions.

In the context of carbon peaking and carbon neutrality, this study tackles these problems by establishing a new framework that can identify economic efficiency and environmental efficiency, where the latter can be further decomposed into performance in pollution reduction and GHG reduction. Additionally, this framework can evaluate the impact of different green governance tools (such as agricultural policies, green technologies, and green finance) on economic and environmental efficiency, which sheds light on a balancing act between environmental protection and economic growth (i.e., food security in agriculture) and between pollution reduction and GHG reduction.

The remainder of the article is structured as follows. Section 11.2 analyzes the green governance goals in China's agriculture. Section 11.3 describes the green governance tools and how they may affect green transition and high-quality development in China's agriculture. Section 11.4 reviews existing studies on the TFP-based framework that evaluate the green transition and high-quality development process. Section 11.5 constructs a new analytical framework that assesses green governance achievement based on a two-step model and is followed by an empirical study in Sect. 11.6. Conclusions and policy implications are given in Sect. 11.7.

11.2 The Goals of Green Governance in China's Agriculture: A Balance Act Between "Pollution Reduction" and "GHG Reduction" in Addition to Food Security

11.2.1 Agricultural Production, Environmental Pollution, and Climate Change

At this stage, the green transformation and high-quality development of Chinese agriculture must address two significant issues: pollution control and GHG emissions control. Figure 11.1 classifies the undesired outputs of agricultural production into three circles. Circle I (the smallest circle in black) covers only CO_2 emissions. Circle II (the middle circle in gray and black) covers all agricultural GHGs, including CH_4 and N_2O emissions, in addition to Circle I. Circle III (the broadest circle) covers all undesired agricultural outputs that include environmental pollution (such as air, water, and soil pollution) in addition to Circle II. Under the premise of ensuring food security, the goal of green governance is to accelerate the green transition and high-quality development. Current "carbon peaking" policies focus on the black area (i.e., CO_2). In contrast, agricultural policies focus on the white area (i.e., environmental pollution), which leaves the gray area (i.e., non-CO_2 GHG emissions), a blind spot.

Moreover, the current focus has been limited to the agriculture production process. However, the modem agricultural production chain, also called the agri-food system, involves the entire productivity system of service before, during, and after production. Environmental pollution and GHG emissions should also be considered and controlled in pre-and post-production stages. Figure 11.2 summarizes the activities that can produce undesirable outputs in the agri-food system.

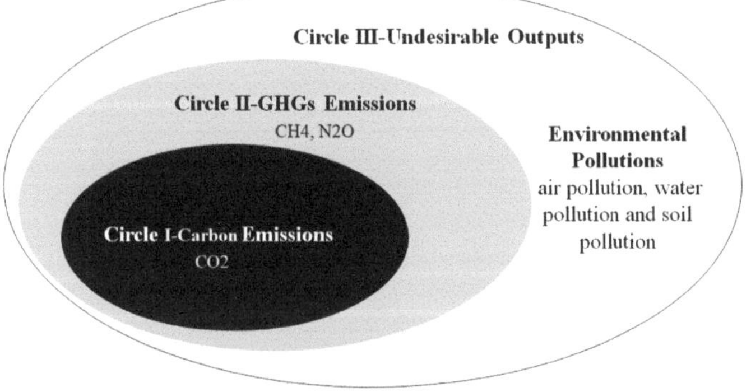

Fig. 11.1 The three circles of undesirable agricultural outputs. *Source* Compiled by the authors

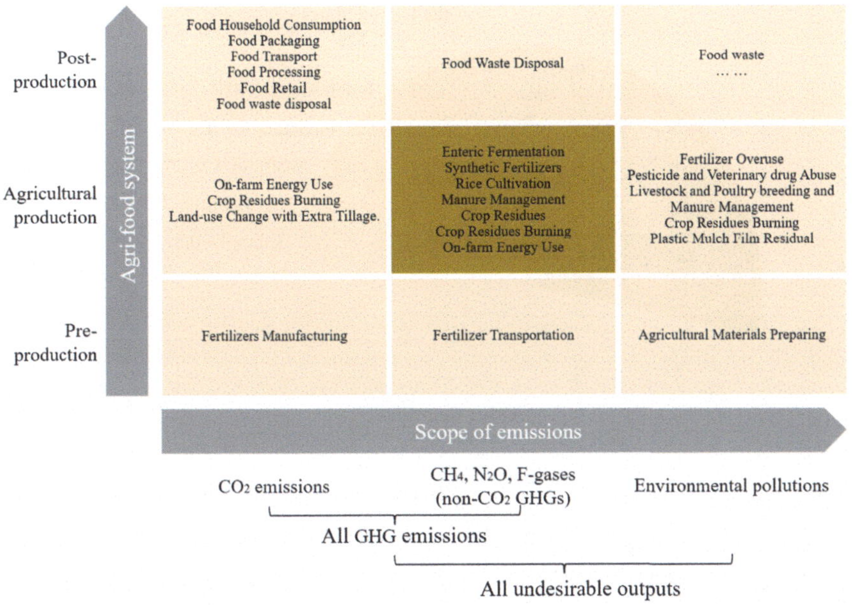

Fig. 11.2 Activities that can produce undesirable outputs in the agri-food system. *Note* The horizontal axis is the scope of emissions, representing CO_2, All GHGs, and All undesirable outputs from smallest to largest. The vertical axis is the agri-food system, representing pre-production, agricultural production, and post-production from bottom to top. The matrix indicates the emissions that occur in the process. It is worth noting that less attention has been paid to the brown circle (non-CO_2 GHG emissions from agricultural production processes). *Source* Compiled by the authors. Regarding the FAO statistics, Gu et al. (2014), Shi et al. (2015), and Guo et al. (2020)

11.2.2 GHG Emissions in Agri-Food Systems

Power, Steel, and Cement are China's largest GHG-emitting sectors. Agricultural production activities have been neglected due to their decentralized and small-scale characteristics. However, two undeniable facts exist about agricultural production and the agri-food system. First, although not a significant CO_2 emitter, agricultural production processes are the primary source of non-CO_2 GHG emissions (mainly CH_4 and N_2O). In particular, CH_4 is a more potent GHG than CO_2. The importance of CH_4 emission reductions was first highlighted in the sixth report of the Intergovernmental Panel on Climate Change (IPCC) in August 2021, showing that CH_4 has contributed to global warming of up to 0.5 °C since the industrial era. Second, the GHG emissions from the entire agri-food system are much larger than the emissions from agricultural production alone.

Agricultural CH_4 primarily comes from animal enteric fermentation, rice cultivation, and animal manure management. In 2018, global agricultural CH_4 emissions amounted to 4.11 billion tons, among which China's agricultural CH_4 emissions

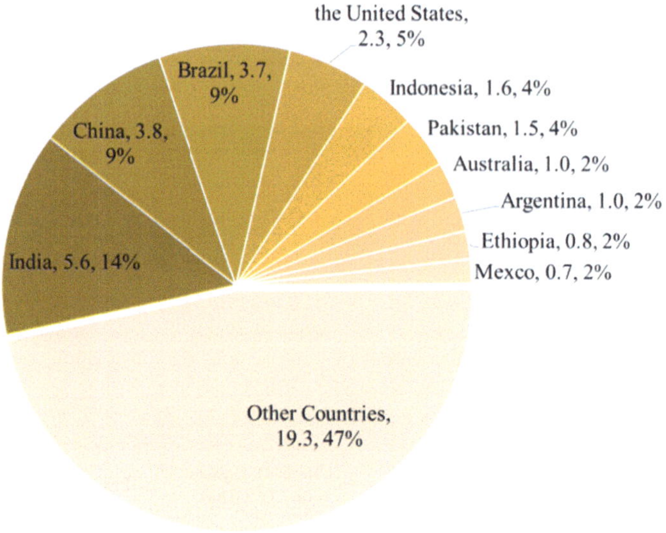

Fig. 11.3 The world's top 10 agricultural CH_4 emitters in 2018 and their share of emissions. *Source* Compiled by the authors. Regarding the FAO statistics

amounted to 0.38 billion tons, accounting for 9.1%, and became the world's second-largest agricultural CH_4 emitter after India (see Fig. 11.3). In China, agricultural CH_4 emissions accounted for 47.1% of agricultural GHG emissions in 2018, with the top emission factor being animal enteric fermentation (see Fig. 11.4).

The Agri-food system refers to the entire industry chain related to agriculture, including agricultural production, food processing, transportation and storage, wholesale and retail, food service and other pre-production, production, and post-production links, which is related to food supply and food security issues and has excellent potential in GHG emission reduction. Globally, the entire food supply chain generates approximately 1/3 of the total human GHG emissions (Crippa et al., 2021; Poore & Nemecek, 2018). The results of Rosenzweig et al. (2020) show that agri-food systems account for up to 21–37% of GHG emissions, with agriculture accounting for 9–14%, land use accounts for 5–14%, and GHG emissions from pre-and post-production-segments of agriculture account for 5–10%. The entire agri-food system chain in China emits 1.9 billion tons of GHG, accounting for approximately 18.4% of the total national emissions in 2018. Moreover, 58% of these 1.9 billion tons of GHG emissions come from the pre-and post-production segments. As a result, besides the agricultural production process, attention should be paid to reducing GHG emissions in other processes, especially food household consumption and food waste disposal downstream and fertilizers manufacturing upstream (see Fig. 11.5).

To summarize, GHG emission reduction is also an essential goal of China's agricultural green governance to achieve green transition and high-quality development, and the entire agri-food system should be considered to deal with the issue of climate change.

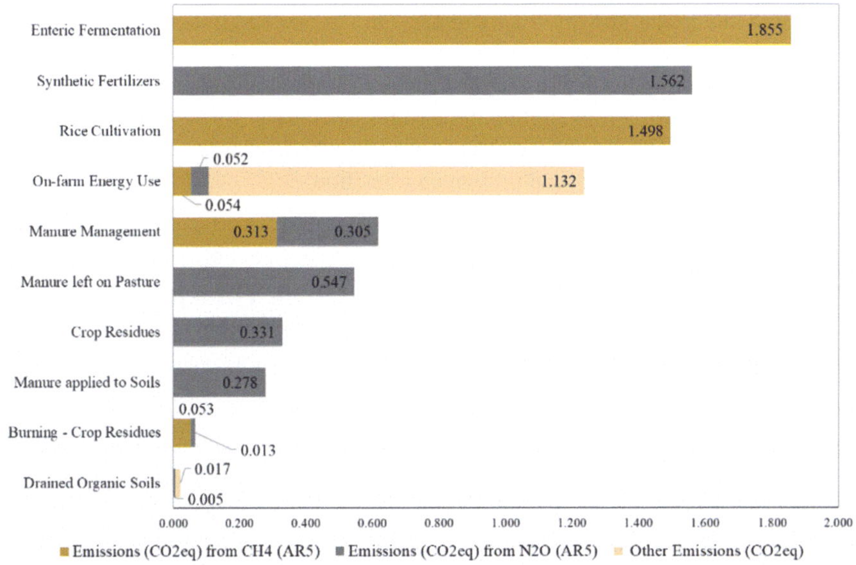

Fig. 11.4 Agricultural production GHG emission inventory of China in 2018 (100 million tons). *Source* Compiled by the authors. Regarding the FAO statistics

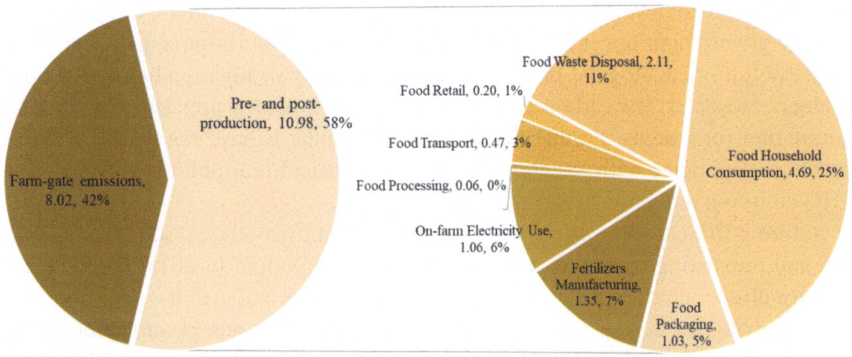

Fig. 11.5 The share of GHG emission from agri-food systems in China in 2018. *Source* Compiled by the authors. Regarding the FAO statistics

11.3 The Tools of Green Governance in China's Agriculture: Institutions, Technologies, and Marketization

As mentioned in the previous section, China's agriculture's green transition and high-quality development aim to prevent environmental pollution and climate change while ensuring food security. The Chinese government has dramatically promoted sustainable and green growth in agriculture. On the one hand, the government has introduced a series of green policies and subsidies to support and reshape agricultural production. On the other hand, the government, along with other market entities, has actively adopted non-institutional measures, including green technologies and green finance as additional green governance tools, which have become the emerging driving forces of China's agricultural green transition.

11.3.1 Green Policy: Policy System for Green Transition and High-Quality Development of Agriculture in China

A series of policies have been enacted to promote the green transition and high-quality development of China's agriculture since 2015, focusing on controlling agricultural non-point source pollution. After the "3060 Targets" were proposed in September 2020, how to establish green, low-carbon, and circular agriculture has gradually become a hot spot for policy attention. This article first summarizes the guiding policy documents of China's agricultural green transition recently (see Table 11.1), from which we can see the change in policy focus. Second, to understand the evaluations of China's agricultural green transition, the policies and their effects on China's agricultural green development are briefly reviewed (see Table 11.2). Generally, the Chinese government has introduced a series of policies on resource use, non-point source pollution, ecological protection, and the supply of high-quality agricultural products. However, few carbon-attainment and carbon-neutral policies exist for agriculture and rural areas. Furthermore, technical standards have not yet been determined, and policies with synergistic effects on agricultural pollution control and GHG emission reduction are unclear enough.

Before 2020, China's agricultural green transition focused on resource conservation and preventing agricultural non-point source pollution. In 2015, the Ministry of Agriculture (now the Ministry of Agriculture and Rural Affairs) took the lead in recognizing the seriousness and urgency of agricultural non-point source pollution in China. It issued the Implementation Opinions on the Battle against Agricultural Non-Point Source Pollution, which proposed "zero-growth action on chemical fertilizer and pesticide use by 2020" and "five major actions" for green agricultural development. The No.1 document of the Central Government in 2016 highlighted for the first time that it would promote green agricultural development in terms of conservation and the efficient use of agricultural resources, management of significant environmental problems, protection and restoration of agricultural ecology, and governance of food safety, to improve the quality, efficiency, and competitiveness of agriculture. Since then, the No. 1 document of the Central Government has put forward opinions related to green agricultural development yearly. The State Council issued the National Agricultural Modernization Plan (2016–2020) in 2016,

Table 11.1 Policies of green transition and high-development of agriculture in China

	Time	Policies	Department Issued
Before the "2030 Target" were proposed	May 2015	*The Implementation Opinions on the Battle against Agricultural Non-Point Source Pollution*	Ministry of Agriculture
	October 2016	*The National Agricultural Modernization Plan (2016–2020)*	The State Council
	September 2017	*The Opinions on Innovating Systems and Mechanisms to Promote Agricultural Green Development*	General Offices of the CPC Central Committee and The State Council
After the "2030 Target" were proposed	February 2021	*The Guidelines on Accelerating the Establishment of a Green, Low-carbon, and Circular Economic System*	The State Council
	August 2021	*The 14th Five-year Plan for Agricultural Green Development*	Ministry of Agriculture and Rural Affairs and other related departments
	October 2021	*The Action Plan for Carbon Dioxide Peaking Before 2030*	The State Council

Source Compiled by the authors

Table 11.2 Specific policies and effects of agricultural green development in China

Type	Start time	Actions	Target pollutant
Economic incentives	2005	*Soil testing and fertilizer recommendation*	Soil and water pollution GHG emissions
	2016	*Cultivated land protection*	Soil degradation and pollution
	2017	*Recycling and processing of agricultural plastic mulch film*	Soil white pollution
Policy experimentation	2011	*Utilization of crop residues*	Air pollution GHG emissions
	2017	*Substituting organic fertilizer for chemical fertilizer*	Soil pollution GHG emissions
	2017	*Utilization of livestock and poultry waste*	Soil pollution GHG emissions
Government regulation	2011	*Green prevention and control of diseases and insect pests*	Soil and water pollution
	2018	*Reduction of veterinary antibiotics*	Soil and water pollution

Source Compiled by the authors

vigorously proposing developing resource-saving, environment-friendly, and ecological conservation agriculture to promote clean production. In 2017, green agricultural development gradually rose to a policy requirement at the national level. The Opinions on Innovating Systems and Mechanisms to Promote Agricultural Green Development issued by the State Office provides programmatic guidance for green transition and high-quality development of Chinese agriculture.

In 2020, the Central Economic Work Conference put the work of the "3060 Targets" as one of the eight essential tasks in 2021 and requested to formulate the action plan for carbon emission peaking by 2030. In February 2021, the State Council promulgated the Guidance on Accelerating the Establishment of a Green Low-Carbon Circular Economic System, which pointed out that green agricultural development should be accelerated in rural areas. In August 2021, the Ministry of Agriculture and Rural Affairs and five other national ministries and commissions jointly issued the 14th Five-year Plan for Agricultural Green Development, China's first particular plan for green agricultural development, putting forward requirements for green agricultural transition from 2021 to 2025.

Besides programmatic policies that establishing macro strategies, many specific policies are enacted to achieve a green growth pattern through agricultural chemical input reduction, the resourceful use of straw and livestock manure, and natural resource conservation (see Table 11.2). Supported by these policies, the green transition and high-quality development of China's agriculture have achieved a good start: (1) Resource use efficiency has been improved; (2) The trend of agricultural non-point source pollution and ecological degradation has been effectively curbed; and (3) the GHG emission reduction from agricultural activities has begun to show results. Specifically, the total use of chemical fertilizers and pesticides nationwide began to decline yearly in 2016 and 2015, respectively, completing the "zero growth" target ahead of schedule. In 2019, the average quality of arable land nationwide was 4.76, an improvement of 0.35 grade over the previous five years. The effective utilization coefficient of agricultural land irrigation water nationwide reached 0.559, an 0.043 improvement over the previous seven years, completing the "13th Five-year Plan" target ahead of schedule. In 2020, the chemical fertilizers and pesticide utilization rate for the three major food crops reached 40.2% and 40.6%, respectively, an increase of 5 and 4% over the previous five years. The comprehensive utilization rate of crop residues reached 86.72%, and the total utilization rate of livestock and poultry manure reached over 75% (Institute of Agricultural Resources and Regional Planning, CAAS, and Chinese Society of Agricultural Green Development, 2021). The national rural biogas treats approximately 1.6 billion tons of livestock and poultry breeding manure, straw, and organic household waste annually. The annual GHG emission reduction is equivalent to over 50 million tons of CO_2eq (Department of Climate Change, Ministry of Ecology and Environment, 2018).

11.3.2 Green Technology: An Important Support for Green Transition and High-Quality Development of Agriculture in China

Innovation is the primary driving force for agricultural growth. Promoting the green transition of China's agriculture must accelerate scientific and technological innovation and strengthen the supply of green agricultural technologies. Compared with conventional yield-oriented agricultural technologies, such as high-yielding seed technologies, chemical fertilizers, and pesticides, green agricultural technologies consider the balance between desirable and undesirable outputs. The Ministry of Agriculture and Rural Affairs promulgated the Technical Guidelines for Green Agricultural Development (2018–2030) in 2018 to further implement the Opinions on Innovative Institutional Mechanisms to Promote Agricultural Green Development and change the direction of scientific and technological innovation. It covers the green inputs, technical modes, and standards. It also divides green agricultural technologies into three stages: research and development (R&D), demonstration, and extension (see Table 11.3).

In the context of the "2030 Target," the General Station of Ecology and Resource Conservation of the Ministry of Agriculture and Rural Affairs released "Top Ten Technical Modes for Carbon Reduction and Sequestration in Agriculture and Rural Areas" in November 2021 (see Fig. 11.6). This document covers critical areas such as carbon emission reduction and sequestration in the plantation industry, pollution reduction and carbon reduction in the livestock industry, emission reduction and sink increase in the fishery industry, and renewable energy substitution in rural areas, involving four GHG emission reduction technologies, four carbon sequestration and sink increase technologies and two renewable energy substitution technologies.

China has researched and extended several advanced technological modes in scientific fertilization, green farming, and water-saving irrigation. As a result of scientific fertilization, in 2019, China's fertilizer application was reduced by 6.19 million tons compared with the peak in 2015, a reduction of over 10%, bringing a total reduction of 56 million tons of GHG emissions in CO_2eq. Using data from extensive field experiments, Cui et al. (2018) found that "integrated soil-crop system management" technology can increase national grain yield by over 30% and reduce environmental nitrogen emissions by 50%, which can meet the dual objectives of food security and environmental protection simultaneously. Huang et al. (2017) estimated the agricultural water use efficiency by upgrading water conservation technology in northern China. They found that the average unit irrigation water use decreased after using water conservation technology, while the crop yield per unit increased. However, although agricultural GHG emission reduction and carbon sequestration technologies are developed and screened, the costs and benefits are yet to be supported by large-scale experimental data, as emission reduction and carbon sequestration technologies are complex and challenging to extend. Meanwhile, the synergistic effect of green agricultural technologies in pollution control and GHG emission reduction at

Table 11.3 Types and stages of agricultural green technology

Technology type	Technology content	Target pollutant
Pre-production: R&D of green inputs	*New varieties with high efficiency and high-quality multi-resistance*	Soil and water pollution GHG emissions
	Environmental protection and efficient fertilizer agricultural drugs and biological agents	Soil degradation and pollution
	Intelligent agricultural equipment with low energy consumption	Air pollution GHG emissions
Production: green production technology	*Cultivated land quality improvement and conservation technology*	Soil degradation and pollution
	Fertilizer and pesticide reduction and efficiency enhancement technology	Soil pollution GHG emissions
	Green production technology of livestock, poultry and aquatic products	Soil pollution GHG emissions
	Aquatic ecological protection and restoration technology	Water pollution Soil pollution
Post-production: green value-added technology	*Low carbon and pollution reduction processing*	GHG emissions
	Intelligent intensive processing technology	Energy conservation

Source Compiled by the authors

the national scale is yet to be evaluated due to the lagging construction of agricultural GHG emission monitoring data.

11.3.3 Green Finance: A Market-Based Mechanism for Green Transition and High-Quality Development of Agriculture in China

Green finance, also known as environmental finance or sustainability finance, refers to the financial services provided to support economic activities for environmental improvement, climate change, and efficient use of resources. That is, project investment, operation, and risk management in environmental protection, energy conservation, clean energy, green transportation, and green buildings. Traditional financial activities in selecting investment and financing projects are often based on profitability, ignoring factors such as resources, environment, and ecology, leading to

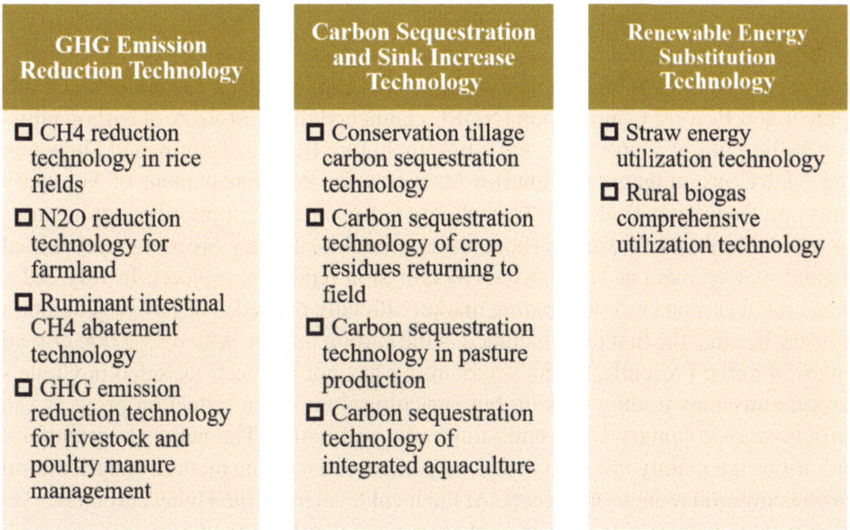

Fig. 11.6 Ten technical modes for carbon reduction and sequestration in agriculture and rural areas. *Source* Agricultural Ecology and Resource Protection Station, Ministry of Agriculture and Rural Affairs, 2021. http://www.reea.agri.cn/stkzszy/202111/t20211122_7782554.htm

further deterioration of environmental problems (Tamazian & Rao, 2010). In contrast, green transition, an intrinsic requirement for sustainable economic growth (Zhang et al., 2011), leans on the driving role of green financial development at the theoretical and empirical logic levels (Bai et al., 2014). The green transition of agriculture requires institutional and technical support and financial and fiscal instruments to build market-oriented and sustainable mechanisms. From the perspective of the trading market and financial instruments, green finance includes two aspects. One is the financial products of green bonds, credit, and insurance. The other is the construction of financial innovations such as emissions trading.

Regarding traditional green financial products, the Ministry of Agriculture and the Agricultural Bank of China issued a Notice on Promoting Financial Support for Agricultural Green Development to support several green agriculture projects in 2017. Local governments have also made explorations in green finance to support agricultural transitions. By improving the green finance policy system, financial institutions are guided to explore diversified green financing patterns actively. In 2020, the high-quality green agricultural development promotion project in Henan Province received a long-term preferential loan of 300 million USD as the first green development fund of the World Bank in China. The city of Huangshan in Anhui Province secured loans of 90.09 million Euros and 50 million Euros from the Asian Development Bank and KFW Bankengruppe for rural point source and non-point source pollution control and the ecological protection of the Xin'an River Basin in Huangshan (Academy of Global Food Economics and Policy et al., 2021).

Regarding green financial innovation, China has been actively promoting and establishing a carbon trading market for nearly a decade. Carbon trading is a collective term for the trading of GHG emission rights. As early as 2011, the National Development and Reform Commission (NDRC) launched the pilot work of carbon emission trading in seven provinces and cities, including Beijing, Tianjin, and Shanghai. The NDRC promulgated the Interim Measures for the Management of Voluntary Emission Reduction Trading of Greenhouse Gases in 2012, supporting applications for agricultural and forestry carbon sinks, animal husbandry breeding, and animal manure management as voluntary GHG emission reduction projects. In July 2021, the national carbon emission trading market officially opened. The power generation industry became the first to be included in the carbon market, with over 2,000 critical emission units. Presently, China's agriculture has not yet been included in China's carbon emissions trading system, but agricultural emission reduction projects can participate in voluntary GHG emission trading activities. The national agricultural authorities are mainly involved in and support research on the method of agricultural carbon emission reduction projects. At the local level, only the Hubei carbon market pilot encouraged projects such as rural biogas to enter the market for trading through the offset mechanism. However, in general, the establishment of agricultural carbon emission reduction markets and the design of trading mechanisms are insufficient. Also, little research exists on the reduction effects of agricultural carbon emission trading.

11.4 Green Transition and High-Quality Development of Agriculture: A Literature Review and Traditional Analytical Framework

In agriculture, TFP is a measure of output per input, which reflects economic efficiency if we only consider the economic output. Measuring high-quality agricultural development based on agricultural TFP has been widely recognized in academia. The traditional analytical framework focusing on green agricultural transition and high-quality development has primarily undergone three development stages: the first stage is the traditional TFP measurement without considering undesired agricultural output; the second stage is to examine the impact of policy reform on traditional TFP; The third stage is to include environmental pollution in the agricultural production function as an input or bad output (also called undesired output), to measure the GTFP of agriculture and reflect the level of high-quality agricultural development comprehensively.

11.4.1 Stage One: High-Quality Development of Agriculture in China from a TFP Perspective

The TFP concept derives from the theory of economic growth. It was developed at the inception of classical economics. The introduction of the Solow growth accounting model in the 1950s provided a benchmark model for quantifying TFP (Solow, 1956). The growth accounting approach uses a production function to estimate the contribution of factors of production and TFP to economic growth. If the contribution of factors of production dominates, it is called extensive growth. In contrast, if the contribution of TFP dominates, it is called intensive growth, a widely used indicator of high-quality development. The derivation process of the formula for calculating TFP using Solow's residual method is as follows:

$$Y = Af(X_n) \tag{11.1}$$

where Y is the total output, A is TFP, $X_n = (x_1, x_2, \ldots, x_n)$ is a vector of different inputs, and $f(X_n)$ is the generalized production function, such as Cobb–Douglas and Translog. According to Eq. (11.1), TFP can be calculated as follows:

$$TFP = \frac{A'}{A} = \frac{Y'}{Y} - \sum_{i=1}^{n} \delta_n \frac{x_n'}{x_n}. \tag{11.2}$$

Besides the classic Solow residual method, Data Envelopment Analysis (DEA) and Stochastic Frontier Analysis (SFA) have become popular methods for TFP estimation (Gong & Sickles, 2020, 2021). Their common advantage is that they can further decompose TFP growth into technological progress and efficiency change. The advantage of DEA is that there is no need to assume the form of the production function. However, there is no disturbance to control the effects of unobservable factors. In contrast, SFA has an error term to capture the noise in the production, but it requires a rigid functional form assumption, which may be invalid in the real world.

The study on the high-quality development of Chinese agriculture from the perspective of TFP mainly started in the 1980s. Scholars have used different methods and data to measure China's agricultural TFP since the reforms and opening up (Chen & Gong, 2021; Kalirajan et al., 1996; Lin, 1992; Wen, 1993). Since the twenty-first century, the research on China's agricultural TFP has been further expanded to achieve a more accurate estimation of agricultural TFP. On the one hand, the econometric models to estimate TFP were further improved. For example, Gong (2018) establishes a varying-coefficient SFA model to relax the functional form assumption, which makes up for the shortcoming of existing SFA models. On the other hand, the input and output data in agriculture are better collected and adjusted. For example, Sheng et al. (2019) estimated the TFP of China's agriculture from 1978 to 2016 using various sources to derive accurate data on inputs such as labor and capital.

They found that the average annual TFP growth rate was 1.9% for the period 1978–2016, explaining 40% of agricultural output growth. However, annual TFP growth in the agricultural sector declined to 0.9% from 2009 to 2016. Overall, although China's agricultural TFP growth has achieved significant improvements, there is still more room for improvement in the quality of China's agricultural development. After estimating agricultural TFP, it is critical to identify further the influencing mechanisms, which are usually investigated by regressing TFP on its determinants (Gong et al., 2021; Yuan et al., 2022).

11.4.2 Stage Two: Technical Change, Institutional Reforms, and China's Agricultural TFP

Technical change and institutional reform are the two most important factors influencing high-quality development in agriculture. From the perspective of technical change, Huang and Rozelle (1996) empirically investigate the impact of technical change on rice yield, represented by hybrid rice varieties. The results show that the technical change could explain 40% of the yield increase in 1979–1984, while in 1985–1990, almost all of the increase in rice yields came from technical change. Fan and Pardey (1997) introduce agricultural research investment into the accounting framework using provincial panel data for 1965–1993 and find that research investment explained 22.2% of agricultural growth during this period. Jin et al. (2002) use provincial data to measure the TFP of the three major staple grains of rice, wheat, and corn and then evaluate the impact of technical changes represented by high-quality seeds on TFP using panel regression and instrumental variables method. The results indicate that technical change is the primary driver of TFP improvement for the three major staple foods from 1980 to1995.

From the perspective of institutional reform, early studies have focused on the impact of the household responsibility system (HRS) (Lambert & Parker, 1998; Lin, 1992; Mcmillan et al., 1989). Lin (1992) uses a traditional production function approach and an SFA approach to decompose crop growth in China and finds that the employment of HRS alone contributes to approximately half of the growth in crop output from 1978 to 1987, which implies the importance of institutional reforms. Moreover, Lin (1992) also points out that the annual TFP growth rate declined from 3.2% in 1978–1984 to 0.7% in 1984–1987. The decline in TFP during 1984–1987 is mainly due to the declining benefits from HRS and the stagnation of further market-oriented reforms. More recent studies have focused on China's imperfect agricultural land system and the Hukou system and explored the impact of institutional distortions on China's agricultural TFP growth. Chari et al. (2021) use the implementation of the 2003 Land Contract Law in China as a quasi-natural experiment. The results show that stabilizing land transfer rights could alleviate the distorted allocation of agricultural land resources to a certain extent. The staggered difference-in-difference results indicate that the total agricultural TFP increased by 7.6% after the reform. Adamopoulos et al. (2022) find that the misallocation of land resources among farmers and the misallocation of workers across sectors are the main obstacles to further increasing aggregate agricultural TFP in China.

11.4.3 Stage Three: Green Total Factor Productivity of Agriculture Considering Undesirable Outputs

Agricultural production processes have had an increasing and significant impact on resources and the environment, such as soil and water resource loss, water pollution, and heavy metal pollution of arable land. The classic measurement of agricultural TFP mainly examines the relationship between agricultural output and traditional input factors such as land, labor, fertilizer, and farm machinery without environmental concern. With rising environmental awareness, some scholars incorporate environmental pollution into the traditional TFP measurement framework to derive GTFP, which is of great theoretical value and practical significance. This study reviews GTFP studies from two aspects: model construction and empirical application.

Two major approaches exist to embedding environmental factors into TFP models: one is introducing environmental pollution as an input variable in the same way as capital and labor inputs; the other is introducing environmental pollution as an undesired output along with desired output into productivity models. Approaches that consider environmental pollution as a production input factor treat environmental pollution as an unpaid input and minimize environmental pollution while minimizing the input (Hailu & Veeman, 2001). However, this approach does not follow the actual agricultural production process, where environmental pollution is not used as an input in the actual production. For example, inputs in agricultural production include fertilizers and pesticides, but the outputs do not include the associated pollution emissions. Therefore, treating pollution emissions as a factor input may create a mismatch between the actual input and output. It is common to include environmental pollution as an undesired output in TFP estimations.

The first wave of agricultural GTFP studies mainly focused on agriculture in developed countries. Reinhard et al. (1999) evaluate dairy farms' technical and environmental efficiency in the Netherlands by considering environmental pollution and capital, human, and intermediate inputs as productive factors used in agriculture. Rezek and Perrin (2004) construct a Malmquist TFP index based on a transcendental logit function and measure it using data from four U.S. plains states for the period 1960–1996, where nitrogen and pesticides are included as bad output. They find that the average annual growth rate of TFP after the inclusion of environmental pollution decreases from 1.25 to 0.98%. Ball et al. (2004) measure the TFP and GTFP of U.S. agriculture by considering the environmental impact of pesticides used in agricultural production as an undesired output. They find that the average annual growth rate of GTFP in U.S. agriculture is lower than that of conventional TFP during 1960–1972, while the average annual growth rate of GTFP is higher than that of conventional

TFP during 1973–1996. Some recent studies have measured China's agricultural GTFP based on the Slacks-Based Measure-DEA model and in the M-L index framework. For example, Lu et al. (2020) use chemical nutrient demand, total nitrogen, and total phosphorus discharged into water bodies to represent agricultural surface source pollution and apply the Slacks-Based Measure super-efficiency model that includes undesired outputs to estimate China's agricultural, environmental technical efficiency from 2011 to 2015. The results show that the average annual growth of GTFP in China's agriculture is 9.5%, mainly driven by green technical change, and that the contribution of agricultural green technical efficiency is limited.

11.5 Green Transition and High-Quality Development in Agriculture: A New Framework

The traditional analytical framework of green agricultural transition and high-quality development are two relatively fragmented research topics. The former focuses on the impact of green policies on agricultural production, and the latter on estimating agricultural GTFP using different methods. It is essential to integrate these two parts into the same framework. Some scholars have incorporated agricultural pollution into the production function and proposed the concept of GTFP, as introduced in the previous section. In the context of the "carbon peaking and carbon neutrality goals," two major problems remain unsolved in existing GTFP studies. First, GTFP is an "all-in-one" index that cannot be further decomposed into environmental and economic efficiency, thus unable to clarify the relationship between environmental protection and economic development. Therefore, building a new model that can identify environmental efficiency and economic efficiency is crucial to better studying green transition and high-quality development in agriculture simultaneously. Second, current agricultural GTFP studies mainly regard environmental pollution (air, water, and soil pollution) as a unique type of undesired output. This study establishes a new framework based on those mentioned above, the "three circle theory" (see Fig. 11.1), where CO_2 emissions and non-CO_2 GHG emissions are considered as undesired outputs in addition to environmental pollution to better evaluate the green transformation process under the "3060 Target."

11.5.1 The Theoretical Foundation of the New Framework

The theoretical basis of classic agricultural TFP is the theory of economic growth, which has experienced three stages: classical growth theory, neoclassical growth theory, and endogenous growth theory. The existing economic growth accounting methods are still based on the neoclassical economic growth theory. This classic framework attributes economic growth to input and TFP growth. However, these two concepts may overlap, as some technological progress is embedded in various inputs. In other words, the quality improvement of inputs is related to TFP growth. Moreover, the theoretical framework does not include the negative externalities of agricultural production, such as environmental pollution.

Both endogenous growth theory and induced innovation theory point out that even if farmers or firms at the micro-level follow the same production function with constant returns to scale, the macro-level production function will show an increasing scale efficiency due to the existence of positive spillovers thanks to "learning-by-doing" and "learning-by-investing." As a result, the output elasticities to labor and capital are not constant at the macro level since the magnitude of the spillovers varies across regions over time. However, most existing TFP methods assume fixed elasticities or constant return to scale. Moreover, classic TFP and GTFP are black boxes, making it difficult to investigate the impact mechanism of TFP/GTFP determinants. The new framework is based on the theories of endogenous growth and induced innovation to solve these problems. In addition, the theory of externalities and public goods is also incorporated to account for environmental pollution and GHG emissions in agricultural production. It is noteworthy that the new econometric method introduced below can be established based on either the traditional foundation (neoclassical economic growth theory) or the new foundation (endogenous growth theory plus the induced innovation theory and the theory of externalities and public goods). The following subsection will introduce the difference between the two.

11.5.2 The Econometric Method of the New Framework

Agricultural GTFP is currently the most common index to measure the level of green transition and high-quality development in agriculture.

$$Y = Bf(X_n, P_{it}) \tag{11.3}$$

where Y denotes the total output, and $X_n = (x_1, x_2, \ldots, x_n)$ is a vector of different inputs, similar to the setup in Eq. (11.2). Moreover, P_{it} represents air, water, and soil pollution, whereas B measures GTFP. Although Eq. (11.3) is considered part of the environmental pollution, two unsolved issues exist: first, the GTFP cannot be decomposed into environmental and economic efficiency. Second, it does not include GHG emissions as undesired outputs.

This study extends the by-production model of desirable and undesirable outputs (Murty et al., 2012) and establishes a new econometric model to tackle the problems above:

$$\begin{cases} y_{it} = f_1\left(x_{it}^b, x_{it}^g\right) - u_{it}^1 + v_{it}^1 \\ P_{it} = f_2\left(x_{it}^b, y_{it}\right) - u_{it}^2 + v_{it}^2 \\ C_{it} = f_3\left(x_{it}^b, y_{it}\right) - u_{it}^3 + v_{it}^3 \end{cases} \tag{11.4}$$

where the first equation of Eq. (11.4) is a production function model of desirable output (agricultural output); the second equation of Eq. (11.4) is a production function model of traditional environmental pollutants, and P_{it} denotes the total amount of air, water, and soil pollution generated in agricultural production; the third equation of Eq. (11.4) is a production function model of GHG emissions, and C_{it} represents GHG emissions generated in agricultural production. x_{it}^{b} represents non-neutral factors of production that may bring pollution, including fertilizers and pesticides. x_{it}^{g} represents the neutral factors of production, such as land and labor. $TE1_{it} = \exp\left(-u_{it}^{1}\right)$ measures economic efficiency, while $TE2_{it} = 1-\exp\left(-u_{it}^{2}\right)$ measures environmental efficiency. Environmental efficiency can be further decomposed into the efficiency of various pollution sources if we establish a determination equation for each of the three pollution sources, including air, water, and carbon pollution. As a result, the first issue, the identification problem of economic and environmental efficiency, is solved. Similarly, $TE3_{it} = 1-\exp\left(-u_{it}^{3}\right)$ measures the efficiency of GHG emissions and can be further decomposed into the efficiency of CO_2 emissions and non-CO_2 GHG emissions, and therefore tackles the second issue that excludes GHG emissions as undesired outputs. If we adopt the neoclassical economic growth theory as our foundation, the functions $f(\cdot)$ in Eq. (11.3) and $f_1(\cdot)$, $f_2(\cdot)$, and $f_3(\cdot)$ in Eq. (11.4) can be modeled as Cobb-Douglas or Translog. If we adopt the endogenous growth theory as our new foundation, $f(\cdot)$ in Eq. (11.3) and $f_1(\cdot)$, $f_2(\cdot)$, and $f_3(\cdot)$ in Eq. (11.4) can be modeled as in Gong (2020a).

Finally, the impact mechanism of various factors on economic and environmental efficiency can be investigated based on the following system of equations:

$$\begin{cases} TE1_{it} = h_1(Z_n) + \varepsilon_{it}^{1} \\ TE2_{it} = h_2(Z_n) + \varepsilon_{it}^{2} \\ TE3_{it} = h_3(Z_n) + \varepsilon_{it}^{3} \end{cases} \tag{11.5}$$

where $Z_n = (z_1, z_2, \ldots, z_n)$ is a vector of factors that may affect economic and environmental efficiency.

11.5.3 The Design of the New Framework

Research on the drivers of green agricultural development has focused on evaluating green agricultural policies, such as reducing agricultural inputs and utilizing crop residues and livestock manure resources. Gerber et al. (2013) and Himics et al. (2018) examine the potential impact of agricultural support policy reform on GHG emissions. Yang et al. (2014) construct a multi-subject farmer and rural environmental management model based on the Swarm platform and analyze farmers' responses to two policies, including payment for environmental services and fertilizer tax. Wu et al. (2018) conduct a random trial to investigate the effect of mutual monitoring and penalty mechanisms on agricultural surface pollution. However, these studies have not reached a unified conclusion. Some scholars are optimistic about the green effect of agricultural policies (Gerber et al., 2013; Himics et al., 2018). Meran and Schwalbe (1987) and Segerson (1988) suggest combining pollution taxes and subsidy policies can significantly improve environmental performance. Godfray and Garnett (2014) argue that governments actively promote the sustainable and intensive development of agriculture, seeking the multi-win goals of yield, efficiency, and environment. Other studies have found that potential policies, such as carbon and consumption taxes, can reduce the impact of global agricultural GHG emissions (Jensen et al., 2019; OECD, 2019).

Another group of scholars has questioned the actual effectiveness of current agricultural green development policies. Cabe and Herriges (1992) and Horan et al. (1998) compare environmental taxes (taxes on pollutant emissions) with input taxes (taxes on agricultural production factors) and find that these two taxes are ineffective in curbing agricultural surface source pollution. Gardner and Rausser (2001) evaluate policies that provide subsidies to farmers who adopt environment-friendly technologies and find that the state is overburdened in the policy implementation process. Mccann et al. (2005) argue that curbing agricultural surface source pollution by defining property rights may face high costs at a practical level. Laborde et al. (2013) use the IFPRI global general equilibrium model to evaluate the impact of agricultural support policies on global GHG emissions and find significant differences in the performance of different subsidy policies.

Considering the debate in the literature and the features of China, it is essential to assess the process of green transition and high-quality agricultural development and investigate the impact mechanism. The former helps examine the achievement and indicates how to accelerate future development. Figure 11.7 proposes a unified framework that can comprehensively investigate the process of green transition and high-quality agricultural development and the impact mechanism. This framework focuses on economic and environmental efficiency as the goals of green governance (the Y variables). It primarily assesses the impact of the tools of green governance (the X variables), including green policy and emerging drivers. There are three advantages of this new framework: (1) it can achieve the decomposition between economic efficiency and environmental efficiency after measuring agricultural GTFP; (2) it systematically decomposes environmental efficiency into the efficiency of pollution abatement and GHG abatement efficiency, which makes it possible to evaluate the process of pollution reduction and GHG reduction, respectively; (3) it can further identify the impact of green policies, green R&D, green finance and other determinants on economic efficiency and environmental efficiency.

The first classification of green agricultural policies is based on how environmental externalities are handled and can be divided into coercive control and market-incentive policies. Since environmental problems often appear as "market failure," the government usually intervenes to some extent. Such intervention mainly solves environmental problems through direct command policies, including zero-growth fertilizer use action plans, and the comprehensive utilization of crop residues. According to Coase's principle, market transactions can be used to solve externalities instead of taxation and other government direct interventions. These policies include the

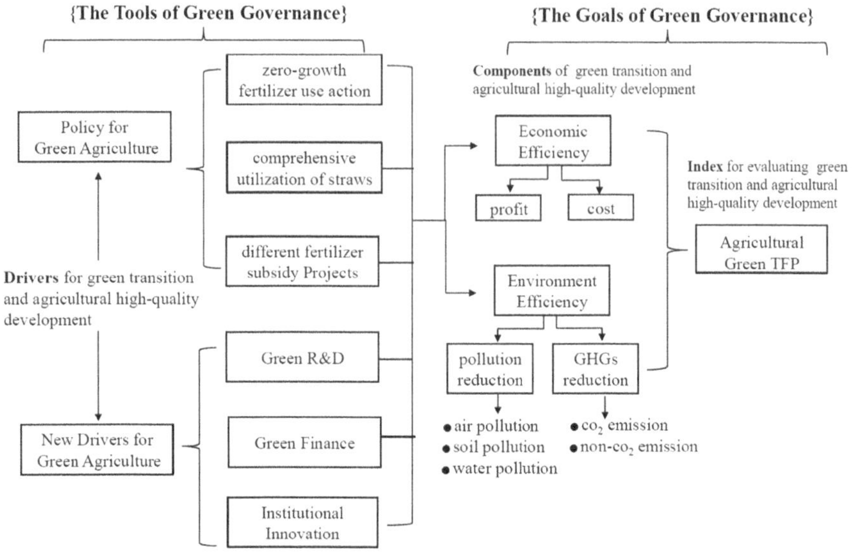

Fig. 11.7 The new frame for research of agricultural GTFP and high-quality development. *Source* Compiled by the authors

formula fertilizer technology subsidy project and organic fertilizer subsidies. The second classification is based on different environmental issues, which can be divided into two types of policies targeting environmental pollution and GHG emission. The existing agricultural green policies mainly address environmental pollution problems, including formula fertilizer technology subsidy projects, organic fertilizer subsidies, and zero-growth of chemical fertilizer use action. In contrast, relatively few policies address GHG emissions.

Meanwhile, existing literature mainly focuses on specific policies for green transition in agriculture, and qualitative studies mostly stabilize the research on emerging green transition tools; it is necessary to examine the effect of green R&D, green finance, institutional innovation, and other emerging drivers on the green transition through quantitative methods. For example, green R&D can reduce nitrous oxide emissions from fertilizer use and CH_4 emissions from rice fields and reduce GHG emissions released from animal regurgitation by adding microorganisms to feed, which is an essential means to achieve green and high-quality development of agriculture in the context of the "3060 Target" goals. Bras (1997) focuses on green R&D and concludes that the development of green R&D has three stages, namely, "design for manufacturing-design for environment-design for life cycle." Jaffe and Palmer (1997) find that the diffusion of green technologies is conducive to "emission reduction and pollution control," thus improving the agroecological environment. Singh et al. (2011) and Forbes et al. (2013) conclude that environmentally friendly agricultural technologies can best use environmental resources, provide the required potential to meet agricultural needs, and contribute to sustainable agricultural development. Cui et al. (2018) find that the theory and technology of "integrated soil-crop system management" can increase national food production by over 30% and reduce environmental emissions of nitrogen by 50%, thus meeting the dual goals of food security and environmental protection simultaneously. This new framework considers economic efficiency, environmental pollution mitigation efficiency, and GHG reduction efficiency as the primary dependent variables. It empirically evaluates the impact of green finance and R&D pilot policies on the green and high-quality development of agriculture through difference-in-difference and regression discontinuity design and other causal identification methods.

11.6 Green Transition and High-Quality Development in Agriculture: An Application of the New Framework

To further demonstrate how to use the proposed new framework, this study presents an empirical study using input and output data from 1978 to 2016 to measure China's agricultural sector's economic efficiency and environmental efficiency. Meanwhile, considering that the public sector plays a significant role in technical innovation and diffusion in China's agricultural sector, this section empirically analyses whether agricultural fiscal expenditure has effectively improved economic and environmental efficiency. The empirical results in this section provide a scientific reference for further optimizing the public finance budget in the agricultural sector, which can promote the green transformation and high-quality development of Chinese agriculture.

11.6.1 Data Sources

The data used in this study are mainly provincial annual input data, desired output data, and non-desired output data for China's agricultural sector from 1978 to 2016. Following Zhou and Zhang (2013) and Zhang et al. (2020) in inputs and output selection for agricultural TFP estimation in China, the desired output variable is the deflated total value of production from farming, forestry, animal husbandry, and fisheries (constant 1980 prices). There are four major inputs: labor is measured as the size of the labor force in farming, forestry, animal husbandry, and fisheries segments (in millions); land means the total agricultural sown area (in a million hectares), fertilizer represents the gross weight of nitrogen, phosphate, potash, and complex fertilizers (in a million tons); and machinery is defined as the total power of machinery used in the agricultural sector (in a million kilowatts).

The undesired output is the key variable to measure Chinese agriculture's green development level. Following the analysis above, this study divides the undesired output into two parts:

First, the total nitrogen, total phosphorus, and ammonia-nitrogen emissions from applying fertilizer in each province from 1978 to 2016 are calculated according to the formula in the Ministry of Ecology and Environment's Handbook on Accounting Methods and Coefficients for Agricultural Sources Production and Emissions. Second, the GHG emission data of China's provincial-level cropping segment from 1978 to 2016 used in this study are from Liang et al. (2021), which is, to the best of our knowledge, the longest span of GHG emission data for agriculture in publicly available databases.

Other control variables include the output value share of the three segments (forestry, animal husbandry, and fisheries), irrigation conditions represented by the ratio of sown areas that can be irrigated, and weather conditions denoted by the share of the cultivated area affected by natural disasters and extreme weather. The data used in this study are mainly from the China Statistical Yearbook and the China Rural Statistical Yearbook. Some data are supplemented by the China Compendium of Statistics 1949–2008 and the provincial-level statistical yearbooks. Since Hainan Province and Chongqing City have some missing data in the expected and non-expected output data, these two provinces are excluded from the empirical analysis in this study. Finally, balanced panel data containing 29 provincial-level units are obtained.

11.6.2 Empirical Models

Based on the model to achieve the decomposition of economic and environmental efficiency in Sect. 11.5.2, the empirical model used herein is specified as follows:

$$\begin{cases} GVAO_{it} = f_1\left(x_{it}^{g}, x_{it}^{b}\right) - u_{it}^{1} + v_{it}^{1} \\ Pollution_{it} = f_2\left(x_{it}^{b1}, GVAO_{it}\right) - u_{it}^{2} + v_{it}^{2} \\ GHGEmission_{it} = f_3\left(x_{it}^{b2}, GVAO_{it}\right) - u_{it}^{3} + v_{it}^{3} \end{cases} \quad (11.6)$$

where the first equation of Eq. (11.6) estimates the economic efficiency of China's agricultural sector; for environmental efficiency, it is divided into two parts, including pollution and GHG emission. $GVAO_{it}$ is the desired output, and x_{it}^{g} denotes neutral production factors, including land and labor. x_{it}^{b} denotes non-neutral factors of production that may generate pollution or GHG emissions, including fertilizers and machinery. $TE1_{it} = \exp\left(-u_{it}^{1}\right)$ represents economic efficiency, and v_{it}^{1} accounts for measurement errors, which is usually assumed to follow a normal distribution.

The second equation of Eq. (11.6) estimates the environmental efficiency of water pollution. $Pollution_{it}$ accounts for the sum of total nitrogen (TN), total phosphorus (TP), and ammonia-nitrogen (AN) resulting from fertilizer usage. x_{it}^{b1} represents the fertilizer that generates the three types of water pollution. $TE2_{it} = 1 - \exp(-u_{it}^2)$ measures the efficiency of water pollution conditions on the desired output, and v_{it}^1 is the measurement error following a normal distribution. The third equation of Eq. (11.6) estimates the environmental efficiency of GHG emissions. x_{it}^{b2} includes fertilizer and machinery that may generate GHG emissions. $TE3_{it} = 1 - \exp(-u_{it}^3)$ measures emission efficiency.

Following Chari et al. (2021), the functions $f_1(\cdot), f_2(\cdot)$, and $f_3(\cdot)$ in Eq. (11.6) are modeled as Cobb–Douglas form. The desired output, undesired output, and input take a logarithmic form. Several methods exist to estimate time-varying u_{it}^1, u_{it}^2, and u_{it}^3 in the panel model setting (Zhang et al., 2022). This study uses three methods from Cornwell et al. (1990), Park et al. (1998), and Kneip et al. (2012) to estimate them, which are widely used in efficiency analysis (e.g., in Gong (2020b) and Yuan et al. (2021)). Compared to the traditional Error Components Frontier approach, all three methods relax the fixed linear trend assumption and are flexible and consistent with China's agricultural production situation.

After estimating China's agricultural sector's provincial economic and environmental efficiency, this study builds regressions to investigate the effect of agricultural fiscal expenditure on economic efficiency and two types of environmental efficiency in Eq. (11.7).

$$\begin{cases} TE_{it}^1 = \beta_0' + \beta_1' AFE_{it} + \beta_W' W_{it} + \theta_t' + \varepsilon_{it}' \\ TE_{it}^2 = \beta_0'' + \beta_1'' AFE_{it} + \beta_W'' W_{it} + \theta_t'' + \varepsilon_{it}'' \\ TE_{it}^3 = \beta_0''' + \beta_1''' AFE_{it} + \beta_W''' W_{it} + \theta_t''' + \varepsilon_{it}''' \end{cases} \tag{11.7}$$

where TE_{it}^1 denotes the economic efficiency of the agricultural sector in province i at year t. TE_{it}^2 and TE_{it}^3 represent the pollution and emission efficiency of the agricultural sector in province i at year t, respectively. The efficiency value ranges from 0 to 1. AFE_{it} represents the agricultural fiscal expenditure in province i at year t, in logarithms. W_{it} denotes several important control variables, including the output share of the forest, animal, and fishery sector, the total sowed areas that can be irrigated (in logarithms), and the share of the agricultural land area that suffered from natural disaster (in logarithms). The term's coefficient β_1 in the three regressions in Eq. (11.7) is the interest of this study. The interpretation of β_1 exploits changes in three kinds of efficiency driven by changes in provincial agricultural fiscal expenditure.

11.6.3 Estimation Results

The most important question this empirical section seeks to answer regards the effect of agricultural fiscal expenditure on economic and environmental efficiency simultaneously. Table 11.4 reports the estimation results of the three equations in Eq. (11.7). Column 1 in Panel A shows that the effect of agricultural fiscal expenditure on economic efficiency is positive and significant. Regarding economic magnitude, our estimate in Column 1, Panel A shows every 1% increase in public financial support for agriculture, increases agricultural economic efficiency by an average of 0.025 percentage points. When we use the PSS or CSS efficiency estimators instead of the KSS efficiency estimators in Panels B and C, the magnitudes of the coefficients of financial support to agriculture are 0.033 and 0.021, respectively, and significant at the 1% level.

Regarding pollution reduction efficiency, Column 2 shows that the increase in public finance for agriculture does not have a positive effect on environmental efficiency, represented by TN, TP, and ammonia nitrogen as agricultural water pollutants. This result remained robust to three different efficiency estimators. Regarding the emission reduction efficiency, however, Column 3 shows that a 1% increase in public finance for agriculture leads to an increase of 0.070–0.088 percentage points of GHG reduction efficiency using three different efficiency estimators (KSS, PSS, and CSS).

To summarize, financial support for agriculture has a positive effect on improving economic and GHG emission efficiency in the agricultural sector but not on the efficiency of water pollutants in the agricultural sector. One possible explanation is that agricultural water pollution is closely related to the intensity of fertilizer

Table 11.4 The impact of public finance on economic and environmental efficiency

	Economic efficiency	Environmental efficiency	
Dependent variable	Production	Pollution reduction	GHG reduction
	(1)	(3)	(2)
Panel A: KSS estimators			
Public finance	0.025*** (0.006) 0.0132, 0.0375]	0.007 (0.013) – 0.0182, 0.0316]	0.072*** (0.010) 0.0515, 0.0925]
Panel B: PSS estimators			
Public finance	0.033*** (0.007) 0.0196, 0.0455]	0.006 (0.013) – 0.0186, 0.0311]	0.070*** (0.011) 0.0490, 0.0915]
Panel C: CSS estimators			
Public finance	0.021*** (0.008) 0.0060, 0.0360]	0.005 (0.013) – 0.0200, 0.0304]	0.088*** (0.011) 0.0660, 0.1109]
Structure	Control	Control	Control
Irrigation	Control	Control	Control
Disasters	Control	Control	Control
Time fixed-effects	Control	Control	Control
Sample size	1129	1129	1129

Notes The dependent variable is economic efficiency for column (1), GHG reduction efficiency for column (2), and pollution reduction efficiency for column (3). Standard errors are given in parentheses, and 95% confidence intervals are given in brackets. Asterisks *, **, and *** denote significance at the 10%, 5%, and 1% levels, respectively

application in the cropping segment. The Chinese government's governance and control of fertilizer application started in 2015. The sample period used in this study is 1978–2016, which means that the government did not take special measures for fertilizer use and its resulting water pollution during most of the sample period, which may be an important reason for the failure of financial support for agriculture.

11.7 Conclusions and Policy Implications

China has made great efforts recently to achieve green transition and high-quality development in agriculture. Economic theory usually uses the output per input to measure development quality. Therefore, TFP/GTFP analysis, measuring the input–output ratio, offers a classic framework for assessing green transition and high-quality development. In the context of the "carbon peaking and carbon neutrality goals," the goal of green governance is to achieve a balancing act between "pollution reduction" and "GHG reduction," in addition to food security. Moreover, besides green policies, the government and other market entities can use non-institutional measures, including green technologies and finance, as tools for green governance. After the goals and tools of green governance are clarified, this study establishes a new analytic framework to investigate better how to use the tools to achieve these goals. More particular, this study introduces the theoretical foundation, econometric method, and design of a new framework on top of the TFP/GTFP analysis and presents how to evaluate the achievement of the goals and how to accelerate the green transition and high-quality development in agriculture in the future. Based on our analysis, several policy implications are given as follows.

Strengthen the monitoring, reporting, and verification system for non-CO_2 GHG emissions, such as CH_4 and N_2O. In terms of non-CO_2 GHG emission reduction, China has made efforts to limit ozone-depleting substances, such as chlorofluorocarbons as early as the Montreal Protocol stage. However, the emission control for CH_4 and N_2O gases is still weak. Also, the construction of monitoring systems is not yet complete, which is not conducive to the scientific understanding of GHG emission problems in various industries and the development of relevant primary research. On the one hand, the government must update the accounting methods and emission factors for non-CO_2 GHG emissions based on Chinese reality. On the other hand, it is necessary to use satellites, drones, and other equipment to monitor non-CO_2 GHG emissions. A cross-validation of the two aspects can guarantee the accuracy of primary GHG emission data.

Enact synergistic green policies to balance pollution reduction and GHG reduction, focusing on non-CO_2 GHG emission mitigation in the agri-food system. Although a series of policies and measures for green agricultural development have been issued in recent years, most focus on pollution reduction. The goal of green governance should transform into a balancing act between pollution reduction and GHG reduction in addition to food security. Moreover, the entire agri-food system should be governance integrated with a series of associated policies, including the pre-production, production, and post-production process.

Develop agricultural carbon neutrality technology standards and accelerate the extension of agricultural emission reduction and carbon sequestration technologies.

Specific technical standards of agricultural carbon neutrality technology should be formulated based on the documents released by the Ministry of Agriculture and Rural Development: the *Technical Guidelines for Agricultural Green Development (2018–2030)* and the "Top Ten Technical Modes for Carbon Reduction and Sequestration in Agriculture and Rural Areas." Governments at all levels should increase fiscal spending on agricultural emission reduction and carbon sequestration technologies popularization.

Accelerate the integration of agriculture into the carbon trading emissions market. Currently, agriculture in China has not been included in the Chinese carbon emission trading system. The inclusion of agriculture into the carbon trading market is feasible at theoretical and practical levels and would be conducive to the synergistic management of agricultural non-point source pollution problems (Jin et al., 2021). In terms of basic research, methodological studies on agricultural carbon emission accounting should be conducted and supported to lay the foundation for agriculture to enter the carbon market. Relevant regulations, accounting, and technical monitoring specifications should be introduced at the policy level. Finally, at the implementation level, a part of the region can be selected as a pilot for agricultural carbon trading emissions to explore the experience actively.

The process of green agricultural transformation and high-quality development should be shifted from a single objective to a multidimensional objective. Currently, China's agricultural transformation and high-quality development needs to clarify the objectives: from the original "pollution control" to the concept of "pollution control and collaborative carbon reduction." This study suggests that agricultural transformation and quality development can be divided into environmental pollution control and GHG emission control. The existing policies, technologies, and markets primarily focus on the environmental pollution generated during agricultural production, such as air, water, and soil pollution. However, insufficient attention is paid to the GHG emissions generated during agricultural production. Along with the "3060 Target," it is necessary to pay increased attention to the latter from the perspective of the agri-food system.

Notes

1. High-quality Development is the fundamental path of China's economic and social development, which was proposed in the Report of the 19th CPC Congress in 2017 that agriculture needs to improve and transform from quantity and scale to high quality to achieve high-quality

development. High-quality development is the fundamental path of China's economic development at this stage. Green transformation, represented by environmental pollution control and low-carbon society construction, is integral to high-quality development. With the introduction of the dual carbon goal, low-carbon development of the economy and society is the key strategic direction of green transformation in the 14th Five-Year Plan period, and the reduction of GHG emissions in various fields of economic and social development is the key measure under the dual carbon policy.

References

Adamopoulos, T., Brandt, L., Leight, J., & Restuccia, D. (2022). Misallocation, selection and productivity: A quantitative analysis with panel data from China. *Econometrica, 90*(3), 1261–1282. https://doi.org/10.3982/ECTA16598

AGFEP (Academy of Global Food Economics and Policy), CARD (China Academy for Rural Development), CIFAD (Centre for International Food and Agricultural Economics), IAED (Institute of Agricultural Economics and Development), and IFPRI (International Food Policy Research Institute). (2021). *2021 China and global food policy report: Rethinking the agricultural food system in the post-epidemic era.*

Bai, Y., Faure, M., & Liu, J. (2014). The role of China's banking sector in providing green finance. *Duke Environmental Law & Policy Forum, 24*, 89–101.

Ball, V. E., Lovell, C. K., & Nehring, R. (2004). Incorporating environmental impacts in the measurement of agricultural productivity growth. *Journal of Agricultural and Resource Economics, 29*(3), 436–460.

Bras, B. (1997). Incorporating environmental issues in product design and realization. *Industry and Environment, 20*(1), 7–13.

Cabe, R., & Herriges, J. A. (1992). The regulation of non-point source pollution under imperfect and asymmetric information. *Journal of Environmental Economics and Management, 22*(2), 134–146. https://doi.org/10.1016/0095-0696(92)90010-T

Chari, A., Liu, E. M., Wang, S. Y., et al. (2021). Property rights, land misallocation, and agricultural efficiency in China. *Review of Economic Studies, 88*(4), 1831–1862. https://doi.org/10.1093/restud/rdaa072

Chen, S., & Gong, B. (2021). Response and adaptation of agriculture to climate change: Evidence from China. *Journal of Development Economics, 148*, 102557. https://doi.org/10.1016/j.jdeveco.2020.102557

Cornwell, C., Schmidt, P., & Sickles, R. C. (1990). Production frontiers with cross-sectional and time-series variation in efficiency levels. *Journal of Econometrics, 46*(1–2), 185–200. https://doi.org/10.1016/0304-4076(90)90054-W

Crippa, M., Solazzo, E., Guizzardi, D., et al. (2021). Food systems are responsible for a third of global anthropogenic GHG emissions. *Nature Food, 2*(3), 198–209. https://doi.org/10.1038/s43016-021-00225-9

Cui, Z., Zhang, H., Chen, X., et al. (2018). Pursuing sustainable productivity with millions of smallholder farmers. *Nature, 555*(7696), 363–366. https://doi.org/10.1038/nature25785

Fan, S., & Pardey, P. G. (1997). Research, productivity, and output growth in Chinese agriculture. *Journal of Development Economics, 53*(1), 115–213. https://doi.org/10.1016/S0304-3878(97)00005-9

Forbes, S. L., Cullen, R., & Grout, R. (2013). Adoption of environmental innovations: Analysis from the Waipara wine industry. *Wine Economics and Policy, 2*(1), 11–18. https://doi.org/10.1016/j.wep.2013.02.001

Gardner, B. L., & Rausser, G. C. (2001). *Handbook of agricultural economics*. Elsevier.

Gerber, P. J., Steinfeld, H., Henderson, B., Mottet, A., Opio, C., Dijkman, J., Falcucci, A., & Tempio, G. (2013). *Tackling climate change through livestock—A global assessment of emissions and mitigation opportunities*. Food and Agriculture Organization of the United Nations (FAO).

Godfray, H., & Garnett, T. (2014). Food security and sustainable intensification. *Philosophical Transactions of the Royal Society B: Biological Sciences, 369*(1639), 20120273. https://doi.org/10.1098/rstb.2012.0273

Gong, B. (2018). Agricultural reforms and production in China: Changes in provincial production function and productivity in 1978–2015. *Journal of Development Economics, 132*(5), 18–31. https://doi.org/10.1016/j.jdeveco.2017.12.005

Gong, B. (2020a). New growth accounting. *American Journal of Agricultural Economics, 102*(2), 641–661. https://doi.org/10.1002/ajae.12009

Gong, B. (2020b). Agricultural productivity convergence in China. *China Economic Review, 60*, 101423. https://doi.org/10.1016/j.chieco.2020.101423

Gong, B., & Sickles, R. (2020). Non-structural and structural models in productivity analysis: Study of the British Isles during the 2007–2009 financial crisis. *Journal of Productivity Analysis, 53*(2), 243–263. https://doi.org/10.1007/s11123-019-00571-8

Gong, B., & Sickles, R. (2021). Resource allocation in multi-divisional multi-product firms. *Journal of Productivity Analysis, 55*(2), 47–70. https://doi.org/10.1007/s11123-020-00595-5

Gong, B., Zhang, S., Liu, X., et al. (2021). The zoonotic diseases, agricultural production, and impact channels: Evidence from China. *Global Food Security, 28*, 100463. https://doi.org/10.1016/j.gfs.2020.100463

Gu, B., Sutton, M. A., Chang, S. X., Ge, Y., & Chang, J. (2014). Agricultural ammonia emissions contribute to China's urban air pollution. *Frontiers in Ecology and the Environment, 12*(5), 265–266. https://doi.org/10.1890/14.WB.007

Guo, Y., Chen, Y., Searchinger, T. D., et al. (2020). Air quality, nitrogen use efficiency and food security in China are improved by cost-effective agricultural nitrogen management. *Nature Food, 1*(10), 648–658. https://doi.org/10.1038/s43016-020-00162-z

Hailu, A., & Veeman, T. S. (2001). Alternative methods for environmentally adjusted productivity analysis. *Agricultural Economics, 25*, 211–218. https://doi.org/10.1111/j.1574-0862.2001.tb00201.x

Himics, M., Fellmann, T., Barreiro-Hurlé, J., Witzke, H. P., Domínguez, I. P., Jansson, T., & Weiss, F. (2018). Does the current trade liberalization agenda contribute to greenhouse gas emission mitigation in agriculture? *Food Policy, 76*, 120–129. https://doi.org/10.1016/j.foodpol.2018.01.011

Horan, R. D., Shortle, J. S., & Abler, D. G. (1998). Ambient taxes when polluters have multiple choices. *Journal of Environmental Economics and Management, 36*(2), 186–199. https://doi.org/10.1006/jeem.1998.1041

Huang, J., & Rozelle, S. (1996). Technological change: Rediscovering the engine of productivity growth in China's rural economy. *Journal of Development Economics, 49*(2), 337–369. https://doi.org/10.1016/0304-3878(95)00065-8

Huang, Q., Wang, J., & Li, Y. (2017). Do water saving technologies save water? Empirical evidence from North China. *Journal of Environmental Economics and Management, 82*, 1–16. https://doi.org/10.1016/j.jeem.2016.10.003

Institute of Agricultural Resources and Regional Planning, CAAS and Chinese Society of Agricultural Green Development. (2021). *China agricultural green development report 2020*. China Agriculture Press (in Chinese).

IPCC. 2013. *In climate change 2013: The physical science basis contribution of working group I to the fifth assessment report of the intergovernmental panel on climate change*, ed. T. F. Stocker, D. Qin, G.-K. Plattner, M. Tignor, S. K. Allen, J. Boschung, A. Nauels, Y. Xia, V. Bex, & P. M. Midgley. Cambridge United Kingdom and Cambridge University Press.

Jaffe, A. B., & Palmer, K. (1997). Environmental regulation and innovation: A panel data study. *Review of Economics and Statistics, 79*(4), 610–619. https://doi.org/10.1162/003465397557196

Jensen, H., Pérez Domínguez, I., Fellmann, T., et al. (2019). Economic impacts of a low carbon economy on global agriculture: The bumpy road to Paris. *Sustainability, 11*(8), 2349. https://doi.org/10.3390/su11082349

Jin, S., Huang, J., Hu, R., et al. (2002). The creation and spread of technology and total factor productivity in China's agriculture. *American Journal of Agricultural Economics, 84*(4), 916–930. https://doi.org/10.1111/1467-8276.00043

Jin, S. T., Han, D. M., Lin, Y., & Hu, J. Z. (2021). Prospect analysis and policy suggestion of agricultural carbon trading under carbon peak target. *Rural Finance Research, 6*, 3–8. https://doi.org/10.16127/j.cnki.issn1003-1812.2021.06.001

Kalirajan, K. P., Obwona, M. B., & Zhao, S. (1996). A decomposition of total factor productivity growth: The case of Chinese agricultural growth before and after reforms. *American Journal of Agricultural Economics, 78*(2), 331–338. https://doi.org/10.2307/1243706

Kneip, A., Sickles, R. C., & Song, W. (2012). A new panel data treatment for heterogeneity in time trends. *Econometric Theory, 28*(3), 590–628. https://doi.org/10.1017/S026646661100034X

Laborde, D., Tokgoz, S., Shutes, L., & Valin, H. (2013). *Assessment framework and operational definitions for long-term scenarios* (Working Paper No. 14).

Lambert, D. K., & Parker, E. (1998). Productivity in Chinese provincial agriculture. *Journal of Agricultural Economics, 49*(3), 378–392.

Liang, D., Lu, X., Zhuang, M., et al. (2021). China's greenhouse gas emissions for cropping systems from 1978–2016. *Scientific Data, 8*(1), 1–10. https://doi.org/10.1038/s41597-021-00960-5

Lin, J. Y. (1992). Rural reforms and agricultural growth in China. *American Economic Review, 84*, 34–51.

Lu, X., Jiang, X., & Gong, M. (2020). How land transfer marketization influence on green total factor productivity from the approach of industrial structure? Evidence from China. *Land Use Policy, 95*, 104610. https://doi.org/10.1016/j.landusepol.2020.104610

Ma, W., Zheng, H., & Gong, B. (2022). Rural income growth, ethnic differences, and household cooking fuel choice: Evidence from China. *Energy Economics, 107*, 105851. https://doi.org/10.1016/j.eneco.2022.105851

McCann, L., Colby, B., Easter, K. W., et al. (2005). Transaction cost measurement for evaluating environmental policies. *Ecological Economics, 52*(4), 527–542. https://doi.org/10.1016/j.ecolecon.2004.08.002

Meran, G., & Schwalbe, U. (1987). Pollution control and collective penalties. *Journal of Institutional and Theoretical Economics, 143*(4), 616–629.

Murty, S., Russell, R. R., & Levkoff, S. B. (2012). On modeling pollution-generating technologies. *Journal of Environmental Economics and Management, 64*(1), 117–135. https://doi.org/10.1016/j.jeem.2012.02.005

OECD. (2019). *Agricultural policy monitoring and evaluation*. https://doi.org/10.1787/agr_pol-2013-en.

Park, B. U., Sickles, R. C., & Simar, L. (1998). Stochastic frontiers: A semiparametric approach. *Journal of Econometrics, 84*, 273–301.

Poore, J., & Nemecek, T. (2018). Reducing food's environmental impacts through producers and consumers. *Science, 360*(6392), 987–992. https://doi.org/10.1126/science.aaq0216

Reinhard, S., Lovell, C. A. K., & Thijssen, G. (1999). Econometric estimation of technical and environmental efficiency: An application to Dutch Dairy Farms. *American Journal of Agricultural Economics, 81*, 44–60. https://doi.org/10.2307/1244449

Rezek, J. P., & Perrin, R. K. (2004). Environmentally adjusted agricultural productivity in the great plains. *Journal of Agricultural and Resource Economics, 29*(2), 346–369.

Rosenzweig, C., Mbow, C., Barioni, L. G., et al. (2020). Climate change responses benefit from a global food system approach. *Nature Food, 1*(2), 94–97. https://doi.org/10.1038/s43016-020-0031-z

Segerson, K. (1988). Uncertainty and incentives for nonpoint pollution control. *Journal of Environmental Economics and Management, 15*(1), 87–98. https://doi.org/10.1016/0095-0696(88)90030-7

Sheng, Y., Tian, X., Qiao, W., et al. (2019). Measuring agricultural total factor productivity in China: Pattern and drivers over the period of 1978–2016. *Australian Journal of Agricultural and Resource Economics, 64*(1), 82–103. https://doi.org/10.1111/1467-8489.12327

Shi, Y., Cui, S., Ju, X., et al. (2015). Impacts of reactive nitrogen on climate change in China. *Scientific Reports, 5*(1), 1–9. https://doi.org/10.1038/srep08118

Singh, J. S., Pandey, V. C., & Singh, D. P. (2011). Efficient soil microorganisms: A new dimension for sustainable agriculture and environmental development. *Agriculture, Ecosystems & Environment, 140*(3–4), 339–353. https://doi.org/10.1016/j.agee.2011.01.017

Solow, R. M. (1956). A contribution to the theory of economic growth. *Quarterly Journal of Economics, 1*(70), 65–94. https://doi.org/10.2307/1884513

Tamazian, A., & Rao, B. B. (2010). Do economic, financial and institutional developments matter for environmental degradation? Evidence from transitional economies. *Energy Economics, 32*(1), 137–145. https://doi.org/10.1016/j.eneco.2009.04.004

The People's Republic of China—Ministry of Ecology and Environment. (2018). *Climate change annual report: China's policies and actions for addressing climate change.*

Wen, G. J. (1993). Total factor productivity change in China's farming sector: 1952–1989. *Economic Development and Cultural Change, 42*(1), 1–41.

Wu, D., Chen, Y., Zhang, W., et al. (2018). How peer monitoring and punishment affect the performance of the group contract: An experimental study on the control of non-point source pollution. *China Agricultural Economic Review, 10*(1), 119–134. https://doi.org/10.1108/CAER-08-2016-0125

Wu, H., Li, Y., Xie, Z., et al. (2021). Estimating ammonia emissions from cropland in China based on the establishment of agro-region-specific models. *Agricultural and Forest Meteorology, 303*, 108373. https://doi.org/10.1016/j.agrformet.2021.108373

Yang, S., Qu, H., Luan, S., et al. (2014). Environmental implications of rural policies in China: A multi-agent model at the level of agricultural households. *Journal of Integrative Environmental Sciences, 11*(1), 17–37. https://doi.org/10.1080/1943815X.2014.883413

Yuan, L., Zhang, S., Wang, S., et al. (2021). World agricultural convergence. *Journal of Productivity Analysis, 55*(2), 135–153. https://doi.org/10.1007/s11123-021-00600-5

Yuan, L., Zhang, Q., Wang, S., et al. (2022). Effects of international trade on world agricultural production and productivity: Evidence from a panel of 126 countries 1962–2014. *International Food and Agribusiness Management Review, 25*(2), 293–309.

Zhang, B., Yang, Y., & Bi, J. (2011). Tracking the implementation of green credit policy in China: Top-down perspective and bottom-up reform. *Journal of Environmental Management, 92*(4), 1321–1327. https://doi.org/10.1016/j.jenvman.2010.12.019

Zhang, S., Wang, S., Yuan, L., et al. (2020). The impact of epidemics on agricultural production and forecast of COVID-19. *China Agricultural Economic Review, 12*(3), 409–425. https://doi.org/10.1108/CAER-04-2020-0055

Zhang, Q., Qian, Z., Yuan, L., et al. (2022). Productivity drain or productivity gain? The effect of new technology adoption in the oilfield market. *Energy Economics, 108*, 105930. https://doi.org/10.1016/j.eneco.2022.105930

Zhou, L. I., & Zhang, H. P. (2013). Productivity growth in China's agriculture during 1985–2010. *Journal of Integrative Agriculture, 12*(10), 1896–1904. https://doi.org/10.1016/S2095-3119(13)60598-5

Chapter 12
Scale Effect and Innovation Effect of New Energy Enterprises' Value-Added Tax Incentives

Chuanwang Sun, Yanhong Zhan, and Boqiang Lin

Abstract Promoting the large-scale development and core technology research of the new energy industry is not only an inherent requirement for the high-quality development of the industry but also an important way to realize China's carbon neutrality goal. Taking the VAT incentive policy as an example, this paper explores the relationship among new energy tax incentives, scale expansion, and technological innovation by constructing theoretical and empirical models, and further analyzes the intrinsic relationship between scale expansion and technological innovation under the policy incentives. There are three main findings. First, the VAT incentive helps promote the scale expansion of new energy enterprises, but does not promote technological innovation at the same time. Second, on the one hand, VAT incentives indirectly promote technological upgrading through positive incentives to the output scale, that is, the output effect. On the other hand, by raising the relative cost of R&D, the scale expansion replaces the technological innovation, that is, the substitution effect, and the substitution effect is stronger. Third, a strong internal innovative foundation and a better external innovative environment make the impact of VAT incentives less pronounced. The findings of this paper have significant implications. The first is to focus on the optimization of new energy tax incentives, focusing not only on industrial-scale development but also on cutting-edge technological innovation. Second, the intrinsic linkage between scale expansion and technological innovation

C. Sun · Y. Zhan
China Center for Energy Economics Research, School of Economics, Xiamen University, Xiamen, China

C. Sun
MOE Key Laboratory of Econometrics, Xiamen University, Xiamen, China

B. Lin (✉)
China Institute for Studies in Energy Policy, School of Management, Xiamen University, Xiamen, China
e-mail: bqlin@xmu.edu.cn

Present Address:
Y. Zhan
School of Economics and Management, Southeast University, Nanjing, China

B. Gong et al. (eds.), *Chinese Governance and Transformation Towards Carbon Neutrality*, Resources, Environment and Agricultural Development,
https://doi.org/10.1007/978-981-97-9996-1_12

in the new energy industry should be paid full attention to distinguish the output effect and substitution effect through the precise regulation of the policy. Third, a favorable space should be created for the transformation of the innovation achievements of new energy enterprises, to promote the high-quality development of the new energy industry.

Keywords New energy · Tax incentives · Scale expansion · Technological innovation · High-quality development

12.1 Introduction

Accelerating the scale development of the new energy industry and the breakthrough of core technology are of great significance for realizing China's carbon peak and carbon neutrality. As the two strategic goals of new energy development, scale expansion lays the necessary foundation for the industrialization of new energy development, while technological innovation provides the intrinsic driving force for the sustainable development of new energy. Stylized facts show that in the early stage of development, the United States, Germany, Japan, and other developed countries mainly take tax incentives, financial subsidies, low-interest loans, and other incentives to support the scale expansion of the new energy industry. At the same time, these incentive policies also influence and change the intrinsic correlation of scale expansion and technological innovation via the output effect and substitution effect. On the one hand, economies of scale and market competition in the process of industrial expansion accelerate technological spillovers, increasing the innovation motivation of enterprises and potential innovation gains, and helping promote the technological innovation of new energy enterprises. On the other hand, due to the naturally positive externality and high-risk nature of new energy technological innovation activities (Wang et al., 2022), the scale expansion incentive policies may also exacerbate the "rent-seeking" and "productive plunder" behaviors of new energy enterprises in the short or medium term. In the process of industrial expansion, as the market space for low-end products expands, enterprises may prefer to increase production at the low-tech level to seek more tax subsidies out of profit maximization, which may lead to the substitution of scale expansion for technological innovation. How to promote the new energy industry through effective policies to achieve common growth in scale and technology at the same time? The answer to this question is not only the focus of policymakers but also the motivation of this paper to study the high-quality development of the new energy industry.

In China, the new energy industry has been subject to a series of fiscal and tax incentives from the government. Among them, the tax incentive policy, represented by the value-added tax (VAT) preferential policy, is one of the most important ways to incentivize the large-scale development of China's new energy industry (Sun et al., 2020). As the largest tax under China's current composite tax system and a major component of the tax burden on enterprises, the VAT, especially changes in VAT policy in the domestic segment, can trigger a significant impact on the economic activities of micro-enterprises (Xu & Chen, 2016). How exactly does the VAT incentive affect the scale expansion and technological innovation of China's new energy enterprises and the intrinsic link between them? Evaluating new energy tax incentives from the dual perspective of scale and innovation is not only conducive to the construction of a policy system for the high-quality development of the new energy industry but also has important significance for the policy design of other emerging industries.

However, there is little literature that studies tax incentives, scale expansion, and technological innovation in a unified framework in the field of new energy development. Studies that explore the evolution of the intrinsic relationship between scale expansion and technological innovation of new energy enterprises based on VAT incentives are even fewer. Existing studies mainly focus on the tax policy and the scale of the new energy industry or technological innovation. Most scholars believe that the fiscal and tax supports issued by the government often reduce costs and increase investment in new energy enterprises (Metcalf, 2010; Uyterlinde et al., 2007). This is conducive to promoting energy-saving renovation and increasing the proportion of new energy use, thus expanding the scale of the new energy industry (Chien & Hu, 2007; Johnstone et al., 2010; Villca-Pozo & Gonzales-Bustos, 2019). Other literature shows that tax incentives are important factors in terms of technological innovation. They can significantly reduce enterprises' R&D costs, but the administrative costs of policy regulations, different incentive designs, and the "free-rider" effect of technological spillovers may somewhat weaken the positive incentives of tax incentives for R&D activities (Bloom et al., 2002; Cappelen et al., 2012; Ernst et al., 2014). Under high-quality development requirements, the new energy industry needs to consider both quantitative scale expansion and qualitative technological breakthroughs. Focusing only on the qualitative or quantitative impacts of industrial support policies not only makes it difficult to form a deep understanding and comprehensive knowledge of the policy effects but also may easily overlook the intrinsic connection between the scale expansion and technological innovation of the new energy industry.

To this end, this paper takes the new energy VAT incentives introduced by the Ministry of Finance and the State Taxation Administration in 2008 as an example, and explores the relationship between the VAT incentives, the scale expansion of the new energy enterprises, and their technological innovation through theoretical analysis and empirical research. In particular, the intrinsic relationship and mechanism of scale expansion and technological innovation under the VAT incentives are focused. Compared with the existing literature, the marginal contributions of this paper lie in three aspects: First, in terms of research design, it focuses on the decomposition of VAT incentives' effect on technological innovation by clarifying the output effect and substitution effect. This study also introduces the differentiated tax burden into the construction and analysis of the theoretical model, which deduces the impact mechanism of the VAT incentives and reveals the intrinsic connection between the scale expansion and technological innovation of the new energy enterprises theoretically. Second, in the empirical study, by identifying new energy enterprises and matching the related data in China's industrial enterprise database, this paper examines the impact of VAT incentives and the output effect of scale expansion. The substitution effect induced by VAT incentives is further discussed in heterogeneity analysis. These investigations provide a more comprehensive micro-explanation of the effects and mechanisms of the new energy VAT incentives. Third, in terms of research significance, the policy effectiveness research and limited analysis carried out in this paper from both qualitative and quantitative perspectives, especially the discussion of the relationship between scale expansion and technological innovation, are not only conducive to the understanding of the tax design and its practical role in the development of China's new energy industry, but also provide theoretical and practical supports for optimizing the incentive policy to promote the new energy industry to shift from low-technology expansion to high-quality development.

The rest of the paper is structured as follows. Section 12.2 introduces the policy background. Section 12.3 is the theoretical model and research hypotheses. Section 12.4 is the empirical design and sample selection. Section 12.5 is the empirical study and result analysis. Section 12.6 further tests the output effect of scale expansion and the heterogeneity effect of tax incentives. Section 12.7 provides concluding remarks and policy implications.

12.2 Policy Background

Scale expansion and technological innovation are two important goals in promoting the high-quality development of the new energy industry in China. In recent years, China's strategic energy development plan has attached increasing importance to the large-scale development of the new energy industry. From the 11th Five-Year Plan to the 14th Five-Year Plan, China's quantitative development target for the proportion of non-fossil energy consumption has increased from 8.1% to 20%. At the same time, with the scale expansion and marketization of the new energy industry, and the increasing international competition, technological innovation for the high-quality development of the new energy industry is becoming more and more significant. Facing the goal of carbon neutrality, how to promote the new energy industry to realize the high-quality development of scale and technology through effective support has become an important issue in the design of industrial policies.

Among several new energy support policies over the years in China, the Renewable Energy Law promulgated in 2005 lays the legal foundation for promoting the development of the new energy industry. Since then, a series of policies to support the new energy industry have been implemented. Among them, tax incentives represented by VAT refunds are one of the main tools used by China to support the development of the new energy industry. In 2008, the Ministry of Finance (MF) of the People's Republic of China and the State Taxation Administration (STA) consecutively issued a VAT refund policy for nuclear power enterprises and a 50% VAT refund policy for wind power enterprises. Five years later, in 2013, the MF and the

STA further included solar photovoltaic (PV) enterprises and new energy automobile enterprises in the new energy VAT incentive policy.

To summarize, the main contents of various VAT incentives for the new energy industry are shown in Table 12.1. It can be seen that China's new energy VAT incentives have the following two obvious characteristics.

First, the VAT refund policies are mainly applied to power generation and sales. Specifically, the new energy VAT incentives for wind power, nuclear power, and solar PV enterprises are mainly focused on the sales of power products, but less on the incentives for the transmission, distribution, and use of new energy power. In addition, unlike other industries (e.g., software, integrated circuits, coalbed methane extraction, etc.) where tax incentives are used not only for production expansion but also for R&D activities, the new energy tax incentives are relatively lacking in promoting technological innovation and technological services.

Second, VAT incentives have obvious temporal and sectoral differences within the new energy industry. As shown in Table 12.1, nuclear and wind power industries were first introduced in VAT incentives in 2008, while VAT incentives for new energy vehicles and solar PV power generation industries have only been implemented since 2013. The differences in the timing and industries of the VAT incentives create good conditions for this paper to further evaluate their impacts. Notably, although the new energy industry also enjoyed other tax incentives such as corporate income tax (EIT), customs duties, and import VAT during the same period, the EIT incentives in the new energy industry were all implemented in 2008 and covered the entire new energy industry without distinguishing between different industries. In addition, although the customs duties and import VAT incentives were only applied to the wind power industry in 2008–2009, they did not have much impact on micro-enterprises behaviors, as the refunded taxes could only be transferred to the national capital fund.

Table 12.1 VAT policies for new energy industry in China

Sub-industry	Implementation time	Main contents
Nuclear power	2008.01	Tax refund after collection and proportional tax returns for the sale of nuclear power products within 15 years
Wind power	2008.07	50% VAT refund for the sale of wind power products
New energy vehicles	2013.08	No VAT is levied on the financial subsidies obtained by new energy vehicle enterprises
Solar PV power	2013.10	50% VAT refund for the sale of solar power products

Source: Public documents from the Ministry of Finance and the State Taxation Administration of China

12.3 Theoretical Model and Research Hypotheses

China's new energy VAT incentives are mainly implemented after 2008, which was the early stage of the development of new energy industry, with notable characteristics such as unstable demand markets, fluctuating price levels, immature technological development, and greater difficulty in innovation (Han, 2012; Qi et al., 2017; Zhang et al., 2013). To accurately analyze the impact of tax policies on the behavior of new energy enterprises, it is important to consider the developmental reality of the new energy industry. Therefore, this paper combines the characteristics of the development stage and the content of the VAT incentives to construct the theoretical model.

First, to theoretically and intuitively examine the impact of VAT incentives on the production expansion and R&D innovation of new energy enterprises, VAT is divided into two categories based on its application stages: one is applied to the circulation of general products (t_q); the other is applied to the circulation of specialized technological products or services dedicated to innovation (t_r).[1]

Second, to comprehensively assess the scale effect and innovation effect of new energy VAT incentives, this paper introduces tax incentives, scale expansion, and technological innovation into a unified theoretical framework in line with Lee (2003) and Zhou et al. (2015). The profit maximization behavior of new energy enterprises is jointly determined by production, sales, and R&D decisions.

On the one hand, the above setting improves the model proposed by Zhou et al. (2015) by introducing differentiated tax burdens into the construction and analysis of the theoretical model. By identifying and decomposing the tax application stages, this paper also advances the analysis of new energy tax incentives to a more microscopic level. On the other hand, this article also expands the research on the relationship between scale expansion and technological innovation under tax incentives. It addresses the shortcomings in existing research that explores the relationship between tax incentives and industry scale or between tax incentives and technological innovation based on frameworks such as game theory, income transfer, or demand-pull analysis (Cullen & Gordon, 2007; Jia, 2014).

Specifically, it is assumed that heterogeneous enterprises i ($i = 1, 2, 3, \ldots, N$) within the new energy industry make production, sales, and R&D decisions based on the following profit-maximizing model.

$$\max_{P,R,K} \pi_i = P_i y_i - \left[\int_0^y c_i(R_i, K_i, L_i)dy + t_q y_i\right] - \left[(1+t_r)R_i - \int_0^R I_{R,i}(t_q, t_r)dR\right]$$
$$s.t.\ y_i \le F_i(R, K, L, P_{input}) \tag{12.1}$$

where P_i is the price per unit of product, R_i, K_i and L_i are the R&D, capital and labor inputs of enterprise i respectively, and y_i is the number of products produced by the enterprise. Among them, K and L are the actual factor inputs, while R impacts the final output by improving the combination of factor inputs and production efficiency. P_{input}

is the price vector of factor inputs. The product's marginal cost of production (mainly refers to the cost of factor inputs) $c_i = c_i(R_i, K_i, L_i)$; t_q is the actual tax burden on the production and sales of a unit of product of enterprise i, t_r is the actual tax burden on the innovation inputs of enterprise i (e.g., the VAT on the introduction of innovative specialized products, the provision of technological services, and other innovation processes), and $I_{R,i}(t_q, t_r)$ is the marginal innovation revenue (e.g., the potential high price of high-tech products, research incentives, and royalties) that an enterprise's products can obtain by reaching the technology level $T_i(R, M)$, and $I_{R,i}$ depends on the effective VAT rates of the different segments at the same time.[2] Further, we assume the profit function is quasi-concave, that scale and innovation effects reduce the marginal cost of production of heterogeneous enterprise i, and that a reduction in the tax rate per unit of product incentivizes R&D by increasing the expected after-tax return on R&D. The concave profit function means that: $y_R \equiv \partial y/\partial R > 0$, $y_K \equiv \partial y/\partial K > 0$; $c_R \equiv \partial c/\partial R < 0$, $c_K \equiv \partial c/\partial K < 0$; $I_{t_q} \equiv \partial I_R/\partial t_q < 0$, $I_{t_r} \equiv \partial I_R/\partial t_r < 0$.

Considering that the demand markets of new energy enterprises often face large uncertainties in the early stage of industrial development. Therefore, we denote

$$y_i = S_i \cdot E(Y) \tag{12.2}$$

where S_i is the market share of new energy enterprise i, $E(Y)$ is the enterprise's expectation of the total market demand, where S_i satisfies:

$$S_i = S_i(P_i, P_{-i}, T_i, T_{-i}, N) \text{ and } S_i'(P_i) < 0, S_i'(T_i) > 0, S_i'(N) < 0 \tag{12.3}$$

That is, the market share of enterprise i is affected by the pricing level of enterprise $i(P_i)$, the pricing level of other competing enterprises (P_{-i}) in the same industry, the product technology of enterprise i (T_i), the technology level of other similar products (T_{-i}), and the total number of new energy enterprises N in the industry. For the sake of simplicity and reasonableness, this paper assumes that each new energy enterprise has a consistent a priori estimate $\Psi(\text{y}) = \text{Pro}(\text{Y} \leq \text{y})$ of the total market demand Y.

In addition, considering that innovation itself is characterized by a high degree of uncertainty, while the R&D process may be affected by other factors, the technological level that an enterprise can achieve after engaging in R&D activities is further expressed as follows:

$$T_i = T_i(R_i, M_i). \tag{12.4}$$

where M_i is the other factors that may affect the R&D and innovation process of the enterprise (e.g., the enterprise's technological capability, the innovation environment in which the enterprise is located, etc.), and there is $T_R \equiv \partial T/\partial R > 0$.

Based on the above assumptions, the expected profit of new energy enterprise i under the condition of profit maximization can be obtained as follows:

$$\max_{P,R,K} E(\pi_i) = E\left\{ P_i y_i - \left[\int_0^y c_i(R_i, K_i, L_i)dy + t_q y_i \right] - \left[(1+t_r)R_i - \int_0^R I_{R,i}(t_q, t_r)dR \right] \right\}$$
$$= E\left\{ \left[(P_i - t_q) \cdot S_i E(Y) - \int_0^y c_i(R_i, K_i, L_i)dy \right] - \left[(1+t_r)R_i - \int_0^R I_{R,i}(t_q, t_r)dR \right] \right\} \quad (12.5)$$

Combining Eqs. (12.1)–(12.5), the enterprise's profit maximization decision problem translates into determining the optimal price level P_i^* and the optimal R&D decision R_i^* (the optimal innovation output T_i^* can be further obtained from R_i^*), so as to obtain the largest market share S_i^* to maximize the profit from sales. While the enterprise's optimal production inputs K_i^* depend on the P_i^*, R_i^*, and the estimation of the form of the production function.

According to the first-order conditions and constraints, it can be obtained that:

$$\frac{\partial E(\pi_i)}{\partial P_i} = \frac{\partial E(\pi_i)}{\partial R_i} = \frac{\partial E(\pi_i)}{\partial K_i} = 0 \quad (12.6)$$

$$y_i = F_i(R, K, L, p_{input}) = S_i E(Y) \quad (12.7)$$

From this, the enterprise's optimal decision set can be solved as $\pi_i^* = \{P_i^*, R_i^*, K_i^*\}$. Where the optimal pricing level is:

$$P_i^* = (c_i + t_q)\frac{\eta^{sp}}{\eta^{sp} + 1} \quad (12.8)$$

The optimal innovation input is:

$$R_i^* = \frac{(c_i + t_q)}{[(1+t_r) - I_{R,i}(t_q, t_r)] + c_{R,i} \cdot S_i^* E(Y)} \cdot \left(-\frac{\eta^{sr}}{\eta^{sp} + 1}\right) \cdot S_i^* E(Y) \quad (12.9)$$

where $\eta^{sp} \equiv \frac{S'(P) \cdot P}{S} < 0$ is the elasticity of market share with respect to product price ($|\eta^{sp}| > 1$), $\eta^{sr} \equiv \frac{S'(R) \cdot R}{S} > 0$ is the elasticity of market share with respect to innovation inputs. Thus, the optimal pricing level P_i^* depends on the production cost per unit of product, the tax burden per unit of product, and the elasticity of market share with respect to the price of the product; While the optimal R&D investment

R_i^* depends on the net marginal cost of innovation, the tax burden on the production and innovation process, the benefits of successful innovation, and the elasticity of market share with respect to innovation inputs and product price.

Based on the relationship between innovation inputs and innovation outputs expressed in Eq. (12.4), the optimal innovation outputs can be obtained as follows.

$$T_i^* = T_i^*\left(R_i^*, M_i\right) \tag{12.10}$$

Based on P_i^* and R_i^*, the optimal market share can be further obtained from Eqs. (12.3) and (12.4).

$$S_i^* = S_i^*\left(P_i^*, R_i^*\right) \tag{12.11}$$

Therefore, the optimal production input is:

$$K_i^* = \mathrm{F}_i^-\left(y_i^*, R_i^*\right) = \mathrm{F}_i^-\left[S_i^* E(Y); R_i^*\right] = \Gamma_i\left(P_i^*, R_i^*\right) \tag{12.12}$$

where $\mathrm{F}_i^-(\cdot)$ is the inverse function of the production function $\mathrm{F}_i(\cdot)$. The optimal output size y_i^* is the multiplication of S_i^* and E(Y).

Since the VAT incentives specifically for new energy enterprises mainly focus on power production, which applies to the circulation of general products (t_q).[3] Therefore, this paper focuses on the impact of t_q change on the production and R&D investment of new energy enterprises.

1. The impact of t_q change on output scale

Denote the total marginal cost of production of an enterprise's product as $MC_i = c_i(R_i, K_i, L_i) + t_q$. Other things being equal, the impact of a change in t_q on output Y depends on the impact of a change in t_q on the enterprise's total marginal cost structure. That is, when t_q falls, the output will increase if the total marginal cost falls. Therefore:

$$sign\left(\frac{\partial y_i}{\partial t_q}\right) = -sign\left(\frac{\partial MC_i}{\partial t_q}\right) < 0 \tag{12.13}$$

As a result, even if enterprises maintain their original R&D investment and technology level, a decrease in the effective tax rate t_q on the production side is favorable to directly incentivize enterprises to expand the scale of output.

2. Impact of t_q change on R&D investment

According to Shephard's Lemma, the demand function for R&D inputs is equivalent to its conditional demand function in the case of profit maximization (Nagatani, 1978; Nie et al., 2010). That is:

$$R_i\left(P_i, p_{input}, t_q, t_r\right) = R_i\left(y_i^*, p_{input}, t_q, t_r\right) \tag{12.14}$$

Therefore,

$$\underbrace{\frac{\partial R_i}{\partial t_q}}_{\text{total effect}} = \underbrace{\left.\frac{\partial R_i^*}{\partial t_q}\right|_{y_i^*}}_{\text{substitution effect}} + \underbrace{\frac{\partial R_i^*}{\partial y_i^*}\cdot\frac{\partial y_i^*}{\partial t_q}}_{\text{output effect}} \tag{12.15}$$

That is, the impact of the declining production-side tax burden on enterprises' R&D investment is jointly determined by the substitution effect and the output effect. This paper further centers on the direction of these two effects.

(1) Substitution effect. From Eq. (12.9), we can get:

$$\begin{aligned}\left.\frac{\partial R_i^*}{\partial t_q}\right|_{y_i^*} &= \frac{\omega_i + I_{t_q}(t_q, t_r)\cdot(c_i + t_q)}{\omega_i^2}\cdot\left(-\frac{\eta^{sr}}{\eta^{sp}+1}\right)\cdot S_i^* E(Y)\\ &= \underbrace{\frac{\omega_i + \phi_i}{\omega_i^2}}_{\text{uncertain symbol}}\cdot\underbrace{\left(-\frac{\eta^{sr}}{\eta^{sp}+1}\right)}_{>0}\cdot\underbrace{S_i^* E(Y)}_{>0}\end{aligned} \tag{12.16}$$

where $\omega_i = \left[(1+t_r) - I_{R,i}(t_q, t_r)\right] + c_{R,i}\cdot S_i^* E(Y) > 0$, representing the difference between the cost and benefit of R&D investment per unit of enterprise,[4] which can reflect the net marginal cost of R&D in new energy enterprises. $\phi_i = I_{t_q}(t_q, t_r)\cdot(c_i + t_q)$, and $\phi_i < 0$ (note that $I_{t_q} < 0$), which represents the additional marginal innovation benefit brought about by the decrease in t_q (this benefit is reflected in the offsetting of the total marginal production cost of the product). Also, because $\eta^{sp} + 1 < 0$, $\eta^{sr} > 0$, and $\omega_i^2 > 0$, $S_i^* E(Y) > 0$, we have:

$$sign\left(\left.\frac{\partial R_i^*}{\partial t_q}\right|_{y_i^*}\right) = sign(\omega_i + \phi_i) \tag{12.17}$$

When $|\omega_i| > |\phi_i|$, the substitution effect is positive, and the VAT incentive, by raising the relative cost of R&D, leads to an inverse change in t_q and the level of enterprises' R&D investment; On the contrary, when $|\omega_i| \le |\phi_i|$, the substitution effect is zero or negative, implying that a decrease in t_q may lead to an increase in the R&D investment.

(2) Output effect. From the setting of the production function, $\frac{\partial R_i^*}{\partial y_i^*} > 0$; combined with Eq. (12.13), it can be deduced that $\frac{\partial y_i^*}{\partial t_q} < 0$, so the output effect is negative, that is,

$$\frac{\partial R_i^*}{\partial y_i^*} * \frac{\partial y_i^*}{\partial t_q} < 0 \tag{12.18}$$

Equation (12.18) also reflects that in the process of tax incentives affecting technological innovation, the output scale has a positive indirect effect. That is, the reduction of the production-side tax rate can enhance the R&D investment of enterprises through the output effect, which is conducive to promoting the technological upgrading of enterprises.

Therefore, the production-side VAT incentives affect the substitution relationship between scale expansion and technological innovation by changing the relative cost of R&D (i.e., substitution effect) on the one hand, and indirectly promoting the technological upgrading of enterprises by positively incentivizing the output scale (i.e., output effect) on the other hand. However, the total effect of a decline in t_q on enterprises' R&D investment R_i is uncertain. When the substitution effect is positive, the total effect depends on the relative sizes of the substitution effect and the output effect; when the substitution effect is zero or negative, a decline in t_q increases enterprises' R&D investment R_i. Similarly, the effect of a decline in t_q on enterprises' technology level T_i (R_i,M_i) is uncertain.

Realistically, it may be more straightforward for new energy enterprises to capture tax incentive gains through scale expansion. Especially for new energy enterprises in the rapid development stage, the high cost and low probability of successful innovation, as well as the short-term market insensitivity to innovation inputs are likely to lead to a certain degree of R&D insufficiency (Zhou et al., 2015). The additional innovation benefits from the decline in the VAT rate only on the production side may be difficult to offset the R&D costs. Consequently, there is a higher probability that $|\omega_i| > |\phi_i|$ (i.e., the substitution effect is positive), and the VAT incentives produce a crowding out of innovative activities of new energy enterprises. The relevant logic is shown in Fig. 12.1.

Based on the above analysis, this paper proposes two hypotheses.

Hypothesis 1: The VAT incentives on the production side are conducive to the scale expansion of new energy enterprises' output.

Hypothesis 2: The impact of VAT incentives on new energy enterprises' innovations is characterized by both substitution and output effects.

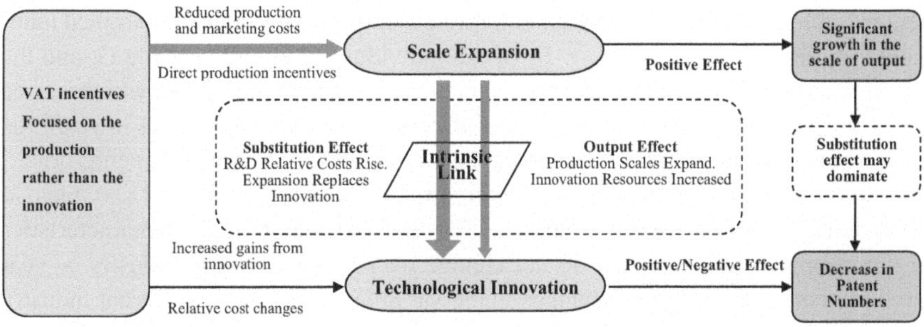

Fig. 12.1 Behavior of new energy enterprises under VAT incentives

(a) Under technology and cost constraints, the substitution effect is likely to be a crowding out of R&D and innovation and dominates both effects, resulting in a negative association between tax incentives and technological innovation in new energy enterprises;
(b) The output effect manifests itself as an incentive for R&D and innovation, i.e., the production-side VAT incentives can indirectly promote the technological upgrading of new energy enterprises by facilitating the scale expansion of enterprises.

12.4 Empirical Design and Sample Selection

12.4.1 Empirical Model

As shown in Table 12.1, China's current new energy VAT incentives have two obvious implementation nodes in the four major new energy sub-industries: wind power and nuclear power have taken the VAT incentives since 2008, while solar PV and new energy vehicle industries have only taken the relevant incentives since 2013. This means that only wind power and nuclear power enterprises were affected by VAT incentives between 2008 and 2012, which provides a good condition for this paper to identify the policy effects by using the difference-in-difference method. By taking wind power and nuclear power enterprises as the treatment group of new energy VAT incentives, and considering solar PV enterprises, new energy vehicle enterprises, and other new energy enterprises as the control group, we can examine the effect of VAT incentives on the scale expansion and technological innovation of new energy enterprises by comparing the differences between the two groups. Hence, this paper sets the following empirical model:

$$y_{it} = \alpha_1 + \alpha_2 G_i \times D_t + \alpha_3 X_{it} + \lambda_i + \mu_{jt} + \varepsilon_{it} \tag{12.19}$$

where subscripts i and t represent enterprises and years, respectively; y_{it} is the dependent variable, serving as a proxy for enterprises' output scale and technological innovation; the interaction term $G_i \times D_t$ of the individual grouping variable G_i and the period grouping variable D_t is the core explanatory variable of interest, which is used to characterize whether the enterprise i is affected by the VAT incentives in year t. Its coefficient α_2 measures the effect of the new energy VAT incentives on enterprises' scale expansion and technological innovation. X_{it} is a vector of control variables. λ_i is the individual fixed effects, controlling for unobservable individual characteristics of the sample enterprises that do not change over time. μ_{jt} is the industry × year fixed effects, controlling for changes in the variables over time in different industry dimensions.

12.4.2 Selection of Variables

For explained variables, this paper uses the gross industrial output (*ind_output*) and revenue (*revenue*) to measure the output scale of new energy enterprises, and the total patent applications (*patent*), non-invention patents (*patentud*) and invention patents (*patenti*) to measure the technological innovation of new energy enterprises. This selection accounts for the fact that total patents encompass various types, each differing significantly in terms of innovation difficulty, patent value, and review processes. Referring to Li and Zheng (2016), this paper distinguishes between utility model patents and design patents (both considered non-invention patents with lower innovation, easier development, and lower value) and invention patents (which are more innovative, valuable, and undergo stricter review). This distinction is used to examine the impact of VAT incentives on different innovation behaviors of new energy enterprises.

The core explanatory variable is the VAT incentives ($G_i \times D_t$), i.e., the interaction term of the individual grouping variable (G_i) and the period grouping variable (D_t) in the above equation. In terms of the control variables, by referring to Cai and Dong (2016) and Zhang and Zheng (2018), this paper introduces variables at the enterprise, industry, and region levels. Variables at the enterprise level mainly include asset investment, capital structure, enterprise age, equity structure, etc. Variables at the industry level are mainly industry concentration, and variables at the regional level include provincial GDP per capita and the GDP share of each industry. The definitions and descriptive statistics of the main variables are shown in Table 12.2.

Notably, this paper also attempts to control for the impact of concurrent policies, mainly including the following three categories: (a) Feed-in tariff (*FIT*) subsidies of renewable energy. To promote the development and utilization of renewable energy, the National Development and Reform Commission (NDRC) has implemented the *FIT* policies of clean energy power generation since 2006. If a new energy enterprise i is affected by the *FIT* at time t, the *FIT* equals to 1, otherwise 0. (b) VAT transformation policy (*VAT_reform*). Since July 2004, China began to implement the pilot reform of VAT transformation in eight industries in the three northeastern provinces. Since then, the scope of the pilot program has been gradually expanded. It has been fully implemented in all industries nationwide since January 2009. If an enterprise i in a certain region is affected by the VAT transformation policy in period t, *VAT_reform* takes 1, otherwise, it is 0. (c) The policy of adding a deduction for R&D expenses (*CIT_ratio*). According to the Enterprise Income Tax Law, R&D expenses related to technological innovation can be deducted at an additional rate when calculating enterprise taxable income. Since the data of R&D expenses in the database of China's industrial enterprises are seriously missing, it is hard to directly obtain the income tax information related to the deduction of R&D expenses. Therefore, this paper uses the CIT rate as a substitute indicator to control the impact of the income tax incentives related to the technological innovation of enterprises.

Table 12.2 Main variables and descriptive statistics

Variable	Definitions	N. Obs	Mean	SD
ind_output	The natural logarithm of the total industrial output of the enterprise (thousand yuan)	17,442	11.169	1.623
revenue	The natural logarithm of the enterprise's operating income (thousand yuan)	19,046	11.088	1.672
patent	The natural logarithm of (Number of patents + 1)	19,046	0.483	0.954
patentud	The natural logarithm of (Number of non-invention patents + 1)	19,046	0.409	0.852
patenti	The natural logarithm of (Number of invention patents + 1)	19,046	0.198	0.585
$G_i \times D_t$	If enterprise i belongs to the wind power or nuclear power industry and enjoys VAT incentives in period t, $G_i \times D_t = 1$, otherwise $G_i \times D_t = 0$	19,046	0.122	0.328
asset	The natural logarithm of total assets (in thousands)	19,046	10.948	1.818
debt_ratio	Total Liabilities/Total Assets × 100%	19,046	0.553	0.257
LTdebt_ratio	Total Long-term Liabilities/ Total Assets × 100%	17,664	0.0546	0.206
FA_ratio	Total Fixed Assets/Total Assets × 100%	19,034	0.326	0.237
age	The natural logarithm of (Corresponding Year − Establishment Year + 1)	19,046	1.967	0.670
ownership	If the proportion of state-owned registered capital of an enterprise exceeds 50%, *ownership* is 1, otherwise 0	19,046	0.0515	0.221
exit	If the enterprise exits in the next period, *exit* = 1, otherwise 0	19,046	0.144	0.352
hhi_revenue	The sum of the squares of the sales share of each enterprise in the sub-industry	19,046	0.117	0.0910
per_GDP	The natural logarithm of GDP at constant prices in 2002	19,046	10.207	0.543

(continued)

Table 12.2 (continued)

Variable	Definitions	N. Obs	Mean	SD
GDP_ratio_1	Primary GDP/Gross GDP × 100%	19,046	0.0838	0.0431
GDP_ratio_2	Secondary GDP/Gross GDP × 100%	19,046	0.515	0.0523

12.4.3 Data Sources and Sample Identification

Due to the small number and scale of new energy enterprises in the early period, as well as the serious lack of relevant data (Zhao et al., 2016), and the fact that the VAT incentives have been gradually extended to other new energy industry sectors since 2013, this paper restricts the sample period to the period of 2003–2012. The enterprise-level and industry-level data used in this paper mainly come from the China Industrial Enterprise Database and the China Patent Database. Among them, the basic information and financial data of enterprises come from the China Industrial Enterprise Database, and the patent data come from the China Patent Database. The regional-level data come from the China Statistical Yearbook (2013).

Most of the new energy enterprises are concentrated in the following five major fields: (a) the production and supply of electricity and heat, (b) general equipment manufacturing, (c) automobile manufacturing, (d) electrical machinery and equipment manufacturing, and (e) communication equipment, computer and other electronic equipment manufacturing (Zhou et al., 2015). Therefore, by referring to Shi et al. (2016), this paper adopts the keywords of the new energy field to identify wind power, nuclear power, solar PV, biomass energy, and new energy vehicle enterprises from the above five major industries. By removing the outliers of total assets, operating revenues, total profits, and other key indicators related to the accuracy of statistical data, this paper finally obtains the unbalanced panel data of a total of 4671 enterprises in the period of 2003–2012, with 1040 enterprises in the treatment group and 3631 enterprises in the control group, which involve 57,114 patents. Among them, 1783 new energy enterprises have applied for patents between 2003 and 2012, accounting for 38.17% of the total number of new energy enterprises in the sample.

12.5 Empirical Tests and Analysis

12.5.1 Scale Effect and Innovation Effect of New Energy VAT Incentives

12.5.1.1 Impact of VAT Incentives on the Scale Expansion of New Energy Enterprises

In the empirical analysis, reasonable control variables can help improve the estimation accuracy, while the selection of unreasonable control variables may lead to inconsistencies in the estimated coefficients. In particular, for micro-enterprise studies, controlling ex-post variables at the enterprise level may lead to the problem of "bad control variables" due to selection bias because ex-post variables may be affected by the policy at the same time after the policy's implementation (Angrist & Pischke, 2009). Therefore, we refer to Chen (2020) and Chen et al. (2021), and control for the enterprise-level variable by multiplying its value (i.e., the predetermined variable) in the year prior to the implementation of the policy (2007) by the time-trend term $f(t)$. The corresponding regression results are reported in Table 12.3. It can be seen that the coefficients on the policy interaction terms $G_i \times D_t$ are significantly positive across the different fixed effects control levels. This result suggests that the gross industrial output and operating revenue of enterprises in the treatment group are significantly increased by the VAT incentives compared to enterprises in the control group. Taking columns (2) and (4) of Table 12.3 as the benchmark regression results, the implementation of the VAT incentives increase the industrial output value (*ind_output*) of the new energy enterprises in the treatment group by 6.77%, and the business revenue (*revenue*) by 6.39%. Consistent with the results of the theoretical model, the VAT incentives promote the output scale expansion of new energy enterprises.

12.5.1.2 Impact of VAT Incentives on Technological Innovation of New Energy Enterprises

The theoretical model has pointed out that the impact of production-side VAT incentives on new energy enterprises' technological innovation is determined by both substitution effect and output effect. Columns (1) and (2) of Table 12.4 report the regression results with the total number of patents (*patent*) of the enterprises as the explained variable. The coefficients of $G_i \times D_t$ are negative in both columns and significant in column (2). Compared to the enterprises in the control group, the total patents of the new energy enterprises in the treatment group decreased by 5.33% after the implementation of the VAT incentives. This result supports a strong positive substitution effect, indicating that R&D innovation levels and the tax burden on the production side move in the same direction. The substitution effect dominates the overall effect of VAT incentives on technological innovation in new

Table 12.3 Impact of VAT incentives on the scale expansion of new energy enterprises

	ind_output		*revenue*	
	(1)	(2)	(3)	(4)
$G_i \times D_t$	0.0728*** (0.0263)	0.0677** (0.0289)	0.0801*** (0.0252)	0.0639** (0.0291)
_const	− 8.494*** (2.944)	− 9.170*** (2.904)	− 10.904*** (3.038)	− 12.267*** (3.221)
Control variables	Yes	Yes	Yes	Yes
ID FE	Yes	Yes	Yes	Yes
Year FE	Yes	No	Yes	No
Industry × Year FE	No	Yes	No	Yes
N	12,678	12,634	14,080	14,030
R^2	0.892	0.893	0.885	0.887

Note: The robust standard errors clustering at the new energy industry-year level are reported in parentheses. The *_const* means constant term. N is the observations. ***, ** and * are significant at the levels of 1%, 5% and 10%, respectively. The above notes are suitable for the following tables unless otherwise specified

energy enterprises. Ultimately, the decrease in innovation due to the substitution effect surpasses the increase in innovation from the output effect, resulting in the VAT incentives having a negative impact on technological innovation. Furthermore, by distinguishing the effect of VAT incentives on non-invention patents (*patentud*) and invention patents (*patenti*) of new energy enterprises, the coefficients of the $G_i \times D_t$ are still negative significantly at least at the 10% level. The above results indicate that the VAT incentives may crowd out the innovative activities of enterprises due to the existence of substitution effect.

Table 12.4 Impact of VAT incentives on technological innovation in new energy enterprises

	patent		*patenud*		*patenti*	
	(1)	(2)	(3)	(4)	(5)	(6)
$G_i \times D_t$	− 0.0476 (0.0290)	− 0.0533** (0.0263)	− 0.0449* (0.0262)	− 0.0489* (0.0251)	− 0.0321* (0.0168)	− 0.0344** (0.0171)
_const	− 8.554*** (3.046)	− 9.514*** (3.197)	− 5.876** (2.681)	− 6.635** (2.854)	− 9.243*** (2.129)	− 9.861*** (2.171)
Control variables	Yes	Yes	Yes	Yes	Yes	Yes
ID FE	Yes	Yes	Yes	Yes	Yes	Yes
Year FE	Yes	No	Yes	No	Yes	No
Industry × Year FE	No	Yes	No	Yes	No	Yes
N	14,080	14,030	14,080	14,030	14,080	14,030
R^2	0.600	0.600	0.571	0.572	0.535	0.535

The above empirical results verify the validity of hypotheses 1 and 2, i.e., the VAT incentives are conducive to promoting the production scale expansion of new energy enterprises, but are difficult to incentivize new energy enterprises to improve technological innovation at the same time. On the one hand, the decline of the tax burden on the production side rather than the technology side has raised the relative cost of technological innovation. On the other hand, it is also closely related to the fact that new energy enterprises in the early stage of industrial development generally face the problems of great difficulty in innovation, low willingness to innovate, imperfect related supporting mechanisms, and so on. In this case, the productive tax incentives may further induce innovation inertia. That is, new energy enterprises are more inclined to scale expansion without increasing innovation inputs under the VAT incentives, which has a negative impact on the innovation outputs of new energy enterprises.

12.5.2 *Discussion of Endogeneity*

12.5.2.1 Omitted Variable Bias

In terms of explanatory variables, the preferential strength and methods of the VAT incentives are directly prescribed by the government rather than chosen autonomously by enterprises. Hence, the VAT incentives are exogenous policies relative to individual corporate profit objectives. As for the control variables, Tables 12.3 and 12.4 have controlled a series of basic information and co-temporal policies that may affect the enterprises' scale expansion and technological innovation, including assets, investment, and capital structure. However, a concern is that China has not only implemented tax incentives for the new energy industry but also given financial subsidies to it. However, the above regressions do not consider the enterprises' subsidy income due to the large number of missing values in the Chinese Industrial Enterprises Database, which may result in omitted variable bias.

Therefore, this paper further controls government subsidies. The regression results are shown in Table 12.5. It can be seen that the coefficients of $G_i \times D_t$ in columns (1) and (2) are significantly positive, while the coefficients of $G_i \times D_t$ in columns (3) to (5) are significantly negative. The VAT incentives still positively contribute to the production of new energy enterprises after accounting for subsidies. Meanwhile, the negative association between tax incentives and enterprises' different innovative activities is enhanced in both magnitude and significance levels. These results support the previous theoretical and empirical analysis, indicating that subsidies do not significantly affect our findings.

Table 12.5 Exploration of endogeneity issues: omitted variable bias

	ind_output	*revenue*	*patent*	*patentud*	*patenti*
	(1)	(2)	(3)	(4)	(5)
$G_i \times D_t$	0.0662** (0.0269)	0.0633** (0.0290)	− 0.0942*** (0.0295)	− 0.0904*** (0.0285)	− 0.0619*** (0.0207)
subsidy	0.0127*** (0.00382)	0.0129*** (0.00383)	0.0220*** (0.00397)	0.0206*** (0.00424)	0.00847*** (0.00273)
_const	− 10.948*** (3.334)	− 14.154*** (3.834)	− 12.632*** (4.661)	− 9.672** (4.132)	− 10.926*** (3.078)
Control variables	Yes	Yes	Yes	Yes	Yes
ID FE	Yes	Yes	Yes	Yes	Yes
Industry × Year FE	Yes	Yes	Yes	Yes	Yes
N	10,118	11,516	11,516	11,516	11,516
R^2	0.897	0.887	0.608	0.581	0.529

12.5.2.2 Reverse Causality

Although controlling for government subsidies can effectively mitigate omitted variable bias, it may induce other endogeneity problems because there may be reverse causality between government subsidies and enterprise behavior. In addition, given that subsidy policy affects enterprises' scale expansion and technological innovation, collusion and rent-seeking may exist between enterprises and the government in the subsidy process (An et al., 2009). To address this, we adopt the approach of Zhang et al. (2015) by constructing instrumental variables based on government subsidies. Using the 2-digit industry in the National Economic Industry Classification as a standard, the study first aggregates annual subsidy income at the enterprise level to obtain the annual total government subsidies at the industry level. Secondly, for a specific enterprise, we subtract its own government subsidy income from the industry's total subsidy income to derive the total subsidies of other enterprises within the industry. The result variable is utilized as an instrumental variable reflecting the subsidy income of a single enterprise. That is:

$$IV{-}subsidy_{it}^{j} = \sum_{m=1\&m\neq i}^{n} subsidy_{mt}^{j} \tag{12.20}$$

where $IV{-}subsidy_{it}^{j}$ represents the instrumental variable of government subsidy income for enterprise i in industry j at year t ($subsidy_{it}^{j}$), and $subsidy_{mt}^{j}$ denotes the total subsidies of other enterprises within industry j excluding enterprise i.

To maintain consistency and continuity, the control variables and samples used in the instrumental variable regression model are the same as those set in the benchmark regressions. Table 12.6 reports the results. When the explained variables are scale variables, the coefficients are significantly positive, while they are significantly

Table 12.6 Discussion of endogeneity: instrumental variable tests

	ind_output	*revenue*	*patent*	*patentud*	*patenti*
	(1)	(2)	(3)	(4)	(5)
$G_i \times D_t$	0.0783** (0.0310)	0.0617* (0.0313)	– 0.0759*** (0.0267)	– 0.0754*** (0.0258)	– 0.0447** (0.0203)
IV-subsidy	– 0.0764 (0.0502)	– 0.0918* (0.0510)	0.0133 (0.0329)	0.0158 (0.0317)	– 0.0158 (0.0308)
Control variables	Yes	Yes	Yes	Yes	Yes
ID FE	Yes	Yes	Yes	Yes	Yes
Industry × Year FE	Yes	Yes	Yes	Yes	Yes
KP-LM Statistic (Identification Deficiency Test)	18.634*** ($p = 0.000$)	21.324*** ($p = 0.000$)	20.526*** ($p = 0.000$)	20.526*** ($p = 0.000$)	20.526*** ($p = 0.000$)
CD-Wald F statistic (weak recognition test)	67.126***	75.399***	67.827***	67.827***	67.827***
N	10,031	11,419	11,375	11,375	11,375

Note: (a) The instrumental variable for subsidy income is the total subsidy income of other enterprises within the same industry (*Ind_sub*). (2) China's Industrial Enterprise Database has some missing values for subsidy data, resulting in the loss of observations when calculating *Ind_sub*

negative when the explained variables are innovation variables. This further indicates that, when taking into account significant concurrent policies within the industry and addressing endogeneity issues, although the VAT incentives can promote the scale expansion of new energy enterprises, they fail to simultaneously incentivize enterprises' technological innovations. Instead, they negatively crowd out the innovation activities of new energy enterprises. In addition, Table 12.6 also shows that the F-statistics of the instrumental variables in the first stage are all significantly larger than the critical value (16.38) at the 10% level, indicating that there is no weak instrumental variable problem (Yu et al., 2020). Meanwhile, the Kleibergen-Paaprk LM (KP-LM) statistic is statistically significant, indicating that the instrumental variables selected in this paper are valid and relevant. Based on the above analysis and considering the numerous missing values in the government subsidy data, the regression analysis in the following sections will exclude the government subsidy variable to retain as many observations as possible.

12.5.3 Robustness Tests

This paper applies several robustness tests to further ensure the credibility and accuracy of our conclusions, including the ex-ante parallel trend test, excluding nuclear power and new energy vehicle samples with large differences in the industry, regressions using non-predetermined control variables, replacing the predetermined variable measurement, excluding frequently changing enterprises, using non-linear regression models, and the placebo test and other robustness testing methods. The regression results all support the findings of this paper.

12.6 Further Discussion

12.6.1 Tests on the Output Effect of Scale Expansion on Technological Innovation

The previous theoretical analysis shows that the total effect of production side tax incentives on the R&D and innovation of new energy enterprises can be decomposed into substitution effect and output effect. The existence of output effect makes the decrease of the actual tax burden at the production side indirectly promote the enterprises' technological upgrading through positive incentives to output. To test this effect empirically, this paper constructs a regression model as shown in Eq. (12.21).

$$
\begin{aligned}
y_{it} = \gamma_0 + \gamma_1 G_i \times D_t \times \overline{M_i} + \gamma_2 G_i \times D_t + \gamma_3 G_i \times \overline{M_i} \\
+ \gamma_4 D_t \times \overline{M_i} + \theta Z' + \lambda_i + \mu_{jt} + \varepsilon_{it}
\end{aligned}
\tag{12.21}
$$

where $\overline{M_i}$ is the enterprise's industrial output ($\overline{output}$) and operating revenue ($\overline{revenue}$) in the year before the policy (2007). Z' is the set of other predetermined control variables and time trend terms excluding $\overline{M_i}$. The rest of the settings are the same as in Eq. (12.19).

Columns (1) and (2) of Table 12.7 report the regression results of Eq. (12.21). It can be seen that the estimated coefficients of $G \times D \times \overline{output}$ and $G \times D \times \overline{revenue}$ are all significantly positive. This result verifies the existence of the output effect, i.e., scale expansion has a positive aspect in the process of VAT incentives affecting the technological innovation of new energy enterprises. The increase in enterprises' production scale can promote technological innovation to a certain extent, thus partially offsetting the reduction of innovative activities caused by the substitution effect in the process of VAT incentives. Furthermore, this paper also replaces $\overline{M_i}$ with the average industrial output and average business revenue of new energy enterprises in all observation periods before the policy to test whether the measurement and the value of $\overline{M_i}$ affect the robustness of the empirical estimation. As shown in columns (3) and (4) of Table 12.7, and the estimated coefficients of $G \times D \times \overline{output}$ and $G \times D \times \overline{revenue}$ are still significantly positive, reconfirming the output effect of the scale expansion of new energy enterprises on technological innovation.

Table 12.7 Output effects of scale expansion on technological innovation

	patent			
	(1)	(2)	(3)	(4)
$G \times D$	− 0.351* (0.189)	− 0.401** (0.185)	− 0.368* (0.191)	− 0.434** (0.187)
$G \times D \times \overline{output}$	0.0283* (0.0170)		0.0305* (0.0177)	
$D \times \overline{output}$	0.0403*** (0.0120)		0.0284** (0.0125)	
$G \times D \times \overline{revenue}$		0.0328* (0.0168)		0.0368** (0.0175)
$D \times \overline{revenue}$		0.0356*** (0.0128)		0.0222* (0.0125)
_const	− 7.865* (4.318)	− 7.897* (4.267)	− 8.012* (4.269)	− 8.132* (4.289)
Control variables	Yes	Yes	Yes	Yes
ID FE	Yes	Yes	Yes	Yes
Industry × year FE	Yes	Yes	Yes	Yes
N	14,067	14,080	14,072	14,080
R^2	0.601	0.600	0.601	0.600

Note $G \times \overline{output}$ and $G \times \overline{revenue}$ were absorbed by individual fixed effects, not reported

12.6.2 Mitigating the Substitution Effect of Scale Expansion on Technological Innovation: Perspectives from the Heterogeneity Analysis

Considering the heterogeneity of policy effects, the impact of VAT incentives on different new energy enterprises in terms of scale and technology may differ significantly. In particular, enterprises in the industry with lower innovation costs and higher innovation awareness may have less incentive to roughly expanse their production under the VAT incentives. Accordingly, the substitution of scale for technology and the negative crowding out of innovative activities by the VAT incentives may also be less pronounced. Given that technological innovation at the micro-enterprise level can originate from both the internal knowledge stock of the enterprise and external incentives, this paper further discusses how the impact of VAT incentives on the production side changes under favorable conditions that reduce innovation costs. The above discussion is conducted from two heterogeneous analytical perspectives: the internal innovation foundation and the external innovation environment.

12.6.2.1 Enterprises' Internal Innovation Foundation

The enterprises' pre-innovation attempts and technology accumulation are important ways for enterprises to increase their knowledge stock and establish and consolidate their innovation base (Zhao et al., 2021). In the empirical analysis, this paper uses the number of enterprises' patents before the policy implementation to assess the relative strength of the innovation foundation of new energy enterprises. Specifically, a binary variable, *pre_innovation*, is used to categorize new energy enterprises into groups. If a new energy enterprise has conducted successful innovation activities before 2008 (the number of patents is greater than 0), it is considered that the enterprise has a certain innovation foundation and is classified as *pre_innovation* = 1; otherwise, it is classified as *pre_innovation* = 0. From the regression results in Table 12.8, the production-side VAT incentives have no significant effect on new energy enterprises that already have a certain innovation foundation (*pre_innovation* = 1). The significantly negative association between VAT incentives and technological innovation occurs only in new energy enterprises with a weak innovation base (*pre_innovation* = 0), and these enterprises also show more significant scale expansion. The underlying implication is that enhancing the innovation foundation of new energy enterprises may help mitigate the imbalance between VAT incentives in stimulating scale expansion and crowding out technological innovation.

12.6.2.2 Enterprises' External Innovation Environment

Enterprises' innovation not only depends on their innovation foundation but also is closely relates to the external innovation environment in which it operates (Wu & Tang, 2016). Therefore, a binary variable, *innov_environ*, is further used to categorize new energy enterprises into groups. Considering that the eastern provinces and cities such as Beijing, Tianjin, Shanghai, Jiangsu, Zhejiang, and Guangdong have better comprehensive innovation environments (Zhong et al., 2017), this paper assigns new energy enterprises located in the above six provinces and cities to *innov_environ* = 1, and the rest to *innov_environ* = 0, and re-conducts the regressions. As shown in Table 12.9, the direct effect of VAT incentives on the scale expansion of new energy enterprises and the negative extrusion of technological innovation are more obvious in regions with poorer innovation environments (*innov_environ* = 0). For new energy enterprises with better external innovation environments (*innov_environ* = 1), the VAT incentives have limited incentive effects on scale expansion and does not show significant crowding out of technological innovation. The underlying implication is that optimizing the external innovation environment may help reduce the negative impact of the production-side VAT incentive on innovation in new energy enterprises.

Table 12.8 Heterogeneity analysis: enterprises' internal innovation foundation

	ind_output	*revenue*	*patent*	*patentud*	*patenti*
	(1)	(2)	(3)	(4)	(5)
Panel A: *pre_innovation* = 1					
$G_i \times D_t$	− 0.0362 (0.0412)	0.00296 (0.0412)	− 0.0813 (0.0691)	− 0.0839 (0.0727)	− 0.0178 (0.0426)
_const	− 12.137*** (3.911)	− 12.925*** (4.023)	− 19.510*** (5.553)	− 15.902*** (5.304)	− 14.736*** (3.804)
Control variables	Yes	Yes	Yes	Yes	Yes
ID FE	Yes	Yes	Yes	Yes	Yes
Industry × Year FE	Yes	Yes	Yes	Yes	Yes
N	3965	4454	4454	4454	4454
R^2	0.910	0.914	0.545	0.522	0.538
Panel B: *pre_innovation* = 0					
$G_i \times D_t$	0.0971*** (0.0359)	0.0784** (0.0385)	− 0.0662*** (0.0198)	− 0.0605*** (0.0171)	− 0.0296** (0.0121)
_const	− 8.010** (3.869)	− 12.524*** (4.108)	− 4.713* (2.538)	− 2.233 (2.084)	− 7.100*** (1.829)
Control variables	Yes	Yes	Yes	Yes	Yes
ID FE	Yes	Yes	Yes	Yes	Yes
Industry × Year FE	Yes	Yes	Yes	Yes	Yes
N	8657	9560	9560	9560	9560
R^2	0.875	0.862	0.345	0.313	0.246

12.7 Research Conclusions and Policy Implications

Currently, China is at a critical stage of energy transformation, accelerating towards a clean, low-carbon, safe, and efficient energy system. To realize the goals of carbon peak and carbon neutrality, new energy is not only a key component of the modern energy system but also an important force to lead and support China's economic and social development. Moreover, it is an inevitable choice and a viable force to guarantee China's energy security. To promote the high-quality development of the new energy industry, it is necessary to improve the policy system supporting the development of new energy, focusing on optimizing the fiscal and tax structure. This includes highlighting the precision, foresight, and effectiveness of policies to better support the industry in achieving both scale expansion and technological innovation. Based on the actual development of China's new energy industry, this paper constructs theoretical and empirical models to focus on the intrinsic relationship between scale expansion and technological innovation of new energy enterprises under VAT incentives. It addresses the core question of whether tax incentives can simultaneously promote both quantity expansion and quality enhancement in new energy enterprises.

Table 12.9 Heterogeneity analysis: enterprises' external innovation environment

	ind_output	*revenue*	*patent*	*patentud*	*patenti*
	(1)	(2)	(3)	(4)	(5)
Panel A: *innov_environ* = 1					
$G_i \times D_t$	0.0469 (0.0377)	0.0607** (0.0301)	− 0.0329 (0.0474)	− 0.0289 (0.0403)	− 0.0317 (0.0318)
_const	− 13.864*** (4.716)	− 15.940*** (4.830)	− 14.747*** (4.759)	− 10.702** (4.298)	− 13.789*** (3.583)
Control variables	Yes	Yes	Yes	Yes	Yes
ID FE	Yes	Yes	Yes	Yes	Yes
Industry × year FE	Yes	Yes	Yes	Yes	Yes
N	7583	8459	8459	8459	8459
R^2	0. 900	0. 898	0. 583	0. 548	0. 532
Panel B: *innov_environ* = 0					
$G_i \times D_t$	0.102** (0.0428)	0.0864* (0.0464)	− 0.106*** (0.0372)	− 0.0953** (0.0361)	− 0.0490* (0.0268)
_const	3.334 (5.111)	− 5.285 (6.691)	− 3.012 (3.287)	− 2.967 (2.834)	− 3.349 (2.822)
Control variables	Yes	Yes	Yes	Yes	Yes
ID FE	Yes	Yes	Yes	Yes	Yes
Industry × Year FE	Yes	Yes	Yes	Yes	Yes
N	5029	5545	5545	5545	5545
R^2	0.886	0.874	0.632	0.616	0.545

This paper finds that VAT incentives are conducive to promoting the scale expansion of new energy enterprises, but the relationship between scale expansion and technological innovation is more attributed to the substitution effect, resulting in a negative crowding out of technological innovation activities. When scale expansion predominantly exhibits a positive substitution effect on technological innovation, VAT incentives increase the relative cost of enterprise technological innovation, thereby causing the tax burden on the production side to move in the same direction as the level of enterprise innovation. The empirical study also finds that the production scale of new energy enterprises increases significantly after the implementation of VAT incentives; however, the number of patents decreases, suggesting that the decline in innovation brought about by the substitution effect outweighs the innovation growth brought about by the output effect.

Furthermore, this paper finds that there is a heterogeneous effect of VAT incentives on scale expansion and technological innovation of new energy enterprises. When new energy enterprises have a strong internal innovation foundation and a better external innovation environment, the substitution effect of scale expansion on technological innovation under the production-side VAT incentive is correspondingly smaller.

Our findings are conducive to understanding the effect of tax incentives on the scale expansion and technological innovation of new energy enterprises from a micro perspective. In addition, our findings also have important revelations for the improvement of the new energy incentives and the high-quality development of the new energy industry. First, tax incentives should be used continuously as an effective financial tool to promote the large-scale development of China's new energy industry. At present, China's new energy industry is in a period of strategic opportunity for rapid development. Facing the new round of the new energy industry expansion, not only the competition of wind power and solar PV enterprises is increasing but also the competition of energy storage, hydrogen energy, fuel cell, and other industries is also escalating. For China to take the lead in the new energy industry in the international arena, it is crucial to effectively utilize policy tools and intensify the continuous implementation of green fiscal and tax policies aimed at carbon neutrality. Especially in the current critical period of China's economic transformation, it is more important to implement more effective tax reductions, fee relief policies, and measures to support and alleviate burdens for the new energy industry.

Secondly, the government should focus on the comprehensive optimization of new energy tax incentives, which should emphasize the large-scale development of the industry and concentrate on key technological innovations. The construction of a new power system with new energy as the main component not only implies the large-scale development and utilization of new energy but also requires technological innovation to ensure high levels of new energy consumption and the safe and stable supply of the power system. Therefore, there is an urgent need to further strengthen the innovation-specific tax incentives based on the existing tax incentives. To further enhance the refined design of tax support policies, precise measures should be implemented in innovation areas such as R&D investment, technology transfer, and technical services for new energy enterprises. Efforts should focus on reducing the cost of technological innovation, promoting proactive initiatives in core technological innovations like smart and digital technologies. These measures help to provide sustainable and resilient support for the high-quality development of the new energy industry.

Thirdly, more attention should be paid to the intrinsic connection between the scale expansion and technological innovation of the new energy industry, and clarifying the output effect and substitution effect. In particular, it is necessary to strengthen market-oriented financial and tax incentives for new energy enterprises' scale expansion, focusing on technical standards restrictions, and being cautious of the negative impact of blind development at low technology levels on advanced technology innovation activities. It could be considered to use the degree of coordinated development between scale and technology as an assessment indicator for the effectiveness of new energy industry development. This approach enhances the positive impact of scale expansion while avoiding its negative substitution effect on technological innovation. By fully leveraging the regulatory function of fiscal and tax policies, it promotes the new energy industry to enhance its quality and increase efficiency, and better facilitate the green and low-carbon transformation of the energy system.

Fourth, in the implementation of support policies for the new energy industry, it is important to comprehensively distinguish between types of new energy enterprises based on internal and external conditions, thereby reducing policy biases caused by heterogeneity. On the one hand, the entry threshold of the upstream of the new energy industry is low, which makes it easy to attract enterprises with lower efficiency and weaker technology. Therefore, in the process of policy implementation, it is necessary to avoid supporting and subsidizing "greenwashing" and inefficient enterprises. It is also essential to focus on guiding new energy enterprises with a weak internal innovation base to invest more in the R&D process of key technologies. On the other hand, China's unbalanced and insufficient development between regions also leads to significant differences in the external innovation environment for new energy enterprises. For regions with a poorer comprehensive innovation environment and a lack of external innovation resources, it is necessary not only to give more talent support and financial support but also to accelerate the improvement of the corresponding scientific research and innovation supporting system. This helps to create a favorable space for the transformation of new energy enterprises' innovation achievements.

Notes

1. Such as the introduction of equipment specialized for innovation, the provision of technical services, and other VAT charges related to the innovation process.
2. An enterprise's innovation may either reduce marginal production costs by improving production efficiency or increase prices by improving product quality. Hence, the tax burden on products at the production side end also affects enterprises' innovation. A lower tax rate per unit of product can incentivize R&D by increasing the expected after-tax return on R&D. For the sake of intuition, L is not discussed in the subsequent model derivation and condition setting.
3. The VAT concessions discussed in this paper are mainly specific tax reduction policies dedicated to the new energy industry. Admittedly, there are some income tax incentives for technological innovation in China, such as lowering the income tax rate for some high-tech enterprises and additional deductions for R&D expenses. However, the target and scope of application of these policies are much wider, especially the R&D expense deduction policy, which is for almost all enterprises including new energy enterprises. In other words, the new energy enterprises studied in this paper are subject to the same strength of the R&D expense deduction policy. Omitting the analysis of the corporate income tax burden in the theoretical model will not affect the conclusions of the model. In the subsequent empirical analysis, this paper further controls the income tax rate of enterprises to eliminate the interference of relevant factors on the empirical results.
4. The total benefits of R&D come from two sources: one is the direct benefits of technological upgrading, such as the benefits of technology transfer; the other is the reduction of marginal production cost per unit of product through the improvement of production efficiency. Note that $c_{R,i} < 0$, so the additional benefit from cost reduction is $-c_{R,i} \cdot S_i^* E(Y)$.

References

An, T. L., Zhou, S. D., & Pi, J. C. (2009). The stimulating effects of R&D subsidies on independent innovation of Chinese enterprises. *Economic Research Journal, 44*, 87–98.

Angrist, J. D., & Pischke, J. S. (2009). *Mostly harmless econometrics: An empiricist's companion.* Princeton University Press.

Bloom, N., Griffith, R., & Van Reenen, J. (2002). Do R&D tax credits work? Evidence from a panel of countries 1979–1997. *Journal of Public Economics, 85*, 1–31.

Cai, J., & Dong, Y. (2016). Banking competition and firms' innovation: Empirical evidence from Chinese Industrial Enterprises Database. *Journal of Financial Research, 11*, 96–111.

Cappelen, A., Raknerud, A., & Rybalka, M. (2012). The effects of R&D tax credits on patenting and innovations. *Research Policy, 41*, 334–345.

Chen, D. K. (2020). Trade barrier reduction and environmental pollution improvement: New evidence from firm-level pollution data in China. *Economic Research Journal, 55*, 98–114.

Chen, S. Y., Zhang, J. P., & Liu, Z. L. (2021). Environmental regulation, financing constraints, and enterprise emission reduction: Evidence from pollution levy standards adjustment. *Journal of Financial Research, 9*, 51–71.

Chien, T., & Hu, J.-L. (2007). Renewable energy and macroeconomic efficiency of OECD and non-OECD economies. *Energy Policy, 35*, 3606–3615.

Cullen, J., & Gordon, R. (2007). Taxes and entrepreneurial risk-taking: theory and evidence for the US. *Journal of Public Economics, 91*, 1479–1505.

Ernst, C., Richter, K., & Riedel, N. (2014). Corporate taxation and the quality of research and development. *International Tax and Public Finance, 21*, 694–719.

Han, X. Y. (2012). Analysis of China's new energy overcapacity problem and policy suggestions: Evidence from wind and solar energy industry. *Journal of Management World, 8*, 171–172.

Jia, J. X. (2014). Tax incentives, corporate effective average tax rate, and firm entry. *Economic Research Journal, 49*, 94–109.

Johnstone, N., Hascic, I., & Popp, D. (2010). Renewable energy policies and technological innovation: evidence based on patent counts. *Environmental and Resource Economics, 45*, 133–155.

Li, W. J., & Zheng, M. N. (2016). Is it substantive innovation or strategic innovation? Impact of macroeconomic policies on micro-enterprises' innovation. *Economic Research Journal, 51*, 60–73.

Lee, C.-Y. (2003). A simple theory and evidence on the determinants of firm R&D. *Economics of Innovation and New Technology, 12*, 385–395.

Metcalf, G. (2010). Investment in energy infrastructure and the tax code. *Tax Policy and the Economy, 24*, 1–34.

Nagatani, K. (1978). Substitution and scale effects in factor demands. *Canadian Journal of Economics, 11*, 521–527.

Nie, H., Fang, M., & Li, T. (2010). China's value-added tax reform, firm behavior and performance. *Frontiers of Economics in China, 5*, 445–463.

Qi, S. Z., Zhang, Q., & Wang, B. B. (2017). Market-oriented incentives to the innovation of new energy companies: Evidence from venture capital and companies' patents. *China Industrial Economics, 12*, 95–112.

Shi, M., Zhang, D. Y., Zou, P. J., & David, B. (2016). Efficiency in the renewable energy sector in China. *Journal of Quantitative & Technological Economics, 33*, 60–77.

Sun, C., Zhan, Y., & Du, G. (2020). Can value-added tax incentives of new energy industry increase firm's profitability? Evidence from financial data of China's listed companies. *Energy Economics, 86*, 104654.

Uyterlinde, M., Junginger, M., Vries, H., Faaij, A., & Turkenburg, W. (2007). Implications of technological learning on the prospects for renewable energy technologies in Europe. *Energy Policy, 35*, 4072–4087.

Villca-Pozo, M., & Gonzales-Bustos, J. (2019). Tax incentives to modernize the energy efficiency of the housing in Spain. *Energy Policy, 128*, 530–538.

Wang, H. W., Zhu, X. T., & Yin, C. X. (2022). Research on the development and the feed-in tarif policy impact of China's photovoltaic industry. *Journal of Quantitative & Technological Economics, 39*, 90–112.

Wu, C. P., & Tang, G. (2016). Intellectual property rights enforcement, corporate innovation and operating performance: Evidence from China's listed companies. *Economic Research Journal, 51*, 125–139.

Xu, W., & Chen, B. K. (2016). Tax incentives and corporate investment: A natural experiment based on the 2004–2009 VAT transition. *Journal of Management World, 5*, 9–17.

Yu, Y. Z., Sun, P. B., & Xuan, Y. (2020). Do constraints on local governments' environmental targets affect industrial transformation and upgrading? *Economic Research Journal, 55*, 57–72.

Zhang, J., Chen, Z. Y., Yang, L. X., & Xin, F. (2015). On evaluating China's innovation subsidy policy: Theory and evidence. *Economic Research Journal, 50*, 4–17.

Zhang, J., & Zheng, W. P. (2018). Has catch-up strategy of innovation inhibited the quality of China's patents? *Economic Research Journal, 53*, 28–41.

Zhang, S., Andrews-Speed, P., Zhao, X., & He, Y. (2013). Interactions between renewable energy policy and renewable energy industrial policy: A critical analysis of china's policy approach to renewable energies. *Energy Policy, 62*, 342–353.

Zhao, G., Zhou, P., & Wen, W. (2021). Feed-in tariffs, knowledge stocks and renewable energy technology innovation: The role of local government intervention. *Energy Policy, 156*, 112453.

Zhao, X., Li, S., Zhang, S., Yang, R., & Liu, S. (2016). The effectiveness of China 's wind power policy: An empirical analysis. *Energy Policy, 95*, 269–279.

Zhong, W. G., Li, L., Lu, J. C., Peng, S. Q., Pan, J. C., Hao, D. H., & Wang, Y. F. (2017). China's Corporate innovation trend index: The environment, strategy, and future of innovation. *Journal of Management World, 6*, 37–50.

Zhou, Y. H., Pu, Y. L., Chen, S. Y., & Fang, F. (2015). Government support and development of emerging industries. *Economic Research Journal, 50*, 147–161.

Chapter 13
Urban Household Water Usage in Adaptation to Climate Change: Evidence from China

Ping Qin, Shuai Chen, Jie-Sheng Tan-Soo, and Xiao-Bing Zhang

Abstract While it has been concluded that climate change poses a significant threat to worldwide supply of freshwater resources, it is unclear if and how demand for water would also be affected. To fill this knowledge gap, we leverage on 'big data' collected using smart water meters from over 40,000 Chinese urban households, spanning nine years and ten provinces to examine the relationship between daily household water usage and climate variability. At the baseline, we find that municipal water is not only a coping mechanism for heat, but its usage is accelerated during heatwave events. Heterogeneity analyses reveal that households from lower-valued properties are more likely to substitute water for electricity to counter heat. Importantly, we find evidence of adaptation behaviors where over time, households are using increasingly more water to cope with high-temperature days. In all, after feeding our results into climate projection models, it is estimated that household water usage will increase by around 7–44% in the long-term (2080–2099) under emissions scenarios of SSP245 and SSP370. Our findings are especially relevant for water-scarce countries such as China as well as developing countries where water is a cheaper and more accessible resource to cope with heat.

Keywords Climate change · Water resources · Chinese households · Adaptation behaviors

P. Qin · X.-B. Zhang
School of Applied Economics, Renmin University of China, Beijing, China
e-mail: pingqin@ruc.edu.cn

S. Chen
China Academy for Rural Development, School of Public Affairs, Zhejiang University, Hangzhou, China

J.-S. Tan-Soo (✉)
Lee Kuan Yew School of Public Policy, National University of Singapore, Singapore, Singapore

X.-B. Zhang
Technical University of Denmark, Kongens Lyngby, Denmark

B. Gong et al. (eds.), *Chinese Governance and Transformation Towards Carbon Neutrality*, Resources, Environment and Agricultural Development,
https://doi.org/10.1007/978-981-97-9996-1_13

13.1 Introduction

The 2018 World Water Development report projected that due to population and income changes, there will be a 20–30% increase in water demand by 2050 (WWAP, 2018). At the same time, global water resources are likely to decrease such that around 3 billion people will live in severely water-scarce area (WWAP, 2018). Amongst the many countries that will be affected by water shortages, China is one of the largest and most vulnerable (Jiang, 2009; Liu & Yang, 2012; Liu et al., 2013). China's current per capita water supply is already lower than world's average as the country has around 20% of the world's population, but only 7% of freshwater resources (Piao et al., 2010). Acute water shortages is apparent in certain parts of the country as China had implemented the largest inter-basin water transfer program in the world to deliver water from the Southern to Northern provinces (Webber et al., 2017). Further compounding this natural constraint are pollution and rising domestic demand. Lack of regulatory oversight has led to several freshwater sources being contaminated to the extent that they cannot be used (Cheng & Hu, 2012). Moreover, rising income and lifestyle changes have drastically increased households' water demand. Zhou et al. (2020) estimated that urban water usage increased from 0.6 kg-m^3 per year in 1975–1992–2.21 kg-m^3 per year in 1992–2013, far out-pacing the rate of change for other water usages.

In this study, we examine a factor that has yet to be explored, but may have a significant impact on future water resources—impact of climate change on household water usage. Numerous earlier studies attempted to predict how climate change would affect China's supplies of freshwater resources (Cheng & Hu, 2012; Piao et al., 2010; Tao et al., 2005). They found that while climate change would have heterogenous impacts on water supply over China, the overall effects are most likely to be negative. However, there are no corresponding studies that examine how climate change would affect household water demand in Chinese settings even though there are ample evidence suggesting that water usage is a function of weather variability (Adamowski et al., 2012; Breyer et al., 2012; Guhathakurta & Gober, 2007; Maidment & Miaou, 1986; Martínez-Espin˜eira, 2002; Praskievicz & Chang, 2009; Ruth et al., 2007; Wong et al., 2010).

One of the main impediments of conducting such research is data that can faithfully reflect daily variations in water usage and temperature, and yet span across long time periods and geography to respectively reflect climate variability and spatial heterogeneity.

Toward this end, we utilize a novel dataset where daily water usage from over 40,000 households (in ten provinces) were collected over the years 2010–2019 using smart meters, to investigate how household water demand is affected by weather and climate variability. After controlling for factors that change in each household at a yearly basis (e. g., income, household composition), and various locational and seasonal conditions, we arrive at the following conclusions. First, we find increasing marginal impacts of water usage with respect to temperature intervals. Compared to a below 5 °C day, water usage increased by around 16 l/household-day at the 5–10 °C interval to 45 l/household-day at the highest interval of above 30 °C. The daily-level dataset also enables us to investigate the accumulative impacts of heatwaves and cold-waves on water usage. We find that households use more(less) water per day for every additional day of a heatwave(cold-wave). Second, there are several pieces of evidence to suggest that households substitute between water and electricity to cope with heat. We find that households from higher-valued properties use relatively more water on lower-temperature days, and relatively less water on hotter days. Similar usage patterns ensue when we demarcate households by average residential electricity usage. Third, we find concrete evidence of long-term adaptation where households use increasingly more water to cope with high heat over time. Putting all these results together, we project that, all else being equal, China's household water usage will increase by around 7.2–43.8% in the long-term (2080–2099) under emissions scenarios of SSP245 and SSP370. This projected increase in water demand would add the water stress that China is already predicted to experience in the future.

Our study is closely related to two major strands of literature.

First, the relationship between weather and household water usage has been an area of active research. Studies in this literature found strong and consistent evidence that household water usage increases with ambient temperature, where the findings are repeated across countries (e.g., United States, Spain) (Breyer et al., 2012; Maidment & Miaou, 1986; Martínez-Espin˜eira, 2002) and climates (e.g., arid, temperate, tropical, etc.) (Adamowski et al., 2012; Guhathakurta & Gober, 2007; Ruth et al., 2007). While the reasons provided for increased water demand on hot days are outdoor usages such as gardening and swimming pools, we also see similar relationships in urban cities such as Hong Kong, Seoul, and Singapore where vast majority of residents live in apartments (Praskievicz & Chang, 2009; Salvo, 2018; Wong et al., 2010). One possible explanation is that urban residents use more water for indoor activities such as laundry and baths on hotter days (Salvo, 2018). To a large extent, this literature was mostly focused on predicting short-term variation in aggregate water demand (i.e., residential, commercial, and industrial) to inform the operations of water-treatment facilities in single location (Ruth et al., 2007). However, because climate change is a long-term phenomenon with highly varied impacts and behavioral adaptations across locations, a richer dataset of micro-level observations over a long period of time is needed to accurately assess the relationship between water usage, and weather and climate. This is especially true for large countries such as China where landscape, climate, and socioeconomic development are highly heterogenous.

The second strand of literature are studies that examine the impacts of climate change on household utility consumption (e.g., Auffhammer, 2014; Auffhammer & Aroonruengsawat, 2011; Auffhammer et al., 2017; Giannakopoulos et al., 2016; Gupta, 2016; Li et al., 2019; Salvo, 2018; Thornton et al., 2016; Wenz et al., 2017). This literature has mostly focused on the impact of climate on residential energy usage, with the exception of Salvo (2018) who used data from Singapore's households to examine both water and electricity usage in response to weather changes. Studies in this literature have established that household electricity usage shares a positive relationship with temperature. Specifically, research conducted in Chinese settings found that households purchased more air-conditioners (Auffhammer, 2014) and consume more electricity when temperature spikes (Li et al., 2019). However, there are no studies conducted in China that examine the relationship between climate change and household water usage. An important distinction of this literature from the former is that it uses careful econometric models to rigorously establish the relationship between temperature changes and household utility usage. In return, their results are more suited for making climate change projections. On this note, we apply methods from climate change-household utilities consumption literature to isolate the impact of temperature on household water usage in China.

This study makes the following contributions to the broad literature on water resources and climate change. First, this is one of the first studies to examine households' usage of water to cope with heat. In turn, our results are applicable not just for our study setting of China, but also for the broader developing world who share similar socioeconomic characteristics. Second, we leverage on the granularity and long time span of the dataset to estimate the extent to which adaptation or behavioral changes have taken place over time. In turn, this allows us to project future water usage under various climate change scenarios, thus contributing to prominent efforts on predicting future water balances and impacts of climate change.

13.2 Methods and Material

13.2.1 Panel Regression

The primary empirical approach deployed in this study is panel fixed-effects regression:

$$y_{ijt} = \alpha + f\left(temp_{jt}\right)\gamma + X_{jt} + \delta_{ij} \cdot year_t + \theta_t + \varepsilon_{ijt} \tag{13.1}$$

where y_{ijt} is daily water usage for household i in county j at calendar date $t.f\left(temp_{jt}\right)$ is a series of temperature intervals to recover non-linear relationship between daily average temperature and water usage. There are seven temperature intervals for average daily temperature and defined as less than 5, 5–10 10–15, 15–20, 20–25, 25–30, and above 30 °C. These intervals are included as binary variables, and thus their associated coefficients (γ) are interpreted as increased water usage for an additional day in the specific temperature interval. From an economics perspective, due to the panel regression structure, (γ) are interpreted as the short-term or direct causal effect of temperature on water usage (Hsiang, 2016).

X_{jt} is a vector of selected daily weather controls (which may affect water usage) up to quadratic terms, including total precipitation, relative humidity, windspeed, hours of sunlight, and atmospheric pressure.

We include a highly flexible series of calendar-date fixed effects (θ_t), where say, 1st January 2010 is a different fixed effect from 1st January 2011. These time fixed-effects serve to control for any temporal or seasonal patterns related to water usage, e.g., households' water usage may vary on weekends, summer months, or public holidays.

As water usage data is collected through smart-meters linked to residential addresses, we also include dwelling-by-year fixed effects ($\delta_{ij} \cdot year_t$). Most other studies in the literature that use microlevel data of utilities consumption (e.g., Auffhammer & Aroonruengsawat, 2011; Li et al., 2019) also employ individual fixed effects to control for any time-invariant factors at the household- or dwelling-level. We further introduce yearly variation in the form of dwelling-by-year fixed effects so that we not only control for time-invariant factors, but also for time-varying characteristics that typically change at the annual-level, such as household characteristics (income and family composition), and community characteristics (water tariffs and local economic development). This set of fixed-effects would also control for varying characteristics due to new households moving into the residential unit. Moreover, $\delta_{ij} \cdot year_t$ is particularly important in this study as we are examining the changing patterns of household water usage in China over the period 2010–2019. In this period, per capita GDP in China has increased by between 5.7 and 10% annually, potentially leading to a large income effect in water usage. Hence, the inclusion of dwelling-by-year fixed effects would help control for changes to water usage due to income.

After controlling for an array of time- and space-varying confounding explanations, the vector of coefficients (γ) are statistically identified by comparing the daily temperature of any city with the average temperature for the remaining sample.

Lastly, ε_{ijt} is an idiosyncratic shock to water usage clustered at the dwelling-level.

A central issue of high-frequency household utilities usage datasets is that some residential addresses may not have any occupants for particular days, are predominantly unoccupied, or may have been repurposed for commercial usages (Auffhammer & Aroonruengsawat, 2011; Li et al., 2019). To remove residences that are mostly unoccupied, we drop the entire year for the household if there is no water usage for more than 60 days (or around 1/6 of the year). Additionally, we drop the entire year for any households if their average daily water usage for the year is less than 0.2 m^3 or more than 0.8 m^3 (respectively at the 5th and 95th percentile of usage). We also exclude any observations where no water usage is recorded. There are two reasons for doing so. First, unlike household utilities such as electricity, it is much more likely observations of "no water usage" indicates that the residential unit is unoccupied on that day. Second, the main purpose of this study is to examine the intensive margin of water usage with respect to temperature. Inclusion of observations with no water usage would entail effects of both extensive and intensive margins. To ensure that the results are not driven by model selection and data cleaning, we conduct several robustness checks in a latter section to test our assumptions.

13.2.2 Long Difference

The temperature regression coefficients in Eq. (13.1) represents the direct or short-term effects of temperature on household water usage. However, the long-term adaptation effect is also of interest to climate change scientists and policymakers. One way to recover both direct and long-term adaptation effects is to estimate a cross-sectional model by aggregating all household data over time. The problem with this approach is that we will not be able to include spatial or temporal controls to account for confounding factors (Hsiang, 2016). Another way to uncover the adaptation effects is by using long-difference model where the dataset is split into two time periods, and the difference between usage is regressed their explanatory counterparts (Burke & Emerick, 2016). Specifically, we estimate the following model:

$$\Delta y_{ij} = \alpha + \Delta f(temp_j)\gamma_{LD} + \Delta X_j + \Delta\varepsilon_{ij} \tag{13.2}$$

where Δy_{ij} refers to difference in average water usage between period 1 (2010–2014) and period 2 (2015–2018), and similarly for the other variables (the year 2019 is excluded from long-difference analysis as we do not have the full year data). The coefficients of interest here is the vector of γ_{LD} which estimates the extent changes in water usage across the two time periods is associated with changes in temperature across the same temporal spectrum. Implicit in this setup is that all household-level time-invariant factors across the two periods has been removed by the differencing. To deliver unbiased estimates of γ_{LD}, we would require $\Delta f\left(temp_j\right)$ to not be correlated with any time-varying factors. This assumption is likely to be challenged by rising income trends in China throughout the study period. As such, we use a second way to quantify adaptation or changing behaviors by combining the short-term approach with long-difference method. We separate the dataset into two four-year periods and conduct individual panel regressions. Accordingly, we can control for changing income over time in panel fixed-effects models by using dwelling-by-year fixed effects. And so any statistical differences between the coefficients from these two models can thus be interpreted as adaptation behaviors.

13.2.3 Projections of Water Usage

To predict future water usage, we first obtain temperature projections from the IPCC-led Climate Model Intercomparison Project. Specifically, we use projections for three distinct scenarios: SSP126, SSP245, and SSP370.

SSP 370 is a high-emissions scenario where there are no GHG mitigation policies. This scenario corresponds to a combination of representative concentration pathway (RCP) 7.0 and shared socioeconomic pathways (SSP) 3. It is projected that temperature in year 2100 will be around 4 °C above pre-industrial levels (Pielke et al., 2021).

SSP 126 represents the policy scenario where governments worldwide succeed in decarbonizing their economies. Similarly, this optimistic scenario corresponds to the combination of RCP2.6 and SSP1. In here, temperature in year 2100 is projected to be around 1.7 °C above pre-industrial (Pielke et al., 2021).

SSP 245 represents a middle-of-the-road scenario where decarbonatization is incomplete, and future temperature is projected to be around 2.8 °C above pre-industrial.

We download county-level daily temperature from 10 different climatic models, for the medium-term (2030–2049) and long-term (2080–2099), and use the average across different projection models as the future temperature (Li et al., 2019). These two time periods are chosen to represent 20 years before the two milestones of mid-century and end-century. In total, there are six distinct scenarios being projected along the dimensions of SSP (126, 245, and 370) and time period (middle- and long-term).

Next, in order to compute changes to water usage, we need to predict how daily weather will change in the future relative to current conditions. We followed Li et al. (2019) by first computing the average number of days in a year that fall within each temperature interval for the time period of 2010–2018 ("current conditions"). Second, we repeat this exercise for the middle-term under SSP126. Third, we then take the difference in each temperature interval between current conditions and the middle-term. These three steps yield the change in number of days belonging to each temperature interval for each year in the middle-term time-period.

This exercise is then repeated for the five remaining combinations of SSP scenarios and time-periods (See Fig. S1 for the change in number of days in each temperature intervals under the six scenarios).

Lastly, changes to household water usage are obtained by multiplying the change in each temperature interval by its corresponding coefficient.

13.2.4 Datasets

The dataset used in this analysis is compiled from two sources. First, household water usage is an unbalanced nine-year (from 1st January 2010–20th May 2019) panel of daily water usage from 41,649 urban households located in ten provinces in China. These ten provinces are mostly located in the heavily populated and economically active Southeastern part of China, and the households are all located in apartment buildings (as opposed to standalone houses). The dataset is obtained from a major company that specializes in installation of 'smart' water meters (Zhiheng Technology, http://www.gszh.cn/). The company do not transact directly with the households as installation of smart meters are often made on behalf of local governments or water utilities companies. Specifically, installation of 'smart' water meters in China mostly occurs through two channels. First, some provinces such as Fujian regulate that new residential constructions need to be installed with 'smart' utility meters. Second, there are many neighborhood renewal projects around China where installation of 'smart' meters is prioritized as part of the program. According to the company, it is estimated that around 20% of all Chinese households have installed 'smart' water meters (in comparison 80% have installed 'smart' electricity meters). Once installed, the meters transmit daily water usage data to the installation company using a combination of radio waves and cellular networks. Each daily observation as provided to us contains the dwelling's water meter ID, water usage, and location specified up to the neighborhood-level (neighborhoods are the urban administrative equivalent of villages in rural areas). As these meters are installed for the purpose of billing household water usage, it is likely water usage is measured with high degree of accuracy. However, to the extent that household water usage data has non-systematic measurement errors, these errors would cause attenuation bias in the regression analyses (i.e., estimated coefficients will tend toward zero) (Wooldridge, 2015).

The second source of data is daily weather Information is obtained from the 337 ground weather stations owned by China Meteorological Data Service Center. We use inverse distance weighting to attribute weather for each county in the dataset (Currie & Neidell, 2005; Deschenes & Greenstone, 2007; Schlenker & Walker, 2015).

The summary statistics are presented in Table 13.1. On average, households use around 0.45 m^3 or 450 *l* of water each day. Days with average temperature between 25 and 30 °C are most common as they account for 28% of all observations. This is because our data are predominantly from the warmer Southern provinces. However, we still observe a wide range of temperature as proportion of days with average temperature between 5 and 10 °C is non-trivial at 10% of all observations.

We plot annual temperature and precipitation to detect if there are significant changes to the climate over the 9-year study period (Fig. 13.1).

We can see that while annual temperature shows a large increase of around 1 °C over the study period (panel A), there is no overall increasing or decreasing trend for precipitation (panel B). Similarly, when regressed over years and county-fixed effects, the coefficients for temperature and precipitation models are respectively 0.14 °C/year (p-value = 0) and 0.61 mm/year (p-value = 0.9). In this regard, even though our study period of nine years is relatively short compared to the conventional time period for defining climate, our data have displayed substantial changes to the main covariate of interest-temperature.

13.3 Results

13.3.1 Daily Household Water Usage

We first regress daily household water usage on daily average temperature to discern the basic relationship between water usage and temperature. The marginal impact or direct effect of average temperature on water usage is positive and statistically significant at around 3.3 l for every °C change to daily temperature. However, evidence from earlier studies of temperature and household electricity usage suggest that it is

Table 13.1 Summary statistics

Variable	Mean	SD	Min	Max
Daily water usage (m^3)	0.45	0.29	0.002	5
Temperature interval (< 5 ∘C)	0.02	0.15	0	1
Temperature interval (5–10 ∘C]	0.10	0.30	0	1
Temperature interval (10–15 ∘C]	0.17	0.38	0	1
Temperature interval (15–20 ∘C]	0.19	0.39	0	1
Temperature interval (20–25 ∘C]	0.22	0.41	0	1
Temperature interval (25–30 ∘C]	0.28	0.45	0	1
Temperature interval (> 30 ∘C)	0.02	0.14	0	1
Heatwaves (days)	0.06	0.58	0	27
Cold-waves (days)	0.08	0.76	0	38
Relative humidity (%)	78.60	10.55	25.28	99.97
Daily precipitation (mm)	4.64	10.73	0.00	316.41
Daily hours of sunlight	4.46	3.80	0.00	13.08
Sea pressure (Pa)	990.83	23.52	791.74	1040.19
Wind speed (m/second)	2.00	1.03	0.02	11.60

Note Number of observations = 28,122,387. Daily water usage is observed at the household level. The remaining weather-related variables are observed at the county-level. Heatwaves count the number of days of a heatwave event, which in turn refers to an event where average temperature is at least 30 °C for three consecutive days. Cold-waves are defined in similar manner, except for days where average temperature is below 5 °C. Days without heatwave or cold-wave are given a value of 0

likely water usage shares a non-linear relationship with temperature (Li et al., 2019). As such, we recategorize daily temperature from a single continuous variable into seven binary variables in temperature intervals of 5 °C, starting from below 5 °C and ending with above 30 °C. As each day is certain to fall into one of the seven mutually exclusive temperature intervals, it is necessary to omit one category of temperature interval to avoid perfect collinearity. In this regard, the lowest temperature interval of less than 5 °C is omitted, and all resulting coefficients should be interpreted with respect to this interval. The results for this regression analysis are depicted in Fig. 13.2 where we see that daily household water usage shares a non-linear relationship with daily average temperature. Daily water usage increases by around 16 l when average temperature is between 5 and 10 °C. The next five intervals respectively record an increasing trend of 30 l, 39 l, 42 l, 44 l, and 45 l. The first inference from these results is that households use more water on hot days relative to cooler days. This finding is also consistent with other studies that examined household water usage in urban areas (Praskievicz & Chang, 2009; Salvo, 2018; Wong et al., 2010). Next, unlike the U-shaped relationship observed in household electricity usage, water usage continually increases with temperature. The most plausible explanation is that electricity is used for both heating and cooling purposes while water is predominantly used to cope with heat.

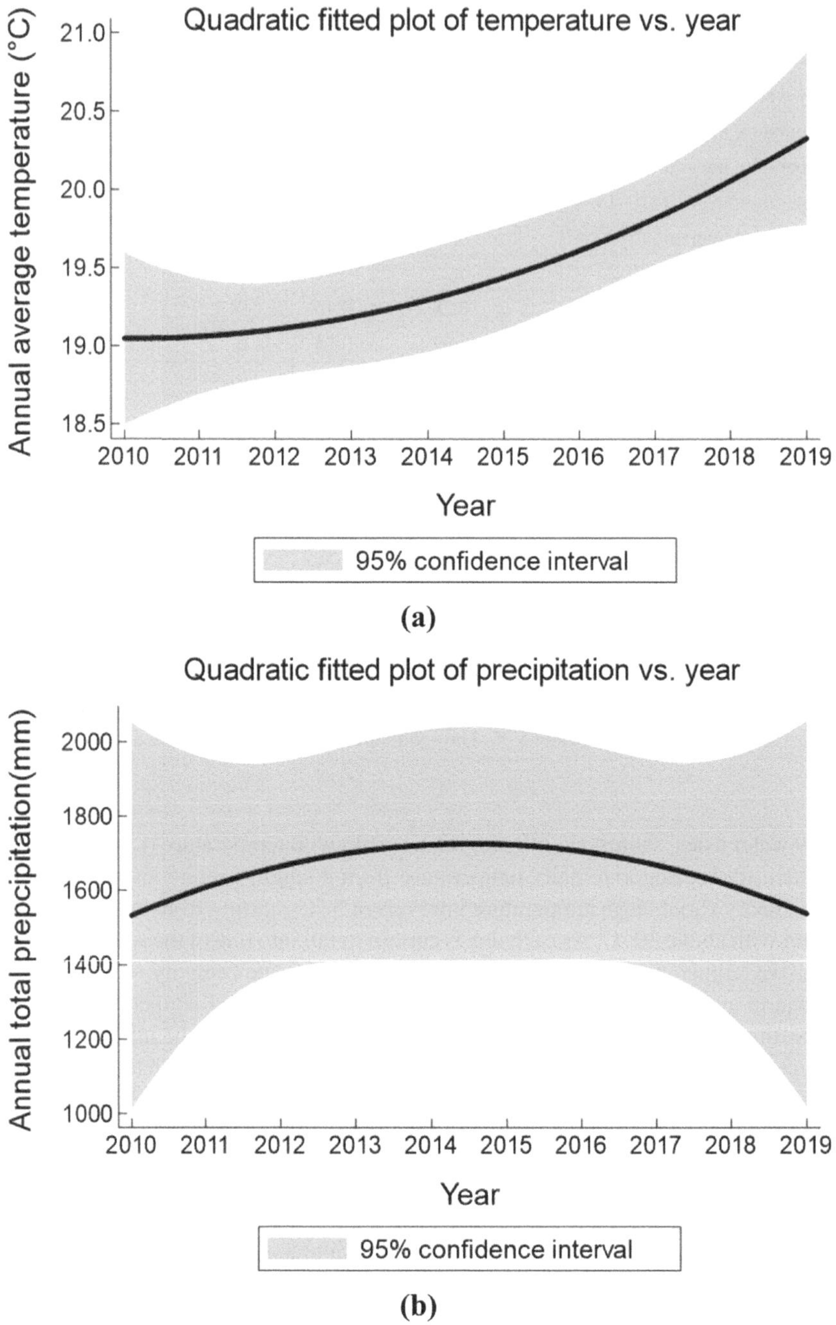

Fig. 13.1 Quadratic fitted plots of weather variables against year (panel (**a**) for temperature and panel (**b**) for precipitation)

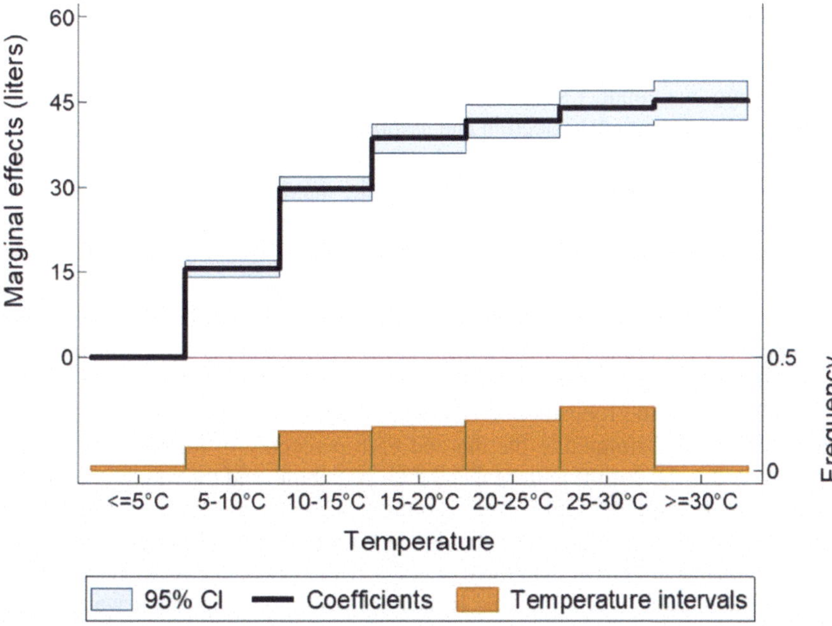

Fig. 13.2 Baseline results of temperature intervals with respect to household water usage. *Notes* This figure shows the estimated coefficients and their 95% confidence bars of each temperature interval on water usage. The omitted temperature interval is < 5 °C, and so that the estimated coefficients of other temperature intervals are interpreted in relation to this omitted reference group (Full results in Table 13.S1)

Second, we exploit the daily-level observations to examine the effects of heatwaves and cold-waves on water usage. Specifically, we want to investigate if there are cumulative effects of prolonged extreme weather. We do so by defining a heatwave event as at least three consecutive days of average temperature exceeding 30 °C. The first day of a heatwave event will take a value of one, second day will take a value of two, and as follows. Similarly, cold-waves are defined as at least three consecutive days of below 5 °C. Regardless of temperature, days without heatwaves or cold-waves are assigned a value of zero. The results in Table 13.S1, Column 2 show that households use increasingly more water as a heatwave prolongs. The coefficient for heatwave is around 0.9 l, and can be interpreted as follows: compared to days without prolonged extreme weather, a household use 0.9 l more water on the first day of a heatwave, 1.8 l on the second day, and so on. In comparison, the effects of cold-wave is a decrease in usage of 2.7 l for every additional day. As climate change is likely to increase heatwaves and decrease cold-waves occurrences in many places, our results show that there will be additional household water demand arising from these events.

13.3.2 Robustness Checks

In this section, we conduct several robustness checks to determine if our baseline results are driven by model selection and assumptions.

First, while some studies have found air pollution to affect water usage (e.g., Salvo, 2018), we did not include air quality in the main specification as there is no consistent metric of measurement for air quality in China for the same data period. The Chinese government relied on Air Pollution Index (API) up until 2013, and switched over to Air Quality Index (AQI) thereafter. Instead, we used part of the dataset where air quality measurement is consistent and found that the coefficients for temperature intervals are statistically similar with or without the inclusion of air quality (Table 13.S2, Columns 2 and 3).

Second, we test the robustness of the data cleaning process in three ways. The dataset is currently trimmed at the 5th and 95th percentile of average daily water usage. We widen the cut-off to the 1st and 99th percentile, and the results are largely similar to the baseline's (Table 13.S2, Column 4). Following Li et al. (2019), we narrow the dataset to exclude household-year with more than 30 days of no water usage. The results are larger than the baseline's. This is expected as we have further restricted the dataset to only include household with more consistent water usage (Table 13.S2, Column 5). To investigate the intensive margin of water usage with respect to temperature, we excluded observations of no water usage. However, one may be concerned that "days with zero usage" are systematically correlated with temperature, e.g., households take vacations during periods of hot weather. As a robustness check, we now include these observations in the estimation by controlling for them using an indicator variable for "no water usage". The coefficients for temperature intervals all retain their statistical significance and are larger than the baseline results (Table 13.S2, Column 6). In all, it is likely that our data cleaning process have the effect of tending our results toward the lower end of the relationship between household water usage and temperature.

Third, we replace household-by-year fixed effects with household fixed effects (the overall year fixed effects are subsumed by existing calendar date fixed effects) to examine if the former are indeed absorbing the impact of changing household income. The rationale is that both temperature and income in China are on increasing trends during the study period, and since both factors are positively correlated with household water usage, temperature may also pick up the effects of income if the latter is not adequately controlled. Toward this end, we see that the temperature coefficients estimated using only household fixed effects are around 7–16% larger than the baseline estimates which included household-by-year (Table 13.S2, Column 7). This disparity in results suggest that the time-varying fixed effects have indeed played an important role in our study as the impacts of temperature on water usage would have been overestimated without their inclusion.

Lastly, the standard error clusters are changed to the date and household-by-year groups respectively. The statistical significance is unchanged for all temperature coefficients (Table 13.S2, Columns 8 and 9).

13.3.3 Heterogeneity Analyses

Findings from climate change-household utilities literature reveal that there is substantial variation in how background environmental and socioeconomic conditions affect household demand for electricity. In this regard, we exploit the wide spatial heterogeneity of our dataset to detect heterogeneous effects along dimensions of temperature, precipitation, property value, and electricity usage.

First, we investigate how background environmental conditions may be correlated with one's behaviors (Auffhammer & Aroonruengsawat, 2011). Households residing in drier climates may exercise more prudence in water consumption compared to households in rainier regions or that households residing in hotter climates may have adapted to higher temperatures. In this regard, we separate locations into 'dry' and 'wet' regions where the former refers to locations with below-median historical precipitation (about 1623 mm annually) and vice versa. Water usage for 'wet' regions is relatively lower compared to 'dry' region at the 5–10 °C interval. However, water usage increases at a much faster rate for the remaining temperature intervals for the former (Fig. 13.3). A growing disparity shows up as households in 'wet' regions use increasingly more water to cope with high heat as temperature increases.

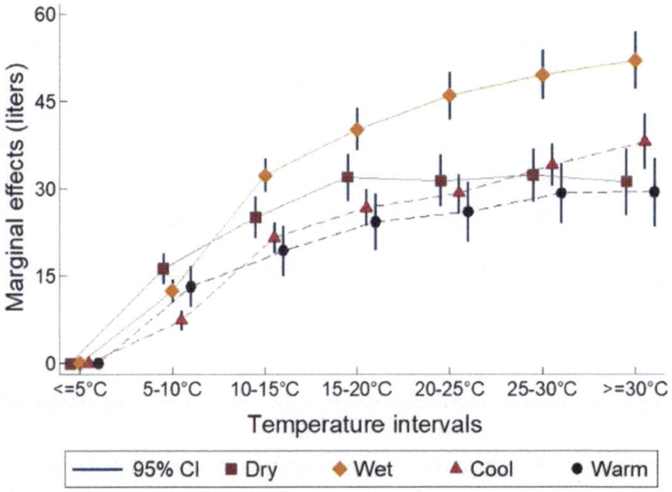

Fig. 13.3 Heterogeneity results of temperature intervals with respect to house-hold water usage (by underlying climatic conditions). *Notes* This figure shows the estimated coefficients and their 95% confidence bars of each temperature interval on water usage. The omitted temperature interval is < 5 °C, and so that the estimated coefficients of other temperature intervals are interpreted in relation to this omitted reference group (full results in Table 13.S3). For easier comparisons, the two solid lines represent "Dry" and "Wet" cities whereas the two dotted lines represent "Cool" and "Warm"

Similarly, we investigate if households living in 'cooler' vs. 'warmer' areas also display different usage behaviors. We record two findings (Fig. 13.3). A between-comparison shows households from locations with above-median average temperature (about 19 °C) use less water for almost all temperature intervals compared to their counterparts in below-median average temperature. A within-comparison shows households residing in 'warmer' regions use roughly the same amount of water to cope with heat on the hottest day compared to the second hottest interval (29I). Such water usage behaviors are contrary to our findings thus far. Both these observations suggest that households from warmer climates have alternate ways of coping with heat, other than using water. One possibility is the usage of air-conditioners where Auffhammer and Aroonruengsawat (2011) found that Californian households from warmer parts of the state consume more electricity on 'hot' days due to presumably wider adoption of air-conditioners.

Second, we examine if water usage patterns are also correlated with economic well-being. When examining both electricity and water usage of Singapore's households, Salvo (2018) found that substitution effects dominate income effects for households in higher-valued residences as they use less(more) water(electricity) compared to those residing in properties of lower value to cope with the tropical heat. When solely examining electricity usage, Li et al. (2019) found evidence of income effect in Shanghai where higher-income households use more electricity to cope with the same level of heat. As we do not have actual measurement of household income, we obtained from various Chinese statistical yearbooks city-level housing value (one administrative level beneath province) as a proxy for economic status. We observe an interesting trend where initially, households residing in higher-valued properties (around US\$1055/m^2) use relatively more water for temperatures between 5 and 20 °C (Fig. 13.4). However, the coefficients for temperature from 20 °C onward is instead larger for households residing in lower-valued properties. This difference is most pronounced at the hottest interval of above 30 °C where households in lower-valued properties use 30% more water to cope with heat. These results are consistent with other studies in the literature who found that wealthier households use more electricity than water to cope with high heat.

Results so far suggest that Chinese urban households residing in warmer regions, and from higher-valued properties may be using electricity as a substitute to cope with heat. In this sub-section, we test this hypothesis by partitioning the dataset by electricity usage. As we do not have information on electricity usage for individual households, we obtain "per capita residential electricity usage" at the city level from various Chinese statistical yearbooks to segregate our dataset into above- and below-median level of usage (around 787 kWh). The results (Fig. 13.4) support our hypothesis as (i) households that use more electricity tend to use more water on lower-temperature days, and relatively less water to cope with heat, and (ii) there is a large increase in water usage on days > 30 °C for the below-median electricity usage group, whereas there is a slight decrease for the above-median group.

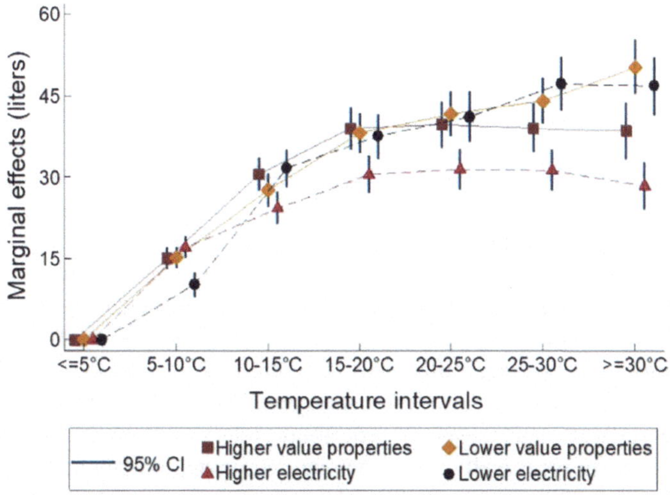

Fig. 13.4 Heterogeneity results of temperature intervals with respect to house-hold water usage (by underlying socioeconomic conditions). *Notes* This figure shows the estimated coefficients and their 95% confidence bars of each temperature interval on water usage. The omitted temperature interval is < 5 °C, and so that the estimated coefficients of other temperature intervals are interpreted in relation to this omitted reference group (full results in Table 13.S3). For easier comparisons, the two solid lines separates cities by property values whereas the two dotted lines separate cities by household electricity usage

13.3.4 Adaptation Behaviors Over Time

The earlier analyses recovered what are known as the direct effects of temperature on water usage. Other than direct effects, it is highly informative for climate change policies to quantify adaptation or belief effects as households may alter their coping behaviors based on past temperature variation. Toward this end, we utilize three different empirical techniques to present a complete picture of how Chinese households adapt to temperature variation.

First, we incrementally aggregate the dataset from daily-level to weekly-, biweekly-, and monthly-level. The key covariates in the aggregated datasets are now temperature bins, which count the numbers of days belonging to the specific interval. From a statistical viewpoint, the coefficients derived from this model can be directly compared to the baseline's as they both measure the marginal impact of an additional day in the temperature interval. However, from a behavioral perspective, the coefficients recovered from the aggregated datasets incorporate adaptation behaviors on top of direct effects compared to the daily-level. As such, we expect the coefficients estimated from the aggregated datasets to be larger than their daily's counterparts as the earlier results on heatwaves suggest that there may be adaptative effects in house- holds' coping behavior. Table 13.2, Columns 2 and 3 respectively presents the results when the data is aggregated to a weekly- and biweekly-level.

In comparison to the daily-level analyses, coefficients for water usage are either flat or decreasing on lower-temperature days. However, we observe a 24% increase in water usage at the hottest temperature interval. Results for the monthly-aggregated data (Column 4) shows similar trends for the lower-temperature days. However, there is a clear departure for the three hottest intervals as the coefficients are around 24–190% larger than their daily-level counterparts. Altogether, these results suggest that the amount of water required to cope with high-heat days may be under-estimated when using daily-level data.

Second, we implement a long-difference (LD) analysis which allows us to recover longer-term adaptation behaviors (Burke & Emerick, 2016; Dell et al., 2014; Hsiang, 2016). This analysis is conducted by splitting the dataset into two 4-year periods, and then regress the average differences between these two periods (see Methods section for detailed description of estimation procedure). The results in Table 13.2 reveal statistically insignificant coefficients for the intervals of < 5–20 °C. In contrast, the coefficients are statistically significant and increasing in magnitude for the two intervals between 25 °C to above 30 °C. One common way of interpreting the LD coefficients is to compare them to their daily-level panel counterparts. The metric $\frac{\beta_{LD}}{\beta_{Daily}}$ measures the extent to which adaptation has taken place. A value of < 1 indicates positive adaptation where less water is used to cope with same level of heat, and vice versa. The "adaptation index" is zero for temperature between 5 and 20 °C. When applied to our results, this means that households have adapted toward using lesser water on days of lower temperatures. Similar to the earlier analyses, the results are clearest for high-temperature days as: (i) the LD coefficients display an increasing trend starting from the 20–25 °C interval, (ii) are larger than the daily-level coefficients, and (iii) are all statistically significant. In all, $\frac{\beta_{LD}}{\beta_{Daily}}$ is computed at around 2.6–2.9 for the intervals of 20 °C to above 30 °C, meaning that between 2010 and 2019, households have adapted to use three times more water to cope with an additional day in these temperature intervals. However, the LD approach may not adequately capture the full adaptation effect as it can only iron out time-invariant household factors. As mentioned earlier, factors such as income is unlikely to have remained constant throughout the study period. More importantly, we would be concerned of confounding explanations if income and temperature vary at similar pulses.

In this regard, a second way of quantifying adaptation or changing behaviors is to separate the dataset into two four-year periods and conduct individual panel regressions. The panel fixed-effects models identify the direct effects for their respective time periods, and any statistical differences between the coefficients from these two models can thus be interpreted as adaptation behaviors. Consistent with the LD model, this set of results show that the marginal impact of temperature on water usage has increased over the latter five-year period (Table 13.2). Specifically, we observe a comparatively smaller increase of around 31%-55% at the lower end of temperature intervals (5–20 °C), and a much larger increase of around 73%-101% at higher temperature intervals (20 °C to above 30 °C). In all, these three analyses consistently show that, after controlling for both time-varying and time-invariant

Table 13.2 Results from regression analyses at different temporal scales

	(1)	(2)	(3)	(4)	(5)	(6)	(7)
	Daily	Weekly	Bi-weekly	Monthly	Long-difference	2014 and before	After 2014
Tem. interval (5–10 °C]	0.0155***	0.0154***	0.0196***	0.0220***	0.0428	0.0131***	0.0174***
	(0.0007)	(0.0006)	(0.0009)	(0.0014)	(0.0348)	(0.0009)	(0.0010)
Tem. interval (10–15 °C]	0.0297***	0.0154***	0.0246***	0.0355***	0.0142	0.0250***	0.0329***
	(0.0011)	(0.0006)	(0.0008)	(0.0012)	(0.0345)	(0.0013)	(0.0013)
Tem. interval (15–20 °C]	0.0387***	0.0233***	0.0296***	0.0343***	0.0682	0.0291***	0.0450***
	(0.0013)	(0.0007)	(0.0009)	(0.0014)	(0.0428)	(0.0016)	(0.0015)
Tem. interval (20–25 °C]	0.0418***	0.0275***	0.0337***	0.0517***	0.0706**	0.0289***	0.0507***
	(0.0015)	(0.0008)	(0.0010)	(0.0016)	(0.0295)	(0.0018)	(0.0017)
Tem. interval (25–30 °C]	0.0441***	0.0355***	0.0451***	0.0652***	0.0923***	0.0278***	0.0559***
	(0.0015)	(0.0009)	(0.0011)	(0.0019)	(0.0321)	(0.0019)	(0.0017)
Tem. interval (> 30 °C)	0.0454***	0.0451***	0.0565***	0.0801***	0.1315***	0.0315***	0.0546***
	(0.0018)	(0.0011)	(0.0015)	(0.0024)	(0.0477)	(0.0022)	(0.0021)
HH-Year Fixed effects (FEs)	Y	Y	Y	Y	N	Y	Y
Month-of-year FEs	N	Y	Y	Y	N	N	N
Calendar Date FEs	Y	N	N	N	N	Y	Y
Observations	28,122,387	7,532,535	3,746,336	1,925,286	38,646	14,650,725	12,134,335
Adj R-square	0.3039	0.6255	0.6570	0.6887	0.0188	0.3090	0.3053

Notes Dependent variable is daily water usage. The following weather variables and their quadratic terms are also included: relative humidity, precipitation, sunlight duration, sea pressure, wind speed. Standard error clustered by household-id in parentheses; *** $p < 0.01$, ** $p < 0.05$, * $p < 0.1$

factors, Chinese households are using increasingly more water over time to cope with high heat.

13.3.5 Water Consumption Projections

One of the central objectives of this study is to project the impact of climate changes on future household water usage. To do so, we use county-level daily temperature projections obtained from ten different climatic models for the period of 2030–2049 (medium-term), and 2080–2099 (long-term). Additionally, we calculate water usage under three different greenhouse gas emissions scenarios of SSP126, SSP245, and SSP370 (commonly referred to as the 'best-case', 'middle-of-the- road', and 'worst-case' emissions scenarios respectively). There are two caveats to these projections. First, our estimate of future water usage is accurate to the extent of uncertainties inherent to climate projection models. Second, these projections are based on current economic and technological conditions, and should be interpreted as estimated under ceteris paribus conditions, where future temperature and it's distributions are the only changing factors, and all other factors remain constant.

Panel A of Fig. 13.5 shows the projected change in water usage for the mid-century projection period of 2030–2049.

First, it is unsurprising that across three emissions scenarios, the change in water usage is smallest for SSP126 as temperature change is projected to be small in this scenario and time period (see Fig. 13.S1). Across the three sets of coefficients-daily, monthly, long-difference water usage is projected to change from − 0.28 to 2.3%. However, we observe an upward trajectory in future water usage for the two other emissions scenarios of SSP245 and SSP370. Due to slower pace of decarbonization, these two emissions scenarios will incur larger temperature changes in the future, especially with increase in number of hot days. As such, water usage is projected to increase by around 3.1–7.7% for SSP245, and by around 3.7–10.4% for SSP370.

Second, water usage for the end-century period of 2080–2099 (Panel B of Fig. 13.5) is forecasted to increase by the largest amount in the SSP370 scenario, followed by SSP245, and SSP126. Specifically, due to accumulated GHG emissions leading to continued rise in temperature, water usage is projected to increase by around 7.8–16.9% even for SSP126 scenario. On the same note, if we fail to reduce GHG emissions sufficiently, it is projected that water usage of Chinese households will increase by an average of 18% (range of 7.2–43.8%) for the two other emissions scenarios.

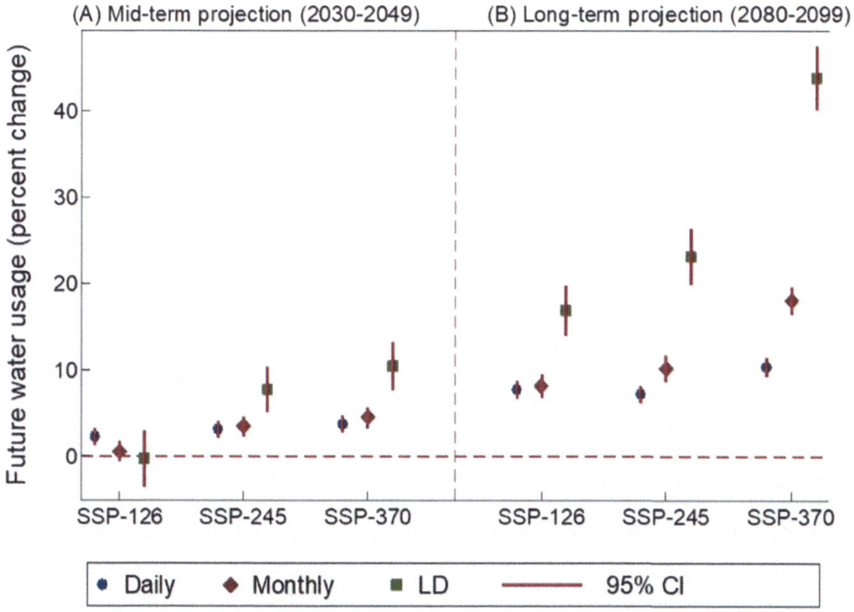

Fig. 13.5 Projected impacts of future warming on water usage. *Notes* This figure depicts the predicted percentage changes in water usage based on mid-term and long-term prediction. The round, diamond, and square represent the projections based on daily estimates, monthly estimates, and long-difference estimates, respectively, while the vertical-line represent their 95% confidence intervals

13.4 Conclusions and Discussions

13.4.1 Summary of Study and Findings

The 2018 World Water Development report projects that global water balance will worsen significantly by 2050 (WWAP, 2018). Additionally, the recent 2020 report highlights the role of climate change in affecting water supply, demand, and quality (UNESCO, 2020). These issues are especially relevant to China where their water resources were already under tremendous stress in the past decades. This problem is likely to exacerbate in future as numerous studies have examined how climate change would affect water supplies in China. However, due to lack of suitable data, there are no corresponding studies on how climate change could affect demand for water in China, or anywhere in the world. We contribute to filling this knowledge gap by leveraging on 'big data' collected using smart water meters to examine the impacts of climate change on urban households' water demand—the fastest growing source of water usage in China (Zhou et al., 2020). Toward this end, we use a daily-level dataset of more than 40,000 households to deliver the first detailed analysis of household water usage with respect to temperature changes.

We find that first, unlike electricity consumption, household water demand increases monotonically with temperature. This is most likely because while households use more electricity during periods of extreme cold or heat, water is mostly used as a coping mechanism for higher temperature.

Second, by exploiting the daily-level observations, we show that heatwaves and cold-waves have accumulative effects as households use increasingly more(less) water for every additional day of heatwave (cold-wave).

Third, we find heterogeneity in water usage patterns along the lines of background environmental conditions and economic status. Our results suggest that water and electricity are likely to be substitutes in coping with heat in China as (i) households residing in warmer climates use less water to cope with heat, presumably due to wider adoption of air-conditioners (Auffhammer, 2014); (ii) compared to their lower-valued properties counterparts, households residing in higher-valued properties use more water at lower temperature intervals (income effect), and less water at the higher temperature interval (substitution effect), and (iii) households in cities with higher electricity usage use less water to cope with heat.

Lastly, using three distinct regression models (i.e., aggregation to different temporal levels, long-difference, by two time periods) we find consistent evidence of long-term adaptation behaviors where over time, urban Chinese households are using more water to cope with high heat. In all, after feeding our results into different emissions scenarios (SSP126, SSP245, and SSP370), it is forecasted that if we fail to sufficiently reduce GHG emissions, Chinese urban household water usage will increase by around 3.1–10.4% in the medium-term (2030–2049), and by around 7.2–43.8% in the long-term (2080–2099). Coupled with the projected reduction in freshwater supplies, increased water usage would add a lot more stress to China's freshwater balance.

13.4.2 Discussions

Our findings have the following policy and research implications. First, China is already facing severe water shortage as their percapita water resources (2072 m^3) is only around 35% of world's average. Moreover, it is projected that the freshwater supplies in China will be further compromised due to climate change and environmental pollution (Cheng & Hu, 2012; Piao et al., 2010; Tao et al., 2005). Our results show that there is a further negative feedback channel on the demand side as climate change induces greater households' water usage. To partially alleviate water shortages, China currently has the largest domestic water transfer program in the world—the South-North Water Transfer Project (SNWTP) (Webber et al., 2017). This costly and ambitious project, when fully completed, will transport more than 40 billion m^3 of water annually from Southern to Northern provinces, and has already attracted controversies for its financial and environmental implications (Berkoff, 2003; Webber et al., 2017; Zhang, 2009). Our findings show that the goals of the SNWTP may be compromised in the future as temperature rises and water usage increases. Our results are especially applicable in this instance as the study area mostly consists of water-providing Southern provinces. This means that even though SNWTP was originally conceived as a long-term solution to alleviate water shortages in the North, it is unlikely that this solution will be sustainable especially if climate changes at a fast pace. Taken together, Chinese policymakers need to step up regulations to protect existing freshwater sources, and possibly use more aggressive price instruments (such as water tariffs) to slow down increase in household demand. On the latter point, despite inherent shortfall in water supply, Chinese residents currently have one of the lowest water tariffs in the world at around US\$0.34/m^3 (world's average is US\$1.35/m^3).[1] As such, there is scope for Chinese policymakers to experiment with strategies such as higher tariffs (especially in well-off cities where income is closer to that of developed countries), behavioral nudges interventions, and information campaign to further regulate residential water usage.

Second, due to constraints in both water and energy supplies, and close dependence in their production, there are growing calls from scholars and practitioners to better integrate these two utility systems, that is, the water-energy nexus (Hamiche et al., 2016). At current, China's electricity and water sectors are largely distinct from each other. However, we show that the relationship between households' water demand and temperature is headed in different directions depending on their underlying electricity usage. A limitation of this finding is that we do not have household-level electricity usage. Combining both water and electricity demand at the household level is a promising and useful area of future research as it would illuminate the extent to which they are related, and help inform Chinese policymakers on integrating water and energy infrastructure, and their pricing.

Third, while conventional logic suggests that water usage would increase with temperature for residential units with grass lawns or swimming pools, we provide strong evidence that even residential apartment units would be affected. These findings are highly relevant in current context as urbanization is advancing at a rapid pace, especially in lower- and middle-income countries (Cohen, 2006; Hannah, 2018). This means that water demand will increase concurrently with local temperature for over three billion population residing in cities (UN, 2019).

Fourth and related, similar to Salvo (2018), we find that households residing in lower-valued properties use more water to cope with heat, suggesting that water is a widely-used coping mechanism for heat for lower-income population. This implies that the policymakers may need to pay more attention to the distributional effect of climate change on water demand, and provide support to the most vulnerable households. Moreover, when generalized to lower-income countries where electricity supply are generally unreliable and air-conditioners mostly regarded as luxury goods, our findings predict that water demand will increase rapidly in cities across the developing world as global temperature rises, thus exacerbating projected water scarcity (Boretti & Rosa, 2019; De Wit & Stankiewicz, 2006; Hijioka et al., 2014; Niang et al., 2014; WWAP, 2018). Due to lack of evidence, current research on climate change impacts have not taken into account of increased water demand (Cisneros et al.,

2014; WWAP, 2018). Our findings show that water usage will increase with rising temperature by a non-trivial amount for large swarth of population. This additional stress on water demand needs to be considered in future reports on water balances projections and impacts of climate change.

Notes

1. IBNet Tariffs DB. Source: https://tariffs.ib-net.org/sites. Last accessed: Dec 10, 2021.

References

Adamowski, J., Fung Chan, H., Prasher, S. O., Ozga-Zielinski, B., & Sliusarieva, A. (2012). Comparison of multiple linear and nonlinear regression, autoregressive integrated moving average, artificial neural network, and wavelet artificial neural network methods for urban water demand forecasting in Montreal, Canada. *Water Resources Research, 48*(1).

Auffhammer, M. (2014). Cooling China: The weather dependence of air conditioner adoption. *Frontiers of Economics in China, 9*(1), 70–84.

Auffhammer, M., & Aroonruengsawat, A. (2011). Simulating the impacts of climate change, prices and population on California's residential electricity consumption. *Climatic Change, 109*(1), 191–210.

Auffhammer, M., Baylis, P., & Hausman, C. H. (2017). Climate change is projected to have severe impacts on the frequency and intensity of peak electricity demand across the United States. *Proceedings of the National Academy of Sciences of the United States of America, 114*(8), 1886–1891.

Berkoff, J. (2003). China: The south–north water transfer project—Is it justified? *Water Policy, 5*, 1–28.

Boretti, A., & Rosa, L. (2019). Reassessing the projections of the world water development report. *NPJ Clean Water, 2*(1), 1–6.

Breyer, B., Chang, H., & Parandvash, G. H. (2012). Land-use, temperature, and single-family residential water use patterns in Portland, Oregon and Phoenix, Arizona. *Applied Geography, 35*(1–2), 142–151.

Burke, M., & Emerick, K. (2016). Adaptation to climate change: Evidence from US agriculture. *American Economic Journal: Economic Policy, 8*(3), 106–140.

Cheng, H., & Hu, Y. (2012). Improving China's water resources management for better adaptation to climate change. *Climatic Change, 112*(2), 253–282.

Cisneros, J., BE, T. O., Arnell, N. W., Benito, G., Cogley, J. G., Do¨ll, P., & Gerten, D. (2014). *Freshwater resources climate change 2014: Impacts, adaptation, and vulnerability. Part A: Global and sectoral aspects. Contribution of working group II to the fifth assessment report of the intergovernmental panel on climate change* (pp. 229–269). Cambridge University Press.

Cohen, B. (2006). Urbanization in developing countries: Current trends, future projections, and key challenges for sustainability. *Technology in Society, 28*(1–2), 63–80.

Currie, J., & Neidell, M. (2005). Air pollution and infant health: What can we learn from California's recent experience? *Quarterly Journal of Economics, 120*(3), 1003–1030.

De Wit, M., & Stankiewicz, J. (2006). Changes in surface water supply across Africa with predicted climate change. *Science, 311*(5769), 1917–1921.

Dell, M., Jones, B. F., & Olken, B. A. (2014). What do we learn from the weather? The new climate-economy literature. *Journal of Economic Literature, 52*(3), 740–798.

Deschenes, O., & Greenstone, M. (2007). The economic impacts of climate change: Evidence from agricultural output and random fluctuations in weather. *American Economic Review, 97*(1), 354–385.

Giannakopoulos, C., Psiloglou, B., Lemesios, G., Xevgenos, D., Papadaskalopoulou, C., Karali, A., & Ioannou, K. (2016). Climate change impacts, vulnerability and adaptive capacity of the electrical energy sector in Cyprus. *Regional Environmental Change, 16*(7), 1891–1904.

Guhathakurta, S., & Gober, P. (2007). The impact of the Phoenix urban heat island on residential water use. *Journal of the American Planning Association, 73*(3), 317–329.

Gupta, E. (2016). The effect of development on the climate sensitivity of electricity demand in India. *Climate Change Economics, 7*(02), 1650003.

Hamiche, A. M., Stambouli, A. B., & Flazi, S. (2016). A review of the water-energy nexus. *Renewable and Sustainable Energy Reviews, 65*, 319–331.

Hannah, R. (2018). *Urbanization*. https://ourworldindata.org/urbanization

Hijioka, Y., Lin, E., Pereira, J., Corlett, R., Cui, X., Insarov, G., Surjan, A. (2014). *Asia. Climate change 2014: Impacts, adaptation, and vulnerability. Part B: Regional aspects. Contribution of working group II to the fifth assessment report of the intergovernmental panel on climate change* (pp. 1327–1370). Cambridge University Press.

Hsiang, S. (2016). Climate econometrics. *Annual Review of Resource Economics, 8*, 43–75.

Jiang, Y. (2009). China's water scarcity. *Journal of Environmental Management, 90*(11), 3185–3196.

Liu, J., & Yang, W. (2012). Water sustainability for China and beyond. *Science, 337*(6095), 649–650.

Liu, J., Zang, C., Tian, S., Liu, J., Yang, H., Jia, S., & Zhang, M. (2013). Water conservancy projects in China: Achievements, challenges and way forward. *Global Environmental Change, 23*(3), 633–643.

Li, Y., Pizer, W. A., & Wu, L. (2019). Climate change and residential electricity consumption in the Yangtze River Delta, China. *Proceedings of the National Academy of Sciences of the United States of America, 116*(2), 472–477.

Maidment, D. R., & Miaou, S. P. (1986). Daily water use in nine cities. *Water Resources Research, 22*(6), 845–851.

Martínez-Espin˜eira, R. (2002). Residential water demand in the Northwest of Spain. *Environmental and Resource Economics, 21*(2), 161–187.

Niang, I., Ruppel, O., Abdrabo, M., Essel, A., Lennard, C., Padgham, J., & Urquhart, P. (2014). Africa climate change 2014: Impacts, adaptation, and vulnerability. Part B: Regional aspects. In V. R. Barros et al. (Eds.), *Contribution of working group II to the fifth assessment report of the intergovernmental panel on climate change*. Cambridge University Press.

Piao, S., Ciais, P., Huang, Y., Shen, Z., Peng, S., Li, J., & Ding, Y. (2010). The impacts of climate change on water resources and agriculture in China. *Nature, 467*(7311), 43–51.

Pielke Jr, R., Burgess, M. G., & Ritchie, J. (2021). *Most plausible 2005–2040 emissions scenarios project less than 2.5 degrees c of warming by 2100*. SocArXiv. https://doi.org/10.31235/osf.io/m4fdu.

Praskievicz, S., & Chang, H. (2009). Identifying the relationships between urban water consumption and weather variables in Seoul, Korea. *Physical Geography, 30*(4), 324–337.

Ruth, M., Bernier, C., Jollands, N., & Golubiewski, N. (2007). Adaptation of urban water supply infrastructure to impacts from climate and socioeconomic changes: The case of Hamilton, New Zealand. *Water Resources Management, 21*(6), 1031–1045.

Salvo, A. (2018). Electrical appliances moderate households' water demand response to heat. *Nature Communications, 9*(1), 1–14.

Schlenker, W., & Walker, W. R. (2015). Airports, air pollution, and contemporaneous health. *The Review of Economic Studies, 83*(2), 768–809.

Tao, F., Yokozawa, M., Hayashi, Y., & Lin, E. (2005). A perspective on water resources in China: Interactions between climate change and soil degradation. *Climatic Change, 68*(1–2), 169–197.

Thornton, H., Hoskins, B. J., & Scaife, A. (2016). The role of temperature in the variability and extremes of electricity and gas demand in Great Britain. *Environmental Research Letters, 11*(11), 114015.

UN. (2019). World urbanization prospects. The 2018 revision. Methodology.
UNESCO. (2020). *2020: United Nations world water development report 2020*. Water and Climate Change.
Webber, M., Crow-Miller, B., & Rogers, S. (2017). The South-North water transfer project: Remaking the geography of China. *Regional Studies, 51*(3), 370–382.
Wenz, L., Levermann, A., & Auffhammer, M. (2017). North–south polarization of European electricity consumption under future warming. *Proceedings of the National Academy of Sciences of the United States of America, 114*(38), E7910–E7918.
Wong, J. S., Zhang, Q., & Chen, Y. D. (2010). Statistical modeling of daily urban water consumption in Hong Kong: Trend, changing patterns, and forecast. *Water Resources Research, 46*(3).
Wooldridge, J. M. (2015). Introductory econometrics: A modern approach: Nelson education.
WWAP. (2018). *The United Nations world water development report 2018: Nature-based solutions for water*. UNESCO.
Zhang, Q. (2009). The south-to-north water transfer project of China: Environmental implications and monitoring strategy 1. *JAWRA Journal of the American Water Resources Association, 45*(5), 1238–1247.
Zhou, F., Bo, Y., Ciais, P., Dumas, P., Tang, Q., Wang, X., & Yin, Z. (2020). Deceleration of China's human water use and its key drivers. *Proceedings of the National Academy of Sciences of the United States of America, 117*(14), 7702–7711.

Part V
Conclusion and Outlook

Chapter 14
Conclusion and Outlook

Binlei Gong

Abstract In this chapter, we review the background of the book, the key issues, the focus of each chapter, and the conclusions. In the face of the seriousness of global climate change and China's proposed "dual-carbon" response strategy, this book is the first to comprehensively and systematically describe the multi-level governance system that China has adopted in realizing its dual-carbon transition. This governance system encompasses the participation of the government, market, industry, and all sectors of society, and emphasizes coordination and cooperation among all levels of government, different sectors, and between domestic and international levels. We find that the government can play an important leading role in the dual-carbon transition. Secondly, making full use of market mechanisms also plays a key role. In addition, industry and agriculture contribute to dual-carbon development by promoting the efficient use of resources and the adoption of green production methods. Finally, raising public awareness and participation in environmental protection is also indispensable to effectively promote the dual-carbon transition process, through publicity and education, social organizations and public participation. Further, we conclude by suggesting some directions for future focus on China's Dual-Carbon governance and transformation, such as global leadership and cooperation, construction and innovation of policy system, development and challenge of carbon trading market, regional governance and industry transformation, residents' participation and social consciousness.

Keywords Climate change · Dual Carbon · Pathway · Foresight

B. Gong (✉)
School of Public Affairs, Zhejiang University, Hangzhou, China
e-mail: gongbinlei@zju.edu.cn

B. Gong et al. (eds.), *Chinese Governance and Transformation Towards Carbon Neutrality*, Resources, Environment and Agricultural Development,
https://doi.org/10.1007/978-981-97-9996-1_14

14.1 Conclusion

Climate change has a serious impact on the global environment and human society now and in the future. China is one of the largest emitters of greenhouse gases in the world, and its carbon reduction measures have an important impact on global climate change and will have a demonstration effect on global climate governance.

China actively plays the role of a great power and fulfills its international commitments to deal with climate change. Carbon peak and carbon neutralization have become the key measures put forward by China to promote sustainable development. At the international level, the realization of the dual carbon goal will have a far-reaching impact on the global carbon emission situation, the global energy market, industrial structure and trade pattern, and promote the cooperation, coordination and development of the cause of global climate governance help to promote the realization of the global sustainable development agenda. At the domestic level, the implementation of carbon emission reduction policies will promote the efficiency of resource utilization, promote the transformation of China's economy to a greener and low-carbon direction, improve the overall environmental quality, ensure people's health and improve the quality of life, and then promote social stability and development.

In this book, we have discussed the top-level design, implementation paths, problems and plans, participants and other aspects of China's dual-carbon goals from different levels.

It is crucial to compare China's experience and performance in climate governance with other nations. From a global perspective, leadership countries are increasingly important, as they can launch innovative climate policies and boost other countries' emulation through international communications. As two top-emitting emerging economies with the largest population, China and India are experiencing heavy industrialization and urbanization and are facing the tradeoff between economic development and carbon emission reduction. Furthermore, China and India play critical roles in fulfilling carbon neutrality worldwide, and they are generally benchmarked against each other in climate ambition. In the Chapter 2, Chen et al. aim to assess China and India's international and domestic positions in climate change mitigation after these two nations became active climate action takers from 2008 to 2021, according to the leadership theory taking structural, entrepreneurial, ideational, and exemplary leadership into account. This paper further employs interest-based and norm-based approaches to identify the driving forces of their leading positions. Although China is generally more inclined to take the leading position, this paper concludes that both countries currently exert substantive leadership, especially in recent international climate negotiation rounds. However, their leadership evolves through different paths: China initially focuses on international rather than domestic leadership positions (symbolic leader), whereas India initially takes the opposite (pioneer). In more recent years, an alignment between international and domestic leadership has been found in both nations, making them both substantive leaders.

Taking into account its role as a leader in the international carbon reduction process and its own national context, and in conjunction with the Belt and Road Initiative, China has proposed a Green Carbon Neutral pathway with its own characteristics. In Chapter 3, Fang et al. focus on this topic. They point out that the Belt and Road Initiative has achieved positive results, but the countries along the route are generally faced with the real challenges of rapid growth in carbon emissions, serious carbon leakage, different challenges of carbon peaking, and a long way to go for carbon neutrality, and that climate change is becoming a constraint to the sustainability of the countries along the Belt and Road. Climate change is increasingly becoming an important factor constraining the sustainable development of countries along the Belt and Road. From the perspective of carbon neutrality, it is of great strategic significance to promote the construction of the "Green Silk Road". To this end, the following countermeasures are proposed in this article: strengthening green and low-carbon cooperation with countries along the Belt and Road at the national level; promoting the construction of a green development system at the Belt and Road level; and proposing a "Chinese program" for climate governance at the global level.

Macro-policy guidance is crucial for leading a nationwide low-carbon transition. In Chapter 4, Zhu and Gong propose the construction of a "1+N" policy system, which will ensure a safe reduction of carbon emissions in the process of realizing the "Dual-Carbon" goal in the face of a series of risks in the economic, financial, and social arenas, as well as a proper handling of the relationship between economic growth and energy conservation. To this end, it is necessary to develop "Dual-Carbon" industries, establish a sound "Dual-Carbon" investment market, increase "Dual-Carbon" technology research and development, and synergistically promote air pollution control and "Dual-Carbon" control through multiple channels to ensure that our country successfully realizes the goal of carbon peaking and carbon neutrality.

How the government, as the visible hand, should play an effective role in the Dual-Carbon governance process? The tournament competition theory is usually adopted to illustrate strong economy-promoting incentives of local officials in China, saying that local government officials are competing for GDP growth to get promoted. Inspired by GDP-based tournament competition, can we adopt tournament competition to accelerate emission reduction? In other words, is it a practical approach to let local government officials compete with each other in achieving the "3060 Target"? The Chapter 5 by Chen et al. points out that tournament emission reduction competition would lead to more emission transfers among provinces in China, which may postpone the carbon peaking target nationwide. The current emission transfers in China are actually "robbing the poor to help the rich" since they accelerate the speed of carbon peaking for progressive provinces at the expense of postponing the peaking times for lagged provinces. The simulation result shows that emission transfers can postpone nationwide carbon peaking time by one year and increase the carbon peaking level by 13%. As a result, differentiated responsibilities should be distributed to various provinces when decomposing the national carbon peaking targets, and more cooperation, rather than competition, should be encouraged among local governments on carbon peaking.

The construction of a clean, low-carbon, safe and efficient energy system is a top priority in promoting China's goal of carbon neutrality. Green development in a long-term perspective needs to inject new theoretical connotations into the coordinated development of the energy system in the traditional sense. In Chapter 6, Lin et al. believe that carbon-neutral energy supply and demand side synergistic development is a new development approach based on the background of green and low-carbon development, which takes into account the deep integration of the energy and low-carbon industrial chain, balanced spatial balance of energy production and marketing, the coupled development of energy technology, the interconnectedness of the energy market and the coordinated guarantee of the policy system. The deep adjustment of the energy system should not only solve the problem of energy supply and demand mismatch in terms of quantity, but also promote the deep coupling of energy supply and demand on the structural system of industry, space, technology, market and system.

In addition to macro policy guidance, the market as the invisible hand also leads the low-carbon transition. The carbon trading market is treated as a crucial market-based instrument to cost-effectively reduce global greenhouse gas emissions. By allowing allowances trading, equal marginal abatement costs across plants are achieved and, therefore, control the overall social costs at a minimum level. In 2021, China officially launched the national carbon trading market for the electricity industry, making it the world's largest carbon market. In Chapter 7, Zheng and Zhang analyze China's electricity market reform and carbon trading market. This study finds that regional targets on carbon emission and energy consumption may hinder cross-regional trading. Moreover, the regulation of the electricity market, including electricity prices and generation rights, will significantly affect the performance of the carbon market. As a result, China should develop its carbon market and simultaneously promote the electricity market. It is crucial to coordinate the carbon and power markets in the new round of power market reform to ensure that policy interaction would not undermine overall economic efficiency. This study supports the idea that the market and the government should complement and coordinate to achieve Climate Neutrality. More specially, we should let the carbon trading market play the decisive role in allocating resources while allowing the electricity reform of the government to perform its functions better.

Although a national carbon trading market covering the power sector has been established, its effectiveness depends on how the power sector develops into a more integrated market. In Chapter 8, Cui et al. assess the impact of power market integration on the cost-effectiveness of carbon pricing in China. The study uses both integrated (regional power market) and segmented (provincial power market) market scenarios to identify possible future reform paths. Using a high-frequency dataset from five southern provinces in 2018, they assess the impact of electricity market integration on the abatement potential and cost-effectiveness of carbon pricing, finding that carbon prices would need to be as high as 200 RMB/tonne to begin to achieve overall carbon reductions. In this case, regional markets are more cost-effective than provincial markets in terms of emission reductions. However, regional markets can also raise potential equity issues. The provincial distribution of carbon emission reductions, as well as the exit of coal power, is more concentrated in regional markets than in provincial markets, suggesting that the socio-economic-environmental impacts of market integration are inequitable. The findings of this article will help improve policymakers' understanding of the interplay between carbon pricing and electricity market reform. This will help harmonize the effective design of carbon and electricity markets and support China's carbon neutrality goals.

Besides the regional governance and policies, sector-level Dual Carbon governance and transition are also essential to achieve "carbon peaking and climate neutrality." As climate change becomes increasingly serious and extreme weather events caused by global warming occur frequently, changes in temperature have a huge impact on industrial production. How to mitigate the impacts of climate change and cooperate with the process of low-carbon transition is an issue worth discussing in the future development of Chinese industrial enterprises. Chapter 9 demonstrates the investigation of Yang et al. on the mechanism of the impact of temperature change on industrial production in China. They find that there is a nonlinear relationship between industrial output and temperature change: higher temperature in summer significantly reduces industrial output, while higher temperature in winter increases industrial output. Average daily temperatures lower or higher than [12 °C, 15 °C) negatively affect industrial output. In addition, seasonal fluctuations in temperature also adversely affect industrial output. Further tests of the impact mechanism show that high temperatures indirectly affect the output of industrial enterprises by reducing their total factor productivity, gross fixed assets, investment and innovation capacity.

In addition to industry, agriculture plays a crucial role in climate change, as it generates significant greenhouse gas emissions and has considerable potential for carbon sequestration. Achieving carbon-neutral agriculture is challenging, but important for meeting future climate goals. Chapter 10 presented by Zhao et al. uses the agricultural sector to investigate the pathway to China's climate neutrality at the sector level. China's agricultural emissions already peaked in 2016, so how to contribute to climate neutrality is the next assignment. This study emphasizes the importance of balancing climate mitigation with other targets. Shi et al. aim to fill the research gap by exploring the approach to climate-neutral agriculture while ensuring food security by 2060. Since China's agricultural carbon intensity is lower than its leading exporters, producing more food enhances food security and contributes to the world's climate mitigation. This paper predicts that the GHG mitigation potential is enormous with proper mitigation measures. On the one hand, by improving management practices for synthetic fertilizers, incorporating residue, reducing or eliminating tillage, and employing organic farming and other climate-friendly farming systems, we can reduce nitrous oxide emissions by 12% in 2030 and 71% in 2060. On the other hand, by taking mitigation measures such as improving forage digestibility, improving manure management, decreasing animal mortality rate, and optimizing flood irrigation and drainage in rice cultivation, we can reduce methane emissions by 18% in 2030 and 76% in 2060. This paper also projects the trend of agricultural

GHG emissions for the next four decades. Finally, they put forth several strategies to push China's agriculture to go climate-neutral.

In addition to reducing agricultural GHG emissions in various regions and sectors, a balance should be striked between "pollution reduction" and "greenhouse gas (GHG) reduction" under the goal of green governance. In terms of the analytical framework, economic growth theory uses total factor productivity (TFP) and updated Green TFP to assess the process of green transition and high-quality development. Chapter 11 coming from Wang et al. investigates how to embed "carbon peaking and climate neutrality goals" into the existing framework of Chinese green governance and identifies its relationship with green transition and high-quality development. Using agriculture as an example, this paper first points out that green governance aims to consider both "pollution reduction" and "GHG emission reduction," in addition to TFP improvement and food security. Moreover, besides green policies, the government and other market entities can use non-institutional measures, including green technologies and green finance, as tools of green governance. After the goals and tools of green governance in climate neutrality are clarified, this paper builds a new analytic framework to investigate further how to use the tools to achieve the goals more efficiently and effectively. The theoretical foundation, econometric method, and design of the new framework are introduced based on the TFP analysis. This framework sheds light on how to evaluate the achievement of the goals and accelerate the green transition and high-quality development in the future.

Enterprises are the main promoters of economic activities, and they drive suppliers and partners in the industry chain to carry out low-carbon transformation through technological innovation and investment in renewable energy projects, forming a benign demonstration effect. In Chapter 12, we will find that promoting technological innovation in the new energy industry is not only an intrinsic requirement for the high-quality development of the industry, but also a key path to realizing China's goal of carbon neutrality. Sun et al., take VAT incentives as an example, and explore the relationship between new energy tax incentives, scale expansion and technological innovation by constructing theoretical and empirical models. The policy implications of this paper include: focusing on the optimization direction of new energy tax incentives, not only focusing on the scale development of the industry, but also focusing on key technological innovations; enhancing the positive impact of scale expansion and weakening the negative substitution of technological innovations through the precise regulation of the policy; and creating a favorable space for the transformation of new energy enterprises' innovative achievements.

Residents are direct participants in the low-carbon transition, and the success of the low-carbon transition requires residents to adopt a low-carbon lifestyle, including reducing the use of energy and water resources and choosing low-carbon products and services. Paying attention to residents' behavior and awareness and understanding their performance in the low-carbon transition can help formulate targeted policies and measures to prompt residents to participate more actively in the low-carbon transition. In Chapter 13, Qin et al. utilize "big data" collected by smart water meters from more than 40,000 urban households across ten provinces in China, spanning a nine-year period, to examine the relationship between daily household water consumption and climate variability. At baseline, this article finds that municipal water use is not only a coping mechanism for high temperatures, but that its use is accelerated when heat waves hit, and that households with lower property values are more likely to cope with high temperatures by substituting water for electricity. Importantly, they find evidence of adaptive behavior whereby households use more and more water over time to cope with hot days. This finding is particularly relevant to water-scarce countries, such as China, as well as developing countries, where water is a cheaper and more readily available resource for coping with high temperatures.

14.2 Outlook

Overall, in the future, we mainly concentrate on these topics when referring to how to achieve "Dual Carbon" goal in China.

14.2.1 Global Leadership and Cooperation

As climate change intensifies, global leadership is crucial. In addition to big countries such as China and India, the role of other countries can not be ignored. Future discussions may focus on how to strengthen global cooperation and establish a more effective international climate governance system. In addition, cross-border cooperation and coordination will be the key to promoting the achievement of global carbon reduction targets.

14.2.2 Construction and Innovation of Policy System

In the field of carbon emission reduction, the construction and innovation of policy system is very important. Future discussions may focus on how to establish a better policy framework, encourage the development of innovative technologies, promote the healthy operation of the carbon market, and strengthen coordination and cooperation between the government and the market.

14.2.3 Development and Challenge of Carbon Trading Market

As an important mechanism to reduce carbon emissions, the carbon trading market will face a series of challenges, such as how to balance the efficiency and fairness of carbon pricing, how to promote cross-regional carbon trading, and how to deal with the relationship between the carbon market and the electricity market.

Future discussions may explore how to address these challenges and promote the development of the carbon trading market.

14.2.4 Regional Governance and Industry Transformation

Regional governance and industry transformation will play a key role in achieving the goal of carbon neutralization.

Future discussions may focus on how to promote cooperation and coordination among different regions, promote the transformation of high-carbon industries to low-carbon development, and how to balance the relationship between economic growth and carbon emission reduction.

14.2.5 Residents' Participation and Social Consciousness

As direct participants in low-carbon transformation, residents' behavior and awareness are very important for the realization of carbon emission reduction targets.

Future discussions may focus on how to improve residents' low-carbon awareness, encourage residents to adopt a low-carbon lifestyle, and how to formulate targeted policies to promote residents to participate in low-carbon transformation.

Epilogue

Global climate change is becoming increasingly serious, and climate problems, including global warming and the frequent occurrence of extreme weather events, pose great challenges to human society and the ecological environment. Under this background, China, as the world's largest emitter of greenhouse gases, bears an important international responsibility. In order to address climate change, the Chinese government announced on September 22, 2020 the landmark Dual-Carbon target, i.e., carbon peaking by 2030 and carbon neutrality by 2060, which demonstrates China's role as a great power. However, China's Dual-Carbon transition faces a number of challenging dilemmas. First, China's rapid economic development has led to high energy consumption and carbon emissions, requiring economic restructuring and energy transformation. How to achieve a low-carbon transition while maintaining sustained economic growth is an issue that needs to be seriously considered and resolved. Secondly, due to China's vast geographic area and large differences in the levels of economic development and energy consumption, achieving the Dual-Carbon goal requires the formulation of differentiated policy measures and the promotion of balanced development among regions. In addition, a Dual-Carbon transition will need to rely on technological research and development and innovation, including innovation in clean energy technology and energy utilization efficiency enhancement, which will require increased investment and enhanced talent training.

Sponsored by the Environment and Energy Policy Research Center, School of Public Affairs, the China Academy for Rural Development at Zhejiang University, as well as the Zhejiang Youth High-level Talent Association, the symposium "Energy, Environment and Economic growth: opportunities and challenges at the stage of High-quality Development" was held at Zijingang Campus of Zhejiang University on November 13–14, 2021. Experts and scholars from universities, scientific research institutions and government departments in related fields gave presentations related to climate change, energy security, carbon emission, and green development. From the papers submitted and discussed in this conference, we have selected 12 of them and compiled a book on this basis.

B. Gong et al. (eds.), *Chinese Governance and Transformation Towards Carbon Neutrality*, Resources, Environment and Agricultural Development,
https://doi.org/10.1007/978-981-97-9996-1

This book provides the first comprehensive and systematic account of the multi-level governance system adopted by China in realizing the Dual-Carbon transition. This governance system encompasses the participation of the government, the market, industry and all sectors of society, and emphasizes coordination and cooperation between all levels of government between different sectors, and between domestic and international levels. We find that the government can play an important leadership and guidance role in the Dual-Carbon transition. By formulating and implementing relevant policies, regulations and planning, the government can promote the process of Dual-Carbon development. Second, the full utilization of market mechanisms also plays a key role. Through measures such as establishing a carbon market and promoting carbon pricing, the market mechanism promotes the innovation and application of low carbon technologies. In addition, the active participation of industry is an indispensable factor in realizing a Dual-Carbon transition. Industry and agriculture have contributed to Dual-Carbon development by promoting the efficient use of resources and the adoption of green production methods. Finally, raising public awareness and participation in environmental protection is also indispensable, and the process of Dual-Carbon transition is effectively promoted through publicity and education, social organizations and public participation. By addressing multiple themes, this book provides a comprehensive understanding and in-depth analysis of the Dual-Carbon transition, and offers scientific guidance and policy recommendations for China's sustainable development and the achievement of Dual-Carbon goals. At the same time, the significance of this book lies in the fact that it provides reference for other countries and regions, and makes a positive contribution to global climate governance.

First, I would like to thank the leaders and colleagues of School of Public Affairs and the Environment and Energy Policy Research Center at Zhejiang University for their generous support to the conference. Second, I am grateful to all the experts and scholars who participated in the symposium "Energy, Environment and Economic growth: opportunities and challenges at the stage of High-quality Development", especially the authors of the 12 papers included in this book, for sharing their unconventional wisdom on Chinese governance and transition towards Dual-Carbon goal. Third, I truly appreciate the students who participated in proofreading this book. They are Zimeng Chen, Shouhan Dai, Yayun Xiao, Yuhe Wang, Xiaoxu Zhi.

This book is supported by the National Natural Science Foundation of China (No. 72161147001, 72173114, 71903172, 72061147002), the Major Project of Philosophy and Social Sciences by the Ministry of Education (2024JZDZ059), the National Social Science Foundation of China (21&ZD092), Humanities and Social Sciences Program of the Ministry of Education (22JJD790075), Mitigate+: Research for Low Emissions Food Systems, China Academy for Rural Development, School of Public Affairs, Office of Global Engagement, Academy of Social Governance, Academy of Humanities and Social Science and the Office of Talent Management of Zhejiang University.

Binlei Gong.

August 2024.

The manufacturer's authorised representative in the EU is Springer Nature Customer Service Centre GmbH, Europaplatz 3, 69115 Heidelberg, Germany. If you have any concerns regarding our products, please contact ProductSafety@springernature.com

Printed and bound by CPI Group (UK) Ltd, Croydon, CR0 4YY
01/10/2026
02225934-0012